Grow
Your
Business

Grow
Your
Business

MARK HENRICKS

Entrepreneur Press
2445 McCabe Way, Irvine, CA 92614

Managing Editor: Marla Markman
Book Design: Sylvia H. Lee
Copy Editor: Lynn Pomije
Production Editor: Megan Reilly
Production Designers: Mia H. Ko, Marlene Natal
Cover Design: Mark Kozak
Illustrator: Neil Shigley
Indexer: Alta Indexing

This publication is designed to provide accurate and authoritative
information in regard to the subject matter covered. It is sold with
the understanding that the publisher is not engaged in rendering
legal, accounting or other professional services. If legal advice or
other expert assistance is required, the services of a competent
professional person should be sought.

ISBN 1-891984-20-9

Library Of Congress Cataloging-in-Publication Data

Henricks, Mark
Grow your business / by Mark Henricks.
p. cm.
Includes index.
ISBN 1-891984-20-9
1. Small business--Management. I. Title.
HD62.7 .H474 2001
658.02'2--dc21
00-011177

Printed in Canada

09 08 07 06 05 04 03 02 01   10 9 8 7 6 5 4 3 2 1

Acknowledgments

Thilis book would never have been completed without the patience, understanding, encouragement, vision and technical skill of Marla Markman. I gratefully acknowledge the writers and editors of *Entrepreneur* and *Start-Ups* magazines and the other publications of Entrepreneur Media from whose work this book is based. That group includes but is not limited to Maria Anton, Peggy Bennett, Janean Chun, Maria Valdez Haubrich, Mike Hogan, Jacquelyn Lynn, Robert McGarvey and Karen Spaeder. I owe a particular debt to Rieva Lesonsky and Karen Axelton for their work on the book *Start Your Own Business*, which precedes this one in time, in spirit and in content. Lynn Pomije's copy editing improved this book enormously but not, if I can help it, anonymously.

Thanks to the many writers and businesspeople who have provided material specific to this book through personal interviews and letters, their own articles and books and other communications. They include David "Andy" Bangs, Karl Egge, Tom Gillis, Seth Godin, James Olan Hutcheson, Patricia Kishel, Jay Conrad Levinson and Karl Vesper. Each of the thousands of entrepreneurs I have talked to during nearly 20 years as a business writer has contributed in some way to this book. I thank all of them for their time, and for the opportunity to discuss with them the businesses they love, and I wish them every success in their own hopes for growth.

As always, Barbara, Kate, Corey and Brady inspire and motivate everything.

Table Of Contents

part two

How Are You Going To Get There? ... 77

part three

After You Arrive. 255

part four

The Next Journey. **371**

Introduction

In the film "Annie Hall", Woody Allen explains to girlfriend Diane Keaton his theory that love affairs, like sharks, have to keep moving forward to stay alive. "What we have here," Allen informs Keaton, "is a dead shark." Is your business a dead shark? If it were to stop growing, some would say yes. A 1999 survey conducted by Pitney Bowes Inc. of nearly 1,400 small-business owners nationwide found that 71 percent wanted their businesses to grow. This book is aimed at making sure that, if you are one of those 71 percent, your business doesn't end up like one of Woody Allen's failed relationships.

Your business career is no movie, however, and perhaps the most important factor in determining your business's growth potential is your personal attitude toward growth. With that in mind, one of the first things you'll do by reading *Grow Your Business* is be able to determine exactly how you feel about growth. Although you may think you already know the answer to this question, approach it with an open mind. You may be surprised to find out that you are more—or less—intrigued by expanding your business than you thought.

Assuming you are interested in expanding your business, the next potential constraint lies in your business's actual prospects for growth. In reading this book, you'll see that a broad array of factors govern the business potential of your company, ranging from the size of its market to the energy of your competitors. This is not meant to be negative—you just have to understand the obstacles before you can overcome them.

Next, you have to create some kind of goal for growth. This does not have to be a grand scheme along the lines of "I'll be a millionaire by the time I'm 30," or anything dull and corporate-sounding like "I'll generate an annual 12 percent return on equity." In fact, a goal for growth may have more to do with your lifestyle than your revenue. Either way, you have to have one.

When you have a goal, you are ready to design a plan to grow your business. You'll consider many elements, including your sales, employees, markets and financing, and formulate a real plan for expanding your business.

The bulk of the book, of course, is about putting your plan into action, from hiring the people you need to finding the funding to pay for growth—and even what to do after your business career is finished. The following chapter-by-chapter summary explains how you will be exposed to all these things.

Chapter 1: Where Are You Now?

This chapter provides practical ways to size up the status of your company, your personal achievements, your financial status, your skills and even your personal satisfaction.

Chapter 2: What Are Your Aspirations?

Desire for achievement has driven many an enterprise's growth, just as lack of drive has kept many others in steady stability. This chapter explains why understanding your aspirations is a vital part of preparing for intelligent growth.

Chapter 3: Picking A Time To Grow

If you look at virtually any great entrepreneurial enterprise, you'll notice that what worked for the company at one time probably wouldn't have worked at another time. This chapter describes different types of timing and the roles they play in growth.

Chapter 4: Setting New Goals

The fact that you're reading this book suggests that you are dissatisfied with the prospects for achieving your growth goals. Sometimes the goals themselves need to change. This chapter describes the role of goals in producing and controlling your business's growth, and how to make them work for you rather than against you.

Chapter 5: Ready To Relocate?

Just as there's a time for growth, there's a place for growth. This chapter explains how moving to a new location has spurred many a company into a long-term expansion, and it also covers alternatives to moving.

Chapter 6: Building A Company Image

Image can provide much (if not all) of the power behind a business expansion. This chapter describes how to assess your image and, if necessary, craft a new one to power your growth.

Chapter 7: Hiring Employees

All growing enterprises are made up of people. This chapter tells how to evaluate your employees, plan for hiring additional workers, and even train someone to someday grow into your own job.

Chapter 8: Using Professional Service Providers

In even the largest and most sophisticated growing companies, some essential business functions are provided by outside professionals. This chapter explains how to ensure that legal, accounting, marketing, management and other professional advisors contribute as much as possible to your company's growth.

Chapter 9: Funding Expansion

When you started your business, you learned how important money was to getting underway. This chapter clarifies the role financing plays in expanding an existing business, as well as the places and ways for you to obtain it.

Chapter 10: Going Global

The opportunity to compete on the global playing field is one many growing companies can't pass up. Why not? As this chapter explains, international expansion offers unique challenges and rewards for the growing company.

Chapter 11: Trade Shows And Conferences

Trade shows have proved vital tools for finding customers and suppliers for countless growing firms. This chapter shows you how to make your company one of them.

Chapter 12: Marketing, Advertising And Public Relations

Marketing skill or lack thereof is often noted as the biggest difference between companies whose growth is extraordinary and those who are just getting by. From creating a media kit to formulating a marketing strategy, this chapter gives you pointers on ways to implement your own growth-oriented marketing plan.

Chapter 13: Setting Up Distribution

Getting products to end users is always critical. The model you select, your packaging and other distribution factors are the topics of this chapter.

Chapter 14: Updating Office Technology

Technology has touched nearly every business today, but if you're intent on maximizing growth, there's probably a way you could improve your use of technology. This chapter covers topics from evaluating your current technology to the importance of training.

Chapter 15: Partnering With Suppliers And Vendors

You can't sell any product unless you can source it, and even service companies get supplies, equipment and other goods from somewhere. This chapter tells you how suppliers and vendors can go from being necessary evils to valuable adjuncts to your expansion plans.

Chapter 16: Innovating For Growth

Innovative new products are the fuel for the most powerful growth engine you can connect to. This chapter shows how new products and services affect growth, how to make decisions to add products, and how to introduce them to the market when they're ready.

Chapter 17: Setting Prices

The prices you charge for what you sell have enormous power to affect your company's growth. This chapter reveals techniques for assessing your pricing and, if necessary, changing your prices to reintroduce growth to a sagging company.

Chapter 18: Customer Service

Paying close attention to your customers is essential to keep your business thriving. This chapter shows why customer service is so important, how to measure your own level of service, and how to pave your path to growth with good customer service.

Chapter 19: Sales Personnel

Sales are what drive a company's growth, and salespeople are the ones who personally bring in the sales. This chapter shows how to evaluate your sales force and improve it to boost your company's growth.

Chapter 20: Other Roads To Growth

Government contracting and strategic alliances are not the first paths to growth most entrepreneurs think of. But, as this chapter explains, they are perfectly viable growth alternatives for business owners who aren't afraid to be unconventional.

Chapter 21: Online Growth Opportunities

This chapter takes the stance that the Internet was almost made to serve small businesses. It outlines the fundamentals you will need to master to successfully sell your business as well as your products and services online.

Chapter 22: Managing People

The big issue for many owners of growing companies is not how to pay for growth, but how to manage the increasing work force necessary to power a growing company. This chapter explains the importance of delegating—and techniques for doing so. It also covers many other personnel details growing companies face—from making workplace policies clear to monitoring employee e-mail and Internet usage.

Chapter 23: Risk Management

Managing risk is an important part of growing your company. In this chapter, you'll see how to use insurance, training, theft prevention and other risk management tools to improve the odds that your company will grow without falling victim to the ever-present risks of doing business.

Chapter 24: Financial Management

It's safe to say that finance is not most entrepreneurs' favorite subject—nor is it most entrepreneurs' strongest subject. But perhaps it should be. This chapter explains how understanding and employing effective tools for managing cash, planning for taxes and other functions of financial management can be an important part of encouraging growth.

Chapter 25: Regulatory Roadblocks

Growing businesses are usually subject to a stream of new regulations as they expand, requiring new licenses and permits as you enter new markets, commence new operations or simply get larger. This chapter shows you where and how to cut through the necessary paperwork.

Chapter 26: Business Travel Tips

Not every small-business owner loves business travel, but most business travel, if done correctly, can spur growth. This chapter shows how to control travel costs, both financial and psychological, and employ alternatives to travel when possible.

Chapter 27: Administering Growing Businesses

As a company grows, staff, forms and policies inevitably increase. This chapter shows you how to keep mushrooming paperwork and administrative trivia from overwhelming you in your quest for growth.

Chapter 28: Beating Business Cycles

You can't sail against wind and tide, and any sensible growth plan takes into account the cycles of business. This chapter shows how to identify, minimize and even benefit from seasonal fluctuations, booms, busts and other business cycles.

Chapter 29: Time And Stress Management

Nobody said growing a business was going to be easy, but it would be nice if the stress associated with the undertaking wouldn't kill you. This chapter shows you how to combat stress and includes tools for improving your (and your employees') time management skills.

Chapter 30: Effective Communications

Time and time again, effective entrepreneurs are described as being good communicators. This chapter shows you how to evaluate your own communications quotient, identifies the components of good communication, and provides workable methods for becoming a better communicator.

Chapter 31: Coping With Competition

Competition almost always increases as your business gets bigger. But according to this chapter, that's not always a bad thing, nor is coping with increasing competition necessarily a daunting task.

Chapter 32: Succession Planning

After you've spent a good chunk of your career building a business, it would be nice to leave it in good hands. This chapter is about why planning for succession is so important and what you should be doing right now to prepare for a successful transition.

Chapter 33: Retirement Planning

A desire for financial security is one of the most common reasons entrepreneurs start businesses. Using the tools and techniques this chapter discusses, there's no reason you can't extend the financial security of being a business owner into retirement, for both yourself and your employees.

Chapter 34: Entrepreneurship Programs

If you're a small-business owner with most of your growth ahead of you, you may want to go back to school to help your expansion. This chapter details what you can learn from continuing education programs, executive MBA programs and other midcareer educational alternatives.

Chapter 35: Franchising Your Business

A business generally can grow much farther and faster by franchising than if it were funded by bank loans or internally generated funds. This chapter tells you how to assess your company's prospects as a franchisor, handle the substantial regulatory requirements and ensure that it all makes financial sense for both you and your prospective franchisees.

Chapter 36: Selling Your Business

The end of your involvement in your business may seem too far off to consider now. But it's never too soon to look ahead to one of the most important events of your business career: selling the business. This chapter outlines the types of exit strategies and ways to implement them.

Appendix: Government Listings

Finally, at the end of the book you will find a Government Listings appendix chock-full of contact information for Small Business Development Centers, Small Business Administration district offices and state economic development offices across the country.

To top it all off, throughout the book, you will find tip boxes containing brief hints, resources, warnings and shortcuts to help you achieve the growth you desire.

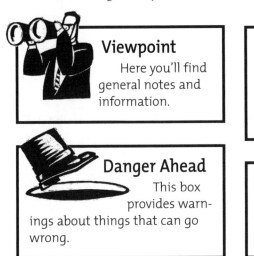

Viewpoint

Here you'll find general notes and information.

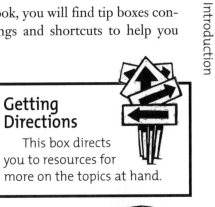

Getting Directions

This box directs you to resources for more on the topics at hand.

Danger Ahead

This box provides warnings about things that can go wrong.

Fast Lane

Practical tips about how to save money, time and other resources.

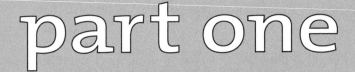

part one

Where Are You Going?

You have to decide where you're going before you can hope to get there. That's a statement most entrepreneurs would readily agree with, but it takes more than a nod of the head to really get a grip on where you want to go with your business. Devising the necessary plan of action, including comparing your current status to your future ambitions, is the topic of the first part of *Grow Your Business*.

To begin at the beginning, you need to figure out where you are now in your personal and business life. Finding out where you're going involves first assessing how well you and your business measure up in terms of income, net worth, personal and employee skills, and overall satisfaction. In Chapter 1, you'll analyze your aspirations, examining how well you're doing in reaching your goals and what you look like next to other businesses in terms of sales, profits, markets, financing, employee skills, and more. In Chapter 2, you'll be asked to assess what you want from growth and, if necessary, revise your growth plans to fit your personal ambitions. You'll learn in Chapter 3 about the necessity of keeping your growth goals in sync with product life cycles and other fluctuations on the business scene. In Chapter 4, you'll work on setting those goals. And in Chapter 5 you'll examine the role that physically relocating your business may play at some point in your journey toward growth. Where you are is more than a matter of your street address, so in Chapter 6 you'll study how your company's image may help or hinder business growth.

Overall, the first part of *Grow Your Business* provides you with a foundation for the later portions, which focus more on what to do than why you're doing it. In Part 2, you'll take your first look at the elements of tactical execution.

chapter 1

Where Are You Now?

*Sense of Where You Are* is a book about a basketball star at Princeton University in the 1960s. The title came from the response the author got when he asked the young athlete how he could consistently make shots when looking away from the basket and heaving the ball over his shoulder. The jock's explanation: "You develop a sense of where you are."

That might have been just another throwaway line if not for the attentive ear of writer John McPhee, but odds are good that Bill Bradley would still have gone on to lead his team to the Final Four in the national tournament, graduate from Princeton and become a Rhodes scholar, win two championships in the National Basketball Association, serve three terms in the U.S. Senate, and run for president.

Maybe your goals as an entrepreneur are more modest than that. Maybe you aren't sure what your goals are. But it's certain that you are somewhere today. Before you can make any decision about how to grow your business, you have to have a sense of where you—and it—are today. Then, and only then, do you have a chance of understanding what it's going to take to achieve your goals.

Sizing Up Your Status

Sizing up your status is a matter of developing a sense of where you are—on several fronts. You need to make a careful diagnosis of the state of your mind, your finances, your skills and your personal satisfaction level just to evaluate yourself. Then it's time to get started on your business. There you need to look at measures such as sales, profitability, assets, employees and growth rates. You can't grow without customers, so next you need to look at your market, checking out its size, potential and competition. Finally, since growth always takes money, you must evaluate your financing, including how much is available to you, in what form and what you'll have to give up to fund expansion.

Viewpoint

Wonder how your earnings as an entrepreneur compare to earnings of employees? U.S. per capita income was $20,120 in 1998, according to the Census Bureau. Median household income was $38,885. The median income for full-time male workers was $35,345 and for full-time females, it was $25,862.

Income

For many of us, how much money we made last year is our way of keeping score. And it's a good idea to know exactly where you stand on the income you're getting from your business before deciding whether or how to grow it. There are several parameters to income besides the amount at the bottom of your pay stub.

Your income may be bit less than your take-home pay suggests. For instance, many entrepreneurs work far more hours than are in a regular workweek to generate the income they receive. If you're one of them, divide your take-home pay by the number of hours you worked. Try to make a hard-nosed assessment of your income. You may decide that growing your business is the best way to boost your own payday.

Net Worth

Your net worth is as important as your income. Every now and then, you should sit down and tally up your personal assets and liabilities, just as you do with your business, to figure out where you stand. Use the work sheet on page 6 to calculate your personal net worth. Enter actual or estimated market values on each line and total just as you would a balance sheet.

Every now and then, you should tally up your personal assets and liabilities, just as you do with your business, to figure out where you stand.

You can grow your net worth through some combination of decreasing liabilities and increasing assets. Why should you care if your net worth grows? One common reason is retirement planning, the topic of Chapter 33. Simply put, the more assets you have, the more comfortable your retirement will be. You may also need a high personal net worth to buy a business, pursue some types of investments, purchase a second home, pay for a child's college education, or for other purposes.

Competencies

What are you good at? What are you not good at? Knowing your strengths and weaknesses will help you make many decisions regarding the growth of your company. To help figure out your pluses and minuses, take the competency assessment quiz on page 7.

Your score on this quiz isn't designed to tell you precisely what to do or how to grow. But it may alert you to opportunities for improvement and suggest growth paths. It would be interesting to take this test, or one like it, once a year and see how you have improved your competencies in the previous 12 months.

Personal Balance Sheet

ASSETS

Cash (bank accounts,
money market funds, CDs, etc.) $_____

Securities (stocks, bonds, mutual funds, etc.) $_____

Real estate (primary residence,
vacation home, etc.) $_____

Vehicles (personal cars and other vehicles) $_____

Household goods and furnishings
(estimated resale value) $_____

Art, antiques, jewelry, etc.
(estimated market value) $_____

Life insurance (cash value) $_____

Company profit-sharing plans
(your personal share) $_____

Pension plan (vested benefits) $_____

IRAs, Keoghs, SEP plans $_____

Your interest in your business $_____

Personal loans payable to you $_____

Other assets (trusts, etc.) $_____

Total Personal Assets $_____

LIABILITIES

Home mortgage $_____

Other real estate mortgages $_____

Car loans and leases $_____

Credit card balances $_____

Unpaid bills $_____

Taxes (federal, state, local,
property and income) $_____

Capital gains taxes (due on investments if sold) $_____

Student loans $_____

Other liabilities (leases, etc.) $_____

Total Personal Liabilities $_____

Personal Net Worth
(total assets minus total liabilities) $_____

Personal Satisfaction

It's easy to see that some entrepreneurs find lots of personal satisfaction in their work. Are you one of them? Start by asking yourself what you mean when you say you're an entrepreneur. Finish the following sentence: "To me, being an entrepreneur means:_____

_____."

What did you write? Some possibilities include:

○ being my own boss
○ taking vacations when I want to, not when someone else says I can
○ being free to do the best job possible
○ having the opportunity to express my creativity through my work
○ making a lot of money
○ working harder than anyone else
○ doing what has to be done
○ a never-ending battle

Competency Assessment Quiz

Score yourself from 1 to 5 (5 being the best) on each item. Don't think too long about each area. There's no right answer for any of them.

Score

○ *Opportunity:* How good are you at spotting and developing opportunities? _____

○ *Organization:* How well can you monitor, organize and develop resources? _____

○ *Strategy:* Can you prepare a vision, set goals and devise strategies to reach them? _____

○ *Social:* Can you communicate and persuade and build relationships effectively? _____

○ *Commitment:* How committed are you to being an entrepreneur? _____

○ *Problem-solving and decision-making:* Can you analyze, learn and innovate in an atmosphere of uncertainty and risk? Can you move when you have only your intuition to guide you? _____

Total _____

As with the competency quiz, there are no right or wrong answers. But what you say about being an entrepreneur can tell you something about how you view life as a small-business owner. You may find out you are pleased with things and want to keep them just the way they are. Or you may discern the need for significant change. Either way, gaining an understanding of what attracts you to entrepreneurship (or, perhaps, repels you from it) is an essential step in plotting your growth strategy.

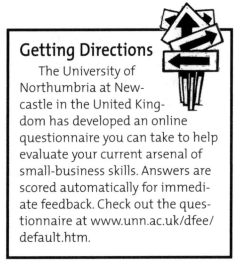

Getting Directions

The University of Northumbria at Newcastle in the United Kingdom has developed an online questionnaire you can take to help evaluate your current arsenal of small-business skills. Answers are scored automatically for immediate feedback. Check out the questionnaire at www.unn.ac.uk/dfee/default.htm.

Benchmarking Your Business

After you've evaluated where you are personally, it's time to benchmark your business. This process can be quite involved, requiring the collection, analysis and comparison of mounds of data on everything from your recent sales growth to production capacity. However, you might want to start the process by simply sitting down, looking around and asking yourself if your business seems to be where it should be right now. Your gut-level intuition of how the business is doing may be more valuable than even the most detailed analysis.

Getting Directions

Not feeling satisfied with your work? *The Inner Game of Work* (Random House) by Timothy W. Gallwey is a book that uses techniques derived from sports psychology to show you how to boost your performance and your enjoyment of work at the same time.

Sales

You probably won't have to consult any financial statements or even think for more than a second or two to recall your business' sales for the most recent month and year. Sales revenue is the most common measure of a business' size and level of success. However, don't stop after you

Mission (Statement) Possible

"**A** mission statement defines what an organization is, why it exists, its reason for being," says Gerald Graham, dean of the W. Frank Barton School of Business at Wichita State University in Kansas. At a minimum, your mission statement should define who your primary customers are, identify the products and services you produce, and describe the geographical location in which you operate.

If you don't have a mission statement, create one by writing down in one sentence what the purpose of your business is. Ask two or three of the key people in your company to do the same thing. Then discuss the statements and come up with one sentence everyone agrees with. Once you have finalized your mission statement, communicate it to everyone in the company. "Post it on the wall, hold meetings to talk about it, and include reminders of the statement in employee correspondence," says Graham.

It's more important to communicate the mission statement to employees than to customers, according to Graham. "The most effective mission statements are developed strictly for internal communication and discussion," says Graham. "Then, if something promotional comes out of it, fine." In other words, your mission statement doesn't have to be clever or catchy—just accurate.

If you already have a mission statement, you will need to periodically review and possibly revise it to make sure it accurately reflects your goals as your company and the business and economic climates evolve. To do this, simply ask yourself if the statement still correctly describes what you're doing.

If your review results in a revision of the statement, be sure everyone in the company is aware of the change. Make a big deal out of it. After all, a change in your mission probably means your company is growing—and that's a big deal.

look at your total sales figure. Break that figure down as much as you can. Looking at your sales by lines of business, product lines, individual products, varieties of individual products, and price points of individual product varieties can be far more useful than just knowing that sales are up.

Details about sales provide you with important information about what's selling, what's not and why. This information, in turn, can give you some helpful ideas and inspiration on how to grow your company in the future.

Profitability

The ability to run a business profitably was rated the top trait of effective business leaders in a study by executive recruiter Korn/Ferry International and *The Economist* magazine's Intelligence Unit. Knowing exactly how profitable you are is a prerequisite to planning for growth. And it's not enough to just know whether you are or are not making money overall. You should also look at your current profitability in light of several ratios, including gross margin (sales minus cost of goods), return on equity (profit divided by net worth), and return on investment (after-tax net profits divided by total assets).

Fast Lane

Use a corporate scorecard to benchmark your business. This is a statement of a half-dozen things that are important to your business. It should be brief enough to fit on an index card and review daily; revise the list as often as circumstances require. Include goals such as "growing 10 percent per year" or "maintaining defect rates below 10 per million."

Assets

Profits aren't the only way to measure a company's success. You should also be aware of how much your company is worth. One way to do this is to check out an updated balance sheet. That figure at the bottom for net worth, representing assets minus liabilities, is a good indicator of whether you have built value in your business—and if you have, how much.

Don't stop your valuation checkup with your balance sheet, either. There are a few other ways to measure value. One of the most important valuation techniques is based on expected future cash flow, or how much cash the company should be able to throw off for you or another owner in the next several years. Businesses are typically valued as a multiple of their future cash flows, but different industries and types and sizes of businesses use a variety of indicators. To find out what rule applies to your industry, check with your trade association.

Market Share

Market share can be like a powerful lever that allows you to virtually specify standards for products, features and even pricing in ways that suit your company's preferences. That's if you have market share. If you lack it, market share can work against you and in favor of your competitors who do have it. So an important part of preparing for growth is making sure you know all you can about how much of your market is yours.

In its simplest sense, your market share is the percentage of the total sales of your product or service that go to your company. Another way to figure market share is to divide your dollar sales of a product by the gross sales of the entire market.

Right off the bat, you can see that you may have different market share for different products or services. Also, your market share for identical products and services will likely vary by market because there is rarely a single monolithic market. For instance, there are domestic markets, international markets, emerging markets and mass markets, just to name a few. Try to break down your markets and products as finely as is practical to get a realistic view of your market share. The results can be an accurate indicator of the most likely direction you should head in to achieve growth.

Employees

Over the past 20 years, there has been a sharp decline in the percentage of publicly traded companies' stock market value that is composed of tangible assets such as inventory, plant and equipment, real estate and cash. Today, intangibles account for about three out of every four dollars in the value of the average publicly traded company.

What are these intangibles? For many entrepreneurs, their most valuable assets, tangible or otherwise, are their employees. Having a work force of skillful, motivated employees is essential to a small company's ability to deal with globalization, shorter product cycles, evolving information technology, and the other challenges of modern business. At the same time, the pressures of competition mean that no company can afford to have more employees on its payroll than it needs.

Getting Directions

Learn more about how your business measures up against others by checking out *Annual Statement Studies,* a massive and detailed comparison of financial data from more than 150,000 businesses' financial statements. Find out more at publisher Robert Morris Associates' Web site at www.rmahq.org.

When you are evaluating your finances, there are many ratios you can apply and calculations you can perform to discern how well you are doing. You can come up with figures for, say, return on investment and compare them with norms to see how finely tuned your organization is. But when it comes to evaluating employees, things are not quite so clear. The basic question you are trying to answer is this: Do my employees have

Fast Lane

One way to create a highly customized evaluation of your work force is to use your best employees to build a benchmark against which you can measure the rest of your work force. If your top two salespeople average 30 percent annual growth in their territories while the rest get just 5 percent, you may have some training and/or hiring to do before you can grow significantly.

the capability to carry out the work that will be required of them if the firm expands? There's no easy answer. You will have to look at a variety of factors. Some key factors used in measuring work force quality include: number of years of education of a typical worker, average length of time a worker has been with your company, and average length of time a worker has worked in your industry. You may also look at defect rates, turnover rates and absenteeism records to determine the quality and motivation of your work force. Work force quality can't be expressed as a single number, but it's a key variable in plotting your company's future growth.

Skills

These days the ability to acquire and manage knowledge and skills is considered as valuable to a businessperson as the ability to raise money and manage people. Before you can accurately evaluate opportunities for growth, you have to get a good feel for whether or not you and your company have the skills to handle new markets, new products and new customers.

The required skills and talents vary widely from industry to industry. While creativity may be highly valued in an advertising firm, it's less useful to a long-haul trucking firm. You likely have a strong sense of the skills necessary to succeed in your business. You are less likely to take a systematic inventory to determine whether and to what extent you and your company possess these skills. Now is a good time to do that.

Start by listing the key skills and traits needed in your industry.

For instance, in an accounting firm, they might be accuracy, integrity, persistence, innovation and general business acumen. Then ask yourself dispassionately how well you, your employees and your company exemplify those traits. You can give yourself a numerical score if you want, but the key is to think in an organized manner about whether you possess the skills you'll need to grow.

Locations

Entrepreneurs in fast-food and similar industries know that these businesses aren't just about providing good products, good service and good prices. They're also about real estate. The companies with the best locations tend to have better sales than their competitors, all other things being equal. So fast-food entrepreneurs fight furiously with other retailers of all stripes to secure the best spots for their restaurants. Location is also important for companies in industries from transportation to health care. Even firms whose operations are relatively location-independent, such as companies providing telephone call-center services, have to think twice about their locations. No matter where they are, they still have to find employees to staff their operations. Here are five factors to use in evaluating your current location:

1. *Quality of life:* Does your current location provide a pleasant work environment?

2. *Labor:* Can you find the workers you need to grow?

3. *Market:* Will the local market provide adequate additional opportunity to grow?

4. *Distribution:* Can you get enough raw materials—and ship out enough finished goods—at your current location?

5. *Business costs:* Are the costs of doing business low enough to support growth where you are?

The answers to these questions will help you determine whether you're going to grow where you are now, or whether another place might be better.

Capacity

Many a business has gotten into trouble by growing beyond its ability. Growth constraints often relate to your capacity to produce the product or service you are selling. For instance, if your factory can't produce more than 1,000 units a day, then that may be the upper limit to your growth plans. Of course, you may be able to expand capacity by outsourcing, building or adding on to your plant. Before you can make these decisions, you need to know what your current capacity is. Here are some questions to ask to figure it out:

○ *Labor:* What's your average productivity per employee?

○ *Equipment:* What's the maximum throughput you can achieve with your existing plant and machinery?

○ *Supply:* Can you obtain more raw materials and supplies than you are getting now?

> **If you have been growing at double- or even triple-digit percentage rates every year, then it may be time to take a breather rather than go in search of faster growth.**

Different businesses will have different answers. They will probably have different questions as well. For instance, a travel agency may have very little limitation on supply when it comes to the airline tickets it can sell to its customers. However, there may be significant limitations on average productivity per employee for that agency. Take a look at your capacity and try to measure it in the way that makes sense to you. The measurements you make will come in handy when you're studying how to grow in the future.

Growth Rates

A business isn't a static entity. It's always growing, shrinking, or just about to change direction and do something different from what it has been doing. One of the most important measures of how you're doing is determining exactly whether and how you've been growing. This affects your future prospects for growth. If you have been growing at double- or even triple-digit percentage rates every year, then it may be time to take a breather rather than go in search of faster growth. On the other hand, if your business has seen declining sales, shrinking markets and overcapacity, then growth may be something you won't be able to accomplish without radically repositioning your company.

Don't stop after looking at the top-line sales growth you've experienced. Also examine whether and how fast you have been adding employees, expanding to more locations and taking on new customers. Find out which products and services have been growing at the fastest rates. Determine whether new staff positions have tended to be in administrative functions or in production or sales. Evaluate all the new locations you've added. Are they in high-traffic spots with strong demographics that are increasing the average quality of your outlets? Or have you been growing without careful planning? Answering these questions will do a lot to guide your plans for future growth.

Measure Your Market

There is one sure-fire limit to growth: Your sales can't grow larger than your market. It's also true that many measures, from the maximum profits you can generate to the top growth rates you can sustain, are dictated by market limitations. So one prerequisite to deciding whether and how to grow is to know how large and what kind of a business your market will support.

Size

Size is perhaps the most important variable of a market, and one common measure of market size is dollar volume. For example, the U.S. recorded music market has a size of about $12 billion, based on the dollar volume of the industry's annual sales. Unit volume is another way to measure your market. For example, each U.S. beer drinker consumes about 88 gallons of brew annually. These markets, like the markets for most mass consumer goods, are clearly large enough to support many businesses, big and small. Overall market size isn't a major limitation on growth for most companies selling into these markets.

Not all markets are so large, however. If you are selling battery-powered electric cars, for instance, your market size is quite small at the moment. There may be room for only a few modest-sized competitors in this market. Also realize that few markets are monolithic, consisting of undifferentiated customers buying more or less identical products. Most markets can be segmented one or more of these three ways:

1. Geographically
2. By product type
3. By end user type

This basically means you are liable to sell more or less in one area of the country compared to another, of one product type compared to another, and to one kind of user compared to another. Segmenting your market in this way is an important part of evaluating it.

Profitability

Not all products or markets are equally profitable. For instance, while the software products Microsoft sells to corporate customers can sport high gross margins of up to 90 percent of sales, a grocery store may have to get by on a margin of just a few percent on its merchandise. Markets and channels also provide varying profitability. Microsoft gets a smaller markup when selling to a channel such as computer manufacturers installing its software on PCs at the factory. Since no business can last forever without profits, you have to get a grip on the profitability of your current market before you can make a decision about pursuing others.

There are several ways to look at profitability. Net after-tax income shows you the bottom line for your whole company. Other measures, such as gross margin (sales minus cost of goods), are helpful when looking at one of several markets that your company may serve. The important thing is to know profitability for the markets you are operating in now. This will provide a clue to what kind of profit levels other markets will have to be able to support if you are to consider them for expansion.

Growth

When markets expand rapidly, the opportunities for new sales increase and competitive pressures dwindle. When a market is growing, you don't have to beat your competitors to grow. You just have to stay even with them. For instance, if a market is growing by 25 percent a year, and you do no more than hang onto your share of it, then your sales will grow by 25 percent as well. While real life is rarely this simplistic, it's definitely true that one of the most promising prospects for any business is to find itself operating in a fast-growing market.

Danger Ahead!

Entrepreneurs have a tendency to believe their product or service is the first of its kind and fail to recognize that competition exists. In reality, every business has competition, whether direct or indirect. You have to recognize this and have a strategy to deal with the competition if you intend to grow.

Competition

Most businesspeople accept it as a given that competition today is vigorous, growing in intensity, and will continue in this fashion for the foreseeable future. However, not all markets are equally competitive or equally attractive to future competitors. A competitive analysis will detail the strengths and weaknesses of your competitors, the strategies that give you a distinct advantage, any barriers you can develop to prevent new competition from entering the market, and any weaknesses in your competitors' service or product development cycle that you can take advantage of.

You can use a simple tool called a competitive matrix to analyze and present your competitive position. Start with a grid, such as a sheet of graph paper. Along one axis of the grid, list yourself and your competitors. Along the other side, list components of product and service offerings such as price, guarantees, availability and other features. Place a check mark in every box where a competitor offers a particular feature. Leave the others blank. You'll be able to see in a glance how you measure up.

Product Cycles

Nothing lasts forever, and products are no exception. Even the longest-lived product had to start somewhere, and sooner or later it will fall out of fashion and disappear. Between introduction and decline, products generally go through stages of growth and maturity. Acceptance and sales growth is slow in the beginning, speeds up during the growth stage, and levels off as a product matures. Profits are best in the growth stage, as advertising costs to build demand and educate consumers are high at first. Later, in the mature stage, many companies sacrifice part of their profits to added promotions. In the declining stage, when demand for an obsolete or out-of-fashion product is weak, discounting often eats up a lot of profit. In technology and fashion industries, product cycles are commonly measured in months, but in slower-moving fields such as kitchen appliances, products may last for years. You should know where your most important products are in the product cycle before making decisions about your future growth direction.

Market research helps you answer the essential question, "How fast will my market let me grow?" You need market research to provide you with information about three critical areas: the customer, the industry and the competition. In researching the industry, look for information on the latest growth trends, changes in customer taste and technology developments. You can use primary research directly from the source—your customers—or secondary research gathered for you by a third party, such as a market research firm, a government agency or a trade group. Customer research should begin with a market survey of users in the demographic or geographical area you are selling to. You'll want to know the spending characteristics of the population, their purchasing power, population, and perhaps other factors, such as unemployment rate. Competitor information comes from a combination of industry and customer research. Don't underestimate the number of competitors out there. Keep an eye out for potential future competitors as well as current ones.

Your Sales Records

Your own sales records are quite likely to prove your most valuable marketing information source. Files of customer purchases with addresses, amounts, dates, products, payment methods, returns, and other information constitute a rich trove of marketing data. You can analyze this information to find out who your best customers are, what they like the most, and what kinds of marketing approaches appeal to them most powerfully. One of the best things about doing market research with your own records is that it's all proprietary. No one else has the same data you do, and there's no information anywhere that is more appropriate to your business. Add in the fact that market research using your sales records is economical, and it's a powerful combination. Do everything you can to capture and analyze information from your own sales.

> Quite often, problems with new products and suggestions for new ones are generated directly or indirectly by salespeople.

Salespeople's Reports

Your sales force is more than a way to push product. It's also a pipeline to your customers. Quite often, problems with new products and suggestions for new ones are generated directly or indirectly by salespeople. That shouldn't be surprising. Who else spends more time with your customers focusing on their needs, problems and objections? You can't assume that valuable market research will automatically flow from salespeople to your marketing department, though. It's your job to make it easy and enjoyable for salespeople to pass on comments, tips, suggestions, complaints and other useful information from customers in the field. Many firms pass on a percentage of the profits from new ideas generated by salespeople as a result of customer input.

Customer Comments

Customers are going to call you, drop by, send you e-mails and visit your Web site from time to time when they aren't there to shop. Instead, they'll be there to impart information. Often, this is in the form of a customer complaint, which you probably won't enjoy hearing. But you should encourage customers to come forth by using suggestion boxes, customer comment forms, e-mail feedback links and toll-free comment lines. Since these are direct, unvarnished comments from the people who are sustaining your business, it makes sense to treat them as if they were gold. Some companies offer financial rewards, such as discounts on future purchases, to customers who take the time to give them a piece of their minds. It's a wise investment for companies in pursuit of growth.

Vendors

Close ties with vendors can make your business more efficient and profitable. Coordinating shipments and cooperating on marketing programs are just a few of the potential rewards of good vendor relations. Your vendors also are likely to be able to give you valuable insight into the needs and trends in your markets. Customers who might not ever say anything to you about a problem could be perfectly willing to pour their hearts out to one of your friendly suppliers. This is especially true of the kind of information you need to hear *most*, such as the motivations of customers who are defecting to your competitors. If you maintain good relations with vendors and gently probe them for information about your markets and customers, your understanding will increase tenfold.

Knowing Your Customers

You can't know too much about your customers. (Well, actually, you can. It's considered an invasion of privacy to gather sensitive personal information about customers, such as where their children go to school or whether they are overweight, without a legitimate need.

But while respecting people's privacy, you definitely need to know to whom you are selling so you can offer them products and services likely to appeal to them.) Key traits you need to know about your customers include their age, sex, address or at least ZIP code, purchase history and, finally, where they learned about you.

Exploring Buying Motivations

Shoppers' buying motivations can run the gamut of human needs, from hunger and security to convenience and style. They are buying from you for some reason—but what is it? Is it because you're the highest quality? Cheapest? You can find out these answers through a combination of customer surveys, sales analysis and competitive analysis. Whatever tools you use, it's important to know why people are buying what you're selling before you embark on a growth strategy. Otherwise, you might try to grow by selling the right product for the wrong reason.

Measuring Customer Satisfaction

Management guru Peter Drucker says, "The real purpose of any business is to create customers." He might have added "satisfied customers," because otherwise you aren't creating customers, you're destroying them. Having satisfied customers is a good indicator that you are poised for future growth. You can leverage a satisfied customer base to generate referrals, accept additional products and services, and perhaps absorb price increases. A company with dissatisfied customers, on the other hand, even if it reports strong sales growth and profits, is unlikely to fare well down the road. You can measure customer satisfaction by checking return rates, warranty activations, repair reports and customer comments.

Evaluating Your Financing

When you were starting up, you may have been more concerned with getting financing—any financing—than with making sure you were getting the right amount and kind of financing. But you can have too much financing just as you can have too little. And you can certainly have the wrong kind of financing if it doesn't fit your business and personal needs. So before making a decision about growing

Danger Ahead!

Can you have too much financing? Some entrepreneurs would say no. But if you raise $10 million for a five-year product development effort and use $1 million per year, you have too much. Those millions are earning a return of a few percent in a money market account instead of the 30 or 40 percent the venture capitalists wanted. You aren't pleasing your investors or helping your business by having more money than you need.

your business, take a look at your current financing and see whether it measures up.

Capacity

You can't assume you can pay your way to growth just because you're doing OK now. To fund any expansion, you will need to include in your estimate many of the same costs you did when you started, possibly including buying inventory, hiring employees, and renting or building space. Depending on the nature of your growth, you may have additional marketing expenses as well. You need to carefully evaluate whether your cash flow will cover the costs of growth. If it won't, arrange for adequate financial capacity in the form of bank loans, lines of credit, equity investors or other sources. And expect the unexpected: Most financing plans add a contingency amount of 15 to 30 percent to cover unforeseen financial needs.

Cost

Not only does it take money to make money, it also takes money to get money. You pay for all financing you get. If you borrow money from a bank or other lender, you'll have to make interest payments. Equity investors don't charge interest—they take ownership. That includes a share of the say in how profits are disbursed, as well as a percentage of the gain if the business is sold down the road. Other forms of financing may carry other costs. For instance, if you borrow from your family, it may mean you have to employ your less-than-exemplary in-law in the front office until the loan is paid back.

Control

Financial costs aren't the only demands of investors. To obtain financing, you will generally have to give up some control of your business. A venture capitalist negotiating from a strong position may demand 51 percent control and a majority of the seats on the board of directors, effectively making it someone else's company instead of yours. A banker will typically have fewer demands. Most liberal are friends and family, who may ask for no control whatsoever. You may have to do some hard self-interrogation before you decide whether or not going after growth is worth giving up control.

Summing Up Your Prospects For Growth

There is no easy answer to whether or not you are ready for growth. Your chances of growing your business successfully depend on a variety of factors, ranging from your personal skills to the state of your market. Furthermore, these factors play off each other. If you lack a sales record that justifies expansion, you're not likely to be able to get the financing you need. Countless recent start-ups have embarked on the road to growth, however. If you want to be one of them, the next thing to do is take a look at your own aspirations.

chapter 2

What Are Your Aspirations?

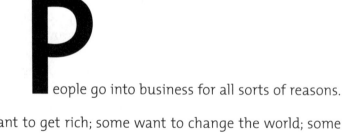

People go into business for all sorts of reasons. Some want to get rich; some want to change the world; some just want to be left alone to work the way they want to. Nobody can say which reasons are best—that depends on the entrepreneur. However, you can say which time is best for deciding what is important to you when it comes to growth. That time is now.

To many people, being an entrepreneur is synonymous with seeking growth. However, not all entrepreneurs are committed to growth. For some, it's the ultimate goal. For others, it's fine if growth happens and fine if it doesn't. The majority of entrepreneurs are somewhere in between. They want growth, but not at any cost. As with so many other things, you don't get growth without somehow paying for it. Whether the bill is in financial, social or personal currency, you're going to have to give something in exchange for growth. So before you embark on an expansion plan, it's essential that you decide what growth means to you, as well as what it's worth to you.

What Does Growth Mean To You?

Japanese firms gradually dominated global markets for cameras, copiers and other products by focusing their efforts on growing market share. Many American corporate CEOs tend to concentrate on increasing their quarterly earnings per share. Who's right? Both are, because growth takes many forms. In addition to growth in market share and earnings, growth may come in the form of sales increases, increases in capacity, and growth in numbers of customers or markets served. Another important kind of growth is growth in net worth.

Sales Volume

Many entrepreneurs gauge their growth largely or even solely by measuring increases in sales volume. It's common to find companies that have annual sales growth targets of a set percentage. And sales volume is, indeed, an important measure of growth for almost all companies. The central activity of any business is making sales, so what better way to figure whether a business is growing than to look at sales? If you choose to measure your growth by sales and to pursue a sales growth-oriented strategy, you are in good company.

Number Of Clients

The 80/20 rule, also known as the Pareto Principle, states that the majority of a business' sales and profits will come from a minority of its customers. In other words, about 80 percent of sales—and even more of profits—are generated by about 20 percent of customers. Using this phenomenon to guide their strategy, many businesses have worked to focus their efforts on the 20 percent of customers who are most active

Danger Ahead!

It's tempting to want growth of all kinds—all at once. However, this is unlikely to happen. It's tough, for example, to increase your profit margins while increasing your market share. Trying to do both means you are likely to do neither. So focus on what kind of growth you want, and go after that rather than trying to achieve all kinds of growth.

and profitable, and divert attention away from the less beneficial masses. If you are in this group, then adding more clients to your existing customer base may be exactly what you don't want to do. Your best bet for expanding sales, profits and other parameters of growth may be to have fewer customers, not more.

It is also possible, however, for businesses to have too much of their sales coming from one or two clients. This is an especially common situation with self-employed professionals who get all or most of their business from selling their services to their former employer. While the Pareto Principle might smile on the efficiencies and simplicity generated by the one-item customer base, it is a risky situation when all your revenues depend on one customer. If that customer decides to go elsewhere, it could be disastrous. If you find yourself in this position, your wisest move may be to seek growth in your customer base above all else, even at the expense of temporarily lower overall sales and profits.

Market Share

Market share is not seen as a major issue by many business owners. This makes sense if you consider the market in terms of its global, national or even regional volume. After all, what market share can a single garden supply store have in the $45 billion national garden supply market? But market share is a bigger issue for small-business owners than it might seem. That garden supply store's gross annual sales of $1 million may represent an imperceptible amount of the national market. But that same annual sales figure might make it the dominant supplier in a small town. Being the dominant supplier of anything in your service area provides you with important advantages in pricing and other key matters. Your competitors are going to have to follow your lead, rather than you having to follow theirs. If you can slice up your market or service area finely enough to see that you have a potential for dominant market share, then growing market share may be the way for you to grow.

Profits

Sometimes, top-line sales growth isn't possible or even preferable. If you're operating in a mature or declining market, it may not be feasible to seek growth in sales volume. Likewise, if, due to competition or other factors, you are being forced to sell your products below cost, losing money on each sale, you are unlikely to want more sales growth! In these situations, it may be best to focus on growth in profits. It's quite possible to grow profits while sales hold steady or even decline. By focusing on products or customers that produce higher margin, by cutting costs or by simply raising prices, you can increase profits significantly on stable sales volume. One of the nice things about growing profits instead of sales is that it isn't likely to require expanding your work force or debt load. Growing your business while simplifying your business is a coup, indeed.

Fast Lane

You don't have to be bent on market domination to use market share as a measure of growth. It's possible, using census figures and other sources, to determine what per capita consumption of many products and services is in a given geographical area. Comparing changes in your sales per capita with overall consumption per capita gives you a quick answer as to whether and how your market share is increasing.

Viewpoint

Sales and profits get the lion's share of attention when it comes to growing your business. But you may also want to pay attention to growing the business's assets. Owning real estate, machinery and other assets won't, by itself, make a successful business. But most businesses that grow over a long period of time have steadily increasing assets.

Net Worth

The greater the net worth of your business, the more flexibility you have in raising money to expand. Why? Lenders usually demand collateral and are reluctant to lend a business more than its worth. A high-value business also gives you flexibility in deciding to pursue other ventures, including retirement, or passing the business along to your heirs, because it's obviously much easier to sell a business that has a high net worth. Net worth can be valuable even when it's not time to sell your business. Being able to place a high valuation on a business may be critical to success when an entrepreneur is obtaining financing, negotiating with a potential new partner or strategic ally, hiring a key employee, setting up an employee stock ownership plan, and at myriad other points. While building net worth is rarely the sole component of a growth plan, it should be part of almost any strategy designed to achieve viable growth.

Ways To Grow

If you've been considering all the different measures of growth, it's probably become obvious that there is more than one way to achieve growth. While one entrepreneur expands by adding new products and markets, another may grow just as well by selling existing products through new locations in existing markets. You can also amplify your enterprise's size by adding to your work force, increasing the productivity of existing workers, or by using other people's production and marketing capacities via the licensing and franchising routes. You can grow rapidly by acquisition, or slowly by methodically diversifying your product line.

New Products

The sexiest kind of growth is based on new products and services. To come up with the next "killer app" that storms the world in a year or two is the dream of many an inventor/entrepreneur. Ideally, growth based on new products yields revenue that are both fast-growing and highly profitable. If your product is advanced enough, you may have a long period of little competition. The income generated by a hot new product can fund development of new products and refinement of your original design, creating a long-term lead on the rest of the field. New products can be expensive to develop, however,

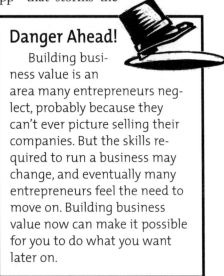

Danger Ahead!
Building business value is an area many entrepreneurs neglect, probably because they can't ever picture selling their companies. But the skills required to run a business may change, and eventually many entrepreneurs feel the need to move on. Building business value now can make it possible for you to do what you want later on.

and many require years of testing and adjustment before they are ready to hit the market. They're also risky, since by definition there is no proven market for a truly new product. But for the right company with the right idea for a new product, there's no more powerful engine of growth than a new product.

New Markets

The Internet chugged along for 20 years as a communications medium for government researchers and university academics. It didn't explode into the mainstream until it caught the attention of a broader group of commercial businesses and general computer users. Introducing the Internet to this whole new market changed not only the Net, but all of business and much of society as well. In the same way, you can achieve high-powered growth without changing your products or services much (or at all). You can also achieve growth if you find different markets where you can sell your products or services. For instance, a local retailer can tap growth by selling to a global market via the Internet. A manufacturer may be able to supercharge sales by introducing mainstream consumers to a product that has been successful in ethnic markets, or vice versa. Some companies find switching to the business-to-business market generates faster growth than selling to end users. The opposite tack may work, too. Even if you don't have any ideas for new products, think about new markets as a way to find growth when you need it.

Fast Lane

It can take several years and many dollars to create a new product. But you may be able to generate significant growth by repositioning existing products or offering them to new markets. Changing the price, packaging or marketing message can be done much more easily—sometimes with superior results—than developing new products.

Adding Locations

For many retailers, growth is measured largely by the number of retail outlets they add each year. That's because sales are likely to be about the same for most locations, so aside from figuring out a way to sharply boost per-store sales, adding new stores is the only way to grow. Adding locations can help you tap new markets, diversify your risk, try out new products, make your advertising efforts more effective, and increase economies of scale for purchasing and marketing. While some superstore retailers have succeeded in recent years with strategies that call for fewer but larger outlets, for most retailers a key measure of success will be growth in number of outlets.

Growing Your Work Force

It's difficult to grow very much without adding to your work force. And increasing the number of employees you have can quickly add production capacity to allow you to grow. You may use new employees to allow you to serve new customers, or to improve service and increase sales to existing customers. Adding employees isn't the cheapest way to grow, however. You'll have to lay out money to recruit them, train them, equip them, provide them with space, and, of course, pay them and provide benefits such as insurance and retirement plans. A significant difference between growth by adding employees and other strategies is that employees can leave your company at any time. If you have trouble retaining workers, growing by hiring could endanger your expansion plan down the road.

Increasing Productivity

You may be able to grow without hiring more workers or opening new locations if you boost the productivity of your existing employees and facilities. You can increase employee productivity by sending workers to training programs or implementing new technology, such as computers, to help them do more in less time. You can increase the productivity of retail outlets by revving up marketing efforts, changing display and seating arrangements, and altering the mix of products you sell. While increasing productivity can be expensive upfront, the beauty of boosting your productivity is that it frequently allows you to maintain or reduce prices while maintaining or increasing margins. And productivity gains tend to be long-lasting compared to the one-shot rejuvenation of a new location or new product.

> ### Danger Ahead!
> Adding new locations indiscriminately can harm rather than help your growth prospects. Even if a new location boasts strong sales, these sales may be cannibalized by your other locations if they are too close together, if traffic flow around the new location tends to divert customers bound for the other location, or if the image of the new location puts off loyal customers of the old spot. Beware the risks of cannibalization before opening new locations.

Licensing

There are few faster or more profitable ways to grow than by licensing patents, trademarks, copyrights, designs, and other intellectual property to others. Licensing lets you instantly tap the existing production, distribution and marketing systems that other companies may have spent decades building. In return, you get a percentage of the revenue from products or services sold under your license. Licensing fees typically amount to a few percent of sales price but can add up quickly. About 90 percent of the $160 million a year in sales at Calvin Klein Inc. come from licensing the designer's name to makers of underwear, jeans and perfume. The only merchandise the New York-based company makes itself, in fact, are its women's apparel lines. Many large corporations, such as the Walt Disney Co., generate less significant proportions of their revenue from licenses. IBM, after energizing its efforts to license its thousands of technology patents a few years ago, now attributes $1 billion a year of its corporate sales to licensing. The downside of licensing is that you settle for a smaller piece of the pie. Calvin Klein-branded products, for example, generate $5 billion in sales a year, the vast majority of which goes to licensees and retailers. At the same time, licensing revenue tends to be high-margin, with almost all the fees from licensing flowing straight to the bottom line.

Viewpoint

One advantage of adding workers is that it can make you popular. The world's leading retailer, Wal-Mart, gets lots of mileage out of the fact that in one recent year the company added 85,000 new Wal-Mart jobs, employs over a half-million people overall and also supports thousands of U.S. manufacturing jobs through its efforts to buy American-made goods. If you are hiring, don't forget to let your community know that you're helping out the local economy.

Franchising

Franchising is a way to grow rapidly when you have inadequate capital to pay for the growth on your own. It's similar to licensing in that the franchisor receives a fee, usually called a royalty, that represents a percentage of the sales generated by businesses operating as franchisees. However, in the most popular form of franchising, known as business-format franchising, what you're licensing is a system of operating a business rather than, say, a cartoon character or a dress

Viewpoint

While franchising can be a low-cost way to expand, it's also likely to be a low-profit way to expand, at least in the beginning. The revenue from early-stage franchising efforts typically pays for little more than the cost of marketing and getting the first crop of franchisees set up. Franchising, therefore, should be looked at as a way to grow rapidly with a long-term payoff.

design. That means you'll have to train and often equip franchisees to operate the business design you have created. And before you can do that, you'll have to have a proven system for doing business with several successful years under your belt. Since it became popular in the 1960s, franchising has provided the expansion method for some of the best-known, largest and fastest-growing companies in the world, including McDonald's restaurants and Century 21 real estate brokerages.

Acquisitions

There's only one way to achieve massive growth literally overnight, and that's by buying somebody else's company. Acquisition has become one of the most popular ways to grow today. Since 1990, the annual number of mergers and acquisitions has doubled, meaning that this is the most popular era ever for growth by acquisition. Companies choose to grow by acquiring others to increase market share, to gain access to promising new technologies, to achieve synergies in their operations, to tap well-developed distribution channels, to obtain control of undervalued assets, and a myriad of other reasons. Acquisition is risky because many things can go wrong with even a well-laid plan to grow by acquiring. Cultures may clash, key employees may leave, synergies may fail to emerge, assets may be less valuable than perceived, and costs may skyrocket rather than fall. Still, perhaps because of the appeal of instant growth, acquisition is an increasingly common way to expand.

How Big Do You Want To Be?

In 1982, a young business reporter strolled through the brand-new factory owned by a Houston start-up that, until recently, called itself Gateway Technology. The company's chief financial officer

A Tale Of Two Burger Joints

In 1921, a pioneering restaurateur named E.W. Ingram opened a restaurant that became the prototype for the very first fast-food burger chain. The restaurant, which he called White Castle, became famous for its small, square hamburgers—known as "slyders" or "belly bombers" to White Castle fans. Though innovative in his concept, Ingram was conservative and traditional when it came to expansion. He avoided borrowing, funded all growth internally and retained ownership of all the White Castle restaurants.

Ingram's growth strategy worked. Today the Columbus, Ohio-based company, still owned and run by Ingram's descendants, has 330 White Castles in the Eastern and Midwestern United States. Slyders are still famous, and the company brings in an estimated $400 million a year in sales and is growing at about 4 percent annually.

About 33 years after White Castle was born, a milkshake mixer salesman walked into a restaurant in Southern California and walked out with an idea for yet another kind of fast-food hamburger place. That salesman's name was Ray Kroc, and the restaurant was, of course, McDonald's—at that time a one-location operation run by two brothers in San Bernardino.

Enthused by the efficiency, hygiene and popularity of McDonald's, Kroc convinced the brothers to let him take over their modest franchising effort. While the brothers were even less interested in rapid growth than E.W. Ingram was, Kroc wanted to turn up the heat as high as it would go. He began franchising restaurants as rapidly as he could, using an innovative new system that gave him much greater control over franchisees than was normal at the time.

Today, Oak Brook, Illinois-based McDonald's is the world's largest fast-food chain, with some 26,000 restaurants in more than 100 countries. More than three out of four units are franchises. In 1999, the company's sales topped $13 billion and were growing at nearly 7 percent annually.

As these two stories illustrate, you can prosper by growing quickly or by growing slowly, but the magnitude of your eventual success is largely determined by whether you are willing to take risks, or whether you prefer to take a cautious approach.

informed the reporter that the organization had the financial structure in place for a $200-million-per-year sales firm. The journalist put this remark down to hubris, doubting that the firm, which had yet to even start up its production line, would ever achieve such a lofty sales number. However, a year later the company had notched first-year sales of $111 million, and three years after that it became the youngest start-up to date to make it to the Fortune 500. Five years from start-up, sales topped $1 billion at the firm, which by then was practically a household name: Compaq Computer Corp.

The point of this story is that it's a good idea to think for a moment about the end of the road. Where do you want to be when you've achieved everything you aspire to in business? What can you reasonably expect? Do you have the right structures, financial and otherwise, in place to support your aspirations? Now is the time to mull these questions over so that when your chance arrives, no matter how unlikely it may appear to others, you will be ready with a solid foundation on which to build your dreams.

Reasons To Grow

Growth is something many entrepreneurs desire without knowing exactly why. Of course, larger companies are more visible and more prestigious, and the opportunity to run a well-known firm may drive many entrepreneurial growth strategies. However, there are sound business reasons, unrelated to ego, that recommend growth to entrepreneurial entities. As firms grow, they can benefit from economies of scale to reduce costs. By adding market share, they can achieve greater flexibility in pricing. And by adding new markets and new products, they can diversify, reducing long-term risk.

Economies Of Scale

Economies of scale refer to a company's ability to reduce its production costs as its sales volume grows. Simply put, the more you make of something, the more cheaply you can make it. Economies of scale include: greater leverage in purchasing raw materials from suppliers, less time and money spent setting up factory lines for different products due to longer production runs of the same products, more negotiating power with labor unions, more experience at reducing errors and simplifying tasks. This powerful lowering of costs as unit volume increases also works for retailers and, to a lesser extent, service providers. One of its most important features is that it tends to reinforce itself. As your costs fall, you can reduce prices, which brings in more business, allowing you to reduce costs even more.

Market Share

The bigger your market share, the more you can set the tone for the market. In the case of monopoly or near-monopoly situations, such as J.P. Morgan held in steel a century ago or Microsoft holds in personal computer operating systems today, you can set prices, control distribution, enforce standards, and otherwise manage the market almost at will. Of course, it's unlikely a small company can enjoy a genuine monopoly position, and true monopolies are likely to draw the attention of the U.S. Justice Department, as they have with AT&T, IBM, Microsoft and U.S. Steel. But through growth, a small company can achieve enough market share to at least play a part with other companies in creating a viable market for customers and competitors.

Diversification

Many small companies are one-trick ponies, betting their entire futures on a single product, a single service, a single location or even a single customer. There's nothing wrong with that in the beginning. A narrow focus lets a start-up concentrate energy on doing one thing extremely well. But as you grow larger, you will find opportunities to add products, services, locations, customers and markets. Diversifying in this way can help your firm weather tough times by providing alternate sources of revenue in the event that your original market dries up, stops growing or is hit by new competition. Most companies that survive for long periods of time find that they have to develop new sources of revenue as tastes change and opportunities evolve. Growth through diversification can help your company have options in place when they are needed.

Limits To Growth

Companies come in all sizes, and there are reasons for that. Sooner or later, you will find yourself up against limits on the size to which you can comfortably expand. Some limits are seemingly hard-wired—you don't see too many 10,000-employee art galleries, for instance. But other limits are more flexible and depend on your industry, your market and your own abilities.

Financing

Access to capital is one of the main limits to growth. It takes money to grow, and if you can't borrow it, raise it by selling equity to investors, or generate it internally, you're going to have a hard time growing. Some industries have steep financial barriers to growth. For instance, if you have one state-of-the-art microprocessor manufacturing plant, you're going to need about $2 billion to expand to a second. Financing limits may also be imposed by the economy, business cycles, market sizes and the presence of competitors—all of which may make it too difficult for you to raise the money you need to expand. It's a rare era, in fact, when financing does not pose a primary limit to growth. Luckily for entrepreneurs around the beginning of the 21st century, this is one of those periods when, as the saying goes, "the money is chasing the deals." Venture capital funds are well-stocked, public equity markets welcome offerings, and banks offer low interest rates. Usually, it is the other way around—entrepreneurs do the courting while financiers play hard to get.

> **Luckily for entrepreneurs around the beginning of the 21st century, this is one of those periods when, as the saying goes, "the money is chasing the deals."**

Competition

A hundred years ago was a very good time to start an automobile company. In fact, hundreds of them were started, and many of them prospered for decades and made the entrepreneurs who founded them very wealthy. Today, however, is a poor time to start an automobile company. The reason is not that people have stopped buying cars. It's that the market is essentially locked up by a number of very large, very powerful competitors. The engineering, manufacturing, marketing and distribution clout of General Motors, Toyota and DaimlerChrysler make it almost impossible for an entrepreneur to effectively compete against them. Not all competitive playing fields are like that, of course. There are many competitors and much opportunity in less mature fields, such as software development, retailing and construction, to name just a few. As a general rule, if there is not much difference between your company and the others in your field, you have good prospects for future growth.

Quality Control

Many entrepreneurs are obsessed with maintaining the quality of their product or service. They feel, with some justification, that "if you want it done right, you have to do it yourself." Clearly, entrepreneurs have to get past this bottleneck if their companies are to grow significantly. But a desire to maintain tight, hands-on oversight of product or service quality can be a legitimate reason to restrain the growth of your company. If nobody truly can do it like you, you have to do it all yourself and limit your company's growth to accommodate your own level of productivity.

Market Size

The size of your markets is a near-absolute cap on your company's growth. Obviously, you can't sell more of anything than your customers want to buy. In fact, with rare exceptions, no company owns 100 percent of any market. So if you are planning to grow your company to, say, $100 million in sales, you first have to pick a primary market that will support a company with that level of sales. Furthermore, that much of the market must be available for you to capture. If your market, or the share of it you can capture, is smaller than your goals, you'll have to switch or add markets, increase your competitiveness or come up with a more modest goal.

Labor Availability

In the economic environment of the past several years, availability of labor has been one of the most important limitations of company growth. Problems finding good employees regularly top employers' lists of frustrating issues. The situation tends to be worse in areas of the country where unemployment is very low, and in industries where particular skills, such as computer programming, are in short supply and high demand. However, the differences are largely a matter of degree. Labor shortages exist today no matter what industry you are in or where you are located. Unless you plan carefully to be able to recruit, retain and maximize the productivity of the employees you need, labor availability will put a significant restraint on your growth.

Think Small

Bigger may not always be better. In some instances, it's a wise strategy to stay small. Here are a few examples, as presented by entrepreneurial expert Karl Vesper in his book *New Venture Strategies*:

○ *When demand is limited by a small national market:* For example, if you're selling crew racing shells or top-quality musical instruments, the small size of your market precludes you from becoming a large company.

○ *When flexibility and innovation are at a premium:* Big companies are efficient, but the many finely tuned practices and policies that make efficiency possible tend to hinder flexibility and innovation.

○ *When close supervision and very careful work without excessive costs are vital:* Fast-food restaurants get by with employees who have a week of training under their belts. If you're running a restaurant featuring an elegant atmosphere and fine cuisine, however, you'll need veteran professional chefs and an experienced waitstaff or risk driving away your clientele.

○ *Where custom or personalized service is important:* Clients often prefer to deal with the person whose name is on the door, which may mean you'll have to limit the number of clients you take on.

○ *Where government policies are designed to aid small firms:* Many agencies at all levels of government set aside certain amounts of their procurement budgets to provide contracts to small firms. Numerous funding programs are set up specifically to benefit small companies. If you rely heavily on small-business set-asides like these, you could be shooting yourself in the foot by growing too large to take advantage of them.

Vesper also notes that these size considerations should not be thought of as negative limitations, but as advantages that small firms have over larger ones in certain situations.

Personal Limits

Organizational theorists say that the largest group of humans that can be managed as a unit is about 150 people. Many business experts see a point at around 100 employees when many growing firms become too much for their founders to comfortably manage. Whether the number is 100, 150 or something else, and whether the relevant factors are organizational or personal, it's clear that there are limits to how large a company almost any entrepreneur will be able to run. If you aren't certain how large a company you can manage, you may need to obtain some additional management training or perhaps hire an outside manager to run the company for you. Alternatively, you may choose to limit your company's growth to a speed or size with which you feel comfortable.

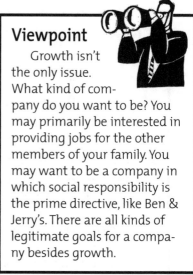

Viewpoint

Growth isn't the only issue. What kind of company do you want to be? You may primarily be interested in providing jobs for the other members of your family. You may want to be a company in which social responsibility is the prime directive, like Ben & Jerry's. There are all kinds of legitimate goals for a company besides growth.

What If You Don't Want To Grow?

A significant percentage of small-business owners are happy with their businesses just the way they are. They're making enough money, building enough value and spending enough time working, and they don't want to grow any larger. These business owners don't necessarily lack ambition. They just may be channeling their ambition into other areas, such as family or hobbies or community activities. There's nothing wrong with this, but if you are such an entrepreneur, you should be aware that there are risks associated with not growing. A firm that isn't growing is likely to become complacent, selling the same things to the same customers in the same way year after year. When change hits, this type of firm is going to find it harder to adjust than one that has been vigorously seeking out new opportunities and new ways of doing things. Just as there are problems with growing too much, you can get in trouble by not growing at all.

chapter 3

Picking A
Time
To Grow

There is a time for everything, and growth is
no exception. If you try to grow at the wrong time, it can be as
serious a mistake as trying to grow too fast or without adequate
financing. Imagine a typewriter manufacturer implementing an
aggressive growth strategy just as the personal computer was
beginning to become the standard for word processing.

It's hard to conceive of any amount of clever marketing, innovative product design or flexible financing that could overcome the sheer misfortune of the timing. That's why timing your growth is as important as any consideration you will make.

Timing your growth plan involves more than making sure you don't get blindsided by some new technology. You have to take into consideration business growth stages, product cycles, market cycles and economic cycles. These cycles take place at all levels, from the level of individual products in your inventory to the economy as a whole.

Business Growth Stages

Businesses, like people, go through life in stages. The best-known business growth model is Greiner's five-stage model, first publicly described by L.E. Greiner in a 1972 *Harvard Business Review* article. Greiner views growth as a series of changes forced by crises.

In phase 1, called "growth through creativity," Greiner posits a "crisis of leadership," during which a youthful organization's founder must begin to delegate authority and accept nonfounder managers. It's at this stage that most entrepreneurs begin to encounter trouble with growth. Greiner's model is designed, however, for large organizations. Entrepreneurs prefer to use a model put forth in 1983 by N.C. Churchill and V.L. Lewis, also in *Harvard Business Review*.

Churchill and Lewis base their model on Greiner's and, like him, describe five stages: existence, survival, success, takeoff and resource maturity. But they focus on the early, perilous days when problems of raising money and delivering product threaten the company regularly. This model is aimed at high-growth companies with the idea that rapid expansion often creates a mismatch between a company's capabilities and its needs. It helps articulate the issues and crises that accompany growth, suggesting what problems are likely to arise and where action may be needed.

An early-stage entrepreneur who studied Greiner's and Churchill and Lewis' models wouldn't worry much

Getting Directions
You can learn more about the five stages of business growth at the Web site for Brigham Young University's Center for Entrepreneurship at http://marriottschool.byu.edu/cfe/resources/5Stages.html.

about problems with internal controls and red tape, for example. Instead, attention would focus on delivering product and raising money because these are problems common to early stages. Using models like these can make all the difference between a solid growth plan and one headed for trouble.

Product Cycles

Products go through life stages—or phases—too. There are usually four: start-up, growth, maturity and decline.

1. *Start-up phase:* During this phase, the introduction of the product takes place, and if there's acceptance, there is usually growing user demand. Education is an issue at this stage; because of this, profits are not usually made at this stage.

2. *Growth phase:* During this time, there is market share growth with strong end-user demand. Quality is a major issue in this stage, and profits begin to appear.

3. *Maturity phase:* Now, market share is strong but end-user demand is leveling off. More attention is paid to price. Most profits are made in this stage.

> **N**ot all products go through the stages at the same rate. For instance, toys and fashion have very short life cycles.

4. *Decline phase:* Increased competition or obsolescence causes a drop-off in demand. Maximizing profits and minimizing costs are key to navigating this stage. Some companies use a harvest strategy in this phase, selling a product—or the equipment to make it—to competitors and redeploying the assets for more promising products.

It is difficult to forecast the length of the cycle or of any one stage. Not all products go through the stages at the same rate. For instance, toys and fashion have very short life cycles, with products moving through one or more of the stages in months or weeks. Consumer technology also typically moves very fast. The reasons are that consumer tastes change, technology changes, and the skills of your employees change. The stages may also occur in a different order. For instance, growth may be followed by decline, or maturity may be followed by renewed growth.

Market Cycles

Christmas decorations are cheap in January. Electricity demand is high in July. These are examples of market cycles, or changes in the pricing, demand or competition for sales that vary over time. There are many types of market cycles. Obviously, electrical usage and holiday decorations are affected by variations in the season of the year. Seasonal cycles affect many products and services, from bathing suits to vacations. Other kinds of cycles also come into play. For example, housing cycles typically move from boom to bust as builders flock to a local market that is undersupplied and then build more homes and apartments than the demand will support. Then they stop building, demand rises to match supply, and the cycle starts over again.

You should identify the cycles that affect your business and then decide when would be the most advantageous way to fit your growth plan into the cycles of your markets. Sometimes you will want to kick off a growth plan just as your market is beginning an upswing. On the other hand, you may want to start while things are at the bottom if your plan will take one or more market cycles to generate momentum.

Economic Cycles

Cycles also affect the larger economy. These business cycles, as economists refer to them, consist of expansions and contractions in a nation's aggregate economic activity. The contractions occur most obviously in the form of recessions, when growth slows across the economy. Expansions appear as booms, when a rising tide seems to lift all boats. One company's boom can be another's bust, since many industries are countercyclical. As with market cycles, the idea is to time your growth effort so that you aren't trying to generate growth when your most prosperous cycle is down.

Timing is the problem. Economic cycles vary widely in terms of their length and severity. Expansions during

Getting Directions
You can stay on top of the latest in economic trends by subscribing to various publications from the National Bureau of Economic Research, 1050 Massachusetts Ave., Cambridge, MA 02138, (617) 868-3900, www.nber.org.

peacetime in the United States average 18 months to three years long. Contractions run from one to two years. The total cycle runs anywhere from two and a half to five years. About the only thing you can count on is that expansions will usually be longer than contractions.

There are also three other fluctuations in economic activity that aren't due to business cycles. Long-term growth trends, such as the growth in U.S. gross domestic product or the persistent upward spiral of inflation, also come into play in making growth decisions. Seasonal fluctuations, which are mentioned in the section in this chapter on market cycles, are also considered separate from business cycles. Seasonal fluctuations in the economy may be affected by considerations such as the date on which Easter falls, which can affect quarterly sales projections at companies that do a lot of business around that holiday. Also, there are purely random events, such as hurricanes, droughts and earthquakes, that can affect the economy.

What Time Is It At Your Company?

Large companies often hire economists or even staffs of economists to help predict changes in markets and economies and guide their investments of corporate resources. For a small company contemplating growth, it's probably just as important to know where you are in terms of your own company's life cycle—and the life cycles of your most important products.

Assessing Your Point In The Cycle

The two most important things for your growth plan when it comes to cycles are assessing at what stage your company is, and where your key products are in their own life cycles. Companies are typically considered start-ups for the first year or two of operation—and established firms after that. However, some firms go through years of developing products, management teams, strategies and other key elements of business operation before they actually commence operations. For these firms, the start-up stage may be short but preceded by a long period of pre-start activity.

Some industries also move faster than others. Today, it's common in the e-commerce world to speak of Internet time, which basically means things happen a lot faster in the e-business world than they do in other arenas. While Internet time is a rather vague concept—there is no formula that says seven years of regular time equal one year of Internet time—it does seem that products and companies that do business on the Internet come and go at a faster rate than in other industries. By comparison, industries such as brick-making or retailing automobile tires may go a decade without comparable change.

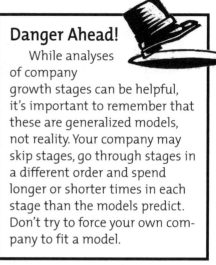

Danger Ahead!
While analyses of company growth stages can be helpful, it's important to remember that these are generalized models, not reality. Your company may skip stages, go through stages in a different order and spend longer or shorter times in each stage than the models predict. Don't try to force your own company to fit a model.

Assessing Market And Economic Cycles

Predicting market and economic cycles is an arcane, difficult art. Economists can't even agree on what causes cycles of boom and bust. Some argue that they are simply self-correcting expansions and contractions in the supply chain; others maintain that interest rates, monetary supplies and trade policies are more important. The National Bureau of Economic Research (NBER) tries to predict the direction of the economy with its index of 10 leading indicators, ranging from new unemployment insurance claims and average hours worked weekly by manufacturing employees to interest rate spreads and consumer expectations. However, even the NBER's leaders don't always indicate accurately. You may do better by using your knowledge of the factors your own industry and business are sensitive to, and making your own gut-level predictions of economic cycles that affect you most directly.

Danger Ahead!
Don't assume you are insulated from broad economic cycles because you operate in a niche industry. For instance, when interest rates rise, they rise for everybody. If you plan to finance growth by borrowing, think through various interest rate scenarios and prepare backup plans, such as alternative financing sources, in case economic cycles jack up rates.

Timing Is Everything

It may seem obvious that the best time to grow is when the business cycle is on the upswing. That's true if your business is the kind that can ramp up production or change direction quickly. But if you're in an industry that requires longer lead times for planning, you may need to begin your growth effort when market and business cycles are at the bottom or just beginning to trend down. The key thing is to be aware that you should not start your growth plan without making an effort to synchronize it with cycles that are larger than your business.

chapter 4

Setting New Goals

"**I**f you don't know where you're going,

you'll probably end up someplace else," Yogi Berra said. A goal is

a way to make sure you don't wind up someplace other than

where you want to be. At its simplest, a goal is just something

you aim for. But goals are powerful contributors to successful

business growth in several ways.

To begin with, the process of setting goals forces you to think through what you want from your business and how growth may—or may not—provide that. This process helps suggest directions for pursuing that growth, which can greatly improve your chances of achieving your goals in the first place.

Goals also give you a framework within which to work. This tends to focus your efforts by helping you rule out actions that will not contribute to achieving the goals you have set. A very important part of that framework is a timetable. Any good goal has a timetable, and that timetable will influence your actions profoundly. For instance, if your goal is to retire by age 50, you'll know that any growth plan with a payoff that won't occur by your 51st birthday is not one you'll consider, no matter how attractive it might otherwise seem.

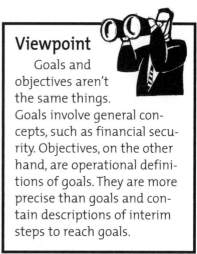

Viewpoint

Goals and objectives aren't the same things. Goals involve general concepts, such as financial security. Objectives, on the other hand, are operational definitions of goals. They are more precise than goals and contain descriptions of interim steps to reach goals.

Evaluating Goals

It's not enough just to have goals. They need to be the right goals and ones that are appropriate to your ambitions and abilities. When entrepreneurs talk about their goals, whether they are for the past year or for a lifetime, the most frequent issue is whether those goals were the best ones to have.

If your goals appear to be holding you back or directing your efforts into unproductive areas, then there is definitely something you can do about it. In fact, setting new goals for yourself and your business is both easy and essential if you're going to grow. When looking at new goals, make sure they have the following qualities:

○ *Specificity:* You stand a better chance of achieving a goal if it's specific. "Raising capital" isn't a specific goal; "raising $10,000 by July 1" is.

○ *Optimism:* Goals should be positive and uplifting. "Being able to pay the bills" is not exactly an inspirational goal. "Achieving financial security" phrases your goal in a more positive manner, thus firing up your energy to attain it.

○ *Realism:* If you set a goal to earn $100,000 per month when you've never earned that much in a year, that goal is unrealistic. Begin with small steps, such as increasing your monthly income by 25 percent. Once your first goal is met, you can reach for larger ones.

○ *Thinking short- and long-term:* Short-term goals are attainable in a period of weeks to a year. Long-term goals can be achieved five, 10 or even 20 years from now; they should be substantially greater than short-term goals but should still be realistic.

○ *Income:* Many entrepreneurs want growth to provide financial security. Consider how much money you want to make each year when planning your growth.

○ *Lifestyle:* This includes areas such as travel, hours of work, investment of personal assets and geographic location. Are you willing to travel extensively or to move if that's what it takes? How many hours are you willing to work? Which assets are you willing to risk?

○ *Type of work:* Your growth plan may require changes in the type of work you do. When setting goals for type of work, you need to determine whether you like working outdoors, in an office, with computers, on the phone, with lots of people, with children, and so on.

○ *Ego gratification:* Face it—many people want to grow their business to satisfy their egos. Owning a bigger business can be very ego-gratifying. You need to decide how important ego gratification is to you and what size business best fills that need.

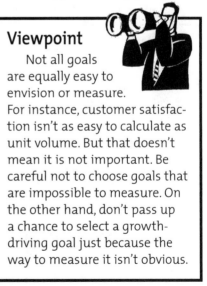

Viewpoint

Not all goals are equally easy to envision or measure. For instance, customer satisfaction isn't as easy to calculate as unit volume. But that doesn't mean it is not important. Be careful not to choose goals that are impossible to measure. On the other hand, don't pass up a chance to select a growth-driving goal just because the way to measure it isn't obvious.

○ *Honesty:* The most important rule of goal-setting is honesty. Building a business with your eyes wide open about your strengths and weaknesses, your likes and dislikes and your ultimate goals allows you to confront dilemmas with greater confidence and a greater chance of success.

Cost-Benefit Analysis

There's no free lunch when it comes to achieving goals. Any goal you set will require some investment of time, effort and money that will cause you to forego other goals. One way you can figure out whether a goal is going to be worth it is to do a cost-benefit analysis. This doesn't have to be complicated. Simply draw a line down the middle of a piece of paper to create two columns. On the left, list the benefits of achieving a given goal. On the right, list what it will cost you to get there. You can simply count the benefits and costs columns and see which has more, or assign weighted scores to each entry and total them at the bottom. You may not want to let this quick and easy analysis make the final decision for you. And, as the example below shows, it may sometimes be the nearest thing to a tossup. But even a simple cost-benefit analysis can give you an idea of whether a given goal is worth investigating further.

Cost-Benefit Analysis

Goal: Open three new offices by year-end

Benefits	Value	Costs	Value
Tap into new markets	5	Have to apply for new bank loan	5
Provide opportunities to promote employees	2	Won't be able to expand home office	4
Achieve economies of scale	6	Not likely to be able to staff new locations easily	3
Total	**13**	**Total**	**12**

Creating A Road Map For The Future

The difference between a dream and a plan is that the first simply expresses a desire to be someone or to achieve something, while the second expresses a method for accomplishing the first. If you really want to achieve your dreams, you need a plan or a map that is going

Getting Directions

Goal Setting: A Worksmart Guide (AMACOM) by Susan B. Wilson discusses the importance of business and personal goals and explains how to set and achieve them. The book contains 11 specific strategies to accomplish goals, including overcoming obstacles and changing counterproductive behavior.

to show you how to get from here to there. A good road map for future growth needs to have the characteristics of specificity and realism, just like a good goal. It should also contain benchmarks to measure your progress and tools to measure how well you're doing.

Setting Benchmarks

An important part of any growth plan is establishing a way to tell when you have reached important points in the process. These mile markers can be composed of any number of indicators. Overall sales revenue is a common one. Many companies recognize the first year they topped $1 million, $5 million and $10 million in sales. Sales is an obvious, important, easily grasped measurement. You can look at sales growth rates and overall sales volume as valuable benchmarks.

Sales, however, are not the only benchmark. You can also look at such critical variables as number of stores, number of customers and transaction volume. Many industries have benchmarks unique to them. For instance, air carriers think in terms of percentage of seats filled and revenue generated per mile flown. E-commerce businesses measure Web page views and time spent on each page. Your business may be concerned with even more esoteric signs, such as percentage of repeat customers or average sale amount per customer.

Not all benchmarks have to do with growth. You can set markers related to cost savings, error rates, employee turnover and many other aspects of your business. The only

Viewpoint

Don't forget to notice when you pass a milestone on your growth trek. When you hit a monthly sales target for the first time or successfully open your 10th new store, stop for a moment and recognize the accomplishment. Give the manager who opened the store a plaque, give a bonus to the salesperson who landed the big account, or simply hold a party to let everyone know you are making progress toward your goal.

characteristics all benchmarks share are that they should be significant, relevant and measurable.

Establishing Measurement Tools

One of the biggest differences between small companies and large ones is the amount of effort each devotes to measurement. Big firms are famous for generating mounds of reports containing measurements of all kinds of performance data. These reports describing what is happening in a company are handy for enterprises with thousands of employees that may be spread all over the globe but still need to be guided in the same direction.

If you're a one- or two-location venture and you've personally hired all the employees and see them every day, doing a lot of measurement and creating reports may seem like a waste of time. And it probably isn't necessary for small firms to spend as much energy tracking performance as it is for big companies. At the same time, most entrepreneurs go out of their way to avoid paperwork. More so than large company executives, entrepreneurs' decision-making is hamstrung by a lack of adequate information about their companies. Although their intuitive knowledge of their companies may be superior to the grasp exhibited by Fortune 500 CEOs, entrepreneurs could generally do a better job of gathering data about their companies. Entrepreneurs often lack enough data to be able to answer questions such as: What is my most profitable product? What are the traits of my best customers? Which types of promotions have the highest payback?

> It probably isn't necessary for small firms to spend as much energy tracking performance as it is for big companies.

You will find your growth plan much easier to implement if—along with setting up financing, hiring and other functions to achieve it—you create measurement tools to tell you how you're doing along the way. These need not be overly complex. You need to decide the things that are most critical to achieving your growth objective and then find a way to measure them. If, for instance, competitive pricing is the main thing you feel will determine your fate in the marketplace, you could assign one employee to make a weekly or daily trip to an outlet where your products are sold alongside those of competitors, just to make sure you're not being undersold. It's easy

Quick-Change Artist

When you are resetting goals, don't forget to update your business plan. You should update your plan at least annually even if you are not considering a major growth initiative. When significant change is on the horizon, it becomes even more important to update your plan. Here are seven reasons to think about updating your business plan. If one applies to you, it's time for an update.

1. *A new financial period is about to begin.* You may update your plan annually, quarterly or even monthly if your industry is fast-changing.

2. *You need financing—or additional financing.* Lenders and other financiers need an updated plan to make financing decisions.

3. *There is a significant market change.* Shifting client tastes, consolidation trends among customers and altered regulatory climates can trigger plan updates.

4. *Your firm develops or is about to develop a new product, technology, service or skill.* If your business has changed a lot since you wrote your plan, it's time for an update.

5. *You have had a change in your management team.* New managers should get fresh information.

6. *Your company has crossed a threshold.* Moving out of your home office, topping $1 million in sales or employing 100 people are perfect examples of prime times to update your business plan.

7. *Your old plan doesn't seem to reflect reality any more.* Maybe you did a poor job last time; maybe things have changed faster than you expected. But if your plan seems irrelevant, redo it.

to overdo measurement, spending valuable resources collecting data that isn't useful. But that doesn't mean all measurement is bad.

Revisiting Goals

The value of a goal lies in the way it provides you with a relatively steady, unwinking light toward which to steer in the fog of everyday business life. But that doesn't mean a goal should be as immovable as a lighthouse. You should periodically take a fresh look at your goals to see if they need to be changed or, perhaps, dumped. Changes in your personal situation, such as a desire to spend more time with family, may cause some goals to become irrelevant to your true desires. Of course, the best reason to scrap a goal is because it has been accomplished.

The last thing you need to know about goals is that they are just that—goals. They aren't preordained events that will occur whether or not you work toward them. In other words, just having a goal of reaching $10 million in sales doesn't mean you'll achieve it. Nor should the accomplishment of a goal be considered absolutely necessary to your personal well-being. Some goals are more important than others, but it's not wise to be so committed to a given goal that, if you don't achieve it or it's not all you hoped it would be, you'll be emotionally destroyed. Remember, as that great philosopher Yogi Berra also said, "The future ain't what it used to be."

chapter 5

Ready To Relocate?

very year, the grass on the other side of

the fence looks greener to many entrepreneurs, and a change of

place looks like the most promising path to growth. So they pull

up stakes and move to a new place, where they hope to find

better odds for business success than they had in their previous

location. They're in good company.

The U.S. Census Bureau reports that approximately 40 million Americans relocate each year, and the U.S. Postal Service processes about 38 million change-of-address forms annually. Although no one keeps a similar count of business moves, given the multitude of valid business reasons for making a move, almost any entrepreneur will, at some time, consider relocating as a way to expand.

Why Location Matters

Businesses commonly cite five main reasons for moving, according to Sharon K. Ward, an economic development consultant in Allentown, Pennsylvania. These are labor and work force issues, the desire to reach new markets, the need to upgrade facilities or equipment, the desire to lower costs or increase cash flow, and considerations about quality of life. For different businesses and at different times, certain concerns are more important than others, Ward notes. But just about all moves can be attributed to some combination of these issues.

Chief among current reasons for relocation is the need for a suitable work force. Unemployment rates are lower than they've been in decades, and the shortage of workers in some occupations, especially those requiring technical expertise, is acute. For firms that need specialized employees, it may be well worth it to relocate to an area where they can easily find these kinds of employees.

When a company finds itself in outmoded or undersized facilities, that's another reason to look at moving. Most businesses start in a small facility, such as the founder's garage, and then move to bigger quarters in the same city, says L. Clinton Hoch, director of location advisory services for DCG Corplan Consulting, a site selection consultancy in West Orange, New Jersey. Later, the business outgrows that location or begins to find fault with its facilities, services, utilities, infrastructure or other features. "Usually only after [a business owner] goes through those stages is he or she ready to make a move out of the original area," says Hoch.

Getting Directions

The Company Relocation Handbook (Oasis Press) by Sharon K. Ward and William Gary Ward is chock-full of tips, tricks, checklists and work sheets to help you decide when and where to move, and how to conduct a relocation so that all goes smoothly.

Cost Issues

Cost is a concern in any business decision, and a move can cure—or create—many cost issues. For starters, the cost of living varies widely among cities. In Little Rock, Arkansas, for example, the cost of living is 13 percent below the national average. At the other end of the spectrum, New York City's costs are more than twice the U.S. average. Theoretically, a move from Manhattan to Little Rock could yield significant savings.

Fast Lane

A move can put a slow-growth business on the fast track. Luigi Salvaneschi, a relocation expert and former executive with KFC, McDonald's and Blockbuster Video, says a location that taps a new market can instantly revitalize many businesses. "People should relocate," he says, "if they see no growth and no future where they are."

But costs involve more than living expenses, cautions Hoch, and differences in geographic costs have leveled out in recent years. Companies often find themselves forced to compromise between staying close to target markets and choosing the lowest-cost facility. That's one reason for the exodus of employees from central cities to nearby suburbs, which, according to the U.S. Census Bureau, resulted in 3 million people leaving the cities, while the suburbs gained 2.8 million in one recent year.

Depending on circumstances, you may have other financial issues to consider. Large companies seeking to build semiconductor factories or auto plants, for instance, often land well-publicized tax concessions worth billions of dollars. Economic development consultant Sharon Ward, a former research and marketing director for the Committee for Economic Growth, a private organization that markets the Wilkes-Barre area of Pennsylvania to businesses, points out that small companies rarely receive such perks because incentives are based on the number of jobs the business will create. However, an entrepreneur may be able

Getting Directions

Check out *Places Rated Almanac* (Macmillan General Reference) by David Savageau and Geoffrey Loftus. You'll find facts on labor markets, cost of living, housing, education, crime, health care, and climate for more than 350 metropolitan areas in North America.

to tap a cash flow windfall by selling a building or land that has appreciated in value, then purchasing or renting lower-cost space.

An even more intangible issue is quality of life. Companies evaluating relocation often look at recreational opportunities, education facilities, crime rates, health care, climate, and other factors when evaluating a city's quality of life. That's another reason deteriorating inner cities are losing businesses, as companies seek an improved quality of life elsewhere. "Maybe it's an unhealthy or unsafe area to live in," notes Ward. "Or it may be hard to recruit workers because of [the location]."

Relocation Results

While moving carries risks, a move can be one of the best things you ever do for your business. When you move or expand to a new location, the odds are stacked in your favor, according to relocation expert Luigi Salvaneschi, who has overseen the selection of new sites

Lease Options

One of the classic business decisions involves balancing the tradeoffs between buying real estate to quarter your business and renting or leasing the space. While each situation offers nuances to consider, the basic difference is that buying requires more upfront capital investment but provides security and the opportunity for capital appreciation. It costs less to get into leased space—and it's easier to get out, too—but monthly payments may be higher, and you may have to find a new place to do business when your lease is up.

One option open to entrepreneurs is to make a personal purchase of property and then lease it to your business. The business gets to deduct the lease payment, while you receive added income.

If you don't want to take on a long-term mortgage to buy office space, consider a lease with an option to own. Terms of this arrangement will allow you to buy the property for a preset sum at the end of the lease. You will be able to lock in a price now and save the expenses of having to move someplace new when you're ready to buy.

for thousands of retail establishments. "Because you've been in business for some time," he says, "you are fully aware of all the problems your current location has. If you have poor traffic and know that's the problem, you look for a new location that has good traffic."

But there are no guarantees in relocation, and as many things can go wrong with a move as can go right. Ward cites a recent study of readers of *Area Development* magazine that identified a number of common mistakes. They included rushing the decision, focusing too narrowly on a few costs, failing to use available economic development services, ignoring quality-of-life factors, missing important environmental or regulatory concerns, and, believe it or not, failing to plan for future expansion. These mistakes can be boiled down to hurrying too much and trying to do a move too cheaply.

Part of the problem is the complexity of these two issues. There's no set time for how long it should take to move, Ward says, and sometimes you don't have a choice. "I've worked with companies that made a decision in three or four months because they didn't have a choice," she says. Others might expend two or three years in the process, with no better results.

Unfamiliar factors complicate cost calculations, adds Salvaneschi. For instance, an entrepreneur must figure in the cost of business interruption. Almost inevitably, a business's productivity will be reduced for a period of days or even weeks after a move. And that's not all. "You may also have some loss of goodwill," he says. "Especially if you've been in that location for many years, you're going to lose some loyal customers."

Expanding Without Moving

Moving is one way to obtain room to expand, but it's not the only one. You may be able to expand by taking in adjoining space, increasing productivity of existing employees and facilities, or by splitting up your facilities in separate locations.

Absorbing adjoining space is probably the most convenient and inexpensive way to add room for more employees and equipment. You save on moving costs, interruption is minimal, and your old customers won't have trouble finding you because you will be in the same place. When you're picking your original location, in fact, it's not a bad idea to consider the availability of adjacent expansion room as one of your criteria. If space next to your current operation becomes vacant at a time when you are considering expanding, you may want to let the owner of the property know you may require more room soon. You may be able to take out an option on the space that will preserve your flexibility.

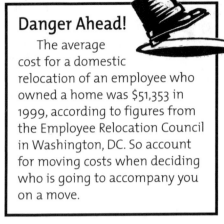

Danger Ahead!

The average cost for a domestic relocation of an employee who owned a home was $51,353 in 1999, according to figures from the Employee Relocation Council in Washington, DC. So account for moving costs when deciding who is going to accompany you on a move.

You may be able to grow your business without moving if you can increase the productivity of your current operation. You can generate more production without adding staff by training your employees to work more efficiently. You can also replace slower machines with faster models, or make alterations to existing equipment to increase output.

Another way to grow without moving your whole company is to split your operation into more than one location. A company that manufactures and sells from a single location can move its warehousing and manufacturing to another facility while leaving its sales outlet in the same place so customers won't have to find it in a new spot. Although the logistics of working from more than one location can be tricky, it's one way to have some of the benefits of moving without all the drawbacks.

Making The Move

Although deciding to move is tough, it's nothing compared to actually making the move. That starts with writing detailed specifications about what your new location must offer. If your main reason for moving is to tap a better labor market, don't get distracted by a favorable lease offered by a prospective landlord or incentives dangled before you by an economic development agency. "You wouldn't want to move to find a well-qualified work force only to find that it's worse in your new location," says Ward.

You'll also need accurate and complete information about the new location before you can commit to moving there. Reference publications such as *The Statistical Abstract of the United States* and magazines such as *American Demographics* are good places to start. You can also subscribe for a month or two to newspapers in the cities you're considering (or read them online) to get a general feel for local circumstances.

Be specific when gathering information from economic development agencies, chambers of commerce, utility companies, real estate brokers, employment agencies, other small-business owners, and so on. Don't ask general questions like "Is there a good supply of affordable office buildings?" Instead, ask "How many 10,000-square-foot blocks of vacant Class A downtown office space exist, and what are the going terms and prices?"

You should also visit all sites on the short list of your targets. "I have a saying: You walk it; you drive it; you fly it," says relocation expert Salvaneschi. Only by walking and driving around a location from various angles can you get a feel for traffic patterns. Aerial views from small planes or helicopters can help you grasp the dynamics of a particular retail zone, he adds.

Making the move itself is another challenge in making the relocation work. It's important to decide what equipment, fixtures, records and other items to actually move. It might be better to dispose of inventory at fire-sale prices rather than pay to haul it across the country.

Once you've decided where, when, what and who you will move, assign someone to be in charge of the relocation. He or she will be very busy with tasks from soliciting bids from movers to keeping employees informed about the plans.

Getting Directions

STAT-USA is a vast online information service with economic, business, social and environmental data generated by scores of federal sources. You can check it out at www.statusa.gov.

In business, as in your personal life, not every move works out. But by looking closely at their reasons for moving and making sure the chosen spot addresses their needs, entrepreneurs increase the odds that the grass really will be greener and that what appears to be a better city for their business will turn out to be the best.

chapter 6

Building
A Company
Image

our company's image is comparable to a

person's personality. It is composed of an infinite variety of

facts, events, personal histories, advertising, and goals that

work together to make an impression on the public. Most peo-

ple think a company like IBM acquired its powerful corporate

image simply by being a powerful corporation.

That's not true—IBM board members, executives and public relations specialists worked long and hard to create an image that would place IBM in the forefront of the business machine industry. If you want to grow—even if you don't want to grow as large as IBM—you need to pay attention to the impression your image is making.

Evaluating Your Image

The key to having an image you can grow with is to match it to your target market. For starters, that involves knowing who your target market is. Second, you have to carefully and consistently build an image around that market.

First determine your target market—the segment of the market that is most likely to purchase your product or utilize your service. A veterinarian's target market may consist of pet owners in a 1-mile radius. The market for an online vendor of hard-to-find videos may consist of film fans who live anywhere and are ready to spend $100 or more to get their hands on a rare movie.

> **If you want to grow— even if you don't want to grow as large as IBM— you need to pay attention to the impression your image is making.**

After you've decided who your target market is, ask questions to develop the image these people will feel most comfortable with. These questions include:

- What is the lifestyle of my customers?
- What are my customers' buying habits?
- Are they budget-conscious?
- Where do they live?
- What features do customers like about my product(s)?
- What features do customers like about my competitors' products?
- What benefits do my competitors list in their promotional materials?
- What benefits does my product have that give my company a competitive advantage?
- How are my competitors' promotional materials designed? What colors are they using? What typefaces are they using?

○ What kinds of packaging are my competitors using?

○ What is the pricing like in the market I am targeting?

Choosing The Right Image

Any mismatches between your image and your target market's needs is likely to be pretty obvious. For instance, if you have an economical image but you're marketing to an affluent customer who spends freely, you need to change that before you can achieve significant growth. Here are some other image selection considerations:

○ *Develop an image that defines your company as narrowly as possible.* Few businesses fail from being overly focused. Many fail by trying to be too many things to too many people.

○ *Make sure you can describe what your image is in a single, clear sentence.* For instance, "Everything In Its Place Inc. is the senior executive's personal organization service." Being able to describe your business in a consistent, memorable fashion is a great way to position your company in your prospects' minds.

○ *Define your image by selecting a coherent, interesting, engaging stationery design for business cards, letterhead and envelopes.* You can echo the colors and typefaces from your stationery in any subsequent marketing materials.

○ *Hire a graphic designer to create a distinctive logo.* Then you can use that logo on all printed materials to express a catchy visual image.

Selecting your image may be driven by a flash of inspiration and insight. More likely, however, it will be an evolution, occurring over months or years as you add layers to your marketing materials and marketing message. Just be sure that each time you make a new image-related decision, it stays consistent with existing marketing materials. That way, you will always present the same image to your customers.

Viewpoint

Few, if any, businesses benefit by presenting a shoddy, low-quality image. Even if you position yourself as the price leader, be sure your marketing materials are professionally produced, your telephone is courteously answered and your employees present a businesslike face to customers. These facets of a successful business image are universal.

Establishing A New Image

Establishing a new image is an ongoing effort. Any time you air an advertisement, mail printed materials, make a sales call, sponsor an event, hire a spokesperson, or even paint your building, you are contributing to the image you project.

Establishing a new image starts, however, with a few major moves that need to be replicated throughout your company. They range from the really monumental, such as changing your company's name, down to the less significant, such as adopting a new corporate slogan or motto. Making these basic decisions about your new image, and then implementing them carefully in everything you do, will go a long way toward establishing a new image for a growing company.

Changing Your Name

What's in a name? If you're in business, the name of your company is probably one of your most valuable assets. An effective name is one that establishes a strong identity and describes the type of business you're conducting. It's not unusual for companies to go through one or more name changes as they grow. Name changes can reflect a change in the focus of your company or a change in the market. In his early years in the footwear business, Philip Knight called his athletic shoe company Blue Ribbon Sports when its business was as a U.S. distributor for Japan-based Onitsuka Tiger. Later, Knight decided to market his own line of shoes, which he named after the Greek goddess of victory, and eventually changed the name of the company to Nike Inc.

Name changes may also be necessary when conflicts arise with names of other companies in the field as you expand into new markets. EBay founder Pierre Omidyar had originally called his online auction service Auction Web. Later, trying to come up with something catchier, he picked Echo Bay. When he tried to register the name for

Danger Ahead! When you embark on a major growth plan, it may be tempting to start by slapping a new name on your business. But name recognition is very valuable and can take years of effort and countless advertising dollars to create. So before you take such a major step, make sure you're not throwing away something of great value without a good reason.

his Web site, however, he found that echobay.com was already taken. He then picked eBay from a list of available Web sites that were similar to Echo Bay.

Choosing a name for a company can be the first step in developing a new identity for the business and estab-lishing a new image. It is the first impression the public will have of your growing company. Today, coming up with a good business name is more difficult than ever because many of the best names have already been trademarked. But with advertising costs and competition on the rise, a good name is crucial to creating a memo-rable business image. In short, the name you choose can make or break your business.

Start by deciding what you want your name to communicate. To be most effective, your company name should reinforce the key ele-ments of your business. Naming consultant Gerald Lewis uses retail as an example. "In retailing," Lewis explains, "the market is so seg-mented that [a name must] convey very quickly what the customer is going after. For example, if it's a warehouse store, it has to convey that impression. If it's an upscale store selling high-quality foods, it has to convey that impression. The name, combined with the logo, is very important in doing that." So the first and most impor-tant step in choosing a name is deciding what your business is.

Should your name be mean-ingful? Most experts say yes. The more your name communicates to consumers, the less effort you must exert to explain it. Alan Siegel, chairman and CEO of Siegelgale, an international com-munications firm, believes name developers should give priority to real words or combinations of words over fabricated words. He says people prefer words they can

Viewpoint
Geographic names are appeal-ing but also limiting. If you name your company after the city you start in, you should ask yourself how easy it will be to expand to another city without changing the name. You may be better off picking a state or region of the country, or avoiding geographic names altogether.

relate to and understand. That's why professional namers universally condemn strings of numbers or initials as a bad choice.

Specific names make sense if you intend to stay in a narrow niche forever. However, if you have any ambitions of growing or expanding, you should find a name that is broad enough to accommodate your growth. How can a name be both meaningful and broad? Naming consultant S.B. Master makes a distinction between descriptive names (like San Pablo Disk Drives) and suggestive names. Descriptive names tell something concrete about a business—what it does, where it's located and so on. Suggestive names are more abstract. They focus on what the business is about. Would you like to convey quality? Convenience? Novelty? These are the kinds of qualities that a suggestive name can express.

Viewpoint

Can you name a company after yourself? There is no reason why you can't, and many companies grow to global size bearing their founders' names. It helps, however, if people can tie the name to the product or service you're selling. So "Joe's Bar & Grill" is probably better than just "Joe's."

For example, Master came up with the name "Italiatour" to help promote package tours to Italy. Though it's not a real word, the name is meaningful. Right away, you recognize what's being offered. But even better, the name evokes the excitement of foreign travel. "It would have been a very different name if we had called it 'Italytour,' " says Master. "We took a foreign word, 'Italia,' but one that was very familiar and emotional and exciting to English speakers, and combined it with the English word 'tour.' It's easy to say, it's unique, it's unintimidating, and it still has an Italian flavor."

Before you start thinking up names for your business to grow by, try to define the qualities you want your business to be identified with. If you're running a hearth-baked bread shop, for example, you might want a name that conveys freshness, warmth and a homespun atmosphere. Immediately, you can see that names like "Kathy's Bread Shop" and "Arlington Breads" communicate none of these qualities. But consider the name "Open Hearth Breads." The bread sounds homemade, hot and fresh from the oven. Moreover, if you diversified your product line, you could alter the name to "Open Hearth Bakery." This change would enable you to hold onto your suggestive name without totally mystifying your established clientele.

Changing Your Logo

To build an image for your business, your company name should become a visual symbol. Think of the big blue letters of IBM, the rainbow-colored fruit of Apple or the bucking-horse symbol of Ferrari. These images immediately convey the traits for which these companies are known—IBM's solid conservatism, Apple's counter-cultural appeal and Ferrari's untamed performance.

Building a good logo requires following the rules of visual communication. These rules involve:

○ *Originality:* Your logo should be original, not imitative. The old rule still applies: Imitation is the sincerest form of flattery. Imitating another company signifies that your company is a follower, not a leader.

○ *Distinction:* The design of your logo should be memorable so that people remember it instantly when they hear your name. "Memorable" doesn't mean distasteful, intentionally offensive or outlandish.

○ *Expression:* Your logo should instantly convey the complexion of the business.

○ *Taste:* While your logo should be memorable, it should also be aesthetically pleasing. It should also translate well abroad. In other words, if you plan to do business in other countries, you need to make sure your logo is not unintentionally offensive.

○ *Marketability:* The logo should be easy to use in advertising, public relations and sales promotion materials. It should serve as the symbol that sums up the entire company.

Keep these rules in mind when developing your logo, and remember that any commercial symbol that doesn't get its message across in a few seconds has failed at what it was supposed to do—communicate the company's line of business and how it regards itself in the marketplace.

Consider how you would like the public to perceive your organization before you proceed with the design of the logo. Do you want your company perceived as conservative? Brash, with a tremendous amount of creative energy? Luxurious and quality-oriented? On the cutting-edge of the industry? These are things you have to decide after you've researched the industry and the competition.

Once you know what type of impression you want to create in the market, you need to convey that in a design. Almost invariably, the simpler the design, the more memorable it will be. That applies to typeface, color and shape. You want an eye-catching design but one the viewer doesn't have to spend a great deal of time interpreting.

Choose a typeface that is representative of the identity you want to project. There are conservative, bold, modern and classic typefaces. Many times, companies develop their own typefaces and trademark them. The idea is to match the typeface with the character of the business.

> **Your use of color should be tied to the message you are trying to convey through your logo.**

Color is generally used to express a mood. Bright colors are used for companies that sell fun products; dark colors are more conservative and serious; and neutral colors project a warm and caring image. Again, your use of color should be tied to the message you are trying to convey through your logo. Many financial services companies use darker colors with a contrasting neutral color. Their intention is to convey a conservative and caring company. On the other hand, toy companies often use bright colors set against neutral backgrounds for their logos.

Shape, of course, refers to the basic form of the logo. Will it be circular? Square? Rectangular? Triangular? You need to decide how your company will be best perceived through the various shapes you have to choose from.

All these elements are then combined to create a logo that expresses the message you want to convey. There are many different types of logos from which you can choose. Some of them are:

○ *Seals:* The name or signature of the company is placed within a geometric shape used as a visual to describe the nature of the company's business.

○ *Monograms:* The company initials are used in a unique manner.

○ *Monoseals:* The initials of the company are worked into a pattern that resembles a seal.

○ *Signatures:* These logos show the company name in a specific and constant style that is often proprietary.

○ *Abstracts:* These are geometric shapes used to make a distinctive visual connection with the company. Abstracts are not descriptive but offer a visual that identifies the company universally.

○ *Glyphs:* These are similar to abstracts, except glyphs are descriptive, relating the company's name, major product lines and business identity in a very visual manner.

○ *Alphaglyphs:* These logos are a combination of graphic objects and the company's initials that describe the company's identity, product lines and business concern.

○ *Wordmarks:* These types of logos are a combination of a glyph and a signature to create a distinctive visual and name device.

Trademark Matters

While a logo is a symbol that expresses the company's image and identity, a trademark is a symbol that's used to stamp the company's identity on its products. Traditionally, it is a symbol of quality. It is a signature of the company that is recognized throughout the industry.

A logo can be a trademark, and many times they are used as such. But a trademark can be a separate symbol from the logo of the company. For instance, the familiar stagecoach symbol marks each GMC product, whether it's a Buick, Chevrolet or Pontiac. The stagecoach is GMC's trademark of quality and excellence but not its logo. On the other hand, "Ford" is that company's logo and trademark.

A trademark is a corporate symbol that contributes to the image the company is trying to build. It is a mark of quality and excellence that identifies that company as the manufacturer. Like the logo, a trademark can be a combination of color, typestyle and shape, or it can be just shape and color, like McDonald's golden arches.

There is also a legal side to the term "trademark." In the legal sense, a trademark is a form of protection of your corporate symbols from use by unauthorized parties. Trademark registration is filed through the Patent & Trademark Office of the U.S. Department of Commerce.

An important point to remember when filing for trademark protection is that a trademark is not a trade name. A trade name identifies the business. A trademark identifies the product. For instance, Entrepreneur Media is a trade name, while Entrepreneur is a trademark for the magazine.

There are generally four types of marks that can be federally registered:

1. *Trademarks* used to identify products
2. *Service marks* used to promote a service
3. *Collective marks* used by organizations or associations to identify themselves

4. *Certification marks* such as UL (Underwriters Laboratory) used to certify that a particular product has met the manufacturing standards of an impartial third-party regulatory group

Although the 1946 Lanham Trademark Act provides a limited amount of protection to companies upon the "first use" of a symbol, you should register a trademark as quickly as possible.

Picking A New Slogan

Using corporate slogans to spur growth is common among America's giant companies. For 17 years, Ford Motor Co. used "Quality is job one," both to convince car buyers of its emphasis on quality and to remind workers of quality's importance. Many others, including Avis ("When you're number two, you try harder") and Charles Schwab ("Helping investors help themselves"), have made the most of slogans, according to Robert Keidel, a writer and organizational consultant in Wyncote, Pennsylvania.

There's no reason why smaller companies can't do the same, says Keidel. In fact, the flexibility, low cost and high effectiveness of slogans make them almost mandatory for companies of any size, he says. The best slogans are mini-vision statements. When carefully crafted, they can effectively convey a company's key characteristics to a variety of audiences, from investors to customers and suppliers to job applicants. "The good ones," says Keidel, "resonate at several levels."

The benefit of a slogan is just that: The same memorable message can be used for many purposes in many different media. A brief, catchy slogan can be placed in advertisements, workplace posters, business cards and even on uniforms and corporate stationery, providing a uniform, constant reminder of what makes the company special.

Among Keidel's favorite management slogans are "You expect more from a leader" (Amoco) and "We help businesses do more business" (Sprint). He's especially fond of "We don't cut corners," used by Hartmann luggage.

Slogans are particularly effective when you're trying to communicate a major shift in strategy. Keidel points to Nike, which is trading in its infamously audacious "Just do it" catchphrase for the softer "I can" at the same it's trying to market more shoes and apparel to women. Similarly, Xerox's "The document company" describes its recent return to its roots after forays into financial services and other unrelated areas.

Slogans may also change to reflect societal shifts, Keidel notes.

Ford, for instance, recently dropped "Quality is job one" because of the perception that in today's marketplace, high quality is a given and is no longer an important marketing variable.

An effective slogan should be brief. Keidel notes that many one-word slogans have been used successfully, including "Exactly" (Hertz). He suggests using a maximum of eight words. Short or long, a slogan should encapsulate the essence of the firm. "It should be unique to the company, and it should represent the cornerstone of the company," says Paul Miesing, a management professor at the University of Albany in New York.

One way to get some guidance about your slogan is to look at the slogans used by competitors. Ideally, yours should say something different from all of them, staking out an area that rivals have ignored. A good slogan should also be memorable. Many of the better ones hook up with some idiomatic saying, such as the Hartmann slogan's reference to cutting corners and Ford's mention of "job one."

But slogan crafting involves more than coming up with a catchy saying. As a mini-vision statement, your slogan should state exactly why you are special as a business and how you'll remain that way. For that reason, slogan designers use some of the same tools vision statement writers do, such as weekend management retreats.

Don't let top management come up with a slogan on its own, advises Andrew DuBrin, management professor at the Rochester Institute of Technology. "It's best if employees have some input," says DuBrin. "That will help you use it as a tool for team-building and motivation." One approach is to solicit employee suggestions through a contest. That was the technique Ford used to select its long-lived "Quality is job one" slogan. However, DuBrin cautions, do not commit yourself to using the contest-winning slogan.

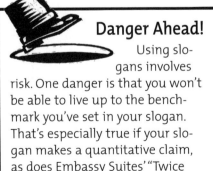

Danger Ahead! Using slogans involves risk. One danger is that you won't be able to live up to the benchmark you've set in your slogan. That's especially true if your slogan makes a quantitative claim, as does Embassy Suites' "Twice the hotel," referring to the lodging chain's claim of charging one-room rates for two-room suites.

Quantitative slogans can be very effective, Keidel says. But if you make a quantitative promise and can't live up to it, you'll succeed only in looking foolish, he warns. You may also err if you come up with a slogan that focuses attention on the wrong things. For instance, it's probably not a good idea to have a slogan dealing strictly with financial matters. "Your cornerstone shouldn't be something like 'Maximizing profit,'" says Miesing.

Slogans can be inexpensive, or they can be very costly. Many large companies spend millions of dollars with ad agencies and image consultants to come up with new slogans. Communicating the new slogans can be expensive too; Ford has budgeted $40 million for the corporate advertising campaign that will roll out its new slogan, "Better ideas. Driven by you." But printing slogans on posters, atop memo pads and in other visible places will work well and inexpensively for smaller companies, says DuBrin.

Not every company is ripe for a new slogan. If your firm is changing direction and is uncertain about where it's going, wait until you have a firm strategy before trying to come up with a slogan to express it. "You need a fair sense of where you're headed," says Keidel. "And you'd better be sure it's something you want to live with for a while."

Image In A Nutshell

Now that you've finished this chapter, you're probably looking at company image in a completely different way. The bottom line is your company's image should seem simple and straightforward. But like a person's personality, your image combines a variety of statements, images, feelings and facts to make a single impression. And only by carefully selecting and managing these components can you expect to make your company's image an ally in your pursuit of growth.

part two

How Are You
Going To
Get There?

Planning is one thing; doing is another. This part of *Grow Your Business* focuses on making sure you can put your plans into action. First, it covers finding people to help you grow your business: In Chapter 7, you'll learn to evaluate current employees and hire the additional workers you'll need to get the work done. Every business can use some outside help, and in Chapter 8, you'll learn to use professional service providers such as lawyers and accountants wisely and well.

The good news about financing growth is that it's a lot easier than financing a start-up. But it's no less important for a growing business to have the proper borrowing and other financial resources in place. Chapter 9 explains how financing plays a role in expanding your company and provides tips on where and how to get what you need. Sometimes you have to go a long way to get what you want—like to the other side of the world. So Chapter 10 covers "Going Global" with a growth plan as big as the planet. Global or not, almost any owner of a growing business has spent some time at trade shows and industry conferences. But has it been time well-spent? Chapter 11 provides you with techniques and tools that will help ensure you can answer that question in the affirmative.

These days, marketing includes almost everything you do that relates to presenting salable products and services to receptive customers. Chapter 12, "Marketing, Advertising And Public Relations," show you how to take on that imposing challenge with an eye toward spurring growth. The topic of Chapter 13, distribution, tends to get short shrift in many expansion plans, but as you'll see, the model you select for distribution and the packaging of your products and services is critical. No less critical is the technology you use to master the ever-increasing flow of information in your business. Chapter 14, "Updating Office Technology," shows you how to select technology, train people to use it and pay for it all.

Customers aren't the only important people in your value chain. You must have reliable, good-quality suppliers and vendors, the topic of Chapter 15, if you're going to generate sustainable growth. One of the things suppliers can do is help you come up with new products and services, one of the most powerful growth creators you can employ, and the topic of Chapter 16.

Pricing is one of those factors that can break you, but if you follow the strategies outlined in Chapter 17, "Setting Prices," you'll find pricing can make you a business owner whose potential for growth is hardly limited at all. Customer service is a topic that's gotten a lot of attention in recent years. Chapter 18 explains why paying close attention to your customers is vital and shows how you can make sure your service is up to the challenge. Speaking of service, most customers' first contact with your company's service is through your sales force. In Chapter 19, you'll learn how to select and hire sales personnel who'll make sure that contact is a revenue-generating experience for your business.

There's more than one way to grow, and the alternatives span tried-and-true choices such as government contracting and strategic alliances, the subjects of Chapter 20, as well as the more up-to-the-minute route of taking your business online. Chapter 21 shows you how to tap online growth opportunities and discusses how to master one of the most promising paths to growth for small businesses.

By the time you finish Part 2, you should be well on your way to putting into action the growth plan you devised in Part 1. In Part 3, you'll learn how to manage the growing business you've created.

chapter 7

Hiring Employees

When you're starting out, it's natural to try to do as much as possible yourself. It's a cost-effective, comfortable, sensible way to do things in the beginning. But as you grow, you'll find yourself stretched thinner and thinner. Eventually, you'll be unable to provide the level of quality and customer service you started with.

When that time comes, you're going to have to make the decision: Do I want to grow enough to hire employees? And if so, how do I add employees in the way that makes the most sense, given my goals and the nature of my business?

Evaluating Your Work Force

Before you can decide whether or not to grow by hiring employees, you need to know what you've already got in the way of help, and whether or not your work force is going to limit or expand your opportunities to grow. Evaluating a work force is more than a matter of counting heads and adding up salaries. You also need to assess the productivity levels of your workers and their training, skills, turnover, absenteeism rates and other factors. This is important for several reasons. To begin with, say you're contemplating adding employees so you can grow. Your evaluation turns up low levels of productivity as well as low levels of training. In this case, you may be better off training the workers you've already got. This could increase productivity enough to give you room for expansion without adding employees.

Do You Need More Employees?

The key to knowing whether and when you need more employees is knowing your employee productivity. Assessing employee productivity doesn't have to be complex. You can quickly calculate companywide productivity by dividing your annual sales volume by the number of employees you have. To get more detailed figures, you can count the number of products handled per time period by each employee. For instance, an auto factory worker may bolt on one bumper per minute. You can calculate this number by dividing the total number of installed bumpers by the number of minutes in a shift, or by measuring how long it takes to put on several bumpers by using a stopwatch.

Measuring productivity is important for service businesses, too. A telephone help line representative may handle one call every five minutes, for example. Once you know your productivity levels, you can compare them to companies like yours to see if you have room to grow by increasing productivity. The simplest way to compare your productivity to other companies is to divide your annual sales by your headcount. Sales-per-employee is a powerful indicator of productivity. You can gain more detailed information such as the number of customer service or sales personnel employed at comparable firms from trade associations, business information sources such as Dun & Bradstreet, and trade and business magazines.

In addition to calculating productivity, you should also examine product and service quality, levels of overtime, absenteeism and turnover. Out-of-line levels for any of these may indicate it's time to do some hiring.

Calculating The Cost Of Hiring

You can't make a decision about adding employees without knowing what it's going to cost to hire them. Salaries and benefits are the obvious costs of having additional employees, and they are the most important ones. But they are hardly the only ones. It also takes money to hire employees, just as it does to compensate them for their work. In addition to the ongoing costs, you will have to budget for some or all of the following one-time hiring costs:

○ Paid newspaper classified advertising to attract job applicants

○ Your own time or staff time to screen, sort and file incoming resumes and applications

○ Time or money (if you use an outside service) to conduct background checks on potential employees

○ More of your time and money to conduct interviews

○ Money to pay travel expenses for candidates who are located in other towns or states

○ Training for new employees to get them up to speed

○ Lost productivity resulting from new employees who do not work out

○ Fees for executive search consultants or recruiters

You probably will not have to pay all these costs for every

> **Danger Ahead!**
> The upfront cost of hiring isn't the only—or even the major—cost of hiring. Once someone is on staff, you may wind up paying for a whole host of things other than salary, insurance and benefits, including severance pay and outplacement training in case things don't work out. So go slowly, and be careful when hiring.

employee. But if you hire a significant number of new workers, you're likely to face all of them sooner or later. Budgeting for them now can help you make a realistic assessment of the costs of growth.

What Kind Of Employees Do You Need?

The traditional full-time employee isn't your only hiring option. In fact, more and more growing companies are turning to alternative arrangements, including hiring temporary employees, part-timers, interns and leased employees. All these strategies can save you money, and some can save you headaches, too.

Leased Employees

Employee leasing lets you add workers without adding administrative complexity. Employee leasing firms manage compliance with state and federal regulations, payroll, unemployment insurance, W-2 forms claims processing, and other paperwork. Some also offer pension and employee assistance programs.

By combining the employees of several companies into one large pool, employee leasing companies (also known as professional employer organizations, or PEOs) can also offer business owners better rates on health-care and workers' compensation coverage. The net effect can be significant savings of your time and money.

While many business owners confuse employee leasing companies with temporary help businesses, the two organizations are really quite different, explains a spokesperson at the American Staffing Association (ASA). "Generally speaking, temporary help companies recruit employees and assign them to client businesses to help with short-term work overload or special projects on an as-needed basis," according to the ASA. With leasing companies, on the other hand, "a client business generally turns over all its personnel functions to an outside company, which administers these operations and leases the employees back to the client."

Employee leasing is a contractual arrangement in which the leasing company is the official employer. Employment responsibilities are typically shared between the leasing company and the business

Look Before You Lease

How can you decide if a particular employee leasing company is right for your business? The National Association of Professional Employer Organizations (NAPEO) makes the following recommendations:

○ Look for services that fit your human resources needs. Is the company flexible enough to work with you?

○ Check for banking and credit references and evidence that the company's payroll taxes and insurance premiums are up to date. Ask to see a certificate of insurance.

○ Ask for client and professional references, and call them.

○ Investigate the company's administrative competence. What experience does it have?

○ Understand how employees' benefits are funded. Do they fit your workers' needs? Find out who the third-party administrator or carrier is, and whether it is licensed if your state requires this.

○ Make sure the leasing company is licensed or registered if required by your state.

○ Review the agreement carefully and try to get a provision that permits you to cancel with short notice—say, 30 days.

For a list of NAPEO member organizations in your area, contact the NAPEO at (703) 836-0466 or write to 901 N. Pitt St., #150, Alexandria, VA 22314.

owner (you, in this case). You retain essential management control over the work performed by the employees. The leasing company, meanwhile, assumes responsibility for work such as reporting wages and employment taxes. Your main responsibility is writing a check to the leasing company to cover the payroll, taxes, benefits and administrative fees. The PEO does the rest.

Temporary Employees

If your business's staffing needs are seasonal—for example, you need extra workers during the holidays or during busy production periods—then temporary employees could provide the flexibility you need to grow. Temporary employees, as the name indicates, are hired

Temporary Heroes

How do you make the most of your temporary workers once they've come on board? For one, "don't treat them any differently from your other employees," the American Staffing Association (ASA) reports. "Introduce them to your full-time workers as people who are there to help you complete a project, to relieve some overtime stress or to bring in some skills you might not have in house."

And don't expect temporary workers to be so well-trained that they know how to do all the little (but important) things, such as operating the copier or answering the phone. "Spend some time giving them a brief overview of these things, just as you would any new employee," advises the ASA.

Another strategy for building a better relationship with your temporary workers is to plan ahead as much as possible so you can use the same temporary employees for an extended period of time—say, six months. Or try to get the same temporary employees back when you need help again. This way, they will be more productive, and you won't have to spend time retraining them.

only for limited periods of time. So they are only there when you need them for specific growth spurts.

Temps also have other advantages. Because most temporary help companies screen—and often train—their employees, entrepreneurs who choose this option stand a better chance of obtaining the quality employees they need.

In addition to offering pre-screened, pre-trained individuals, temporary help companies can help contain your overhead and save time and money on recruiting efforts. The cost of health or unemployment benefits, workers' compensation insurance, profit-sharing, vacation time and other benefits doesn't come out of your budget, since many temporary help companies provide these resources to their employees.

A growing number of entrepreneurs use temporary workers part time at first to get a feel for whether they should hire them full time. As a result, many temporary help companies have begun offering an option, temporary-to-full-time programs, which allow the prospective employer and employee to evaluate each other. Temporary-to-full-time programs match a temporary worker who has expressed an interest in full-time work with an employer that has similar interests. The client is encouraged to make a job offer to the employee within a pre-determined time period if the match seems like a good one.

Part-Time Personnel

Another way to grow flexibly and inexpensively is by hiring part-time workers. You will save money right off the bat with part-timers because you are not legally required to provide part-timers with medical benefits—although, of course, you may.

What are the other benefits to you? By using permanent part-timers, you can get more commitment than you'd get from a temp but more flexibility than you can expect from a nine-to-fiver. In some industries, such as fast food, retail and other businesses that are open long hours, part-timers are essential for filling the odd hours during which workers are needed.

Students provide one traditional source of part-time employees. These workers are typically flexible, willing to work odd hours and don't require high wages. High school and college kids like employers who let them fit their work schedules around the changing demands of school.

Although students are ideal for many situations, there are some potential drawbacks. A student's academic or social demands may come first, crimping your scheduling style. You'll need to be firm and set some standards for what is and is not acceptable.

Students aren't the only part-timers in town, however. Retirees are another, often overlooked source of part-time employees. Often, seniors are looking for a way to earn some extra money or fill their days. Many of these people have years of valuable business experience that could be a boon to your company. Seniors typically have excellent work ethics and can add a note of stability to

Danger Ahead!

While many entrepreneurs hire a temporary worker for just that—temporary work—some may eventually find they'd like to hire the worker full time. Some temporary help firms, however, charge an additional fee any time a temp becomes full time. Defining your employment needs upfront with the temporary help firm can help you avoid such penalties.

Intern Appeal

Some colleges encourage students to work, for a small stipend or even for free, through internship programs. Student interns trade their time and talents for learning marketable job skills. Every year, colleges match millions of students with businesses of all sizes and types. Since they have an eye on future career prospects, the students are usually highly motivated.

Does your tiny, one-person office have anything to offer an intern? Actually, small companies offer ideal learning experiences for interns since they typically have a great variety of job tasks and offer a chance to work closely with senior employees.

Keep this in mind: In most cases, offering routine secretarial or "gofer" work won't get you an intern; colleges expect their interns to learn specialized professional skills. Hold up your end of the bargain by providing meaningful work. Can you delegate a direct-mail campaign? Have an intern help on photo shoots? Ask her to put together a client presentation?

Check with your local college or university to find out about internship programs. Usually, the school will send you an application, asking you to describe the job's responsibilities and your needs in terms of major, skill level and other qualifications. They will also send you the resumes of students they think could work for you.

The best part of hiring interns? If you're lucky, you'll find a gem who'll stay with your company after the internship is over.

your organization. And keep in mind that if a lot of your customers are seniors, they may prefer dealing with employees their own age.

Parents of young children may also represent a qualified pool of potential part-time workers. Many stay-at-home moms and dads would welcome the chance to get out of the house for a few hours a day. Often, these workers are highly skilled and experienced.

Finally, one employee pool employers swear by are people with disabilities. Workers from a local shelter or nonprofit organization can excel at assembling products or packaging goods. In most cases, the nonprofit organization will work with you to oversee and provide a job coach for the employees. To find disabled workers in your area, contact the local Association of Retarded Citizens office or the Easter Seals Society.

Outsourcing Options

Outsourcing has become a major trend in human resources over the past decade. It's the practice of sending certain job functions outside a company instead of handling them in house. More and more companies, large and small, are turning to outsourcing as a way to grow while restraining payroll and overhead costs. How to make it work?

First, make sure the company you're hiring can really do the job. That means getting (and checking) references. Ask former or current clients about their satisfaction with the client. Find out what industries and what type of workload the firm or individual is accustomed to handling. Can you expect your deadlines to be met, or will your small business's projects be pushed aside if a bigger client has an emergency?

Also, make sure you feel comfortable with who will be doing the work and that you can discuss your concerns and needs openly. Ask to see samples of work if appropriate (if you're using a graphic design firm, for example).

Independent Contractors

One outsourcing option is hiring independent contractors. Instead of hiring an in-house bookkeeper, you might outsource the job to an independent accountant who comes in once a month or does all the work off-site. Independent contractors can be more flexible and lower in cost than outsourcing firms. As with outsourcing firms, however, before hiring an independent contractor, make sure the individual you use can do the job.

Evaluating Your Own Recruiting Attractiveness

While you're investigating your local work force and assessing your existing employees, evaluate your own recruiting attractiveness. Compare the wages and benefits you offer to average local rates and benefits plans.

Don't end the examination at workers' wallets. Also take a look at the quality of your work environment compared to what you know of other local employers. A good job in one city may be considered a lousy one in another and vice versa. It all depends on what other employers are offering and how you stack up.

Filling Different Positions

You can't grow efficiently by merely increasing your headcount. You have to fill the right jobs or your growth will stall. Start deciding what types of positions to fill by identifying the bottlenecks in your organization. You can do this by examining the various functional departments in your company and finding out where each is contributing to poor performance.

Production Personnel

If you are constantly shipping orders late and having to turn customers away, you probably have a bottleneck in production. In this case, additional production workers are needed. Plan to hire more shop foremen or other line supervisors to oversee the additional production workers. That's especially important if you are adding enough workers to require another shift.

Marketing Personnel

If your shortfall is in sales, or if you lack the personnel to market to promising new opportunities, it might be time to add marketing employees. You may also need to staff up if you are facing new marketing initiatives from competitors or changes in your core markets.

If you simply have more prospects than you can handle, consider hiring salespeople and sales managers. If you don't know which markets to attack, or your products and services seem misaligned with the market's needs, consider hiring mar-

Danger Ahead!

The IRS has stringent rules regulating exactly who is and is not considered an independent contractor. If you consider a person an independent contractor, and the IRS later reclassifies him or her as an employee, you could be liable for that person's Social Security taxes and a wide range of other costs and penalties.

86-ing The Old 9-To-5

The days when all jobs consisted of 40 work hours spent in eight-hour chunks Monday through Friday are over. Today, an increasing number of employees work flexible schedules from a variety of locations and even share jobs. Employees like these arrangements, and they can be advantageous for the right entrepreneur as well. Here are some of the most notable flexible work arrangements and the key characteristics of each:

○ *Flextime* is the most popular flexible work option with both employers and employees. It lets employees set their starting and quitting times within limits determined by management.

○ *Job-sharing* lets two people share the responsibilities of one full-time position. It's basically a form of part-time work that provides you with the equivalent of one-full time employee while giving the job-sharing employees the ability to keep their careers on track while allowing more time for family responsibilities or other activities.

○ *Compressed workweek* arrangements let employees work 40 hours in fewer than five days. Most commonly, this means four 10-hour days each week. Advantages to employees include an extra day off and lower commuting costs per week. Many employers report higher productivity from employees working compressed workweeks.

○ *Telecommuting employees* work from home during some of their scheduled hours. Telecommuters often come into the office one or two days each week. This lets them go to meetings and stay in touch with co-workers.

keting professionals such as market researchers, product developers and market testing experts. On an even more strategic level, you may need more public relations staff if your public image is deteriorating or if you are fielding more inquiries from the media and the public than your existing PR people can handle.

Management Personnel

As you grow, you will inevitably wind up delegating and handing off jobs to other managers. (See Chapter 22, "Managing People," for more on delegating.) At some point, you'll find yourself needing additional management personnel to hand off jobs to. Symptoms of a management shortfall include too many decisions being handled by nonmanagement personnel, employees coming to you asking for direction and a general lack of coordination among your departments.

To help your company grow to its full potential, it's important to add professional managers to your crop of homegrown supervisors, promoted technicians and others for whom management is a secondary skill. It may be hard to discern the difference in performance of a professional manager whose education and experience is all aimed at leading others, but over time the difference can be significant.

Inside Job

You can find good people both inside and outside your company. Deciding which way to go if a position becomes available in your organization may come down to examining the inherent advantages and disadvantages of hiring from outside vs. promoting from within.

When you promote your employees, you send a powerful positive signal to other workers that says they have the potential to advance. It may also be less costly to promote current employees, since you can pocket money you'd otherwise spend on recruiting and, in some cases, training. You don't have to worry about current employees fitting into a new corporate culture, either.

However, promoting from within may be a bad idea if you are trying to add a skill that no one in your company possesses. Outside employees bring new perspectives and can help change a company's culture, if that's what you're interested in.

Although promoting from within isn't always a good idea, you should make it a habit to at least consider internal applicants. Promoting existing employees builds morale, reduces turnover and enhances teamwork. When you develop your own leaders, you know more about their capabilities and weaknesses than if you hire an unknown quantity from outside. If you constantly seek to cultivate replacements for key positions from within your organization, you'll always be ready with the right person for the right job.

> ## Viewpoint
> Whenever possible, look for employees you can cross-train into different job responsibilities. A welder with college courses in engineering and a secretary with human resources experience are workers one small business has successfully cross-trained. Cross-trained employees can fill in when others are absent, keeping costs down.

Many experts say that 100 employees is a threshold for requiring senior-level professional management. Depending on your personal management aptitude, this may even include placing a professional manager in your own job and bumping yourself upstairs to a chairman's or CEO's job. More important than abiding by any arbitrary headcount, however, is for you to realize you have limits and be alert for any opportunity to improve your company's vision, capabilities and performance by adding professional management.

Should You Fill The CEO Shoes?

The CEO of a growing company extends his influence throughout the enterprise and, to a large extent, determines the company's success. He serves as the overall director of operations, marketing and finance. He makes tough strategic decisions. He selects and deploys the senior management team. More than anyone else in the company, the CEO must exhibit technical expertise, people skills, intelligence, energy, a strong work ethic, openness, and humility.

Perhaps the most important skill a CEO possesses is the ability to acquire, inspire and retain the production, marketing, management and other personnel the company needs to succeed. Many employees are more loyal to the person at the top than they are to a company, and given the importance of getting and keeping top employees, there is no greater indication of the importance of the role played by the CEO. If you are up to the role of CEO in your com-

> ## Viewpoint
> Looking to fill an important position but dreading the hassle of hunting for candidates? Executive recruitment firms, also known as "headhunters" or search firms, can find qualified professional, managerial and technical candidates for you. Search firms charge a percentage of the employee's first-year salary.

Family Affair

Want to get good employees and tax savings, too? Consider putting your family members to work for you.

Hiring family, especially your children, can enable you to move your family's income out of a higher tax bracket into a lower one. It also enables you to transfer wealth to your kids without incurring federal gift or estate taxes.

Even preteen children can be put to work stuffing envelopes, filing or sorting mail. If their salaries are reasonable, they're considered earned income and are not subject to the "kiddie tax" rules that apply to kids under age 14. And if your business is unincorporated, wages paid to a child under age 18 are not subject to Social Security or FICA taxes. That means neither you nor your child has to pay these taxes. A final plus, employed youngsters can make tax-deductible contributions to an individual retirement account.

Be sure to document the type of work the family member is doing, and pay him or her a comparable amount to what you'd pay another employee, or the IRS will think you're putting your family on the payroll just for the tax breaks. Keep careful records of hours worked, and make sure the work is necessary to the business.

Your accountant can suggest other ways to take advantage of the situation without getting into hot water with the IRS.

pany, the position is yours. If not, it may be time to consider putting someone else in the job.

Administrative Personnel

Any time you add a significant number of employees, you will need to add office support staff. When there are more people calling and more phones, you may need an additional receptionist, for instance. The same goes for payroll clerks, benefits administrators and other office staff. Once your administrative roster gets large enough, you will want to add an office manager to supervise them. Office managers can relieve you of nonessential tasks such as ordering supplies and checking time cards.

Entrepreneurs are often reluctant to beef up administrative staff. But secretaries, file clerks, data-entry personnel and administrative assistants are more than paper-shufflers. Your receptionist, for instance, often makes the first and most lasting impression people get of your company. Make sure you have a good administrative staff— and enough administrative employees to cover your business's changing needs.

Hire Power

Hiring employees is a vital skill for an entrepreneur with growth as a goal. By all means, do as much as you can when you're starting out—that's the way you build sweat equity and learn your company's ins and outs at every level. But as you grow, be ready to add employees. If you keep your growth goals in mind and carefully consider the nature of your business and your needs, you can strategically add workers who will help your business be all it can be.

Using Professional Service Providers

fter you've owned your own business

for a while, you know how to run it. You've probably done every-

thing from answering the phones to hiring a general manager,

and you can justly claim to know your business inside and out,

in general and in detail. In case there's any operation you can't

personally undertake, one of your employees probably can.

There are, however, exceptions to this rule. Highly technical matters of law, accounting, management and marketing are usually best handled by outside experts. Attorneys, accountants and management and marketing consultants have specialized knowledge about niche areas that you couldn't—and shouldn't—hope to duplicate either personally or in the form of an in-house employee.

Having access to legal, accounting and other expertise is important to help your business grow as rapidly and efficiently as possible. Given enough time, you may be able to master the intricacies of law and finance. But why bother? Hand these duties off to professional service providers. They can do them faster and more effectively than you ever could. Besides, your skills are needed in helping your business expand.

Legal And Accounting Help

Why do you need a lawyer to grow? It's generally worthwhile to consult an attorney before making any business decision that could have legal ramifications. These decisions could include setting up or altering the terms of a partnership or corporation, checking for compliance with regulations in new locales where you hope to do business, negotiating loans to fund expansion, obtaining trademarks or patents, preparing buy-sell agreements, tax planning, drawing up or revising pension plans, reviewing business forms, negotiating and drawing up documents to buy or sell other companies or real estate, reviewing employee contracts, exporting or selling products in other states, and collecting bad debts. Many of the same considerations apply to the use of accountants by growing firms. You should at least consider running by an accountant any decision that could have accounting or financial ramifications.

You probably started your

Viewpoint

If the thought of a temp brings to mind a secretary, think again. Today, temporary agencies offer employees in a variety of professional and technical fields, from engineers, editors and accountants to computer programmers, bankers, lab support staff and attorneys. If you need more than an occasional consultation and less than a full-time permanent employee, look into professional temps.

business with a lawyer and an accountant available to answer questions, help draw up documents, and solve the inevitable problems of launching a new company. Now that you've been underway for a while and success seems to be a given, shouldn't you keep working with the professionals who helped you get here? Not necessarily, because the needs of a growing business are different from those of a start-up. The professional service providers who aided you in the beginning may not be good matches for your current needs.

Giving your professionals a checkup is largely a matter of assessing your need for professional services and judging whether your current advisors measure up. When you were starting up, issues such as the legal form your business would take—sole proprietorship or partnership, for example—were pressing. Today, you may be looking at how you should structure an international subsidiary. The odds are good that the attorney you started with won't be able to provide you with one-stop service as your business grows.

> **The professional service providers who aided you in the beginning may not be good matches for your current needs.**

Likewise, accounting problems in the beginning, when your business was funded entirely with your own personal savings, may have revolved around little more than making sure you filed state and federal payroll tax forms and income tax returns properly. As you grow, however, you'll have to deal with depreciating plant, equipment and real property, setting up financial controls and, most likely, the tax laws of entities beyond your start-up state and city. Even if your original accountant was a whiz at the jobs you needed early on, it's not likely that you and your accountant will continue to grow in the same directions.

Marketing And Management Consultants

When it comes to marketing and management, many entrepreneurs are on firmer ground than when venturing into accounting and law. But nobody knows everything, even about general management and marketing. There's nothing wrong with admitting that and seeking outside help in an effort to execute your company's management and marketing as skillfully as possible. In narrow disciplines, such as managing mergers and acquisitions and marketing to ethnic groups, the use of an experienced specialist makes even more sense. And even if you feel there is nothing you don't know about a topic, hiring outside experts will allow you to do things you wouldn't ordinarily have time for and don't want to hire permanent employees for.

Fast Lane

When considering legal needs, take a look at legal services plans. A modest monthly fee makes you a member of a legal services plan and entitles you to prepaid consultations with an attorney on contract reviews and disputes, incorporation, wills, tax laws and more. Your prepaid attorney can write letters and make phone calls to collect debts, and you can get reduced fees for more complicated legal matters like patents, trademarks and copyrights.

Hiring a consultant is different from hiring almost any other kind of employee, and it's different from purchasing most outsourced services, too. For one thing, consultants are expensive. They can cost anywhere from several hundred to several thousand dollars a day. Make sure you know what the consulting fees will be and exactly what you will get for paying them. Consultants should provide a more customized solution to your business problem than most outsourced providers. Make sure any consultant you hire asks lots of questions about your needs and listens to your answers. Be sure your description of your needs is specific, and avoid consultants with preconceived notions about solutions.

Upgrading Professional Service Providers

Referrals are the best way to get a new professional service provider. The best source of referrals is other entrepreneurs. Make a point of asking people in the same business sector (service, retail, restaurant, manufacturing, etc.) for referrals. You can also get good referrals from other professionals. That is, ask your accountant for an attorney's name and your attorney for an accountant's name. Other

Liability Check

More than 80 million lawsuits are filed in American courts annually. That doesn't mean that your business will be the target of a lawsuit, but it does suggest the need for you to evaluate your business's legal liability.

As your business grows, you should occasionally reassess your exposure to liability claims. Growing companies naturally become more exposed to various kinds of risks. For instance, liability claims resulting from employment, such as charges of discrimination or wrongful termination, tend to increase as your work force grows. Following are some of the major areas of liability exposure you should evaluate:

○ *Employment:* The larger and more diverse your work force, and the more turnover you have, the greater your exposure to employment-related liability lawsuits will be.

○ *Accidents and injuries on your premises:* If a delivery person trips on your steps and breaks a leg, you may be sued for medical and other costs.

○ *Vehicle-related liability:* If an employee driving a company car gets in an accident, the company could be held liable for damages and injuries.

○ *Product-related liability:* If you manufacture any type of product, you may be liable for injuries or accidents resulting from poor workmanship or labeling.

○ *Errors and omissions liability:* You may be sued for damages resulting from a mistake in the work your company does if, for instance, you accidentally delete a customer's important computer file.

○ *Directors and officers liability:* If you have a board of directors, they may be held personally liable for actions taken by the company.

When it comes to liability, every company is different. For instance, a restaurant that uses hot-oil fryers may be considered a different liability risk by an insurance company than one that bakes its food in ovens. By giving your business a legal checkup, you'll decrease the chances of your particular liability proving to be a disastrous weakness.

service providers, such as recruiters and bankers, are also good sources. Don't forget to ask suppliers and customers. Trade associations can also be good places to find names of professional service providers.

The Interview

Once you are outfitted with a few referrals, contact several to gauge their interest in you and your interest in them. Then personally interview at least three prospects.

At your first interview with a professional service provider, be ready to describe your business and its legal, accounting or other needs. Take note of what the provider says and does, and look for the following qualities:

○ *Experience:* Although it's not essential to find an expert in your particular field, it makes sense to look for someone who specializes in small-business problems as opposed to, say, maritime law. Make sure the professional is willing to take on small problems; if you're trying to collect on a relatively small invoice, for example, will the lawyer think it's worth his or her time?

○ *Understanding:* Be sure the professional is willing to learn about your business's goals. You're looking for someone who will be a long-term partner in your business's growth. Does the professional understand where you want to be tomorrow and share your vision for the future?

○ *Ability to communicate:* If the lawyer speaks in legalese or the accountant uses lots of arcane financial terms without bothering to explain them, look for someone else.

○ *Availability:* Will the professional be available for conferences at your convenience, not his or hers? How quickly can you expect emergency phone calls to be returned?

○ *Rapport:* Is this someone you can get along with? You will be discussing matters close to your heart with this person, so make sure you feel comfortable doing so. Good chem-

Viewpoint

Independent accountants or small accounting firms can provide personalized service, while a Big Five firm offers more services and can lend prestige to your company, smoothing the way to raising capital and establishing credit.

Fast Lane

Don't use an accountant to pay the bills, make bank deposits and the like. A bookkeeper is just as effective and is much less costly.

istry will ensure a better relationship and positive results for your business.

○ *Reasonable fees:* Attorneys, accountants and other professionals charge anywhere from $90 to $300 (or more) per hour, depending on the location, size and prestige of the provider. Shop around and get quotes from several providers before making your decision. However, beware of comparing one provider with another on the basis of fees alone. The lowest hourly fees may not indicate the best value; an inexperienced professional may take twice as long to complete a project as an experienced one will.

○ *References:* Don't be afraid to ask for references. What types of businesses or cases has the attorney worked with in the past? Get a list of clients or other professionals you can contact to discuss competence, service and fees.

Evaluating Credentials

Some jobs, such as auditing financials to satisfy the requirements of lenders or investors, simply must be done by a professional with specific credentials. A certified public accountant is a good example. If you are looking for legal advice, you certainly want an attorney with a juris doctor or equivalent degree who is a member of the bar.

You have more flexibility in looking for other credentials. The initials MBA after a person's name suggest that, as the holder of a master's of business administration degree, that person is well-trained. However, highly experienced people may be just as effective even if they lack the diploma and the initials. Evaluating the worth of credentials can be tricky. Check with associations such as the American Bar Association, the American Institute of Certified Public Accountants, or the government agency in your state charged with granting CPA credentials.

Negotiating Fees

The professional services marketplace is a buyers' market these days. Here are 10 steps to keep your costs in check without hurting your chances of growing:

1. *Choose the right professionals.* The key is to match your needs with the skills and resources of the provider. Most small-business owners simply don't need a large, major-city law firm or international accountant. The overhead expenses of such megafirms are passed on to their clients in the form of high hourly rates. Instead of a big name, look for small-business expertise.

2. *Examine your fee agreement.* Once you find a professional with whom you feel comfortable, read the fee agreement letter carefully. Focus on hourly rates, expenses such as postage and photocopying, and travel time. Ask candidates for a sample of their standard fee agreement for your review. Be suspicious of any professional who balks at this request.

3. *Use paralegals and bookkeepers as part of your professional team.* Certain legal tasks are straightforward enough that utilizing a paralegal instead of a business lawyer can result in significant savings. The same goes for using a bookkeeper instead of an accountant.

4. *Do your own footwork.* Keeping organized records, indexing volumes of documents and writing out memorandums can reduce your professional fees significantly. Professionals will do all this for you—but at their hourly rates, and on your tab.

5. *Meet with your professionals regularly.* At first, this may not seem to be a very effective way to keep fees down, but you'll be amazed at how much it actually reduces both the number of phone calls your provider has to make and the endless rounds of telephone tag.

6. *Use your attorney as a coach for minor legal matters.* When you have a customer who owes you money and refuses to pay, do you turn the case over to your lawyer? Some entrepreneurs do, but some handle small legal matters on their own by using their attorneys as coaches. Lawyers can be very effective in coaching you to file lawsuits in small-claims court, draft employment manuals, and complete other uncomplicated legal tasks.

7. *Demand and examine monthly invoices.* While most professionals are diligent about sending out monthly invoices, some wait until the bill is sufficiently large. If yours doesn't bill in a timely manner, ask for a breakdown of the time spent and costs incurred to date, and for similar monthly invoices to be sent thereafter. When the invoice comes, check the work description to be sure you weren't inadvertently billed for work performed for another client.

8. *Negotiate prompt-payment discounts.* If you're paying a retainer fee, request that your bill be discounted by 10 percent. (A retainer fee

is an amount of money that acts as a fee pre-payment; the remainder is refunded to the client.) Even if you didn't pay a retainer, negotiate a prompt-payment discount if you pay your fees within 30 days of your invoice date. You may not get as much of a discount using this method, but even a 5 percent discount on your monthly legal fees can add thousands of dollars per year to your business's bottom line.

9. *Don't make impromptu calls to your professional.* Most attorneys bill under a structure that includes minimum time increments for repetitive functions such as phone calls. This means when you call your lawyer for a quick question, you'll be subject to a minimum time increment for billing purposes. For instance, if you place four impromptu calls a week to your professional at a minimum time increment of a quarter-hour per call, you'll get a bill for an hour of your lawyer's time—even though you only received five minutes' worth of advice! Keep a list of subjects you need to discuss, and make a single call to discuss them all.

10. *Negotiate outcome-based fee arrangements with attorneys.* Although this is a relatively new concept in the legal market, more and more firms agree to such arrangements in this competitive marketplace. An outcome-based fee arrangement is a risk-sharing plan. Simply put, if your lawyer accomplishes a particular favorable outcome, the bill is adjusted to increase the fees by a preset formula. But if the outcome is not favorable, the final bill is adjusted downward (though not eliminated.)

Writing Professional Service Contracts

Get everything in writing when dealing with professional service providers. Your written agreement should cover the scope of the services to be rendered, the duration of the agreement and the fees. The fee schedule should state whether fees are to be based on an hourly, daily or project rate, and who is responsible for paying expenses. You should consider having fees based

Fast Lane

Don't make cutting ties with an unsatisfactory professional more painful than necessary. If you have a cancelable contract, simply notify your service provider you are exercising that right. If your arrangement is less formal, you may drop him or her a note stating that you will be using someone else from now on. Be firm but polite—there is no sense in burning bridges.

at least in part on performance to protect you from having to pay top rates for shoddy work.

Your agreement should also specify who will be performing the work for your company. Some professional services firms have certain people whose primary job it is to solicit business, while others do the actual work. However, you may not want a lower-level attorney or junior accountant working on your project.

Finally, the contract should explain how the agreement can be ended prematurely, typically with some kind of notice to the other party. This will allow you to get out of an unsatisfactory contract without having to pay the full amount.

What's In It For You?

Having access to top legal, accounting and other professional service expertise is essential to your business's long-term health. With these professionals on your side, you can deal effectively with legal, tax and financial issues that might require years of study to master. So instead of trying to do a professional's job, stick to doing what you do best—growing your business.

chapter 9

Funding
Expansion

ou can't grow unless you have money to
invest in growth. That may seem strange at first. After all,
growth is supposed to generate additional sales and profits,
right? That's true, but before you can increase sales, you usually
have to increase your current assets, such as inventory and fixed
assets such as a plant and equipment.

Rapid growth means hiring more people, furnishing more offices and perhaps renting new quarters. Since there is usually a time lag between the moment you need to invest in growth and the moment you receive the resulting sales and profits, you need money before you can grow.

Financing expansion can take many forms. You can use your own money, borrow from friends and fami-

Danger Ahead!

When sales rise too rapidly, you may find yourself in a cash crunch as suppliers from whom you've ordered large quantities of materials to fulfill orders demand payment before you receive checks from customers. This kind of unrestrained growth spiral has driven many a company into bankruptcy. Lining up financing in advance and managing your growth can prevent it.

ly, use internally generated funds, approach equity investors or tap banks and other lenders. The sources for funding growth are generally the same sources you may have used to start your business. In many cases, you will go back to the same sources to pay for expanding your company. The good news is that it's easier to fund growth in an existing business than it is to fund a start-up.

Types Of Expansion Financing

As you learned when you were looking for start-up capital, there are many places to go when seeking money for business. As you probably also learned, only a few of those places are right for any given business. Selecting the right type of expansion financing is largely a matter of matching your needs to the restrictions of the source. Each type of financing has its own strengths and limitations.

Personal Sources

Self-financing in the form of personal and family savings is the No. 1 form of financing used by most small-business owners. It's low-cost and has other advantages. For instance, when you approach other financing sources, such as bankers and venture capitalists, they will want to know exactly how much of your own money you are putting into the venture. After all, if you don't have enough faith in your business to risk your own money, why should anyone else risk theirs?

Here are some of the sources of personal and family financing you should consider for growing your business:

○ *Personal line of credit, including credit cards:* Although credit card financing is expensive, it can work for emergencies and small amounts.

○ *Home equity loan secured by your personal residence:* Interest rates are low, but you may lose your home if you can't repay.

○ *Cash-value life insurance:* Interest rates are reasonable on loans against cash-value policies, and you don't have to make payments because the loan will be repaid from proceeds of your insurance in the event of your death.

○ *Individual retirement account (IRA) funds:* Laws governing IRAs let you withdraw money from an IRA as long as you replace it within 60 days. It's not a loan, so there's no interest, but if you pay it back late, you'll have to pay a 10 percent penalty plus taxes.

"Friends And Family" Financing

Friends, relatives and business associates are popular sources for financing the growth of small businesses. There are two main advantages to friends and family financing.

1. The all-important issue of the character of the borrower is moot—these people already know you.

2. Depending on from whom you are borrowing, repayment terms may be extremely flexible, and you may not even have to pay interest.

The downside is that, if worse comes to worse and you can't repay the loan, the people who will be hurt will be friends, family and business associates. Make sure you explain the risks involved in investing in a growth business before accepting financing from friends and family. Otherwise, their wish to help you out may lead them to do something that could damage your personal relationship as well as your mutual finances.

> **Danger Ahead!**
> When borrowing from friends or family, don't forget to put it in writing. Make sure it's clear exactly how much money you need, what you'll use it for and how you'll pay it back. And draw up a legal agreement stating that the person will indeed put money into the business.

Internally Generated Funds

One of the most advantageous ways to finance growth is through earnings your business is creating and that you retain. The only cost to using retained earnings is the interest you would receive if you kept the earnings in a bank account. Since this amount is likely to be much less than you will earn by successfully investing the funds in growing your business, plowing retained earnings back into your business is usually a smart move.

One risk to financing with internally generated funds is that you will divert too much of your current profits into expanding the business. This can starve your business and create more trouble than if you financed with a more costly source or never tried to grow at all. Make sure you aren't robbing Peter to pay Paul when you finance with retained earnings, and that your investments in inventories, marketing efforts, production staff and other outlays required for the existing business are maintained.

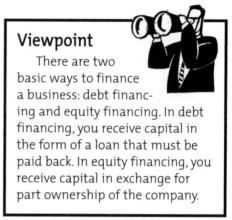

Viewpoint

There are two basic ways to finance a business: debt financing and equity financing. In debt financing, you receive capital in the form of a loan that must be paid back. In equity financing, you receive capital in exchange for part ownership of the company.

Viewpoint

The term of an installment loan will always correlate to its use. A business cycle loan may be written as a four-month installment loan and would carry the lowest interest rate since the risk to the lender is from one to seven years (the typical length of a business cycle). In contrast, real estate and renovation loans may be written up to 21 years.

Bank Loans And Lines Of Credit

Banks exist to lend money, so it's no surprise that banks offer a wide variety of ways to fund growth. Here is a look at how lenders generally structure loans, with common variations.

○ *Line of credit loans:* The most useful type of loan for the small business is the line-of-credit loan. This is a short-term loan that extends the cash available in your business's checking account to the upper limit of the loan contract. You pay interest on the actual amount advanced from the time it is advanced until it is paid back. Line-of-credit loans are intended for purchases of inventory and payment of operating costs for working capital and business cycle needs. They are not intended for purchases of equipment or real estate.

○ *Installment loans:* These bank loans are paid back with equal monthly payments covering both principal and interest. Installment loans may be written to meet all types of business needs. You receive the full amount when the contract is signed, and interest is calculated from that date to the final day of the loan. If you repay an installment loan before its final date, there will be no penalty and an appropriate adjustment of interest.

○ *Balloon loans:* These loans require only the interest to be paid off during the life of the loan, with a final "balloon" payment of the principal due on the last day. Balloon loans are often used in situations when a business has to wait until a specific date before receiving payment from a client for its product or services.

○ *Interim loans:* Interim financing is often used by contractors building new facilities. When the building is finished, a mortgage on the property will be used to pay off the interim loan.

○ *Secured and unsecured loans:* Loans can be secured or unsecured. An unsecured loan has no collateral pledged as a secondary payment source should you default on the loan. The lender provides you with an unsecured loan because it considers you a low risk. A secured loan requires some kind of collateral but generally has a lower interest rate

> **A** secured loan requires some kind of collateral but generally has a lower interest rate than an unsecured loan.

than an unsecured loan. The collateral is usually related to the purpose of the loan; for instance, if you're borrowing to buy a printing press, the press itself will likely serve as collateral. Loans secured with receivables are often used to finance growth, with the banker lending up to 75 percent of the amount due. Inventory used to secure a loan is usually valued at up to 50 percent of its sale price.

○ *Letter of credit:* International traders use these to guarantee payment to suppliers in other countries. The document substitutes the bank's credit for the entrepreneur's up to a set amount for a specified period of time.

SBA Loans

The U.S. Small Business Administration (SBA) provides loan guarantees to entrepreneurs, promising the bank to pay back a certain percentage of your loan if you are unable to. Banks participate in the SBA program as regular, certified or preferred lenders. The most basic eligibility requirement for SBA loans is the ability to repay the loan from cash flow, but the SBA also looks at personal credit history, industry experience or other evidence of management ability, collateral and owner's equity contributions. If you own 20 percent or more equity in the business, the SBA asks that you personally guarantee the loan. After all, you can't ask the government to back you if you're not willing to back yourself. The SBA offers numerous loan programs for growing businesses.

○ *The 7(a) Loan Guaranty Program* is the primary SBA loan program. The SBA guarantees up to $750,000 or 75 percent of the total loan amount, whichever is less. For loans of less than $100,000, the guarantee usually tops out at 80 percent of the total loan. A 7(a) loan can be used for many business purposes, including real estate, expansion, equipment, working capital or inventory. The money can be paid back over as many as 25 years for real estate and 10 years for working capital. Interest rates are a maximum of 2.75 percent if over seven years.

○ *The SBA LowDoc Program* is a special 7(a) loan promising quick processing for amounts less than $150,000. "LowDoc" stands for low documentation," and approval relies heavily on your personal credit rating and your business's cash flow. LowDoc loan proceeds can be used for many purposes. Applicants seeking less than $50,000 are required to complete only a one-page SBA form. Those seeking $50,001 to $150,000 submit the same short form, plus supply copies of individual income tax

Getting Directions

You can tap all the latest information and resources about the Small Business Administration's many financing programs, including downloading application forms, at the SBA's Web site at www.sbaonline.gov. Also, check out the Guaranty Loan sites at www.sba.gov/financing and www.sba.gov/banking.

returns for the previous three years and financial statements from all guarantors and co-owners. The SBA guarantees a 36-hour turn-around on these loan requests.

○ *The SBA Express Program* is a close cousin of the LowDoc, also offering loans of up to $150,000. However, SBA Express gets you an answer more quickly because approved SBA Express lenders can use their own documentation and procedures to attach an SBA guarantee to an approved loan without having to wait for SBA approval. The SBA guarantees up to 50 percent of SBA Express loans.

> The CAPLine program includes variations for small companies that can't meet requirements for other financing.

○ *CAPLine loans* provide working capital through a selection of revolving and nonrevolving lines of credit. CAPLine loans are guaranteed by the SBA up to $750,000 or 75 percent of the total loan amount, whichever is less. The CAPLine program includes variations for seasonal businesses, companies that need credit to complete a large contract, and builders and small companies that can't meet requirements for other financing.

○ *The SBA's Minority and Women's Pre-Qualification Loan* programs help women and minority entrepreneurs pre-qualify for loans of up to $250,000. Private intermediary organizations chosen by the SBA help eligible entrepreneurs complete a loan application. With the SBA's guarantee attached, the bank is more likely to approve the loan.

○ *The Microloan program* helps entrepreneurs get very small loans, from less than $100 to $25,000. The loans can be used for machinery and equipment, furniture and fixtures, inventory, supplies and working capital, but not to pay existing debts. Microloans are administered through nonprofit intermediaries using SBA funds. Terms are usually short, and application turnaround time is less than a week.

○ *The CDC-504 Loan program* provides long-term, fixed-rate loans of up to $1 million for financing fixed assets, such as land and buildings. CDC-504 Loans are made through nonprofit Certified Development Companies. The program is designed to enable small businesses to create and retain jobs.

Trade Credit

For many businesses, trade credit is an essential tool for financing growth. Trade credit is the credit extended to you by suppliers who let you buy now and pay later. Any time you take delivery of materials, equipment or other valuables without paying cash on the spot, you're using trade credit. One drawback to trade credit is that it can be expensive. A supplier who offers a 2 percent discount on bills paid within 10 days, with the full or net amount due in 30 days, is actually charging a 36 percent annual rate of interest.

Angel Investors

An angel investor is an individual who invests his or her own money in an entrepreneurial company. This distinguishes them from

They Like It Like That

Not all investors and lenders are looking for the same thing. Some are interested in preserving capital and generating interest income, while others are willing to risk everything for a shot at great wealth. Knowing what financing sources want can make the difference between getting financing and having to do without.

Bankers are looking for interest income from a loan, along with a high likelihood that the loan will be repaid. They don't want to control the business other than making sure it meets loan convenant standards, and they take collateral in lieu of repayment only as a last resort.

Venture capitalists want very high rates of return, usually through a sale of the company to another firm or the public via a stock offering. They usually want to have lots of input into how the business is run because they're willing to take risks others avoid.

Angel investors vary widely, but they are typically willing to accept risk and demand little or no control in return for the chance to own a piece of a business that may be valuable someday.

Family and friends may be motivated more by personal concerns, such as showing that they care for the small-business owner, than by financial issues. They often fail to appreciate either risks or potential returns. They may ask for no control but later demand it if things go sour.

institutional financiers, who invest other people's money. Angels come in two varieties: those you know and those you don't know. They may include professionals such as doctors and lawyers, business associates such as executives, suppliers and customers, and even other entrepreneurs. Unlike venture capitalists and bankers, many angels are not motivated solely by profit. Particularly if your angel is a current or former entrepreneur, he or she may be motivated as much by the enjoyment of helping a young business succeed as by the money he or she stands to gain. Angels are more likely than venture capitalists to be persuaded by an entrepreneur's drive to succeed, persistence and mental discipline.

Initial Public Offerings

Large amounts of capital have been raised in recent years by small companies that went public. Initial public offerings (IPOs) have made instant billionaires of entrepreneurs such as Yahoo!'s Jerry Yang and Broadcast.com's Mark Cuban. The same IPOs flooded the coffers of the companies with millions if not billions of dollars.

Going public isn't for every firm, however. The ideal candidate for an IPO has both a well-established track record of steadily growing sales and earnings, and operates in an industry that currently is in the news. You may be able to go public if you have a whole lot of one of these characteristics and not much of the other—for instance, little earnings but lots of public interest have characterized many biotech and Internet-related IPOs in recent years.

The stringent requirements for IPOs leave out most companies, including those that don't have audited financials for the last several years, as well as those that operate in slow-growing or obscure industries such as car washes and paper clip manufacturing. And IPOs take lots of time. You'll need to add outside directors to your board and clean up the terms of any sweetheart deals with managers, family

Getting Directions

The Angel Capital Electronic Network (ACE-Net) is an online network that helps accredited angel investors find entrepreneurs in need of capital. It's sponsored by the Small Business Administration and the University of New Hampshire. Learn more at www.sbaonline.sba.gov or https://ace-net.sr.unh.edu/pub, or contact the SBA's Office of Advocacy at (202) 205-6533.

or board members as well as have a major accounting firm audit your operations for several years before going public. In other words, if you need money to grow today, an IPO isn't going to provide it.

An IPO is also probably the most expensive way to raise money in terms of the amounts you have to lay out upfront. The bills for accountants, lawyers, printing and miscellaneous fees for even a modest IPO will easily reach six figures. For this reason, IPOs are best used to raise amounts at least equal to millions of dollars in equity capital.

Employee Stock Ownership Plans

Employee stock ownership plans (ESOPs) allow owners of privately held companies to share ownership with their employees. Technically, ESOPs are defined-contribution employee benefit plans that invest primarily in the stock of the employer company. As such, most ESOPs distribute the stock to employees as a benefit, rather than selling employees the shares. ESOPs are commonly used to give retiring owners a way to cash out all or part of their holdings without selling the entire company. But creating a market for shares of the company can also be used to raise funds for expansion. ESOPs are easy to set up and are used by thousands of employers.

Venture Capital

Venture capitalists represent the most glamorous and appealing form of financing to many entrepreneurs. They are known for backing high-growth companies in the early stages, and a lot of the best-known entrepreneurial success stories owe their growth to financing from venture capitalists.

Venture capitalists (VCs) can provide large sums of money, advice and prestige by their mere presence. Just the fact that you have obtained venture capital backing means your business has, in venture capitalists' eyes, at least, considerable potential for rapid and profitable growth.

VCs make loans to—and equity investments in—young companies. The loans are often expensive, carrying rates of up to 20 percent. Unlike banks and other lenders, venture capitalists frequently take equity positions as well. That means you don't have to pay out hard-to-get cash in the form of interest and principal installments. Instead, you give a portion of your or other owners' interest in the company in exchange for the VCs' backing.

The catch is that often you have to give up a large portion of your company to get the money. In fact, VC financiers so frequently wrest majority control from and then oust the founding entrepreneurs that they are sometimes known as "vulture capitalists." But VCs come in all sizes and varieties, and they aren't all bad.

Venture capitalists typically invest in companies they anticipate being sold either to the public or to larger firms within the next several years. Companies they'll consider investing in usually have the following features:

○ Rapid, steady sales growth

○ A proprietary new technology or dominant position in an emerging market

○ A sound management team

○ The potential for being acquired by a larger company or taken public in a stock offering

Venture capitalists seek very high rates of return; a 30 percent to 50 percent annual rate of return is typical. To generate these returns, they look for firms with proprietary technology, distribution systems or product lines that other companies might want to possess.

SBIR Grants

Small Business Innovation Research (SBIR) grants aim to stimulate technological innovation among small businesses. They let small businesses propose research projects designed to meet the federal government's R&D needs. If approved, the research projects may receive grants of up to $75,000.

Financing On The Internet

The Internet has changed countless things about business, including finance. While the use of the Internet as an information resource for business topics, including finance, is old hat, there are many other ways you can use the Net to help you get the money you need to grow. Here are some of the proven and just-emerging ways to get financing on the Net:

○ You can apply for loans, lines of credit and corporate credit cards online at the Web sites of many large banks, including Citibank (www.citi.com), Chase Manhattan (www.chase.com), and Wells Fargo (www.wellsfargo.com).

○ You can get information about how to fill out loan applications, write business plans and more from the Small Business Administration's site (www.sbaonline.gov), among others.

○ You can look for investors through finance site message boards, chat rooms and online databases at sites such as ACE-Net, the Angel Capital Electronic Network, at https://ace-net.sr.unh.edu/pub.

New tools for raising money on the Net are constantly emerging. In 1995, for instance, the Securities and Exchange Commission began allowing companies to transfer prospectuses to investors electronically via the Internet. All told, the Internet is a promising new frontier for companies raising money to expand.

Direct Public Offerings

Direct public offerings (DPOs) allow you to sell stock directly to the public without the registration and reporting requirements of an initial public offering. DPOs are specifically designed to let small businesses access the public capital markets with less cost and complexity than is involved in IPOs.

DPOs typically raise amounts of less than $1 million, but you can raise up to $25 million with a DPO under certain circumstances. You can also advertise and promote the sale of your own stock if you hold a DPO, something other public companies are forbidden to do.

DPOs' main limitation is the lack of a secondary market for securities. That means the stock of a DPO company is illiquid, so shareholders may have difficulty finding buyers for their shares in the event they want to sell. That's not necessarily bad for you, but it can be a deterrent to investors.

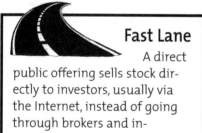

Fast Lane

A direct public offering sells stock directly to investors, usually via the Internet, instead of going through brokers and investment houses. It's inexpensive, fast and well-suited to small, growing companies.

SCOR Offerings

Small Corporate Offering Registrations (SCORs) let small companies raise money by issuing stock directly to the public without the help of an underwriter, as is used with IPOs, who buys the stock and resells it to the public. SCORs feature much less complicated regulatory oversight and document filings compared to standard IPOs and can be used to raise amounts of up to $1 million.

Selecting Your Financing Source

Choosing among the many possible sources of financing may be as simple as going with the only option that will take you. Ideally, you'll have a choice of several options. And at least to start with, you should have a good idea what would be your preferred form of financing so you can go after the most comfortable choices first.

Your options will be dictated by several considerations, including how much money you need, how long you'll need it, what you'll need it for, and how much control you're willing to relinquish. For instance, if you need to raise several million dollars, then venture capital, a stock offering or perhaps a well-heeled angel investor will be your best bet. On the other hand, if you need only $10,000, one of the SBA's Microloans may be your best bet. Financing lasting more than a few years is usually going to come from equity investors such as venture capitalists, angels or friends and family, unless you are financing real estate, when a bank loan would be suitable.

The reason you need the money will also come into play. A bank is unlikely to lend you money to allow you to increase your salary—that is going to have to come from someone with personal interests, such as an angel or family member. That same family member, on the other hand, will be unable to help if what you need is an international letter of credit to wrap up an across-the-border deal. Matching your financing source to your need will eliminate many possibilities.

Control is another issue. If you want to maintain maximum control of the business, stick to family, friends and bank financing. Angels, venture capitalists and public markets are much more likely to want to see themselves or their hand-picked henchmen in the driver's seat.

Estimating How Much You Need

When you started your business, you had to estimate the amount you needed to get going by combining your personal living expenses with start-up costs and outlays required to keep the business running. It's easier now because presumably all you have to worry about are ongoing expenses and expansion costs.

Thoroughness and caution are the keys to making a useful calculation of how much you'll need to expand. Use the work sheet on page 121 to figure out how much you'll need. To start, list all expenses related to running your business, as well as expanding it, in one column of a ledger pad or spreadsheet. Then add two more columns, labeled expansion costs and ongoing costs. In a separate area, place two lines labeled estimated income and other sources of funds.

Add up expenses projected for the coming year, including expansion and ongoing costs in the subtotals and total expenses lines. Put your estimated net income for the coming year in the estimated income line. Place the total of other sources of funds, such as savings and loans, in the other line and add these two together. Now subtract the total expenses from this amount. If the number is negative, this represents approximately how much financing you'll need to pay for expansion.

Wrapping Up

There are many places to look for financing for your growing company. You can look to the same sources that helped you start your business or tap savings, profits, friends and family, banks, venture capitalists, or the stock market. Whatever you do, you'll find it a lot easier to fund a growing company—and grow a company that is well-financed.

Expansion Financing Work Sheet

Item	Expansion Costs	Ongoing Costs
Advertising		
Transportation costs		
Dues and membership		
Equipment		
Fixtures		
Furniture		
Insurance		
Licenses and permits		
Loan payments		
Office supplies		
Postage		
Printing		
Rent		
Shipping		
Telephone		
Utility deposits		
Legal and professional fees		
Start-up inventory		
Replacement inventory		
Cost of goods		
Maintenance		
Entertainment		
Travel expenses		
Owner's salary		
Wages and salaries		
Employee benefits		
Miscellaneous		
Contingencies		
Subtotals		
Total Expenses		
Estimated Income		
Funds From Other Sources		
Total Income		
Total Expansion Financing Needed		

chapter 10

Going Global

The American market for almost everything is huge, but it's not large enough for many entrepreneurs. For these growth-minded business owners, the rest of the world is their oyster. Seeking international growth by going global as an importer-exporter offers opportunity aplenty. Some of the specific advantages presented by successfully growing globally include:

○ You can extend the sales life of existing products and services by finding new markets to sell them in.

○ You can reduce your dependence on the markets you have developed in the United States.

○ If your business is plagued by destabilizing fluctuations in your markets due to seasonal changes or demand cycles, you can even out your sales by tapping markets with different or even counter-cyclical fluctuations.

○ You can exploit corporate technology and know-how.

○ Finally, by entering the global marketplace, you'll learn how to compete against foreign companies—and even take the battle to them on their own ground.

The overriding reason to go global, of course, it to improve your potential for expansion and growth. And there are too many international opportunities for us to catalog them all here—or even in a much longer book than this one. The obvious opportunities are the markets in Canada, Mexico, Europe and Japan. But those only scratch the surface. There are many other fast-growing, less competitive markets.

Just spin the globe and you can find an opportunity to sell something, somewhere. Unearthing the right opportunity for you involves more work, of course. This chapter will get you started on that work.

The Pitfalls Of Exporting

Along with promise, going global carries an equally heavy load of peril. From chasing too many opportunities to getting whacked by currency fluctuations, the game of international expansion has many threats that domestic-only businesspeople never see. You can grab the brass ring of growth by going global, but only if you avoid the pitfalls.

Viewpoint

Despite stringent laws and numerous restrictions, some business opportunities with Cuba are authorized for U.S. individuals. American businesses can invest in foreign companies that conduct business in Cuba as long as the U.S. investor only holds a minority stake in the foreign company.

Chain Reaction

Picture this: A Minneapolis native moves to Siberia to open a chain of restaurants based on an American staple hardly anyone there has ever heard of. Sound outlandish? Not to 32-year-old Eric Shogren. In the summer of 1996, he opened the doors of his first New York Pizza restaurant in Siberia. Today, the chain boasts seven locations throughout Novosibirsk, a city of approximately 1.4 million people. Despite the obvious achievement, Shogren is the first to admit the difficulties inherent in such a venture. "Sometimes I tell people it's a rewarding experience if you can do it," he says, "but it falls into that category of 'Don't try this at home.'"

With the right frame of mind, however—and the right resources—you can boost your chances of launching a successful chain on foreign soil. Because it's a difficult venture to undertake alone, Shogren brought in his two brothers, Brad and Mike, as partners. It's also essential to hook up with the right foreign company before launching a business overseas: Locals can provide cultural and bureaucratic know-how that only comes with first-hand experience.

Beyond language and cultural barriers, financing will be a problem if you don't obtain strong backing at home first—especially when you've relocated thousands of miles away to a place like Eastern Europe, where banks either fail on a regular basis or penalize borrowers with sky-high interest rates.

Another stumbling block? Staying grounded about your goals. When you've taken an innovative product to a foreign land where opportunities abound, the temptation to expand too quickly is all too real.

Which is not to say that obstacles should deter those with a knack for international business. The main thing to remember? You'll have more difficulties than you expect, says Shogren. "But the rewards are out there," he adds. "I suppose if it were easy, everybody would be doing it."

The moment you've been waiting for has finally arrived, and you're ready to export your product. Now what? Your first order of business is to heed the hard lessons learned by those who have gone before you. Many have blundered, but that doesn't mean you have to.

Ready, Set, Go Global?

Experts agree that growing a business in America is risky enough. But what if your aspirations prompt you to debut your concept in a foreign land instead? Wesley Johnston, professor of marketing and director of the Center for Business and Industrial Marketing at Georgia State University in Atlanta, highlights the factors that can either make or break your business when you try to grow by going global. Here are key questions to ask yourself:

O *Will the product sell well in the targeted culture?* Think market research. The good news is most American products and services are embraced overseas. But if many of your potential consumers are lactose-intolerant, you'd want to steer clear of opening an eatery that sells only cheese pizza, says Johnston.

O *Is your target market familiar with your product or service?* If not, be prepared to invest a lot of time and money in consumer education. On the flip side, if you're the first one to introduce a new and exciting concept, "the product then becomes synonymous with your company name or chain," Johnston explains.

O *Do you feel comfortable in that country?* Since you'll probably have to live there temporarily to operate the chain in its early stages, you'll need a working knowledge of the language and culture.

O *What is the infrastructure like?* Can you get Western-style accommodations and support? How good are the roads? Are your supplies guaranteed? What about the reliability of hot water?

If you don't get the answers you want with the first foreign market you're considering entering, that may not mean your idea is poor—just that you picked the wrong place. "It's a big, big world out there," Johnston says. "I don't think there's any one idea that won't work somewhere."

Below are some of the most common exporting mistakes, according to John E. Cleek, program director at the Bloch School of Business Administration at the University of Missouri in Kansas City.

O *Failing to plan your strategy:* "Small businesses are particularly vulnerable to this problem, but larger ones are often guilty of the same mistake," says Cleek. "It takes far more time to extract yourself from problems created by lack of planning than it would to do it right the first time."

○ *Chasing inquiries the world over:* Just because dozens of countries show interest doesn't mean you're ready to market your product everywhere. Patience is key. "It takes discipline to respond to an inquiry from a country about which you know very little," Cleek says.

○ *Assuming if it works in America, it will work anywhere:* Not true—you need to tailor your sales and marketing efforts to each country. Don't ignore the cultural differences that shape the marketplace. The same goes for pricing, shipping, payment terms and packaging.

○ *Assuming business will be done in English:* Familiarize yourself with the local language. Says Cleek, "It is the height of ignorance to expect other people to learn our language to buy from us."

Currency Fluctuations

Today almost all entrepreneurial strategies for international expansion should take currency fluctuations into account. Often, the number of dollars it takes to equal a unit of a particular foreign currency can make the difference between a deal worth doing and a deal that would be a disaster.

When the dollar is weak against a foreign currency—it takes more dollars than usual to buy a unit of the foreign currency—it strengthens exporting entrepreneurs in a few ways. If the entrepreneur keeps prices level, those prices look lower to a buyer dealing in, say, Japanese yen or Mexican pesos. "When a foreign distributor is buying from a U.S. entrepreneur in U.S. dollars, he can buy more," says Frank J. Gaudio, head of the Consumer and Industrial Products Tax practice in the Midwest for PricewaterhouseCoopers.

Getting Directions

TradeNet Export Advisor is a one-stop, online link to government help for businesses getting started in exporting. The Web site, sponsored by several government agencies including the Department of Commerce, includes a wealth of directories, tutorials, databases and other tools. Learn more at www.tradenet.gov.

Aggressive exporters can take advantage of the currency edge to raise their prices, which could still look cheaper than before. Long-range strategists, on the other hand, might hold the line on prices and seek to gain volume. "If I keep my prices fixed and the dollar drops, it makes my product less expensive, so using my current pricing strategy, I can actually gain market share faster than when my prices were higher," says Mark Weaver, associate professor of management and marketing at the University of Alabama in Tuscaloosa, Alabama.

> "If the dollar drops, you are more competitive in the international market, but the cost of doing business over there goes up."

Currency fluctuations also have a downside. Many entrepreneurs who sell to Mexico, for instance, have seen the buying power of their customers shrivel as the peso plunged against nearly all currencies. The same can be said of currencies around the world at some time or another.

H. Maimin Co. Inc. is in the textile equipment manufacturing business, not currency trading. But 70 percent of the family-owned, 30-person Kent, Connecticut, company's output is exported. As a result, company officials practically have second jobs trying to keep track of the relative worth of a whole basket of currencies. Maimin sells to more than 50 countries around the world, so its sales are affected greatly by currency fluctuations.

Back in 1993, Turkey was an important market for Maimin. But around the end of that year, the Turkish currency crashed. While it took only 12 lira to buy a dollar in November 1993, currency traders were demanding a rate of 40 lira to the dollar by January 1994.

In a few months, the relative price of Maimin's dollar-denominated prices tripled to his Turkish buyers. Perhaps more important, no one knew where the Turkish national economy was headed. For months, Maimin's Turkish sales were almost completely stalled. They've now picked up again and are trending just as strongly as ever, according to company officials. But it took six months for the currency to stabilize.

Weak dollars also raise the actual cost of overseas travel when currency translations are accounted for. "If the dollar drops, you are more competitive in the international market, but the cost of doing business over there goes up," notes Mark Rice, director of the Severino Center for Technological Entrepreneurship at Rensselaer Polytechnic Institute in Troy, New York.

Unfortunately, few entrepreneurs are equipped with a strategy for dealing with currency fluctuations. The University of Alabama's Weaver cites a study of U.S. and Norwegian exporters that found fewer than 7 percent of the companies did anything to manage currency risk. "It's a little frightening to me that 93 percent of the exporters out there are exposed to the changes in the direction of the currency," he says.

The simplest way for exporters to deal with currency risk is to insist that all deals with foreign partners be done in dollars. However, that can drive away potential customers who prefer to do business in their local currency.

Another approach is to use financial instruments called currency futures to hedge against currency fluctuations. These instruments let an exporting entrepreneur make an agreement to trade a certain number of dollars for a certain number of another currency units at a specified date in the future. It's equivalent to locking in the current exchange rate, or another one the entrepreneur feels is more realistic, until the deal is done and the money actually changes hands. Any international bank, or any bank with a foreign correspondent, can provide assistance in purchasing currency hedges.

Goldie Paine, owner of Amerex Fire International Inc., a Trussville, Alabama, fire extinguisher exporter, nearly had to shut down a fledgling distribution operation in England several years ago when the pound plunged against the dollar. Now she plays futures between the dollar and the English pound on a regular basis. Typically, she tries to lock in her exchange rate for the next eight to nine months. But currency changes remain a daily object of attention.

Fast Lane

You can quickly get the latest currency exchange rates by using the Universal Currency Converter, a Web-based tool that instantly converts pounds, marks or other units of currency into U.S. dollars or vice versa. Visit www.xe.net/ucc.

"I get up every morning and look at the financial pages to see what the exchange rate is," says Paine. "Then I know whether I'm going to have a good day."

Collection Difficulties

In America, getting paid for your work is relatively straightforward. You sign a contract, complete the job, present the invoice or purchase order, and wait for payment. Getting paid for products or services when exporting isn't so simple. In fact, before you sell a single item, it would behoove you to take a crash course in "Export Payment Methods 101" (check with your local small-business development office or export council).

Don't let all the new terms and definitions scare you, advises Susan Corrales-Diaz, whose Orange, California, company, Systems Integrated, manufactures automated controls for electric power and water management equipment. She knew almost nothing about exporting when she started 17 years ago, but today she exhibits an impressive knowledge of what it takes to collect overseas.

"I didn't know very much at all when we started," remembers Corrales-Diaz with a rueful laugh. "One of my more seasoned salesmen had experience in China, so we decided to go into that market, where we knew there was a good infrastructure."

To educate herself, Corrales-Diaz began attending seminars and reading books. She learned about a variety of ways to get paid but quickly discovered that until you are actually using them, their applications can be difficult to understand. Here's a rundown of what she learned:

○ *An open account* is "the easiest and most dangerous way [to obtain payment for exports]," says a spokesperson at the U.S. Commerce Department's Trade and Project Finance Division. You may do a [credit check] to make sure the customer has enough money and to see what their payment record is, but basically you don't go beyond that. Then you hope in 30, 60 or 90 days that you'll receive payment.

This method robs you of legal recourse if your foreign buyer decides not to pay. "Open accounts should be reserved for your very best customers or countries you feel are very stable," advises the Commerce Department.

An open account is "the easiest and most dangerous way to obtain payment for exports."

○ *Documentary collection* involves sending an overseas bank the title documents for the goods to be exported and a blank check (called a draft) along with instructions not to surrender title until the buyer signs the draft.

"The draft has the amount of money [due to you] filled in and a space for the buyer to sign," reports the Commerce Department, adding that the draft can be a sight draft paid immediately or a time draft paid a certain number of days after it's signed. The draft is drawn up by you after negotiating conditions with the customer, such as what bank to send it to, what documents to include (for example, bill of lading, invoice, insurance, pro forma invoice), when and how payment will be made, and where to ship the goods.

The drawback to this method is that the buyer may refuse to sign the draft, and because a bank is not a collection agency, your goods may just sit on the dock. "The advantages are that it's a convenient, well-understood mechanism that is cheaper to use than obtaining a letter of credit," reports the Commerce Department, adding that this method works best with small and medium-sized orders.

○ *A letter of credit* is the second most secure way to recover payment for your exports, according to the Commerce Department. "There are two kinds of letters of credit, and they can be used for many different things," says a spokesperson at the Export Managers Association of California. "The standby letter of credit is used to collect [if] someone doesn't do something [such as ship the goods or pay the invoice] on time. It can be used as a form of insurance, a performance bond, or even as collateral with a bank."

The commercial letter of credit is usually what the exporter receives from the buyer's bank as payment once proof the order has been completed is assembled. Letters of credit are usually tailored to each transaction and can include information such as how much the order cost, when, how and where it will be shipped, what inspection certifications should be included, and who pays for what.

All this should be agreed on beforehand in a pre-letter-of-credit contract or agreement because any deviation requires amending the letter of credit, which can be extremely time-consuming and expensive.

"The letter of credit is safe because it's issued by a commercial bank and can be created to follow the regulations of the International Chamber of Commerce (ICC)," according to the Export Managers Association of California. "The ICC 500 is a standard set of rules that banks worldwide play with. No lawyers are needed to enforce the letter of credit."

○ *Credit cards* can also be a viable way to accept payment. Exporters don't necessarily need to have a customer's card in hand, according to a Visa spokesperson. Once they have merchant status, all they need is the customer's card number and selected other information to call in for point-of-purchase verification.

Steve L. Abrams, senior vice president of MasterCard International, says the company's Purchasing Card can be a good option for export payments. "We created this card to facilitate small purchases, which we define as those under $100,000."

The American Express card offers several benefits for use in export payment as well. Lack of a preset spending limit is one plus; also, if you process the transaction electronically, you could receive payment within three business days.

○ *Cash*, of course, is always an option. "The safest payment method, although it's not commonly used," according to the Commerce Department, "is cash in advance." He adds that exporters should use cash only for small-ticket items. Have the buyer send a check in U.S. dollars, and then ship the goods express mail.

While getting cash upfront may be the ideal way to receive payment for exporting, it does not give customers the payment flexibility you may need to attract them, nor does it give you a competitive edge.

According to Corrales-Diaz, there are myriad ways to combine the various payment methods. "Our letter of credit is [combined] with a sight draft," she says, "but you can also have a letter of credit with a time draft or an open account backed by a standby letter of credit." She stresses that personal understanding of the drafts and letters of credit can't replace working with a knowledgeable, experienced international banker who can explain the nuances of each method.

"All these different payment methods have degrees of risk associated with them," says Corrales-Diaz. "As a seller, you should understand what your competitors are doing in a country and then choose payment methods [that allow you to compete] yet protect you as much as possible."

Political And Economic Risk

Few nations have experienced governmental and economic systems as stable and long-lasting as those in the United States. As a result, many U.S. companies that venture overseas are completely unprepared for overseas instability. If an economic crisis impacts your business, take the following steps:

○ *Assess your financial capability.* "If you're able to [endure] a tough time, stay in the market. If you can't, get out," says importer-exporter Robert D. Hisrich. His warning: "If you leave, you'll probably have to strip your company, getting maybe 10 cents on the dollar for your [equipment and merchandise]. No one will pay market value in a crisis."

○ *Obtain information.* "Information on the local economy is critical," says Forrest Old, vice president of marketing for the Asia-Pacific, Canada, Latin America and receivables management services of Dun & Bradstreet. "Use the nearest U.S. Chamber of Commerce organization. Consult information providers such as D&B and Equifax. A good local partner also comes in handy. You'll need somebody on the ground who can tell you what the status is there."

○ *Save your client base.* "You're going to lose customers—the question is how many," Old says. "Develop a customer-retention strategy. You might extend more liberal terms, accept partial payments or negotiate alternative [deals]."

○ *Acquire legal representation.* "Hire local lawyers," Old advises. "You are going to need someone to help collect payments that are owed to you. You'll also have breach-of-contract issues to deal with."

○ *Shed weight.* When the ruble went deep-sea diving, one of Hisrich's companies took a hammering—but Hisrich didn't bail out. "I cut my staff from seven to three," the wine and clothing trader says. "You can also scale back your marketing efforts. If you can get by with a bare-bones operation, do it."

○ *Remain focused on your goals.* Says Old, "The [thing to do] in an emerging market is to put yourself in a position of greater growth opportunity than you would in a mature market. If you can get through the tough times, you could have the rapid penetration you were after in the first place."

Protecting Against Overseas Risk

As an international entrepreneur, you face risks every day you do business. The cargo you're exporting could fall off the ship, or it might get stolen in transit. Or maybe a customer went out of business and didn't pay for the last shipment you delivered. Even acts of nature can throw a wrench into an otherwise smoothly functioning global business. So if you have not already, it is time to consider whether or not you are prepared for what the future might bring.

Insurance offers protection, peace of mind and much more. "The reason you use [insurance] to mitigate risk is to increase your business," says Jeffrey Meyer, executive director of the VanAndel Global Trade Center in Grand Rapids, Michigan. "It's a means by which you can go into more risky markets to get more business, and that makes your business more competitive."

The types of coverage available to exporters are numerous and include cargo insurance (to protect your goods in transit), credit insurance (to protect against non-payment), fire and theft insurance, and foreign investment and trade risk insurance (for confiscation or expropriation of your property overseas).

Policies can be purchased separately or in a package deal offered by many insurers. To determine the kind of protection

Danger Ahead!
Laws in other countries are not the same as American laws, and many times the legal systems are so different that parties to international trade agreements have difficulty understanding one another. However, you should never enter into an agreement to buy, sell or trade anything across borders without a legal document describing the deal.

you will need, consider each country and situation individually, and research the risks involved. You may even want to talk to a professional consultant. But no matter what, says Meyer, "You have to insure your cargo. After you get past that, you're looking to see whether you need to insure your receivables [and so on]."

Of course, certain situations allow for a degree of chance. If you have a relationship with a customer in a politically stable country, such as the United Kingdom, you might choose to forgo credit insurance. But it probably would not be a good idea if you are shipping to Africa, which insurers consider to be the riskiest part of the world.

The cost of insurance depends on many factors, such as where you are shipping cargo, who your customer is, how valuable the goods are, and the means by which you ship. And policies, which expire anywhere from after one transaction to after one year, should be continually reviewed. Says Meyer, "If you want to do it right, you should match your risk management tools to the situation."

How To Go Global

Doing business around the world can seem a long way from doing business in your hometown. But each year countless small businesses make the trek. Like most long journeys, going global can be boiled down to a series of steps. Here are the six basic steps to going global:

1. *Start your campaign to grow by international expansion by preparing an international business plan to evaluate your needs and set your goals.* It's essential to assess your readiness and commitment to grow internationally before you get started.

> **It's essential to assess your readiness and commitment to grow internationally before you get started.**

2. *Conduct foreign market research and identify international markets.* The Department of Commerce is an excellent source of information on foreign markets for U.S. goods and services.

3. *Evaluate and select methods of distributing your product abroad.* You can choose from a variety of means for distributing your product, from opening company-owned foreign subsidiaries to working with agents, representatives and distributors and setting up joint ventures.

4. *Learn how to set prices, negotiate deals and navigate the legal morass of exporting.* Cultural, social, legal and economic differences make exporting a challenge for business owners who have only operated in the United States.

5. *Tap government and private sources of financing—and figure out ways to make sure you are getting paid.* Financing is always an issue, but government interest in boosting exporting and centuries of financial innovation have made getting funding and getting paid easier than ever.

6. *Move your goods to their international market, making sure you package and label them in accordance with regulations in the market you are selling to.* The globalization of transportation systems helps here, but regulations are still different everywhere you go.

Getting Directions

The Small Business Administration Office of International Trade helps advise small businesses and coordinate SBA export-related activities, including making hundreds of loans annually to exporters. The SBA also runs the Export Legal Assistance Network, which consists of international trade attorneys who give free initial consultations on export matters to small businesses.

Financing Help From The Export-Import Bank

As with any growth plan, expanding internationally requires financing. And growing globally requires special capabilities when it comes to finances. One of the most popular sources of financing for businesses expanding overseas is the Export-Import Bank of the United States. The Ex-Im Bank, as it's commonly known, is an inde-

Culture Club

One big difference between doing business domestically and internationally is culture. According to Hilka Klinkenberg, founder of Etiquette International in New York City, less than 25 percent of U.S. business ventures abroad are successful. "A lot of that is because Americans don't do their homework or because they think the rest of the world should do business the way they do business," she says. Klinkenberg offers the following tips to avoid making costly mistakes in international business meetings:

○ *Build a relationship before you get down to business.* "That entails making small talk and getting to know one another without [immediately] getting into business discussions," she says.

○ *Don't impose time limits.* Says Klinkenberg, "Keep [the meeting] as open as possible because it adds strength to your negotiating position."

○ *Do your research.* Learn at least a few pointers and facts about the country; it shows you respect your potential partners' cultural heritage. Also, get comfortable with the basic words in their language.

○ *Bring your own interpreter.* If they provide the interpreter, warns Klinkenberg, "the interpreter is going to have the other person's [interests] at heart, not yours."

○ *Understand body language.* "People think [body] language is universal—it's not," she says.

○ *Dress with respect and authority.* This should be self-explanatory. If it's not, seek the help of an image expert.

pendent U.S. government agency that has helped finance overseas sales of more than $300 billion in U.S. goods and services since 1934.

The Ex-Im Bank guarantees working capital loans for U.S. exporters and guarantees repayment of loans or makes loans to foreign purchasers of U.S. goods and services. It also offers U.S. exporters credit insurance to protect against nonpayment by foreign buyers.

To get Ex-Im Bank help, your product or service must have at least 50 percent U.S. content. The bank will finance the export of all types of goods or services except for most military-related products.

Fast Lane

You may be able to grow internationally without becoming an actual exporter. Many small companies tap international opportunities by means of strategic alliances with foreign firms or U.S. exporters. You may also be able to invest in foreign firms and buy a share of an international market without ever setting foot or shipping a product there.

Finding A Foreign Distributor

As tricky as it can be to obtain financing for a global expansion program, finding foreign business partners can be even tougher. If you can find foreign distributors for your product, you will be able to simply sell them your products and let them worry about reselling them at a profit in their domestic markets. Distributors are nice because they can offer foreign customers top-notch service and are easier for you do deal with because they typically buy enough of your product to build up an inventory.

You may be able to find a foreign distributor by simply looking around your home city or state for a foreign company with a U.S. representative. Trade groups, foreign chambers of commerce in the United States, and branches of American chambers of commerce in foreign countries are all good places to start your search for a foreign distributor.

International business consultants can provide valuable help the first few times you are trying to evaluate a foreign distributor. If you prefer to do the job yourself, look for the following when assessing in a foreign distributor:

○ You can eliminate many foreign distributor prospects by deciding whether you need a stocking or nonstocking distributor. Stocking distributors are generally larger firms that will commit to purchasing an inventory of your product.

○ If your product requires a salesperson knowledgeable about technology and other special aspects of your product, you will obviously require a distributor who can provide that type of sales force.

○ The best distributor will be one with a track record selling to the companies or consumers who are target markets for your product.

○ Unless you are fluent in the language of the country you are selling to, you should choose a distributor who can speak your language well.

○ You will want prompt, competent responses to your requests for information or service. Make sure your phone calls, faxes and e-mails are answered in a timely, satisfactory fashion.

○ Meet your prospects in person, and, as always, get and check references.

Global Warning

To break into an international niche, leave your sledgehammer at home and bring your ballet slippers instead. "You can't just take your product somewhere and try to force it on everyone," says Chip Hearn, COO and owner of Peppers, a Rehoboth Beach, Delaware-based hot sauce company that generates approximately $2.5 million in annual sales via the Internet, catalogs and retail stores.

Hearn learned the hard way not to make market assumptions. At a recent international food expo, he wanted to gain entry points into major island groups such as the Bahamas. Inspired by the abundance of dishes made with fresh fruit, he developed a new fruit-based hot sauce. The buyers at the expo hated it but told him they liked hot sauces. He whipped out one of his several hundred existing sauces and promptly found a brand-new market. Says Hearn, "You've got to be prepared to adapt, to think on your feet, and to try to find the best angle to make the sale."

Making NAFTA Work For You

When you're looking for international opportunities, it is important for you to consider various trade agreements between countries. The North American Free Trade Agreement (NAFTA) is an agreement between the Unites States, Canada and Mexico to lower trade barriers, level playing fields, boost cross-border investment and protect intellectual properties. While that may sound vague, the reality is anything but. In the first three years after NAFTA was introduced, total North American trade increased from $293 billion in 1993 to $420 billion in 1996, a 43 percent gain. Canada has long been the United States' biggest trading partner, and from 1986 to 1993, trade with Mexico more than tripled, making Mexico an almost equally big opportunity for U.S. exporters.

Getting Directions

Contact your regional office of the Export-Import Bank by calling (800) 565-3946 or by checking out the agency's Web site at www.exim.gov.

Taking advantage of NAFTA may require significant adjustments on your behalf. Here are some questions to ask before you make a serious effort to do business within the NAFTA framework:

○ Will I need to change my products to conform to Canadian or Mexican business or consumer tastes and preferences?

○ Will I need to change my products' packaging, labeling or other characteristics to conform to Canadian or Mexican safety, environmental or other regulations?

○ Will my human resources needs change? For instance, will I need to hire more Spanish- or French-speakers?

○ Do I have products facing tougher competition domestically that might prosper in NAFTA markets?

Despite the likelihood that you'll have to make adjustments, the opportunities emanating from NAFTA are many. The U.S. Department of Commerce has ranked 40 industries as the ones with the best prospects for export growth. The 40 industries range from advertising services, agricultural machinery, and equipment and apparel to telecommunication equipment, textile fabrics, toys, and games. There's room for almost anything you make or sell to benefit from NAFTA's protective umbrella, and the future looks bright. By 2009, NAFTA is expected to accomplish its ultimate goal: the elimination of all North American tariffs.

Importing

International trade involves more than shipping U.S. products overseas. For many products, foreign sources of supply can provide higher quality, lower cost or some other desirable feature in comparison to U.S. sources. For instance, Italian shoes, French wines and Japanese cameras are widely available in the United States because of their recognized superiority in some respects to domestic alternatives.

Fast Lane

Your efforts to export to Canada and Mexico will be leveraged enormously if you speak Spanish or French—or can hire someone fluent in those languages.

Importing doesn't have to be limited to goods, either. Many companies have grown by importing services in imaginative ways. For instance, a large quantity of the data-entry work that used to be done in the United States is now done by workers in countries such as India and China. The companies for whom this work is being done have effectively imported the data-entry services of international workers.

Getting Directions

There are lots of great books on going global. Some of the best for entrepreneurs include *Exporting, Importing and Beyond: How to Go Global With Your Small Business* (Adams Media) by Lawrence W. Tuller, *Building an Import/Export Business* (John Wiley & Sons) by Kenneth D. Weiss, and *How to Start an Import/Export Business* (Entrepreneur's business start-up guide No. 1092).

At one time, identifying sources of products to import was a serious challenge for American importers. But vast improvements in the global telecommunications network have greatly eased that task. Today anyone with a computer and a modem can do Web searches to locate suppliers virtually anywhere in the world. Furthermore, they can communicate with those suppliers, exchanging specifications and requirements far more easily, swiftly and conveniently than ever before. If you have an idea for importing a product made in another country, it should be easy to find a supplier who can sell it to you. Here are tips for finding a source of products to import:

Getting Directions

You can learn which countries and products get low- or no-duty treatment at the U.S. Customs Service Web site at www.customs.ustreas.gov.

○ Start by focusing on countries whose imports to the United States are granted favored status. This means lower import duties and lower costs for you.

○ Once you have selected countries as likely sources, contact trade representatives at the appropriate embassies. They should be able to provide you with lists of manufacturers of the products you're interested in.

○ Attend foreign and domestic trade fairs where companies seeking to export to the United States are exhibitors.

○ Read U.S. and foreign newspapers and magazines, scanning for advertisements and articles about products you might want to import.

The Internet is having a large impact on the way international business is conducted. This impact is especially significant when it comes to finding leads for international trade partners. You can look at TradeNet, the U.S. government's online trade-matching service, for numerous links, databases, message boards and other tools for finding products to import and other opportunities to grow your business internationally.

Fast Lane

Begin your international expansion by looking for sources of products that are already being successfully imported to the United States. This will make the learning process easier, and later you can look for exclusive sources that will be more profitable.

Once you have identified some likely sources of products to import, make contact with the company and begin gathering information. You'll want to obtain samples of products and, of course, discuss prices and terms of payment. Take special care to check the quality of the products—the United States is a sophisticated marketplace, and shoddy products that might succeed elsewhere will be shunned here.

As in any circumstance where you're checking out a new prospective supplier, ask for references. Get a referral to a company that has dealt with this supplier before, and call to check them out.

Shipping procedures are a paramount concern when moving products long distances. High-value items may be shipped by air, but many

Danger Ahead!

You need a license to import many products. For instance, the import of many agricultural products, including dairy products, plants and animals, requires an import license. If you attempt to import products without appropriate licenses, your goods may be held or even confiscated.

products come by ship. This often means transit times measured in months, with the associated risks of missing market opportunities. Make sure your supplier understands your requirements for delivery and that the shipping procedure chosen will do the job. Once you are happy with the arrangements, have an attorney experienced in international trade review the contract.

Why Go Global?

International expansion is not necessarily the best way to grow your company. The U.S. market is big enough for most small businesses to expand almost indefinitely. But entering the international arena can protect you against the risk of decline in domestic markets and, most important, significantly improve your overall growth potential.

Trade
Shows And
Conferences

xhibiting at a trade show is an excellent

way to find customers to help your business grow. According to

a study conducted by the Center for Exhibition Industry

Research (CEIR), 86 percent of show attendees were the deci-

sion-maker or influenced buying decisions, yet 85 percent had

not been called on by a salesperson before the show.

Trade shows are also economical ways of getting sales. The CEIR reports that closing a sale that begins with contact at a trade show runs about half the cost of closing a sale that doesn't have the exhibition advantage: $550 and 1.4 sales calls compared to $997 and 3.6 sales calls.

Finally, trade shows are popular, and it's easy to find one that fits your industry and your company's needs. *Tradeshow Week* lists more than 1,700 annual trade shows in its directory, from the American Bankers Association Convention to the World Alzheimer Congress 2000. You can search for exactly the show you want at *Tradeshow Week*'s online directory at www.tradeshowweek.com.

Viewpoint

There are so many trade shows that you could probably visit one a week all year long. How many should you go to? Four a year, or one each quarter, is a recipe many entrepreneurs find to be a good schedule, according to Jay Conrad Levinson, author of *Guerrilla Marketing*.

Getting The Most From A Trade Show Or Conference

When you're looking to grow your business, a trade show can be a great place to gather information—whether you're seeking new customers, suppliers or contacts for your business. Exhibitor booths are manned by distributors, franchisors, business opportunity sellers, banks, phone companies, Internet service providers, and even the Small Business Administration—all of whom are eager to assist you. Some trade shows even offer seminars on a variety of business-related topics.

But trade shows can be overwhelming, with dozens of exhibitors all competing for your attention. To get the most out of a show, you need to know what to expect and how to sort through the many offerings.

Advance Planning

You'll improve your trade show experience by planning ahead. Obtain a map of the exposition floor and make notes of the booths you want to visit. "A good show will have a floor plan," says Helen C.

Testing The Waters

Foreign buyers are very interested in U.S. products. They carry a certain panache," says trade consultant Peggy Baird. "But your product must have proven demand in the foreign market you're pursuing."

One way to find out if that demand exists is by exhibiting your product at trade shows. "Foreign buyers attend domestic trade shows," says Baird. "They'll tell you if they have an interest in your product. They're savvy about their exchange rates and can tell you immediately if your product is priced competitively for their market."

You also need to make sure your American-made product fits your foreign buyer's body size, housing needs or lifestyle. For example, hair dryers, television sets and other types of American-made equipment that operate on 110-volt and 60-cycle current will work in Canada but not in Japan and Europe, where electrical equipment operates on different voltages and cycles.

Product quality is another key consideration. An item that chips, fades, shrinks or doesn't operate properly won't be accepted in foreign markets. Some foreign buyers won't accept a product with even the slightest imperfection.

Once you've tested your product for marketability, consider how you will ship it overseas. Also, assess your production capacity to ensure you can adequately fill a large foreign order.

Brown of Aston, Pennsylvania, who attends trade shows regularly. "If you have that, you can plan in advance which exhibits you want to hit."

The most important things at any trade show are the exhibitors and the attendees. Of these two, the more important are the exhibitors. You want to pick a trade show that has lots of exhibitors to draw attendees. Equally important, you want them to be the right kind of exhibitors.

Exhibitors without attendees aren't worth much. High-quality attendees are the lifeblood of any successful trade show. Keep in mind that sheer number of attendees is not the only issue. A show that attracts a relatively small number of attendees who happen to be exactly the type of people you are looking for might easily be more successful at helping you grow than a bigger show with a broader group of attendees.

As part of advance planning, you should decide on an objective for the show. For instance, you may be attending to generate sales leads. You may be interested in testing or introducing a new product. Conducting demonstrations, identifying new applications, obtaining customer feedback, even studying the competition—these can all be legitimate reasons for attending or exhibiting at a trade show. And don't forget the opportunity to recruit new employees, distributors or dealers for your products.

Getting Directions

To find out about trade shows in advance, contact your local chamber of commerce or professional business organizations. They can tell you what's coming before the shows are announced in the paper, giving you time to arrange your schedule to attend the show.

You should also do some training to make sure you get the most from your booth or your interactions with exhibitors. You may go so far as to write a script for people staffing your booth to present to visitors. Qualifying is an important part of speaking to people at trade shows. You can spend a lot of time talking to the wrong people. So make sure you know who you want to talk to, whether it's a potential customer, supplier, dealer or other contact, and make sure you spend as much time as possible interacting with the target people.

At The Show

Once you're at the show, you'll have to make some important decisions about how you'll spend your limited time investigating what may appear to be a nearly infinite spectrum of prospects. In addition to floor plans, most shows provide booklets with descriptions of the exhibits, as well as a listing of the times, topics and featured speakers of any seminars or panel discussions, so that attendees can better plan their time.

Fast Lane

If your time at a show is limited, plan a one-time walk-through by visiting booths in order so that you can cover everything you want to see in a single sweep through the floor. Not only is this a timesaver, it's an energy-saver as well—too much walking on hard convention center floors can be exhausting.

On your first day at the show, you'll want to get a feel for what's actually there. Helen Brown suggests that first-time

Home On The (Trade Show) Range

Ron Sievers had never been to a trade show before he started his homebased landscaping and irrigation business in 1988. But the owner of R & D Irrigation & Landscaping Inc. in Apopka, Florida, decided a local landscaping show would be a good source of ideas and perhaps help him locate some new plant suppliers. He found what he was looking for and more—including a new Bobcat skidsteer loader—and is sold on the idea of attending shows.

"I was surprised at the number of vendors there," says Sievers, 60. "I didn't think much about what a Bobcat would have to do with landscaping, but it has a whole lot to do with it, and we bought one from the people at the show."

No matter what industry you're in, trade shows and conventions are an excellent source of information. Exhibitors are eager to show off their latest products and convince you how such items can enhance your business. And for many homebased business owners, these shows may be your only opportunity to meet face to face with a sizable number of prospective suppliers and customers in a short period of time.

Check with your industry and professional associations for information about upcoming shows. Ask for a list of exhibitors in advance so you can decide which companies you definitely want to contact before you get there. Like Sievers, keep an open mind while you're at the show—you may find an unexpected sales or productivity tool. And be willing to travel to attend the right show. It could be one of the best investments of time and money you can make for your business.

attendees systematically walk through the entire show once, briefly looking at each exhibit. From there, they can choose which exhibits they want to visit again for more detailed information. A seasoned trade show attendee, Brown says this is how she approaches most shows. "I hit every exhibit table," she says. "That means I don't stop and chat. I walk quickly and pick up all the materials."

If an exhibitor tries to pressure her, Brown says she has a tight schedule to maintain and that she'll be in touch later. "The next booth might have something better. If you commit to the first one,

you'll miss out," she says, adding that this is another reason to go through the show quickly once before talking to exhibitors.

During her second pass-through, Brown stops to talk, asks questions, and gathers additional information only from those booths she believes have the potential to provide her with customers, equipment, vendors or other valuable products and services.

Getting Directions

You can check for background information on trade show contacts with the Federal Trade Commission online at www.ftc.gov, or by calling (800) 554-5706.

Don't take anything you see at face value. Brown recommends checking references and contacting the Better Business Bureau in the state where a particular company's headquarters are located. If a company has had a history of customer complaints, for instance, you can either eliminate it from consideration or ask more pointed questions later. If you feel hesitant about asking questions, remember what's at stake: If you avoid asking a question now, you might be sorry later.

A shy attendee can lead into specific questions by asking something general about an exhibit, Brown says. Exhibitors are happy to talk. "They're hungry for you to ask questions," she says. "They want to grab your attention."

If you don't want to wait in line at a crowded booth, you can leave a business card. Most exhibitors encourage attendees to drop off their cards by leaving a box or bowl out for cards, and many even hold drawings, offering prizes ranging from food baskets to computer systems.

Getting Directions

"Tradeshow U" is a seminar on the basics of trade show booth management. The $95, three-hour seminar covers everything from attracting people to your booth and establishing goals to doing publicity. Learn more at www.gesexpo.com, or contact GES Exposition Services at (702) 263-2791 or tradeshowu@gesexpo.com.

Because exhibitors pay a lot of money to participate in trade shows, they want to get the most for their money. That means they will take the time to contact you later. By waiting for them to contact you after the show, you'll be able to ask questions without feeling rushed or on the spot.

Following Up

Making the most of a trade show doesn't end when you walk out the convention center door. Once Brown gets home, she sorts through the bags of items she gathered at the show. She starts with the freebies—such as pens, hats and mugs—given out by exhibitors. "I start with the goodies and give them all away," she laughs. "Then I sort through the information."

Brown immediately discards any information not of interest to her. Then she makes notes and sorts the remaining information packets according to what they can offer her. She then writes letters, makes follow-up calls and sets up meetings with organizations.

Making The Most Of Your Own Exhibit

In addition to attending trade shows as a visitor, you may also want to exhibit. If you do, you'll want to make sure your exhibit is as effective as possible. As a trade show exhibitor, you have about five seconds to catch an attendee's eye before he or she passes your booth. Five seconds. With this kind of attention span, making the most of the graphics at your exhibit is not just smart marketing—it's do or die.

There's intense competition for the eyeball at trade shows. The days of simply tacking up a sign with your company name on it are over. That kind of display is fine if you're as recognizable as Wal-Mart, but if you're Magnet Products Inc., you had better be prepared to tell people who you are and what you do.

Here are a few suggestions for perking up your trade show graphics:

○ Develop a unique proposition and use it as a headline. Example: "Sales automation software that decreases selling time by 25 percent."

○ Make your graphics bold and attractive so they command attention even from a distance.

Fast Lane

Exhibiting at a trade show can cost $2,000 and up just for booth rental at a small show. Total expenses for booth, travel, exhibits and staff will probably top $10,000. But you may be able to trim costs significantly by subleasing a corner of a large booth belonging to one of your partners, suppliers or even customers.

○ Make sure that your display addresses the commonly asked questions, "What does your company do?" and "What are you showing here?"

○ Build brand identity by coordinating display graphics with sales literature, including pre-show promotions and follow-up mailings.

Also, be sure to keep up with the latest technology in trade show displays. Computer-generated graphics and reusable, portable displays can improve your image and save you money.

chapter 12

Marketing, Advertising And Public Relations

nybody can process an order for products or services, but it takes a real businessperson to create a customer. And customers are what power growth. Without customers, in fact, you don't have a business at all. You just have a lot of inventory, employees and fixtures. The tool you use to create customers is marketing, including advertising and public relations, to let the world know you are there and what you stand for.

Effective marketing is often what separates rapidly growing companies from slow-growing or stalled companies that started at the same time, serve the same market and offer similar merchandise. Companies such as Gillette, Frito-Lay and Coca-Cola have succeeded in highly competitive mass markets for consumer goods because, while they certainly produce competitive products, they out-market their rivals. If you expect your business to grow to any size, you will have to become an effective marketer, advertiser and promoter of your business. In fact, you are likely to grow to the extent that you master marketing, and no more.

How To Develop And Run A Marketing Campaign

A marketing campaign isn't something that comes to you while you're taking a shower. Successful campaigns tend to be carefully researched, well-thought-out and focused on details and execution, rather than resting on a single, grand idea.

Planning a marketing campaign starts with understanding your position in the marketplace and ends with details such as the wording of an advertisement. You may also want to include decisions about uniforms, stationery, office décor and the like in your marketing plan.

Keep in mind that your plan is not supposed to be a prison. You have to leave room to make changes as you go along because no plan can perfectly capture reality. But you should also be able to commit fully to implementing your plan—or some future version of it—if you want to take a strong step toward growth.

Revising Your Marketing Plan

A growing business needs a new marketing plan just as it needs a new business plan. The steps in revising your marketing plan are similar to those required to create a marketing plan from scratch.

First, you need to redefine your product or service. Describe your product or service and its features and benefits in detail. Focus on how it differs from the competition. Concentrate on key features of your offering, including pricing, service, distribution and placement. In other words, know what you are going to be selling more of and why more people are going to buy it.

Second, look at the various market segments into which you hope to introduce—or expand demand for—your product. Decide what type of buyer is most likely to purchase it. Now describe your target customer in detail in terms of demographics: age, sex, family composition, earnings, geographical location, lifestyle, purchasing patterns, buying objections, and the like. Know exactly who will be driving your growth.

> **Find out what your target customers read and listen to, and spell out your promotional objectives.**

Third, create a strategy for communicating the message that will produce growth. Find out what your target customers read and listen to, and spell out your promotional objectives. Do you want people to recognize your name or know where you're located? Decide how often you'll need to—and can afford to—expose customers to your message to create the growth you desire.

Choosing The Proper Media

You're not going to reach new markets and new customers by advertising in the same old places with the same old message. That doesn't mean you have to buy a full-page ad in *The Wall Street Journal* or a 60-second commercial during the Super Bowl. Like most small companies, you will be more likely to grow by finding a niche, not by trying to sell to the mass market. Your customers' location, age, income, interests and other information will tell you what media will reach them. Target your advertising as narrowly as possible to the media that will reach your best customers. Then gradually broaden your reach to attract new customers.

For instance, if you were selling computer networking equipment to small companies, you might advertise in *Entrepreneur* magazine as well as some business-oriented computer magazines. If you wanted to broaden your market to home networkers, you could add media aimed at homeowners. Like any aspect of running a business, marketing involves a measure of trial and error. As your business grows, however, you'll quickly learn which advertising media are most cost-effective and draw the most customers.

Print Advertising

The print ad is the basic unit of advertising, the fountainhead from which all other forms of advertising spring. There are two principal publication categories to consider for print advertising.

The first, newspapers, have a positive and a negative side. On the plus side, you can get your ad in very quickly. On the downside, newspapers usually have a shelf life of just 24 hours. Therefore, if you run your ad on Monday, you can't depend on anyone to discover that ad on Tuesday. As the saying goes, "Nobody wants to read yesterday's news." If your budget allows for multiple insertions—that is, running your ad more than once—do so. Regular exposure of the ad builds recognition and credibility. If some of your prospects see but don't respond to your first insertion, they may well respond to your second or third. If you have confidence in your ad's message, don't panic if the initial response is less than you wanted. More insertions may bring a better response.

Viewpoint

When considering print advertising, don't forget the standby of small businesses: the Yellow Pages. Yellow Pages ads have a long shelf life and a broad distribution. The main problem with Yellow Pages ads is distinguishing your business from the sea of competition. Make sure you draft an ad with a strong, attention-getting headline if you want to use the Yellow Pages to help grow your business.

The second type of print publication is magazines, for which there are specialty categories of every kind. Advertising in this type of publication allows you to target special-interest groups. Another advantage of magazines, especially monthlies, is that they have a much longer shelf life than newspapers; they're often browsed through for months after publication. So your ad might have an audience for up to six months after its initial insertion. Moreover, readers spend more time per sitting with a magazine than a newspaper, so there's more chance they'll run across your ad.

Radio And TV Advertising

Many entrepreneurs believe that radio and TV advertising are beyond their means. But while national TV advertising is usually out of the entrepreneur's price range, advertising on local stations and on cable television can be surprisingly affordable. Armed with the right information, the small-business owner may find that TV and radio advertising deliver more customers than any other type of ad campaign. The key is to have a clear understanding of the market so the money spent on broadcast advertising isn't wasted. Make sure you know what your advertising is supposed to achieve, set a reasonable budget, get all the feedback you can from other entrepreneurs, station advertising sales people and others, and your broadcast ad campaign can prove a powerful growth producer.

Fast Lane

You could never afford to run a 30-minute commercial for your business. But on public access cable television, you can almost certainly put on a 30-minute infomercial promoting yourself and your business. For instance, the owner of an antique shop could host a weekly show on finding, restoring and pricing antiques. A car repair specialist could host a weekly car care show. The possibilities are endless.

The cost of producing your commercial is a major issue with broadcast advertising. TV stations usually charge you to produce your commercial (prices range from about $200 to $1,500), while radio stations will put your ad together for free.

These broad categories only scratch the surface of the advertising opportunities out there. Try to find out what media are available, and determine which will work best. Finally, come up with a way to evaluate the results of your communications—market surveys, sales analyses and the like. Then run some tests, and see which ones bring the growth you're after.

Creating A Press Kit

If you haven't put together a press kit for your firm, now is a good time to consider it. A press kit—also called a media kit—is a prepared package of information you can send out to members of the press. As you grow, you may come to the attention of local or national media and need a way to quickly and completely communicate key facts about your company. The press kit provides a simple solution to this need. A complete press kit contains the following:

○ *A brief company biography:* This should be a one- or two-page summary of what you do and what makes you special. It should be a quick reference guide to your organization and include your full company name, address and contact information, mission statement, organizational structure, products and services, locations, number of employees, and relevant financial information.

○ *Short biographies of senior management:* Each one will include full name, title, education, professional affiliations and awards, family and community involvement and awards. A paragraph or two per person should be sufficient.

○ *A sheet of testimonials with comments from customers:* You may also include awards and citations.

○ *Reprints of newspaper and magazine articles, printouts of Web sites and references to television and radio shows your company has been mentioned in:* Articles and media exposure lend tremendous credibility to your company.

Viewpoint
Advertising budgets can be hard to figure, but they should be tied to gross sales. Plan to devote 2 percent to 5 percent of anticipated gross sales to your annual advertising budget.

○ *Photos of products, people, facilities or other important parts of your company:* This will help put a face on your company.

○ *Something to put it all in:* Make it something like a pocket folder with your logo on the cover.

Adding Public Relations To Your Marketing Mix

As your business grows, it naturally becomes a more prominent element in your community and your industry. That means that what it does naturally becomes more worthy of notice. And that means improved opportunities for using public relations as a bigger part of your marketing mix. PR is an excellent tool because it gives you exposure you don't have to pay for directly. The term "directly" is chosen carefully here. True, you may not have to cut a check to a broadcaster or publisher when your company is mentioned in a news report. But good PR rarely happens without effort. Getting good publicity usually requires careful planning, persistent effort, and, often, spending money for press release mailings, copywriters and public relations consultants.

The good news is, as the founder of a growing company, your are in a prime position to be listened to by consumers and the news media. All you have to do is let others know you exist and that you are an expert source of information or advice about your industry.

Viewpoint

Your talents for copywriting and ad design may have helped you get your business off the ground. But now that growth, not just survival, is the goal, you should consider handing the jobs of advertising copywriting and design off to a professional. No matter how creative you are, a commercial copywriter or graphic designer can vastly improve almost any ad created by an entrepreneur.

Being regarded as an industry expert can do wonders for your business. But how can you get your expertise known?

○ Start by making sure you know everything you can about your business, product and industry.

○ Contact experts in the field and ask how they became experts.

○ Talk to as many groups as possible. (If public speaking strikes fear in your heart, you'd better get over it. This is one skill you're going to need as an entrepreneur.) Volunteer to talk to key organizations, service clubs, business groups or anyone else who might be interested in what you have to say. Do it free of charge, of course, and keep it fun, interesting and timely.

Fast Lane

Instead of a full press kit, you can use a quick, one-page fact sheet consisting of a bulleted list. It should be easy to fax and, if stored electronically or as a Web site page, easy for the media to open, print, copy and e-mail to others.

○ Contact industry trade publications and volunteer to write articles, columns, or opinion pieces. (If you can't do that, write a letter to the editor.)

○ Offer seminars or demonstrations related to your business (a caterer could explain how to cook Thai food, for instance).

○ Host—or appear as a regular guest or contributor to—a local radio or TV talk show.

Do all this, and by the time you contact media people and present yourself as an expert, you'll have plenty of credentials.

Developing A New Marketing Pitch

Marketing powerhouses such as Coca-Cola, McDonald's and Ford have the clout to make their messages—such as the McDonald's slogan "You deserve a break today"—part of everyday language. Yet from time to time, these companies decide to get rid of an old message and come out with a new one. Your company may not grow to global size, yet its path to growth will likely also be marked by a series of marketing pitches. As all companies grow and change, their marketing messages change as well. Here are solid reasons for developing a new marketing message:

○ *Your old message has become irrelevant.* Nike's "Bo knows" message, built around two-sport superstar Bo Jackson, lost its meaning after Jackson became injured and left professional sports.

○ *The message doesn't differentiate you any longer.* If your competitors are now routinely offering the things you used to stress in your message, it's time for a new one. Ford's "Quality is job one," for instance, was a good message when the company started, but quality isn't as big an issue as it was when Ford began its campaign.

○ *The message has developed some sort of negative connotation.* One company that called itself Area Industrial Disposal Services grew quite well in the early 1980s but found that it needed to change its message—which often used the company's acronym instead of its full name—after knowledge of the AIDS epidemic became widespread.

○ *Your target market is the same, but its characteristics have changed.* If your loyal customers are getting older, richer, further advanced in their careers or otherwise changing with the march of time, then your marketing message will probably have to evolve or risk being seen as out of touch with the times.

○ *Your old message simply isn't working.* Test it by using focus groups and surveys. Does it appeal to your target audience? If not, for whatever reason, you need a new one.

Fast Lane

Create a positioning statement for your company to help you sum up where you fit into the market-place. In one or two sentences, describe what distinguishes you from your competition. Use this positioning statement in all your marketing communications.

○ *You've shifted your target market.* If you started out going after consumers and are now focusing on business clients, your marketing message likely needs to change.

Netting Customers

These days, online advertising deserves consideration as part of the marketing mix for many companies. There are several useful ways to advertise online, from slipping text boxes into electronic newsletters to sending e-mail solicitations to customers who want to receive them. But the primary means of online advertising is the banner ad. These rectangular boxes of text and graphics float at the top of countless Web sites. Most Web advertisers agree banner ads are an excellent way to get company names and messages in front of the masses, and studies have linked Web banners to higher brand awareness and consumers' incentive to buy.

That doesn't mean Web banners should be your only ad channel. Nor are Web banners useful for all businesses. One problem is that nobody's really sure what type of businesses Web banners are best for. A recent report by Forrester Research showed advertisers are baffled by the impact of their banner ads and, in particular, are dissatisfied with the methods sites use to track responses. "Media sites and advertisers resoundingly agreed: Ad measurement on the Internet is a mess," the report states. Reasons cited for messy ad tracking included hyped expectations, a lack of agreement on standards, technology obstacles, and a fragmented ad delivery process.

Online ad agencies and ad software companies are pushing for standards to resolve these issues. In fact, a bona fide movement is underway—specialists are perfecting technology that would measure ads' effectiveness and count the number of click-throughs (people who click on a banner ad to reach an advertiser's site). Soon ad software companies will also be able to track users' demographic and behavioral characteristics.

Does the Internet provide a foolproof way to measure the ad responsiveness it initially promised? Obviously not. But with industry standards and technology hurdles being addressed, Web advertising may soon live up to advertisers' high expectations.

Reaching New Markets

One of the most effective ways to grow your company is to tap into new markets. These can be markets that haven't existed until recently, such as the markets for Web site development software and electronic books that sprang up in the 1990s, or just markets that are new to your firm. Many companies' growth prospects practically exploded when they accessed a new market for existing products and

Brown-Bag-Budget Marketing

"**Y**ou don't have to spend a lot of money to have effective marketing," says Martin R. Baird, author of the book *Guaranteed Results*. "If you can accomplish one small, simple marketing effort every day, it's amazing what kinds of results you can get." Baird's tips:

○ *Speak at community events.* Offering your expertise at public occasions is an easy way to get the word out about your business. You'll maximize your impact and lend credibility to your product or service.

○ *Ask customers for referrals.* Generating referrals from current customers is one of the best ways to market your business. Don't forget to query your vendors (they're likely to have many contacts) and explain to your customers exactly what kinds of referrals you're looking for and how they can help.

○ *Spend two days in your customers' shoes.* To find out what your customers really want, visit a wide range of businesses they're likely to frequent. Observe how customers are treated, as well as the kinds of services that appear important to them; then adapt your business accordingly.

○ *Offer gift certificates.* They're an easy, low-cost way to generate immediate revenue you can put to use until they're cashed in. Always ask your customers if they'd like to purchase a gift certificate.

○ *Offer free samples.* If you can get someone to try your product or service, chances are they'll buy it later. Have employees pass out product samples in front of your business; if you provide a service, offer free services on a trial basis.

services. If you are committed to growth, checking out opportunities to market to new customers should be a priority.

Why New Markets Require New Strategies

You may be able to sell existing products or services into new markets without significantly modifying the products or services themselves. However, it's likely that you will have to alter your business strategy when you try to penetrate a new market. For instance, if the new market is larger but more competitive than the one you are currently in, you may have to adjust your pricing strategy to give your business leverage to take market share from entrenched rivals.

Pricing isn't the only key part of your strategy you may have to alter. New markets often require new marketing messages, new packaging, new value propositions and new product names. You can't comprehend the adjustments necessary for penetrating a new market unless you understand that market. Knowing a new market usually requires careful study, including conducting market research, consumer opinion polls, competitive surveys and test marketing.

Marketing remains as much art as science, and there is no certain way to tap new markets or increase sales to existing ones. But fast-growing companies are, almost without exception, companies that are effective marketers. To generate long-lasting, consistent growth, developing marketing, advertising and promotional skills has to be a priority.

Setting Up
Distribution

istribution is one of the famed "four P's"

of marketing. It falls under the umbrella of "place" and, along with

the other P's of product, price and promotion, can easily make the

difference between a successful growth plan and one destined

for failure. At its simplest, distribution refers to where the prod-

uct is when a potential customer has a buying opportunity.

For instance, if customers primarily come across your product in retail drugstores, then retail drugstores are your main distribution channel.

There are many ways to distribute products and seemingly more being invented, improved or popularized all the time. For instance, a few years ago Internet distribution of software was rare, whereas now it's becoming one of the most widely used methods. Time-tested means of distribution include retail outlets, wholesalers, salespeople, telemarketing and direct mail. These major methods of distribution often feature their own variations. For instance, you can distribute your product through orders placed by television viewers of commercials, infomercials, sponsorships of televised events, and other shows. Often, selecting a new distribution channel is the key to jump-starting growth in a company. So you need to choose wisely when deciding on the means of distribution you will employ in your growth plan.

Viewpoint

The four P's of marketing were popularized around 1960 by an advertising executive named Jerome McCarthy, who distilled them from the even older "Marketing Mix" equation used by Borden's Inc. in its marketing efforts. The four P's are widely used today, although some modern marketers add additional P's, such as one for customer service "processes."

Distribution Models

When deciding how to distribute your product, use the traditional distribution model as a starting point. The conventional distribution model has three levels: the producer, the wholesaler and the retailer. This is a time-tested system with many well-established members at all levels.

The conventional distribution model, however, calls for all parties in the channel to protect their own best interests. Thus, retailers are pitted against wholesalers, and wholesalers try to best producers. This web of conflicting interests sometimes works to the detriment of the entire system. For instance, a producer may try to bypass the wholesaler and go straight to retailers, prompting the wholesaler to retaliate by dropping the producer's products.

The primary alternative distribution channel is direct distribution.

This is the model Dell, Avon and many other successful companies use. It calls for you to sell and deliver your product yourself, using your own salespeople and warehouses. Going direct can cut significant costs from the system because you don't have to provide a profit for intermediaries such as wholesalers and retailers. But slicing two steps from the traditional distribution channel tends to alienate wholesalers and retailers. Before you decide to go direct, make sure you don't need these other channels of distribution—because if you decide to use them later, they may not be available to you.

There are many ways to modify traditional distribution. For instance, as in the above example, a producer could use a two-level distribution framework by selling direct to retailers and cutting out only the wholesalers. A retailer could do the same thing by going directly to manufacturers—this is one of the strategies Wal-Mart has used so effectively. Look around you at the many ways your competitors and people in other industries set up their distribution channels. One of these models may well be right, with some modification, for you.

Selecting A Model For Growth

Often, your choice of a distribution plan will be dictated—or at least strongly influenced—by various factors relating to your product, your customers and the way they will use it. For instance, if your product—or the new one on which you hope to build your growth plan—is perishable, then the need to provide refrigerated storage and transport will significantly restrict your choices of distribution methods. Size is another issue. If your product takes up a lot of display space, this consideration will weigh heavily when you are selecting ways to transport and display it. That is why automotive dealerships are usually located outside

Danger Ahead! It's tempting to see your market as everybody and your best place for distribution as everywhere. But small companies with limited means need to select the forms of distribution that will work best for them. Focusing your distribution efforts on the channel most suited to your product and plan will produce better results than trying to be all things to all methods of distribution.

Judging A Book By Its Cover

Packaging is more than a pretty face. Your package design may affect everything from breakage rates in shipment to whether stores will be willing to stock it. For example, displayability is an important concern. The original slanted-roof metal container used for Log Cabin Syrup was changed to a design that was easier to stack after grocers became reluctant to devote the necessary amounts of shelf space to the awkward packages. Other distribution-related packaging considerations include:

○ *Labeling:* You may be required to include certain information on the label of your product when it is distributed in specific ways. For example, labels of food products sold in retail outlets must contain information about their ingredients and nutritional value.

○ *Opening:* If your product is one that will be distributed in such a way that customers will want to—and should be able to—sample or examine it before buying, your packaging will have to be easy to open and to reclose. If, on the other hand, your product should not be opened by anyone other than the purchaser—an over-the-counter medication, for instance—then the packaging will have to be designed to resist and reveal tampering.

○ *Size:* If your product must be shipped a long distance to its distribution point, then bulky or heavy packaging may add too much to transportation costs.

○ *Durability:* Many products endure rough handling between their production point and their ultimate consumer. If your distribution system can't be relied upon to protect your product, your packaging will have to do the job.

central business and shopping districts, where costs for display space for cars and trucks would eat up profits.

Another concern when it comes to selecting a distribution method is the way the product is bought. For instance, clothing shoppers usually want to try garments on before purchasing them. So your means of distribution is going to have to include a nearby fitting room, like the ones found in department stores. Many products are best sold with the help of a live demonstration, so if your product is one of those products, your distribution plan will have to include some way of conducting these demonstrations. Multilevel network marketing plans, for instance, often include excellent opportunities to demonstrate products in front of live audiences. If your product is often bought on impulse, then it will be better off distributed in a manner that will display it in a high-traffic area such as in the checkout line at a grocery store.

The characteristics of your customers may also dictate distribution. If customers buy your product frequently, there will be more outlets for its distribution. Videotape rental stores outnumber swimming pool contractors, for example, because people may rent several videos a week but only build a new pool every few years. The distance the customer is willing to travel to purchase your product or service is another key consideration. If you have a one-of-a-kind item in short supply and high demand, you may be wise to limit distribution to your own location. This will give you ultimate control over costs and pricing because highly motivated customers will be willing to travel to you to get what they want.

The way customers will use your product cannot be overlooked, either. For instance, if you are selling complex computer software that requires considerable training before customers can use it effectively, your distribution scheme must include significant amounts of post-sale support, perhaps through company-owned stores, an in-house sales and support staff or carefully selected franchisees.

Getting New Distribution

Distribution is often one of the biggest question marks when it comes to launching a new product. When Ronn King started a company to make a new type of paint mixer, the toughest part wasn't

Getting Directions

Check out *The Encyclopedia of Associations* (Gale Research), which lists nearly 23,000 U.S. nonprofit associations, along with a wealth of contact information and other data. Though the printed book costs more than $500, many local libraries carry it.

coming up with the idea—or even figuring out how to manufacture it. The toughest part was persuading retailers to stock it. Most national retail chains would rather buy 100 products from one supplier than one product from 100 different suppliers. So small manufacturers have a tough time breaking into the game, says King, co-founder of Site-b in Spokane, Washington.

King's company makes a paint-stirring device called the Squirrel Mixer. More than 275,000 were sold worldwide in a single year through such major stores as Home Depot. The inventor's success came with the help of distributors and independent sales representatives. These allies can pioneer your product into new geographic areas, get it into stores that won't even talk to small manufacturers, and provide valuable services, such as fast order fulfillment. But distributors can be as difficult to woo as retail buyers. Winning them over takes time, research and hard work. Here are nine steps to distribution success:

1. *Get your product market-ready.* "Most new manufacturers aren't prepared to go to market," says Joseph Coen, president of ASKCO Marketing Services in Kure Beach, North Carolina. Coen's company serves as a matchmaker between manufacturers and distributors to food, drug and gift retailers. Before going to market, manufacturers must resolve issues ranging from the most appealing packaging to the best way to ship their products, he says. They must also find a price consumers will pay that still means good profit margins for retailers, distributors and themselves. "The product needs to have a point of difference," Coen says. "If the product is lotion, the only difference is the fragrance and maybe a few ounces [more product] per bottle. The manufacturer must create a perceived difference with packaging or marketing." New manufacturers must prepare sales materials that tell retailers the product's benefits and its statistical information, such as how much space it needs in the warehouse and on the shelf. Production capacity is also a major issue, Coen says. "You can't sell to Wal-Mart unless you're ready to manufacture millions of units."

2. *Understand whom you're selling to.* Most manufacturers don't sell directly to consumers. Instead, the manufacturer's marketing strategy must aim at sales through dealers or distributors. Most manufacturers, distributors and independent sales reps deal with a narrow range of products. They know each other and refer work to each other. That worked to King's advantage when he first tried to sell to retail chains. Several turned him down, but one buyer referred him to a manufacturer's representative who carried dozens of products for many companies. That rep took on the Squirrel Mixer and referred King to reps in other areas. A distributor or sales rep wants to carry products that sell in high volume. If you can't promise huge sales, you might have to lure distributors with high profit margins, King says. If you can't raise the retail price, that extra margin will come out of your profit. "It sounds expensive," King says, "but compared with the cost of reaching customers yourself, it's not."

3. *Target your market.* One way to focus your marketing is with targeted mailing lists, which you can often find through trade associations. If you use such lists for direct-mail advertising campaigns, plan to send out at least three separate mailings and then follow up with phone calls, advises John Metscher, a business analyst with the Central Ohio Manufacturing Small Business Development Center in Columbus. "One mailing is a waste of money. Don't give up; you'll be surprised at the results," says Metscher. He also recommends advertising in carefully selected trade journals targeted at the industries most suited to your product.

4. *Create demand.* The manufacturer—not the distributor or retailer—must make consumers want to buy a product. That can involve cooperative advertising campaigns with retailers, display stands, signs, fliers, brochures and other marketing materials, Coen says. "Each year, about 25,000 new mass-market items are introduced," he says. "The manufacturer must do everything possible to encourage [consumer] acceptance."

5. *Prove your product will sell.* A new company may have to prove its product will sell before distributors and major retailers take notice, King says. He first started selling the Squirrel Mixer by mail order and to a few local retail stores to prove consumers would buy the device. "Distributors' sales forces started seeing the Squirrel Mixer in several stores and asked [the stores] about it," King says. "Even then, the distributors didn't call us. We had to call them."

6. *Ask questions.* Many new manufacturers don't know where to look for distributors and sales representatives. King found many of his by asking questions. He asked retail buyers for names of distributors, he called manufacturers of similar products and asked whom their distributors and sales representatives were, and he studied industry magazines for names and ads. Many trade groups have distributors and reps as members.

7. *Attend trade shows.* "Take an exhibit booth, either by yourself or in partnership with another company with complementary products," Metscher says. As with other marketing efforts, choose a trade show targeted to your market. At the show, collect business cards from prospective distributors or sales reps and follow up after the show is over. Even if you can't afford your own booth, attend the shows that target your industry. "Shows are good places to network and identify the people and companies that will buy your products," Metscher says.

8. *Select distributors and sales reps carefully.* Ask others in your industry for referrals to good sales reps and distributors. When considering reps, ask for their credentials and references. Look for reps and distributors who carry similar but noncompeting products and who sell to the same geographic territory and type of retailers that carry your type of product. Distributors usually buy some of your product and store it at their warehouses. Good ones fill orders quickly and accurately and help build a market for your product. Independent sales reps do not buy your product, but they should aggressively sell your product in markets you can't reach.

> **C**hoose a trade show targeted to your market. Even if you can't afford your own booth, attend the shows that target your industry.

9. *Find private-label partners.* Even though King has succeeded in getting the Squirrel Mixer into thousands of stores, attracting distributors "continues to be a problem for small companies, even when you prove you have a good product," he says. That's one reason he allows some major paint companies, such as Hyde Manufacturing and Red Devil, to put their brand names on his mixer.

Private-label deals let companies with built-in distribution networks, such as grocery stores, sell products manufactured by

Before You Sign On The Dotted Line...

You can't assume distributors will live up to their end of the deal. Before you sign on with a distributor, know what to expect from the relationship by asking these questions:

○ *What are the distributor's credentials and background?* Check references.

○ *Does the distributor cover a territory you want to reach?* Does the territory compete with those of your other distributors?

○ *What other products does the distributor carry?* Are they compatible with yours? Do they target similar customers?

○ *How well does the distributor know the market and its potential?*

○ *What are the terms of the distribution agreement?* Are they too costly? Distribution terms vary widely and depend on the details of the product and market. For instance, a computer equipment distribution deal that called for the distributor to provide post-sale support for the products would naturally be more expensive for you. Look at expected volume, markups, commissions and fees for additional services, and come up with a total that leaves you with an adequate profit.

○ *What are the terms for terminating the agreement?* A typical agreement allows for the deal to be canceled with 30 days' notice by either party.

others under their own brand names, often including manufacturers with their own brand names. You may be able to get your product into wider distribution under a private label more quickly than if you relied on your own brand.

Managing Your Distributors

The relationship between a product's manufacturer and its distributor is a two-way street. Each must fulfill certain tasks to get the product to market and keep it on the shelves. The manufacturer's role includes the following jobs:

○ Make a quality product.

○ Use advertising and other means to create demand for the product.

○ Provide marketing materials.

○ Have the capacity to fill any order the distributor gets.

○ Offer incentives to distributors' sales forces.

○ Provide technical support or other quality customer service.

You also need to be aware of your responsibility to not undercut your distribution network. That means that when customers call you directly, you should pass their orders on to your distributor or sales rep.

Distributors also have specific responsibilities in the manufacturer-distributor relationship. The distributor's role includes the following jobs:

○ Respond quickly when the manufacturer passes on sales leads.

○ Provide storage for products prior to sale.

○ Fill customers' orders quickly and accurately.

○ Assist in building a market for the product.

○ Give customer feedback to the manufacturer.

Few companies that manufacture products are prepared to distribute them. But without adequate distribution, growth is impossible. If you have ambitious growth goals, examine your existing distribution channels to see if they can be improved. Better distribution can easily make the difference between stagnation and growth.

chapter 14

Updating Office Technology

usinesses existed before there were computers, fax machines, telephones and copiers, but few entrepreneurs these days would want to try to grow a company without the advantages modern information technology can bring. Merely having access to the Internet—with its myriad opportunities for finding customers, building brands, researching

suppliers and communicating with employees and others—can easily justify updating the technology in an office. For many companies, having the appropriate office technology can make the difference between a successful expansion and one that falls flat on its face.

Evaluating Your Current Technology

As important as technology is, that doesn't mean you always have to have the latest version of equipment. Here's how to evaluate your current technology to see whether it's time to upgrade:

Computers are likely to need upgrading as a result of a software update. If you have recently begun using a new version of an important software package and your computers' performance seems unsatisfactorily slow, it may be time to buy new hardware. Otherwise, you can and probably should make do with what you have. Don't delay buying new computers just because the ones you have are only a few years old, though. During that span of time, performance of the models on the market typically doubles. Forcing customers and employees to wait on slow computers can cost you far more than a new system would.

Telephone systems should be upgraded quickly if a problem develops, because they are your lifeline to your customers and suppliers. If customers complain about being kept on hold, or about phones not ringing or not being answered, you may need to add lines, improve your answering system or perhaps hire more telephone operators. If you expect your call volume to surge sharply, perhaps because of an upcoming new product launch or seasonal buying, you may want to upgrade your phone system before trouble starts.

High-end copiers can cost more than a whole office full of computers. Today's models are increasingly interchangeable with printers, thanks to the new gen-

Fast Lane

You may be able to buy a much nicer piece of office technology than you'd expect if you explore refurbished machines. Computers, copiers, printers and phone systems that have been checked out and, if necessary, repaired by a manufacturer or authorized service outlet can be as reliable as brand-new equipment, at a significant discount from the new price.

Buy, Buy, Lease?

As quickly as technology becomes obsolete, it sometimes makes sense to rent instead of buy your next round of upgrades. You can rent or lease most kinds of office technology, including computers, printers, copiers and phone systems. Here's how your options stack up:

○ *Buying:* Buying your equipment costs more upfront. If you're buying on an installment plan rather than paying cash, monthly payments are usually higher. It may be comforting to know you own your equipment rather than rent it, but you may find yourself with an out-of-date machine right as you put the last check in the mail.

○ *Leasing:* If you're like many small businesses, you are willing to lease costly technology that is likely to become quickly outdated. Leasing lets you get higher-end, more costly gear while reducing upfront outlays. Monthly payments will also usually be lower than those for credit-purchased equipment. Maybe most importantly, however, you're transferring the risk of obsolescence to somebody else. If that high-end PC is a clunker by lease's end, just hand it back to the owner and get a new model. Check the terms of your lease carefully. Scrutinize your options for the end of the lease. You may be able to buy the equipment for a small additional fee if you want to.

eration of digital, network-ready copiers. Some late-model digital copiers will also scan documents and send faxes. But fancy features don't mean you need one of these costly machines. Upgrade your copiers when you experience or foresee a significant increase in the volume of copies you produce. Extras such as automatic document feeders and staplers are nice but probably not worth upgrading for.

Improving Your Technology

The great thing about the march of technology is not so much that the equipment keeps getting cheaper. It's that it keeps getting better. To put it another way, a decent computer has cost around $2,000 for more than a decade. This year's decent PC is, of course, far more powerful than the one of 10 years ago. But it costs the same amount. What that means is that waiting until prices fall to upgrade your technology is usually a mistake. If what you have isn't cutting it, you should probably buy an upgrade sooner rather than later. Six months from now, a midrange computer is going to cost you the same amount; it'll just be a somewhat better machine.

One exception to this "buy now" rule is when you absolutely need a specific technology that has been introduced very recently. Most new gadgets go through a steep price decline after an initial phase of high pricing. If you need something that is currently the latest thing but you can live without it for a while, you can save significant amounts of money by waiting to purchase until several months after it debuts.

Expanding Your Phone System

A lot of small businesses start with a single phone on a desk or kitchen table. It may be the same line the entrepreneur uses for his or her home. As a business grows, one of the first pieces of technology to grow along with it should be the phone system. At first, you may add another line so your home office can have a dedicated phone. Then you may add a fax or computer data line. A second line for incoming calls is likely to become a necessity. Then, as you hire employees, you'll need more lines and more stations.

At this point, most businesses opt for a key service unit, commonly known as a KSU or key system. Key systems offer more flexibility than multiline residential-type systems, along with features such as call transfer and hold. But they can be costly and difficult to upgrade or expand.

The next step for most businesses is a private branch exchange (PBX). These in-house telephone switches cost a lot more than key systems but have much greater capacity, features and complexity.

The new kid on the block is the PC-PBX, also sometimes called

Danger Ahead!

Don't neglect service contracts if you are buying a computer network, feature-laden phone system or high-end copier. These complex systems can cost you $100 an hour or more to repair when they break. Investigate terms of service contracts you are offered, and don't be afraid to negotiate, but don't reject them out of hand either. You can grow with confidence if you know you are covered if your equipment breaks.

telecommunications servers or communications servers. These are basically desktop PCs running special software that allows them to provide many of the services of a PBX. PC-PBXs are cheaper, more flexible and easier to use than PBXs and provide a number of services, such as the ability to make voice phone calls over the Internet.

A phone system built around a PC-PBX costs around $500 per line, a fraction of what most PBX systems will run you. PC-PBXs also typically use standard analog phones—the type sold virtually everywhere. PBXs often require you to buy a digital phone, at around $300 and up, for every one of your extensions. Finally, PC-PBXs are much easier and cheaper to upgrade and maintain when you need to move a phone, add lines or otherwise change things. All told, PC-PBXs represent a highly viable third alternative for many small to midsized offices with up to 150 lines.

Upgrading Your Computers

Moore's Law is a high-tech rule of thumb that says the speed of a computer microprocessor doubles about every 18 months, while its price is sliced in half. Basically, that means every couple of years, your computer hardware is going to be out of date, at least in some sense. What matters, of course, is not whether your computer is still the fastest in town but that it's still doing the job you need it to. Typically, after two to four years, a computer truly is obsolete because it will no longer run the latest version of the software you use on it.

When you start to upgrade computers, don't start by looking at ads from the computer stores. Instead, study your needs. Ask yourself:

○ *What software am I going to run?* How often is it upgraded? What is the software publisher's recommended system configuration? This will usually come phrased in terms of the slowest processor, least memory, oldest version of operating system and smallest hard drive a computer should have to run the software.

○ *What features will I use most often?* If you don't need stereo sound, a big monitor or modem, you shouldn't buy them.

○ *What financing is available?* You can frequently buy a computer on an installment plan or, if dealing with a large retailer, with an interest-free 90-day loan. Check the fine print—on some seemingly appealing deals, if you miss a payment, the interest rate skyrockets.

○ *Who is going to fix it if it breaks?* Ideally, you'll buy your machines from a company with a local service center that can handle most repairs. Alternatively, some vendors offer on-site repair or even overnight replacement. Consider a service contract if you are buying a large number of computers, since having more of them increases the odds that something will break.

Improving Your Internet Access

Surfing the Internet can be a "hurry up and wait" experience when you're using a standard 56K modem to access it. But there are faster ways to get on the Net that you may want to consider if your business does a lot of Web work.

Cable modems use the cable television network to connect users to the Internet. They offer very high download speeds of up to several megabits per second and cost less than $100 per month. The coaxial wiring needed to provide cable Internet access already passes 97 percent of American homes and offices. Drawbacks include the cost of modems (around $200) and the fact that cable television providers still don't offer the service everywhere.

Digital subscriber line (DSL) is a fast access method offered by local telephone and other companies. There are several varieties of DSL, but the most popular is ADSL, or asynchronous DSL. It generally offers top download speeds of up to 8 megabits per second but only 1 megabit-per-second upload speeds. DSL modems cost $200 and up, installation runs $100 and up, and a typical service offering is $50 per month for a 1.5 megabit-per-second connection. Phone companies promise to make DSL widely available in the next few years.

Satellites provide Internet access using the same orbiting system that sends you direct-broadcast video programming. Direct broadcast Internet service uses a dish measuring 18 to 21 inches to receive signals, and a phone line to return your commands. Direct satellite access offers peak download speeds of just 200 to 400 kilobits per second but is available virtually everywhere. Sign-up and equipment charges are less

Viewpoint

You may not need fast Internet access if your main use of the Internet is for e-mail. Fast access speeds up Web surfing significantly, but short e-mail documents won't download significantly faster with a high-speed connection than with a standard 56K phone line modem. Caveat: If you regularly receive files such as music or video clips attached to your e-mail, a faster hookup will be a significant boon.

Speed Trials

Here are estimates of how much time it would require for you to download the *Encyclopedia Britannica*—which is about 44 million words long—depending on your Internet connection:

○ *28.8K modem (28.8 Kbps)*: 1,222 minutes
○ *56K modem (56 Kbps)*: 628 minutes
○ *ISDN (128 Kbps)*: 275 minutes
○ *Cable modem (500 Kbps)*: 70 minutes
○ *High-speed DSL (12 Mbps)*: 2.9 minutes

than $500, and monthly rates range from $20 to $130, depending on your service plan. You must have a regular modem and telephone line to send commands and other data to the network.

Integrated services digital networks (ISDNs) have been around a long time and offer twice the speed of the fastest analog modems, about 128 kilobits per second, but are relatively slow compared to newer technologies. Service costs around $80 per month, including a voice line, and modems run $200 or so. ISDN lines are tricky to install, however, and the service still isn't available everywhere.

Still not fast enough? You can get a T1 or T3 line offering megabit-per-second speeds—but at monthly costs of up to five figures. If you're running an Internet service provider or major Web site, you may someday select leading-edge OC12c technology. Today it's used in portions of the Internet backbone, the very high-capacity main lines that carry e-mail and other traffic between the Internet's data centers, and can move data at more than half a gigabit per second.

The Role Of Training

Buying new technology is usually just the beginning. If employees aren't trained on how to use the new equipment, your business won't get the full benefit of your investment. You can get employees trained in almost any technology, at any level and any subject. For instance, your employees may need lessons on how to use a PC if they haven't been exposed to computers much. Even highly experienced users may need training to use the latest programming and networking tools.

Start your search for training by quizzing the company that sold you the technology. Many vendors have on-staff professional trainers who can come to your site to train employees on using new technologies. If not, they can probably refer you to a local firm that offers appropriate training. You can also look in the business Yellow Pages under "Training Programs" and "Training Consultants."

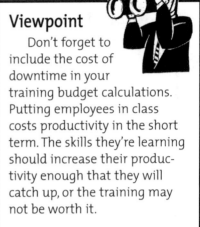

Viewpoint

Don't forget to include the cost of downtime in your training budget calculations. Putting employees in class costs productivity in the short term. The skills they're learning should increase their productivity enough that they will catch up, or the training may not be worth it.

Always make sure technical training material is up to date. Studying obsolete manuals is like buying obsolete computers. You should also make sure instructors are credited as, for instance, Microsoft-Certified Systems Engineers.

You can choose from various types of training: Classroom training with a live instructor can be done at your business or off-site, in the form of a short tutorial or continuing series of classroom lessons. Having an instructor on hand helps learners get questions answers.

If you can do without a live teacher, check out video-based training. Class starts when you insert a prerecorded tape into a VCR. Students take notes and follow along in workbooks, just like with live teachers. Video courses can be repeated any time and are low in cost.

Computerized training can be delivered in a classroom with PCs on desks, or via the Web. Internet classes let students choose the time, place and pace of learning. Some are taught by an instructor who communicates over the Net. Students can mix, mingle and discuss lessons in online chat rooms.

Why Technology Is Crucial

A few years ago, having access to technology could provide you with a significant advantage over the competition. Today, you will likely have to work hard just to maintain enough technological know-how to keep the playing field level. In any event, staying on top of the information technology you use in your office will remove one significant barrier to the growth you desire.

chapter 15

Partnering With Suppliers And Vendors

uppliers are essential to almost every business. Without raw materials to make what you sell or manufacturers to provide what you resell, you will have a tough time growing. There are also many supplies and services your business consumes as part of general overhead, from paper clips to Internet access.

Suppliers and vendors—the terms are used interchangeably here—can do much more than merely supply you with the materials and services you need to do business. They can also be important sources of information, helping you evaluate the potential of new products, track competitors' actions and identify promising opportunities. Vendors can turn into partners, helping you cut costs, improve product designs and even fund new marketing efforts. If you don't make selecting good suppliers and vendors a part of your growth plan, you're likely to regret it.

Evaluating Your Suppliers And Vendors

Suppliers can be divided into four general categories.

1. *Manufacturers:* Most retailers buy through company salespeople or independent representatives who handle the wares of several different companies. Prices from these sources are usually lowest unless the retailer's location makes shipping freight costly.

2. *Distributors:* Also known as wholesalers, brokers or jobbers, distributors buy in quantity from several manufacturers and warehouse the goods for sale to retailers. Although their prices are higher than a manufacturer's, they can supply retailers with small orders from a variety of manufacturers. (Some manufacturers refuse to fill small orders.) A lower freight bill and quick delivery time from a nearby distributor often compensates for the higher per-item cost.

3. *Independent craftspeople:* Exclusive distribution of unique creations is frequently offered by independent craftspeople who sell through reps or at trade shows.

4. *Import sources:* Many retailers buy foreign goods from a domestic importer, who operates much like a domestic wholesaler. Or,

Getting Directions

Sometimes suppliers will contact you through their sales representatives, but more often, particularly when you're starting out, you'll need to locate them yourself—either at trade shows or wholesale showrooms and conventions, or through buyers' directories, industry contacts, the Business-to-Business Yellow Pages, and trade journals.

depending on your familiarity with overseas sources, you may want to travel abroad to buy goods.

What Makes A Good Supplier?

A lot of growing companies focus on one trait of their suppliers: price. And price certainly is important when you are selecting suppliers to accompany you as you grow your business. But there's more to a supplier than an invoice—and more to the cost of doing business with a supplier than the amount on a purchase order. Remember, too, that suppliers are in business to make money. If you go to the mat with them on every bill, ask them to shave prices on everything they sell to you, or fail to pay your bills promptly, don't be surprised if they stop calling.

After price, reliability is probably the key factor to look for in suppliers. Good suppliers will ship the right number of items, as promised, on time so that they arrive in good shape. Sometimes you can get the best reliability from a large supplier. These companies have the resources to devote to backup systems and sources so that, if something goes wrong, they can still live up to their responsibilities to you. However, don't neglect small suppliers. If you are a large customer of a small company, you will get more attention and possibly better service and reliability than if you are a small customer of a large supplier. You

> **If you are a large customer of a small company, you will get more attention and possibly better service and reliability than if you are a small customer of a large supplier.**

should also consider splitting your orders among two smaller firms. This can provide you with a backup as well as a high profile.

Stability is another key indicator. You'll want to sign up with vendors who have been in business a long time and have done so without changing businesses every few years. A company that has long-tenured senior executives is another good sign, and a solid reputation with other customers is a promising indicator that a company is stable. When it comes to your own experience, look for telltale signs of vendor trouble, such as shipments that arrive earlier than you requested them—this can be a sign of a vendor that is short on orders and needs to accelerate cash receipts.

Don't forget location. Merchandise ordered from a distant supplier can take a long time to get to you and generate added freight charges quickly. Find out how long a shipment will take to arrive at your loading dock. If you are likely to need something fast, a distant supplier could present a real problem. Also, determine supplier freight policies before you order. If you order a certain quantity, for instance, you may get free shipping. You may be able to combine two or more orders into one and save on freight. Even better, find a comparable supplier closer to home to preserve cost savings and ordering flexibility.

Finally, there's a grab bag of traits that could generally be termed competency. You will want suppliers who can offer the latest, most advanced products and services. They'll need to have well-trained employees to sell and service their goods. They should be able to offer you a variety of attractive financial terms on purchases. And they should have a realistic attitude toward you, their customer, so that they're willing and eager to work with you to grow both your businesses.

Making A Change

Having fewer vendors is usually better than having many vendors. Reducing the number of vendors you deal with cuts the administrative costs of working with many. Closer relationships with fewer vendors allow you to work together to control costs. Getting rid of troublesome vendors can quickly increase the efficiency of your purchasing and administrative staffs. So how do you decide when to change vendors? Here are keys areas to consider:

○ *Unreliability:* When a vendor's shipments start arriving consistently late, incomplete, damaged or otherwise incorrect, it's time to consider looking for a new one. Every company has problems from time to time, however, so check into the matter before dumping your vendor. Vendors can experience temporary difficulties as a result of implementing a new product line, shipping procedure or training program. If you stick with a vendor through a rugged interval, you may be glad you did. They might be more willing to see you through a future cash flow crunch.

○ *Lack of cost competitiveness:* Sometimes vendors fail to change with their industries. When your vendor's rivals start coming in with bids for comparable goods that are lower than your existing supplier's, you need to investigate. Point out the issue to your existing supplier and ask for an explanation. If you don't like what you hear, it may be time to consider taking some of those offers from competing suppliers.

○ *Insularity:* Some suppliers will let you visit their plants, talk to their workers, quiz their managers, obtain and interview references, and even examine their financial statements. These are the kinds of suppliers you should seek out. The more you know about your suppliers, the better you can evaluate whether you should continue to do business with them. If they shut you out, perhaps you should cut them off.

○ *Extra-sale costs:* The number at the bottom of the invoice is only the beginning of the cost of dealing with suppliers. You have to lay out money beforehand to draw up specifications, issue request for proposals, evaluate them, check references, and otherwise qualify your suppliers. You have to place the order, negotiate the terms, inspect the goods when they arrive, and deal with any shortages, damage or other errors. Finally, you may have to train workers to use the newly arrived goods or purchase more equipment and material to make use of them. While some of these costs are inevitable, some are traceable to individual suppliers. If too many costs are being tacked onto the sale, check out some other suppliers.

> **While some costs are inevitable, some are traceable to individual suppliers. If too many costs are being tacked onto the sale, check out some other suppliers.**

Getting New Suppliers

Getting new suppliers starts with researching potential vendors, just as you would do if you were looking for customers. You can get lists of potential suppliers from trade groups, directories and other suppliers, to name a few sources.

Once you have compiled a list of possible suppliers, ask for quotes or proposals, complete with prices, available discounts, delivery terms and other important factors. Don't just consider the terms; investigate the potential supplier's financial condition, too. Ask for customer ref-

> ### Danger Ahead!
> By the time you decide to get rid of a supplier, you may be annoyed enough to want to give them a piece of your mind. Resist the urge. The day may come when you need this supplier again, either because your needs change or because their capabilities improve. Don't burn any bridges.

erences, and find out from them how well the supplier has performed. If there have been any problems, ask for details about how they were resolved. Every supplier relationship hits bumps now and then; the key is to know how the rough spots were handled. Was the supplier prompt and helpful in resolving the problem, or was the vendor defensive and uncooperative?

Communications with prospective suppliers should be open, courteous and firm. In other words, tell them exactly what you need, when you need it and why. You'll need a bottom-line figure for the total cost and a firm date when delivery can be expected. Don't feel bad about demanding on-time deliveries and accurate invoices. Stay in touch with suppliers to learn about delays, opportunities to substitute more suitable goods, issues related to quality, prospects for improving products, and potential savings.

Suppliers often establish minimum orders for merchandise, and this minimum may be higher for first orders to cover their cost of setting up a new account. Some suppliers also require that you purchase a minimum number of items per order. A supplier who requires a minimum order that represents a year's supply to you is going to cost you a lot in inventory and shrinkage. On the other hand, a supplier that will sell you a month's worth at a time will allow you to spread your orders out much more conveniently and economically. All other things being equal, the second type is a more attractive supplier.

> ### Getting Directions
> Once good source for finding suppliers is the *Thomas Register of American Manufacturers* (Thomas Publishing). This directory lists manufacturers by categories and geographic area. You can find one in most libraries.

Carefully evaluate your suppliers' quotes, terms, promises and general attitudes. Those who are willing and able to help you grow will be worth the trouble it takes to identify them.

Changing Your Supplier Relationship

You may not need to find new suppliers to get a new deal. You can usually get discounts, obtain improved service and receive other features you need by making a request of your current suppliers—although it may not be as simple as merely asking. Here are some of the options and negotiating strategies for turning mediocre suppliers into top-shelf ones.

○ *Getting discounts:* If you walk into a department store and purchase a pair of shoes, you'll pay the same price any other shopper would. But business-to-business commerce is more complicated. Businesses that sell to other businesses commonly have a whole range of quoted charges, offering discounts of 50 percent or more depending on the quantity purchased, the terms, the length of the relationship, and other considerations. You may be able to comfortably conform to some of these requirements, qualifying you for a lower price. To find out, ask about discounts and what is necessary to earn them. You may be able to get anything from an interest-free loan in the form of trade credit to a substantial discount for paying early.

○ *Improving service:* It is the rare businessperson who knows exactly what is happening in all parts of his company at all times or what is going on with all his customers. You probably don't, and you shouldn't assume your suppliers do, either. If you have a service-related problem with a supplier, bring it to someone's attention. If you don't get satisfaction, move up the chain of command until you do get what you want or are as high in management as you can get. Odds are, someone will be concerned and possess enough authority to remedy the situation. Only if you ask for better service and don't get it should you sever the relationship.

> ## Viewpoint
>
> Some suppliers use a first-in, first-out system to decide who gets served next. Others focus on large orders first. If you suspect you're being shunned, specify a cutoff date on your next order. If the supplier wants the deal to stand, they'll have to ship your order by that date or it becomes void.

○ *A better relationship:* Not every customer wants to buddy up to suppliers, so the fact that your suppliers aren't offering to work closely with you to improve quality, reduce defects and cut costs doesn't necessarily mean they don't want to. They may be under the impression that you are the reluctant one. So if you want a tighter working relationship with suppliers, let them know. You may also drop a hint that those who don't want to work with you may see some of their orders being diverted to those who are more agreeable. Either way, you'll know whether it's your supplier's reluctance, or their perception of your reluctance, that's getting in the way.

Behind Every Growing Business...

You aren't likely to grow without good suppliers. If you can't rely on timely shipments and fair terms from your vendors, your customers are going to have a hard time relying on you. Having solid, supportive vendors behind you, on the other hand, can make you a more effective competitor than you would be on your own. So take care to choose and keep good suppliers. Your company will be glad you did.

chapter 16

Innovating
For Growth

Innovative new products are the fuel for the
most powerful growth engine you can connect to. You can grow
without new products—AT&T sold essentially the same tele-
phones for decades while becoming the world's largest
telecommunications concern—but most small companies will
find it difficult to grow at all, much less rapidly, without a constant stream of new products that meet customer needs.

Making The Decision To Add Products

How do you know when you need new products? Early detection of a problem with existing products is critical. The following eight symptoms of a declining product line will provide clues far enough in advance to help you do something about the problem before it's too late. Not all symptoms will be evident in every situation, but you can start suspecting your product line when more than just one or two crop up.

1. *You are experiencing slow growth or no growth.* A short-term glitch in product sales can happen any time. If, however, company revenue either flattens or declines over an extended period, you have to look for explanations and solutions. If it isn't the economy or some outside force beyond your control, if your competitors didn't suddenly become more brilliant, if you still have confidence in your sales force, and if there are no major problems with suppliers, examine your product line.

2. *Your top customers give you less and less business.* It may not be worth your trouble to determine your exact market share when a rough idea of where you stand will suffice. But knowing how much business you get compared to your competitors is critical. Every piece of business your competitors are getting is business you aren't getting—and may never get. If your customers' businesses are growing and the business you get from them isn't, your product may be the culprit. Chances are, someone else is meeting your customers' needs.

3. *You find yourself competing with companies you've never heard of.* If you've never heard of a new competitor or don't know much about them, watch out! They've found a way to jump into a market with new products and technology that could leave you wondering what hit you. It might not be that your product has a fundamental flaw. It's more often the case that someone has brought innovation to the industry. You earn no points for status quo thinking. Although Southwest Airlines revolutionized the way airlines do business, when it was initially just buzzing around Texas, the industry paid the company little attention. Eventually, however, Southwest brought innovation and creativity into scheduling, routing and customer service—all this in an industry known for slothlike change and rampant me-tooism.

4. *You are under increasing pressure to lower your prices.* No one likes to compete strictly on price. When your product is clearly superior and offers more value than lower-priced competitors, you don't have to. Everyone understands that great new products eventually run their course and turn into commodities. One day, a customer tells you she can't distinguish the benefits of your widget from those of one or more of your competitors, and now you're in a price squeeze. If you want the business, you have to lower your prices to stay competitive. If that was where it ended, things might stabilize, although at a lower price level. But lower prices usually mean lower profit margins, which usually mean less investment in keeping the product current, which means more price pressure, lower margins...and so it goes.

5. *You experience higher-than-normal turnover in your sales force.* Good salespeople want to win customers so they can make more money. When they have trouble competing, they can't win customers or make money. So they look for new opportunities and challenges that will bring them what they want. You will always have turnover, but heavy turnover is a symptom of something very wrong. It could be an ill-advised change in the compensation scheme or a new sales manager coming in with a negative attitude. But it could also be that members of your sales team are frustrated because they are having trouble selling your products. When business owners start to pressure their sales forces to get order levels up, morale drops because the salespeople know there isn't much they can do.

> **You will always have turnover, but heavy turnover is a symptom of something very wrong.**

6. *You see fewer and fewer inquiries from prospective customers.* We all dread the time when the phone stops ringing and prospects stop coming in. When your advertising or other forms of promotion aren't creating the results you want, and you see fewer positive results from the money spent, something could be wrong with the way customers see your company. An obsolete product line positions you as an obsolete company.

7. *Customers ask for product changes you can't or don't want to make.* Here's a not-too-subtle sign that your product may no longer meet market needs. There will be times when you have to decide whether filling a customer's request is in your company's best

interests. When customers say "I want it this way," you may want to say no because you doubt you could ever recover the costs of the change, even by raising the selling price. But when the customer says "I want it this way, and it's standard at ABC Widgets," you should suspect you aren't keeping up with changing customer needs. When your competitors have leapt ahead of you in features and benefits, you must either catch up or leap ahead of them with innovations of your own, or you'll fall so far behind you become a marketplace postscript.

8. *Some of your competitors are leaving the market.* In the short term, this sounds great. Your competitors drop out, and you pick up the business they leave behind. The pie is shrinking, and as it does, business gets better than ever. But beware: This is a classic signal of a declining market. Nobody walks away from a growth business. Vibrant growth markets attract new competitors; they don't discourage them.

Implementing Your Idea

If you decide to develop new products as part of your growth plan, you are in good company. Small companies like yours contribute at least half of the major industrial innovations occurring in the United States, according to the Small Business Administration. At the same time, approximately one-third of all new products are unsuccessful, and in some industries the percentage of failures is much higher. The way to increase your chances of coming up with good ideas is to follow the tested track to new product development success.

New product development can be described as a five-stage process, beginning with generating ideas and progressing to marketing completed products. In between are processes where you evaluate

Danger Ahead!
Cannibalization describes what happens when customers who would have purchased one product are diverted to another, newer product from the same company. Some companies do this intentionally to phase out obsolete products. However, it can happen accidentally, turning a once-viable product into an also-ran with no net gain to your company. Make sure new products aren't likely to lure customers from your other offerings.

Dance With The One You Came With

If you find yourself faced with a declining product line, the correct action may not be to rush to develop new products. Here are a few other options:

○ *Do nothing.* This attitude says "The business has run its course, and it may be time to move on." One of the beauties of continuing to sell in a business you think has little future is that you can stop investing in it. Instead, you can simply squeeze it for all the profit you can get. The resulting boost to your bottom line can provide funds to start a new, more promising business or, eventually, develop new products in a different field.

○ *Look for niche markets.* There are still companies out there that make vacuum tubes, typewriter ribbons, dot matrix printers, vinyl records and perhaps even buggy whips. Demand for a product rarely falls to zero. There are always customers who will continue to buy obsolete products to keep from making major changes in the way they've always done things. The beauty of serving a niche market well is that you could end up having it virtually all to yourself. If this happens, you will be able to maximize profits—perhaps far more than you would be able to do with a different product entry that commands only a modest share of a fast-growing market.

As a rule, new product development drives growth. But rules are made to be broken. Don't rush to abandon the tried-and-true products that have helped you grow your company so far unless you've carefully evaluated all the options. In business, as in ballrooms, sometimes it's best to dance with the one you came with.

and screen product ideas, take steps to protect your ideas, and finalize design in an R&D stage. Following are details on each stage:

Generating Ideas

Generating ideas consists of two parts: creating an idea and developing it for commercial sale. There are many good techniques for idea creation, including brainstorming, random association and even daydreaming. You may want to generate a long list of ideas and then whittle them down to a very few that appear to have commercial appeal.

Evaluating And Screening Product Ideas

Everybody likes their ideas, but that doesn't mean others will. When you're evaluating ideas for their potential, it's important to get objective opinions. For help with technical issues, many companies take their ideas to testing laboratories, engineering consultants, product development firms, and university and college technical testing services. When it comes to evaluating an idea's commercial potential, many entrepreneurs use the Preliminary Innovation Evaluation System (PIES) technique. This is a formal methodology for assessing the commercial potential of inventions and innovations.

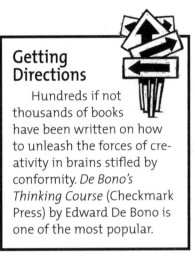

Getting Directions

Hundreds if not thousands of books have been written on how to unleash the forces of creativity in brains stifled by conformity. *De Bono's Thinking Course* (Checkmark Press) by Edward De Bono is one of the most popular.

Protecting Your Ideas

If you think you've come up with a valuable idea for a new product, you should take steps to protect it. Most people who want to protect ideas think first of patents. There are good reasons for this. For one thing, you will find it difficult to license your idea to other companies, should you wish to do so, without patent protection. However, getting a patent is a lengthy, complicated process, and one you shouldn't embark on without professional help; this makes the process expensive. If you wish to pursue a patent for your ideas, contact a registered patent attorney or patent agent.

Many firms choose to protect ideas using trade secrecy.

Getting Directions

You can learn more about the Preliminary Innovation Evaluation System from the Innovation Institute at Rte. 2, Box 184, Everton, MO 65646, or Wal-Mart Innovation Network Innovation Center, 901 S. National Glass Hall, College of Business Administration, Southwest Missouri State University, Springfield, MO 65804. You can also call the Wal-Mart innovation center at (417) 836-5671.

This is simply a matter of keeping knowledge of your ideas, designs, processes, techniques or any other unique component of your creation limited to yourself or a small group of people. Most trade secrets are in the areas of chemical formulas, factory equipment, and machines and manufacturing processes. The formula for Coca-Cola is one of the best-recognized and most successful trade secrets.

Made Fresh Daily

Here are practical things you can do to make sure your products stay fresh and viable:

○ *Keep current with technology changes.* The word processor ensured the demise of the typewriter, and voice messaging has changed the way people use the telephone. While your product line may not have the global impact these developments have, changes in technology will always affect your business. Isn't it better to lead the way than to react to events?

○ *Anticipate changing customer needs.* If you want your customers to keep buying from you, you have to let them know you will be there to fulfill their changing requirements. Customers have a way of not knowing exactly what they want. When they finally make their choice, they will go with the supplier who is there with the right product at the right time.

○ *Track your competitors' actions.* Keeping on top of what your competitors are doing means you'll find out when they make effective product developments. If they get to the market before you do, there's a good chance you'll end up the loser. Organize some sort of competitive-intelligence-gathering system that will help you keep track of what they're doing.

○ *Keep up to date with changing trends in the marketplace.* How many clothing manufacturers saw the "casual Fridays" trend coming? If you were a maker of men's suits, wouldn't it have been nice to see into the future before you experienced a 20 percent decline in sales? There's no substitute for keeping your eyes and ears open. Improve your awareness of the market around you. Participate in trade associations and business roundtables. Know all you can know about your customers and your customers' customers.

Finalizing Design— Research And Development

Research and development is necessary for refining most designs for new products and services. As the owner of a growing company, you are in a good position when it comes to this stage. Most independent inventors don't have the resources to pay for this costly and often protracted stage of product introduction. Most lenders and investors are trapped by a Catch-22 mentality that makes them reluctant to invest in ideas until after they're proven viable in the marketplace. If you believe in your idea, you can be the first to market. R&D consists of producing prototypes, testing them for usability and other features, and refining the design until you wind up with something you think you can make and sell for a profit. This may involve test-marketing, beta testing, analysis of marketing plans and sales projections, cost studies, and more. As the last step before you commit to rolling your product out, R&D is perhaps the most important step of all.

Fast Lane

Not all new products must be radical departures from the norm. Many times, you can fire up growth with a line extension or a new product that adds some relatively minor feature to an existing product or line of products. Line extensions can include such things as different packaging, colors, sizes and flavors.

Getting Directions

The U.S. Patent and Trademark Office's Web site at www.uspto.gov is an excellent first stop for patent information of all kinds, including lists of registered patent attorneys and agents, details on the difference between patents, copyrights and trademarks, and more.

Promoting And Marketing Your Product

Now that you have a ready-for-sale product, it is time to promote, market and distribute it. Many of the rules that apply to existing products also apply to promoting, marketing and distributing new products. However, new products have some additional wrinkles. For instance, your promotion will probably consist of a larger amount of customer education, since you will be offering them something they've never seen before. Your marketing may have to be broader than the niche efforts you've used in the past because, odds are, you'll be a little unsure about the actual market out there. Finally, you may need to test some completely new distribution channels until you find the right place to sell your product.

Setting Prices

The prices you charge for what you sell have an enormous ability to affect your company's growth. They can lure some customers and drive others away, produce profits from declining products and turn cash cows into money-losing dogs. These results can be produced by either lowering or raising prices.

Results depend not on whether your prices increase or fall, but on your market, your product, your competition, your goals, and the precise mechanism you employ to adjust prices.

Evaluating Your Current Prices

Prices fluctuate constantly for some things, such as food and gasoline, and remain about the same for others over years or even decades. Some products seem to have rapidly changing prices, but in reality the prices don't change much—it's the products that change. For example, look at personal computers. The price for a midrange personal computer has been about $2,000 for many years, despite the fact that the computer you paid $2,000 for last year can now be bought for less than half that.

Whether you are in an industry with rapidly changing prices or pricing that seems set in concrete, it's a good idea to evaluate your pricing periodically to see if you could generate some growth by tinkering with it. There are several ways to decide what your prices should be. They include matching the competition, charging whatever the market will bear, and marking up from your own costs.

Competitive pricing seeks to match what others charge for the same product or service. All pricing has to take competitors into account. When you are a small company in a large market, you will almost be forced to follow others' lead on pricing. That means pricing your product neither very far above or below what others charge. As you grow larger, you will be able to exert more independence in pricing, especially if you can differentiate your offering as exceptionally high in value. You can take the lead in pricing, by forcing others to match your low prices, when you gain enough experience and volume to truly become the low-cost producer.

Using the cost-based pricing technique, you calculate what it costs to produce your goods or services—including such items as salaries and ben-

Fast Lane

Try letting customers buy at today's lower prices for a while. Pre-announcing a price increase acts like a trade promotion, encouraging people to stock up now before the price goes up. You may have to place a limit on purchases so you don't get too much sales volume at the old price.

efits, materials and supplies, and sales and overhead—and then add whatever amount you think is appropriate for your gross profit margin. Some businesses, such as those that perform repairs, have prices explicitly based on adding a preset profit margin to whatever it costs to do the job. However, customers are generally not concerned about what it costs you to provide a good or a service. So while costs have to be a consideration in your pricing, your costs are rarely justification for higher prices in the marketplace.

> **If you have more business than you can handle, raise prices. If you are sitting around with nothing to do, reduce prices.**

The main thing you should be concerned about with pricing is neither what others are charging nor what it costs you to compete. It is maintaining a proper balance of supply and demand. Simply put, if you have more business than you can handle, raise prices. If you are sitting around with nothing to do, reduce prices. If competitors follow suit, you may have to discount again until you capture enough business to sustain your operation. If you can't reduce prices enough to make money, you will have to cut costs somehow.

Various tactics can be used within these strategies. Skimming is the practice of charging high prices, usually for new products, to take advantage of the willingness of early adopters to pay more. Skimming can allow you to recoup development costs of new products and services. Buying market share is what companies call it when they charge initially low prices with the intent of getting people to try their product and, hopefully, like it enough to pay more for it later on.

Managing the competing interests of supply, demand, cost and competition is a lot to ask. But pricing is up to the challenge. Finding the sweet spot between your cost and the highest price customers will tolerate, given existing competition, requires near-constant tinkering with prices, observation of the results, and frequent analysis of what you could do better.

How To Raise And Lower Prices

The decision to raise or lower prices is a tough one, with many ramifications for your business. But the decision whether or not to change prices is not as important as the decision about how to accomplish the change. To put it another way, two companies who change prices on the same products by the same amount may get widely different results depending on how they implement the new policy.

Raising and lowering prices effectively involves careful attention to timing. It requires knowing how to affect your customers' perception of the value inherent in what you are selling. It forces you to study and accurately predict reactions from your competitors.

Deciding How Much To Change Prices

Sometimes businesses announce major price hikes, even doubling their previous rates. One theory is that a single large price hike will get the pain over with. Businesses may also announce large price hikes when they've experienced major increases in the price of a key ingredient or cost component. A company that is being overwhelmed by sales volume from an unexpectedly popular product may jack up prices to reduce demand to a manageable level.

However, most price hikes are done in stages on the theory that customers will be accustomed to higher prices over time and be willing to tolerate them as they become more loyal. A series of smaller hikes may not even be noticed by customers who would be seriously put off by a single large one.

If you have more than one product, consider raising prices on some items while leaving the others the same, or even lowering them. Some customers are sensitive to the slightest price hikes for a particular item while mostly ignoring other increases. Automobile dealers use this fact to their advantage by cutting prices on cars as low as possible and attempting to make much of their profit on accessories like fancy paint jobs, about which customers are less price-sensitive.

Danger Ahead!

It's against the law to conspire with competitors to set prices. It's a crime to advertise prices as being lower than prices that didn't exist before, or to say prices are wholesale when they aren't.

Picking The Right Time

If you decide to raise or lower your prices, you must pick the right time. If you're lowering prices, choose a time when the change will have the most impact; if you are raising prices, choose a time when you'll encounter the least resistance. Your business's seasonality, growth stage and sales cycle affect your choice.

Many retailers, for example, raise prices seasonally, usually in the fall when Christmas is near and rushed shoppers pay less heed to prices. A brand-new store early in its growth stage might delay a price hike, however, in a bid to gain market share. Meanwhile, a computer store catering to businesses is likely to ignore the holidays and time prices changes to coincide with new model introductions, which are more important to its sales cycle.

It may be tempting to put off raising prices until after a busy season ends. After all, higher volume may make up for lower per-unit revenues. Gouging should never be a part of your price-raising strategy. But the time to raise prices is when your product or service is in demand.

Changing Value And Price

Prices don't exist in a vacuum. Like the earth under your feet, a price is supported by the value the customer perceives in the product or service to which the price is attached. Thinking about price and value in this way makes it clear that this is at least a two-dimensional problem. That is, you can change the pricing and leave the value alone, or you can change the value and leave the pricing alone. You can also change both value and pricing or leave them both alone. Any one of these changes can be tailored to have the same impact on your bottom line, at least on an individual unit basis, but they may have vastly different effects as perceived by customers.

An example of changing the price without changing the value is when a grocery store holds a sale on a popular consumer item. A case of Coca-Cola is a well-recognized commodity; shoppers have a firm idea of what a dozen cans of Coke are worth. If a retailer charges less than that amount, shoppers will be attracted. Charge more and shoppers will be repelled, all other things being equal.

Just Say "No"

If a dentist asks Peter Chwalisz to handle his tax return, he'll get a referral to another accountant, while a doctor asking for the same will get an appointment. If you want Chwalisz, president and co-owner of a five-person Missassauga, Ontario, accounting firm, to do your taxes after April 30, you'll get a nice discount compared to people who want to file earlier.

What may sound whimsical is sound business practice, says Chwalisz, a student of an emerging discipline called revenue management. He's found he makes money on doctors' returns but loses on dentists, Chwalisz explains. And he cuts prices May 1 because it's the day after the Canadian filing deadline.

"You have to charge more when there's bigger demand, but if someone wants to save money, he can," Chwalisz says of his deadline-tied pricing scheme. And of turning down certain clients, he says, "you don't do the jobs that are not profitable, period."

Revenue management is making sure you sell the right product to the right customer at the right price to maximize profitability, according to Robert Cross, an Atlanta consultant and author of *Revenue Management* (Broadway). RM, as it's often called, can help almost any business succeed and may be essential to survival in some cases, Cross says.

"There are a lot of things you can do to differentiate your company, but all of them can be matched or surpassed by your competitors," says Cross. "But one of them will make you invincible to competitors—having a strong revenue stream. There's nothing like a huge revenue stream to wash away a lot of problems."

Many businesses change value without changing price. For instance, cans of ground coffee have slowly shrunk from 1 pound to around 13 ounces. This has allowed coffee makers to maintain the perception of holding prices steady or even reducing them, while they are in reality increasing the per-ounce charge for ground coffee. Shoppers who notice such shenanigans may resent them. But if a competitor makes a value change, many companies feel they have to follow suit or be perceived as high in cost.

You can complicate the picture by changing both value and price

Danger Ahead!

Be wary of simply extracting value without lowering prices. Consumer goods sellers may have gotten away for years with packaging products in smaller and smaller sizes with no cut in price. But that has sensitized many shoppers to the trick. If you consistently do this, people may form an unfavorable impression of your company and its practices.

simultaneously. For instance, a grocer could raise prices on Cokes but include a free insulated can holder with every purchase of two or more cases. Changing value and price simultaneously may confuse customers, so it's a good idea to figure out which element is most important—the value of the can holder or the extra prices on Cokes, to continue the example—and stress that in promoting the offering to the marketplace.

Many businesses get the best long-term results from increasing price and value. Others find that they can cut their own costs while increasing value and thereby offer an almost irresistible proposition to customers—a powerful recipe for growth, indeed. But the key lesson about value and price is that these elements can be adjusted to move demand and increase sales without changing what it actually costs you to make a product. Careful attention to what happens when you move pricing and value points can show you the way to pain-free, profitable growth.

chapter 18

Customer
Service

It's tempting to focus all your energy on making new sales and pursuing bigger accounts. But paying close attention to your existing customers, no matter how small they are, is equally essential to keeping your business thriving. Closing and finalizing the sale is only the beginning. Closing the sale sets the stage for a relationship that, if properly managed, can be mutually profitable for years to come.

The key to doing more business with your existing customers, as well as attracting new ones through word-of-mouth recommendations, is customer service. Customer service means different things to different companies and in different industries. In some instances, good customer service may consist of no more than a friendly smile and a wave goodbye after the sale. In others, good customer service may involve years of follow-up, technical support, parts and repair service, training, updates, and more. In any case, customer service is an important part of making sure existing customers stay—and return to buy again.

How To Measure Your Customer Service

Excellent customer service is more than what you say or do for the customer. It also means giving customers a chance to make their feelings known. Here are some suggestions for finding out what your customers want—and what they think about your customer service:

○ *Attend trade shows and industry events that are important to your customers.* You'll find out what the competition is doing and what kinds of products and services customers are looking for.

○ *Nurture a human bond, as well as a business one, with customers and prospects.* Take them out to lunch, dinner, a ballgame or the opera. In a relaxed social atmosphere, you'll learn the secrets that will allow you to go above and beyond your competition.

○ *Stay abreast of trends; then respond to them.* Read industry trade publications, be active in trade organizations, and pay attention to what your customers are doing.

○ *Ask for feedback.* Survey your customers regularly to find out how you're doing. Send postage-paid questionnaire cards or letters, call them on the phone, or set up focus groups. Ask for suggestions and then fix the trouble areas revealed.

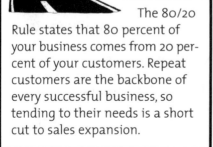

Fast Lane

The 80/20 Rule states that 80 percent of your business comes from 20 percent of your customers. Repeat customers are the backbone of every successful business, so tending to their needs is a short cut to sales expansion.

I Can't Get No Satisfaction

Studies show that the vast majority of unsatisfied customers will never come right out and tell you they're unsatisfied. They simply leave quietly, later telling everyone they know not to do business with you. So when a customer complains, don't think of it as a nuisance—think of it as a golden opportunity to change that customer's mind and retain his or her business.

Even the best product or service receives complaints now and then. Here's how to handle them for positive results:

○ Let customers vent their feelings. Encourage them to get their frustrations out in the open.

○ Never argue with a customer.

○ Never tell a customer "You do not have a problem." Those are fighting words.

○ Share your point of view as politely as you can.

○ Take responsibility for the problem. Don't make excuses. If an employee was sick or a supplier let you down, that's not the customer's concern.

○ Immediately take action to remedy the situation. Promising a solution and then delaying it only makes matters worse.

○ Empower your front-line employees to be flexible in resolving complaints. Give employees some leeway in deciding when to bend the rules. If you don't feel comfortable doing this, make sure they have you or another manager handle the situation.

Whatever you do, don't rest on your laurels. Regularly evaluate your product or service to be sure it is still priced, packaged and delivered correctly.

Improving Your Customer Service

When you're a start-up with few employees and few customers, it's easy to stay on top of what customers want and what they're getting. But as you add more customers and employees, you add links to the customer service chain. That creates the potential for growth and the potential for poor service along the way. That's why creating a customer service policy and adhering to it is so important. Here are some steps you can take to ensure that your clients receive excellent service every step of the way.

○ *Put your customer service policy in writing.* These principles should come from you, but every employee should know what the rules are and be ready to live up to them. This doesn't have to be elaborate. Something as simple as "the customer is always right" can lay the necessary groundwork, although you may want to get more detailed by saying, for instance, "any employee is empowered to grant a 10 percent discount to any dissatisfied customer at any time."

○ *Establish support systems that give employees clear instructions for gaining and maintaining service superiority.* These systems will help you outservice any competitor by giving more to customers and anticipating problems before they arise.

○ *Develop a measurement of superb customer service.* Don't forget to reward employees who practice it consistently.

○ *Be certain that your passion for customer service runs rampant throughout your company.* Employees should see how good service relates to your profits and to their futures with the company.

○ *Be genuinely committed to providing more customer service excellence than anyone else in your industry.* This commitment must be so powerful that every one of your customers can sense it.

○ *Share information with people on the front lines.* Meet with your employees regularly to talk about improving service. Solicit ideas from employees—they are the ones who are dealing with customers most often.

○ *Act on the knowledge that what customers value most are attention, dependability, promptness and competence.* They love being treated as individuals and being referred to by name.

Principles of customer service are all very well, but you

Getting Directions

One of the most popular books on boosting customer service is *Delivering Knock Your Socks Off Service, Revised Edition* (AMACOM) by Kristin Anderson and Ron Zemke. It gives concise advice to businesses of all sizes about what to do, what not to do, and how do to it if you want to deliver world-dominating customer service.

need to put those principles into action with everything you do and say. There are certain "magic words" customers want to hear from you and your staff. Make sure all your employees understand the importance of these key phrases:

○ *"How can I help?"* Customers want the opportunity to explain in detail what they want and need. Too often, business owners feel the desire or the obligation to guess what customers need rather than carefully listening first. By asking how you can help, you begin the dialogue on a positive note (you are "helping," not "selling"). And by using an open-ended question, you invite discussion.

○ *"I can solve that problem."* Most customers, especially business-to-business customers, are looking to buy solutions. They appreciate direct answers in a language they can understand.

○ *"I don't know, but I'll find out."* When confronted with a truly difficult question that requires research on your part, admit that you don't know the answer. Few things ruin your credibility faster than trying to answer a question when you are unsure of all the facts. Savvy buyers may test you with a question they know you can't answer and then just sit quietly while you struggle to fake an intelligent reply. An honest answer enhances your integrity.

○ *"I will take responsibility."* Tell your customer you realize it's your responsibility to ensure a satisfactory outcome to the transaction. Assure the customer you know what he or she expects and will deliver the product or service at the agreed-upon price. There will be no unexpected changes or expenses required to solve the problem.

○ *"I will keep you updated."* Even if your business is a cash-and-carry operation, it probably requires scheduling and coordinating numerous events. Assure your customers they will be advised of the status of these events. The longer your lead time, the more important this is. The vendors customers trust the most are those that keep them apprised of the situation, whether the news is good or bad.

○ *"I will deliver on time."* A due date that has been agreed upon is a promise that must be kept. "Close" doesn't count.

○ *"Monday means Monday."* The first week in July means the first week in July, even though it contains a national holiday. Your clients are waiting to hear you say "I deliver on time." The supplier who consistently does so is a rarity and will be remembered.

○ *"It'll be just what you ordered."* It will not be "similar to," and it will not be "better than" what was ordered. It will be exactly what was ordered. Even if you believe a substitute would be in the client's best interests, that's a topic for discussion, not something you decide on your own. Your customer may not know (or be at liberty to explain) all the ramifications of the purchase.

❍ *"The job will be complete."* Assure the customer there will be no waiting for a final piece or a last document. Never say you are finished "except for…."

❍ *"I appreciate your business."* This means more than a simple "Thanks for the order." Genuine appreciation involves follow-up calls, offering to answer questions, making sure everything is performing satisfactorily, and ascertaining that the original problem has been solved.

Neglecting any of these steps conveys the impression that you were interested in the person only until the sale was made. This leaves the buyer feeling deceived and used, and creates ill will and negative advertising for your company. Sincerely proving you care about your customers leads to recommendations and repeat sales.

Hiring

Good customer service starts with hiring good customer service representatives. Because your employees are the ones most directly responsible for dealing with customers, making sure you have the right kinds of employees is essential to providing good customer service. Many companies perform personality testing to make sure they are hiring people who will remain friendly, upbeat and helpful in the face of occasionally disgruntled customers.

When it comes to customer service, technical ability is less important than having the right attitude. Therefore, when companies are testing to identify top-notch customer service people, they tend to look more for people with "will do" attitudes than those with "can do" skills.

Personality isn't the whole story

Fast Lane

One good way to make sure you are hiring people who will be able to provide good customer service is to hire those who have worked for organizations known for excellent service. You probably know companies like this in your industry or community. Firms known nationwide for customer service excellence include Southwest Airlines, Nordstrom, Charles Schwab, Lands' End and American Express.

The Extra Mile

These days, simply providing adequate customer service isn't enough. You need to go above and beyond the call of duty to provide customer service that truly stands out. Going the extra mile is especially important when a customer has complained or if there is a problem with a purchase. Suppose an order is delayed. What can you do?

○ Call the customer personally with updates on the status of the order and expected arrival time.

○ Hand-deliver the merchandise when it arrives.

○ Take 20 percent or 30 percent off the cost.

○ Send a note apologizing for the delay...tucked inside a gift basket full of goodies. These are all ways of showing the customer you're on his or her side.

Going above and beyond doesn't always mean offering deep discounts or giving away product. With a little ingenuity and effort, you can show customers they're important any time. Suppose you've just received the newest samples and colors for your home furnishings line. Why not invite your best customers to a private showing, complete with music, appetizers, and a coupon good for one free hour of consultation?

Emergency orders and last-minute changes should be accommodated whenever possible, especially for important occasions such as a wedding or a big trade show. Customers remember these events, and they'll remember your flexibility and prompt response to their needs, too.

Being accessible also wins loyalty. One entrepreneur who runs a computer chip company has installed a customer service line on every employee's telephone, from the mail room clerk on up. This means every caller gets through to a real person who can help him or her, instead of getting lost in a voice-mail maze.

Customer loyalty is hard to win and easy to lose. But by going above and beyond with your customer service, you'll soon see your sales going above and beyond those of your competitors.

in checking to see if your employees are capable of giving excellent customer service, though. You should also try to find out whether new and existing employees understand the levels of customer service that are part of your policies. You need to see whether they have the right tools and skills to provide that level of service, and whether they are being encouraged, by compensation and other motivators, to resolve customer issues. You don't have to do a lot of testing—just asking some questions and listening to the answers should give you a good idea whether the people who are providing your customer service have what it takes to do the job well.

Training

Good customer service is made, not born. Most companies find that employees require training to provide good customer service. Some of the areas in which employees often get help from customer service training include:

○ *Stress management:* It's not easy to be the interface between an angry customer and a balky accounting department. Training on how to manage and relieve stress will help customer service representatives keep their cool under pressure.

○ *Empathy:* Often, good customer service consists of little more than putting yourself in the other person's shoes. However, this isn't always easy. Training employees on how to look at a problem from the customer's viewpoint goes a long way toward helping improve customer service.

○ *Conflict resolution:* Many times, customer service representatives spend their time resolving conflicts such as those between a customer's demands and a company's policies. Training on identifying issues, finding compromises and presenting alternatives can help.

○ *Listening:* Often, the only thing a customer wants is to feel understood. Learning how to listen effectively is not a widely held skill. However, it can be taught, and listening training is a common feature of many customer service courses.

Using Guarantees To Boost Customer Service

When you're casting about for ways to boost customer service, don't neglect guarantees. Guarantees are one of the most powerful marketing statements you can make, especially for new companies, says marketing

Getting Directions

The American Management Association holds seminars on numerous topics, including customer service training, in many locations across the country. To find out when a customer service seminar will be held near you, go to www.amanet.org or call (800) 262-9699.

consultant Sunny Baker. "It's creating a relationship that says 'We stand behind our product,'" she says.

While building customer loyalty, guarantees also lead to excellent feedback. Customers demanding guarantee payouts point directly to weaknesses in the system. While you may have to pay to make things right for disgruntled customers, in return you will be purchasing invaluable information about where things are going wrong.

Baker says making good on customer returns isn't a cost—it's a learning opportunity. "Make sure you use those returns to your advantage," she says. "If products start coming back, you need to know that."

Few companies get maximum payoff from guarantees, says Christopher Hart, author of *Extraordinary Guarantees*. The problem, according to Hart, is that their guarantees are weak, watered-down or tied up in fine print, Ideally, a good guarantee is unconditional, easy to understand, meaningful, easy to invoke, and quick to pay off.

As an example, he holds up the guarantee offered by cataloger Lands' End, which says its products are "Guaranteed. Period." Additional words in the guarantee advise buyers that this means they can return anything at any time for any reason. That's very comforting to a customer.

A meaningful guarantee has to really repay a customer for the trouble your product or service caused. Even a 100 percent refund may not do that if the cost of the product is small compared to the inconvenience, for instance, when a leaky ballpoint pen ruins an expensive suit. Sometimes, Hart says, you may have to offer to pay more than you received.

Before you decide whether your guarantee should be unconditional or specific, money-back or more, ask your customers what

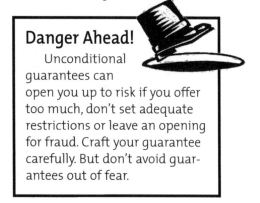

Danger Ahead!

Unconditional guarantees can open you up to risk if you offer too much, don't set adequate restrictions or leave an opening for fraud. Craft your guarantee carefully. But don't avoid guarantees out of fear.

Fast Lane

Contact management software such as Symantec's ACT! or GoldMine FrontOffice from Front Range Solutions can quickly, easily and inexpensively do wonders for customer service by reminding you automatically of everything from a big client's birthday to an important sales call.

is important to them. Xerox Corp. once considered offering buyers of its office copiers a 90-day, unconditional, money-back guarantee. It sounded great until Xerox asked customers what they wanted. Most corporate purchasing agents said they didn't want the money back; that would just make them look like they had made a mistake buying a Xerox. What they really wanted was a guarantee of a replacement if any problem cropped up. So Xerox crafted a guarantee to replace any copier that had a major service problem within three years of purchase.

"The guarantee concept is frightening," Hart warns. But that fear can be good. Properly harnessed, it forces an entire organization to focus on customers and set clear goals for customer service.

Using Follow-Up In Customer Service

One important tool for generating repeat business is following up. Effective follow-up begins immediately after the sale when you call the customer to say "thank you" and find out if he or she is pleased with your product or service. Beyond this, there are several effective ways to follow up that ensure your business is always in the customer's mind.

○ *Let customers know what you are doing for them.* This can be in the form of a newsletter mailed to existing customers, or it can be more informal, such as a phone call. Whatever method you use, the key is to dramatically point out to customers the excellent service you are giving them. If you never mention all the things you are doing for them, customers may not notice. You aren't being cocky when you talk to customers about all the work you have done to please them. Just make a phone call and let them know they don't have to worry because you handled the paperwork, called the attorney or double-checked on the shipment— one less thing they have to do.

○ *Write old customers personal, handwritten notes frequently.* "I was just sitting at my desk and your name popped into my head. Are you still having a great time flying all over the country? Let me know if you need another set of luggage. I can stop by with our latest models any time." Or if you run into an old customer at an event, follow up with a note: "It was great seeing you at the CDC Christmas party. I'll call you early in the New Year to schedule a lunch."

○ *Keep it personal.* Voice mail and e-mail make it easy to communicate, but the personal touch is often lost. If you're having trouble getting through to someone whose problem requires that personal touch, leave a voice-mail message that you want to talk to the person directly or will stop by his or her office at a designated time.

○ *Remember special occasions.* Send regular customers birthday cards, anniversary cards, holiday cards…you name it. Gifts are excellent follow-up tools, too. You don't have to spend a fortune to show you care; use your creativity to come up with interesting gift ideas that tie into your business, the customer's business or his or her recent purchase.

Fast Lane

E-mail gives you a fast, convenient and reliable way to stay in touch with customers. You can even set your computer to automatically send e-mails wishing customers happy birthdays or responding to routine communications with boilerplate messages such as "I'll get right to it." Don't neglect to collect customers' e-mail addresses.

○ *Pass on information.* If you read an article, see a new book, or hear about an organization a customer might be interested in, drop a note or make a quick call to let them know.

○ *Consider follow-up calls as business development calls.* When you talk to or visit old clients or customers, you'll often find they have referrals to give you, which can lead to new business.

With all your existing customers can do for you, there's simply no reason not to stay in regular contact with them. Use your imagination, and you'll think of plenty of other ideas that can help you develop a lasting relationship.

chapter 19

Sales Personnel

hen you're starting out, you may be sales manager, marketing director and lone salesperson all in one—plus filling whatever other spots exist on the organizational chart. As you grow, however, you'll find you need additional people to handle specialized jobs. These will someday include a chief financial officer and vice president of operations, among others.

But one of the first specializations in which you're likely to need to hire is sales. This makes sense because sales are what drive your company's growth. All other things being equal, the more salespeople you have, the more sales you will generate. So adding sales personnel and improving your existing sales staff are essential parts of growing your company.

Evaluating Your Sales Force

Maybe your sales force is fine the way it is. Maybe not. How can you tell? Evaluating your sales force is an important step in the process of deciding whether and how to grow your sales team. If your existing sales force is fine and will be more than adequate to fuel future growth, you still might need some additional training or perhaps a revamped compensation package. On the other hand, your sales force may need to grow by a few heads, or you may choose to stay the same size but have different people filling the sales positions.

Step one in evaluating your sales force is to decide what you want it to do for you. For some companies that do most of their selling through mail order or the Internet, a sales force is strictly an option. In this case, you may expect your sales force to handle only the larger accounts, leaving the smaller orders to customer service personnel and order-takers. For other companies, however, the salesperson is the most visible—and perhaps the only—outward manifestation of the company seen by customers. This type of salesperson carries a heavy load. He or she has to uphold the company's image, hold the customers' hands, interface with delivery and repair departments at headquarters, and, of course, get the sale.

It will not require a lot of thought for you to come up with a good description of what you want your sales force to do. Make sure you're not evaluating your sales force based on some other company's needs. For instance, if your salespeople are primarily charged with following up on leads generated by your advertising, don't penalize

Fast Lane

You can get a quick read on how effective a salesperson is likely to be by looking for the common traits of great salespeople. These include having high personal integrity, having an outgoing personality, possessing relationship savvy, and, last but not least, displaying sales ability.

them if they aren't making a lot of cold calls. Once you decide what jobs your sales force is intended for, simply check their performance against the requirements. The key measure when it comes to evaluating a sales force is sales productivity.

Measuring Sales Productivity

The simplest measure of sales productivity is the dollar amount of sales per salesperson. That's easy enough to figure out: Just divide the volume of sales by the number of salespeople on staff. That will give you an average sales productivity figure and let you know how the average salesperson in your organization is doing. More useful, though, is to know how each individual salesperson is doing compared to the average. You may have a handful of relatively productive people who are carrying the load for a raft of underperformers. This is the kind of information you'll need to know to decide whether to make a change.

Be warned, though: Sales productivity may involve more than simply generating dollars of sales. Your sales force may be moving a lot of product now but costing you sales later by alienating customers with poor service. They may be making promises you can't deliver on, overburdening your production and shipping departments. They may be selling a lot of the wrong products (items with low margins or high support costs) while ignoring your more profitable lines. Check to see if certain salespeople have large numbers of returns or tend to sell to customers who don't pass credit checks. These salespeople could be costing you more than they're worth.

Hiring Salespeople

Adding salespeople can result in steadily increasing sales. This can free you up to spend time and energy on other tasks. Hiring salespeople could also hurt sales, erode profits, damage valuable customer relationships, and destroy your image in the marketplace. The difference between these two scenarios is the difference between hiring the right salespeople and the wrong ones.

Salespeople are not just the people responsible for building your bottom line. They're also your front-line troops, the ones with the most daily contact with your customers. With those caveats in mind, it's important to not only grow your sales force, but to grow it properly.

To start with, understand that there may not be any truly bad salespeople. There may just be good salespeople in the wrong positions. To hire the right salesperson for the job, you have to understand and be able to describe what the job is. That means clarifying whether this sales position is intended to immediately generate sales or perhaps develop contacts for a sales cycle that may stretch into months or years. Do you want someone who is a closer or one who takes more of a consultative approach? Matching your company's sales needs and selling style to your new hires is the first step in getting good salespeople.

Few salespeople are motivated by altruism, and misunderstanding your company's compensation package is one of the main reasons for sales staff dissatisfaction and turnover. For all potential new hires, explain precisely what the compensation plan is. In addition, clarify the territory, your performance expectations, any training you will offer, and any sales tools you will provide. You should also provide candidates with a thumbnail description of the market and the competition. Then you'll know that you have explained the opportunity accurately to anyone who is interested.

Don't stop by describing your needs. Imagine the ideal salesperson for the job, including his or her personality, experience, energy level, reputation and abilities. You may not find someone exactly like that, but if you don't know what you want, the odds of making a bad hiring decision are very high.

Only now should you actually start looking for salespeople. But before dashing out a three-line ad and calling the classified department of your local newspaper, consider some other options:

○ *Look internally.* You may have

Getting Directions

The Fast Forward MBA in Hiring by Max Messmer (John Wiley & Sons) is a well-organized and concise reference guide on finding and keeping good employees. It covers many topics, from absenteeism to work force diversity.

Under Your Thumb?

In these days of outsourcing everything, many companies continue to keep their sales forces in-house. There are plenty of opportunities for having outside salespeople hawk your product, but there are many advantages to keeping the sales function internal.

Inside salespeople work for you as employees so you can expect their full attention and dedication to calling on customers, answering queries and handling problems. Because they work for your company, they should know a good deal about opportunities for cross-selling additional products and services to existing customers when they are placing orders. Since they're on staff for the long haul, you can afford to train them to be knowledgeable and courteous when dealing with customers. Inside salespeople can be shaped the way you want them—to go after large sales or focus on after-sales service—as you and your strategy dictate.

Outside salespeople, such as manufacturer's reps, have one shining quality that distinguishes them from in-house people: They're cheaper. Because you don't have to pay a salary and benefits to third-party salespeople, you can afford more of them. This may allow you to reach more markets and customers than if you were relying solely on the salespeople you can afford to hire as permanent, full-time employees. The problem with outside salespeople is that they may be selling similar and even competing products, so you could lose sales.

technical, support, operations or administrative people who would and could successfully move into sales. Post the ad on a bulletin board and see what happens.

○ *Ask for employee referrals.* Chances are your existing employees know the kind of people who would be happy working for you. They may be able to suggest some people for you to contact.

○ *Network with suppliers, customers, colleagues, advisors and social contacts.* This can be cheaper, faster and more reliable than advertising to the general public.

○ *Check with professional associations.* They may have job lines to help members find employees.

○ *Try online advertising.* The speed, searchability and freshness of online job banks make them attractive options for both candidates and employers.

○ *Check with your local college.* You may be able to hire a recent graduate who is enthusiastic, effective and less expensive than a seasoned professional.

○ *Contact headhunters.* Headhunters specializing in sales personnel aren't cheap, but when labor markets are tight, it may be worth the cost to find a solid salesperson.

○ *Consider using temporary and staffing services.* Temporary and staffing services can provide you with sales and marketing personnel on a temporary, temp-to-perm, or permanent direct-hire basis.

Manufacturer's Reps

Manufacturer's representative, broker and agent are terms used to describe independent sales agents who work on commission. You don't pay them a salary, just a percentage of what they sell. Manufacturer's reps offer a practical, cost-effective alternative to a direct sales force for many growing companies. There are more than a half-million reps in North America, most selling to targeted markets in select geographic regions. Reps know their markets because they call on local buyers regularly and have established working relationships.

Getting Directions

If you're interested in learning more about manufacturer's reps, contact the Manufacturers' Agents National Association at P.O. Box 3467, Laguna Hills, CA 92654-3467, or check out the agency's Web site at www.manaonline.org.

Using reps can provide you with many of the benefits of having a satellite office in the location—including knowledge of local markets and rapid access to large accounts—without your incurring large fixed costs. With reps, sales costs are always a fixed percentage of sales. The downside is that reps typically handle many different products. Some may be complementary to yours, while others may compete. A typical manufacturer's rep earns a 5 percent commission on sales, although that amount varies widely depending on the product, market and sales volume.

Telemarketers

Telemarketers who contact your customers by phone can provide customer service, answer questions and follow up on previous ship-

Danger Ahead!

Hiring salespeople to be paid purely on commission sounds economical but may turn out to be more costly than paying salaries. Commission-only salespeople may experience wide swings in personal income and have trouble budgeting and getting personal loans because of it. As a result, top-notch salespeople rarely take commission-only jobs.

ments as well as take orders. One of telemarketers' most useful jobs is generating qualified leads. Because you contact customers using phone numbers, it's easy to track results from a telemarketing effort. You can build your own telemarketing operation in-house or contract with a third-party call center.

Of course, you need not decide to go with only one form of sales force. Many entrepreneurs effectively deploy a mix of inside and outside sales forces, sales reps and telemarketers. The challenge is managing conflicts, including turf wars and cannibalism.

Sales Managers

It's never easy to hand over responsibility for an important management job to someone else, but delegating accounts to your sales manager may be the toughest thing you'll ever have to do. After all, you've won over these customers. How can you be expected to happily shift the responsibility for servicing them to somebody else? But hiring a sales manager is an important part of your business's growth. It's unreasonable to expect to be able to make a dozen sales calls a day, direct other salespeople and run the company at the same time. Once you hire a sales manager, you will be able to greatly reduce your sales calls and eliminate managing salespeople, and devote the balance of your time to the jobs you're uniquely qualified to handle, like devising the company's strategy.

A good sales manager has to be able to:
○ Oversee salespeople
○ Develop sales strategies and plans
○ Set targets for the sales team
○ Monitor sales performance
○ Personally handle key customers
○ Prepare sales reports and other reports

○ Report directly to you or a superior in marketing

Typically, you will want a sales manager with experience both selling and managing. Sales managers should be well-versed in the computer or other technical skills required to manage your department

---

The Greatest Show On Earth

After cold calls and follow-ups have gotten you an opportunity to make your pitch, you want that pitch to be as effective as it can be. Here are steps to make your sales presentation a success.

○ *Know your customer's business.* Potential clients expect you to know their business, customers and competition as well as you know your own.

○ *Write out your sales presentation.* Talk about the three major selling points of your product or service.

○ *Make sure you're talking to the right person.* When you're setting the appointment, always ask "Are you the one I should be talking to?"

○ *Build rapport.* Find out if you have a colleague in common. Get a little insight into the company and the individual so you can make the rapport genuine.

○ *Ask questions.* Don't jump into a canned sales spiel. The most effective way to sell is to ask the prospect questions and see where he or she leads you.

○ *Take notes.* Write down key points you can refer to later during your presentation.

○ *Learn to listen.* A good rule of thumb is to listen 70 percent of the time and talk 30 percent of the time. Don't interrupt.

○ *Eliminate objections.* When a prospect raises an objection, don't immediately jump in with a response. Instead, show empathy by saying "Let's explore your concerns." Ask for more details about the objection.

○ *Close the sale.* There's no magic to closing the sale. If you've followed all the previous steps, all you should have to do is ask for the customer's order.

After the sale, always follow up with a thank you, and don't forget to ask for a referral.

Getting Directions

You can access scores of free articles, studies, speeches and more material on hiring, training and making the most of sales managers at the Web site for Sales & Marketing Executives International at www.smei.org. Write to this worldwide organization at: P.O. Box 1390, Sumas, WA 98295-1390, or call (770) 661-8500

and demonstrate your products. He or she should have good leadership and communication skills and have a proven record of growing sales in past positions. If you have a specific problem you want your sales manager to address, such as difficulty reaching larger corporate customers, you will want to have someone with expertise in that area.

Dividing Up Territories

A sales territory is a segment of your market that you have assigned to a salesperson or a group of salespeople. While a sales territory is usually described as a geographic area—states west of the Rockies, for instance—it should be thought of as a group of customers and should be serviced with close attention to customer type. Some territories aren't geographical areas—customers over $1 million in annual sales, for example. These "territories" may be assigned to product or account specialists, such as those focusing on large accounts, rather than to the people who would otherwise own them because of their geographical territories.

Few things are as loaded as the assignment and division of sales territories. Salespeople tend to think all the good prospects are in others' territories, while all their best customers have been gerrymandered into someone else's territory. When dividing up territories, you want everyone to feel they got a fair shake, but at the same time, you have to be realistic. You want to match salespeople with territories based on things other than strict equity. For instance, if your salespeople vary widely in talent and energy level, you don't want to give everyone comparable sales territories. It makes sense to divide territories to make the most of everyone's abilities. If a salesperson is great at dealing with midsized accounts, save big prospects for someone who will do well there. Therefore, the key to good sales territory design is appropriate balance.

Just Sold!

As your business grows, so will your need for additional sales personnel. Remember: The more salespeople you have, the more sales you will generate. So don't make the mistake of thinking you can grow your business without growing your sales force—one way or another—right along with it.

chapter 20

Other Roads
To Growth

The classic way to grow a business is to develop products for businesses or consumers, find markets for those products, and use the profits to hire more employees and acquire more equipment, and then develop new products and markets to repeat the process. Keep at this process long enough, and you will wind up a large company. But there are ways to grow other than by coming up with ideas for selling things to business and consumer markets. Selling to the government (as either a prime contractor or a subcontractor) and strategic alliances are both viable ways to expand that lie outside the usual strategies for growth.

Government Contracting

The United States government is the world's largest customer. Each year, the federal government and its various agencies procure more than $300 billion of everything from airplanes to zippers. For many products and services, the U.S. government is the biggest buyer on the planet. Uncle Sam is also an attractive customer for a few other reasons:

○ The government makes its needs publicly known through such media as the *Commerce Business Daily*, a publication listing numerous government contracting opportunities. This is quite different from most markets, which you have to thoroughly research to identify needs.

○ Government sales are conducted in an open environment where there are many rules to ensure that the process is fair.

○ The government frequently buys in very large volumes and over a long period of time. That kind of customer can provide a solid foundation for growing your company.

Getting Directions

Read the *Commerce Business Daily* for free online at http://cbdnet.gpo.gov. Study the Federal Acquisition Regulations, a set of rules controlling how the government buys, at www.arnet.gov/far. The General Services Administration, an organization that oversees a lot of U.S. procurement, is an another important stop at www.gsa.gov.

○ Laws set aside all or part of many contracts for small businesses, women-owned businesses, minority-owned businesses, and other firms the government wants to support.

○ Having the U.S. government as a customer gives your business a stamp of approval. If you can meet the government's standards for quality, price and service, odds are good you can meet other customers' requirements.

There are downsides to selling to the government as well. It can be

Fast Lane

You can sidestep many of the hassles of winning a government contract if you subcontract with the main or prime contractor. Prime contractors, ranging from large defense contractors to companies that may be smaller than yours, do most of the work to land the government job. Then they may hire you to fulfill all or part of it. Find prime contractors by perusing many of the same resources you would to sell directly to the government.

hard to find the proper purchasing agent among the thousands employed by various branches and agencies of the federal government. In addition, the rules and paperwork are daunting. The good news is that there are many sources of help. The Small Business Administration's Web site, at www.sba.gov, is one good place to start looking for help selling to the government.

And don't restrict yourself to selling to the federal government. State and local governmental entities, including cities, counties, school districts and others, actually purchase more goods and services than the federal government. There are more of them and they're smaller, but these government customers can provide alternative tracks to growth that are just as viable as the opportunities in Washington, DC.

Strategic Alliances

Many allies are small, says Mitchell Lee Marks, co-author of *Joining Forces*, a book on business partnerships. This statement is supported by a recent survey of CEOs of small, fast-growing companies in which 90 percent reported forming alliances.

Small businesses in search of growth favor alliances because they can quickly and inexpensively provide access to technology, expertise, marketing, production, distribution and other capabilities. Studies show businesses that participate in alliances grow faster, increase productivity faster and report higher revenues than abstainers.

Alliances are excellent for testing the waters before a full-scale merger. Because no ownership changes, it's easy to back out, notes Marks. Another advantage to alliances compared to mergers or acquisitions is that you can participate in several at the same time.

Synergy is the benefit most alliances are after. If you have a product but lack distribution, you may seek synergy by allying with a

Decent Proposal

Every year, corporations, foundations and government agencies dispense billions of dollars in grants to companies for addressing issues these organizations are interested in. Writing good grant proposals is a valuable skill. You can learn much of what you need to know to write a successful proposal by talking to the agency offering the grant. The main parts of a grant proposal are:

○ *Abstract:* This brief summary, about a half-page long, should clearly describe your proposed project like an executive summary of a business plan.

○ *Needs statement:* This describes the situation or problem your proposal will address, including supporting evidence. It should focus on the problem you hope to solve with the grant money and make the case that the problem is fixable, that this is the appropriate agency to take on this problem, and that the problem is significant enough to warrant funding

○ *Project description:* This part of the proposal describes the project, explaining how it will solve the problem. It should convince the reader that your way is the best way.

○ *Goals:* This section should describe the desired outcome of your project. Discuss both long-range goals and specific, short-term objectives, as well as the precise effect to be achieved and the means you will employ. It should be reasonable, measurable and bound to a specific time frame.

○ *Action plan:* The action plan is a step-by-step description of sequential activities that must be completed to achieve the objectives. It should clearly and specifically say who will do each step, what will be done and when.

○ *Evaluation:* This describes how the project will be monitored and its results evaluated. It should cover the criteria for measuring progress, say who will be conducting the evaluations, and tell when evaluations will be held.

○ *Budget:* This is where you tell how you will use the money you receive. It should be within the amount you are asking for, be realistic, and include only eligible expenses. Make it detailed enough to satisfy anyone's curiosity on the question of how the money will be spent, and make sure everything adds up.

Danger Ahead!

Choose allies carefully. If you hook up with someone known for unethical practices, you may damage your reputation even if you do nothing wrong. Be wary of losing proprietary information such as customer lists, secret processes, marketing strategies and product formulations. And never let an ally take over any job that's central to your business.

---

company that has good distribution and no competing product. Companies that own technologies that can be combined with yours to create a compelling product are also potential allies. In international alliances, one company can provide local market skills while another supplies imported products or technologies. Allies may also benefit by purchasing cooperatively, marketing jointly, combining research and development, co-sponsoring training, or agreeing to set standards in a new technology.

Yet it requires skills to maintain healthy alliances. Three out of four corporate alliances disappoint, producing higher costs or lower returns than expected, according to Marks.

Seeking Allies Successfully

Allying well is almost as difficult as marrying well. Here are keys to finding and making a match that will last:

○ *Plan first, pick later.* You should know exactly what traits your ally needs before you start looking for one.

○ *Network.* The most likely place to find an ally is among customers, suppliers, competitors and other professional associates.

○ *Look for synergy.* A combination of allies should add up to more than either does separately.

○ *Value trust more than competence.* An expert ally you can't trust is no ally at all.

○ *Listen to your gut.* Check a potential ally's credit rating, financial reports and reputation in the industry, but trust your feelings when it comes to the final decision.

○ *Identify benefits, including synergistic effects.* Make sure the benefit isn't lopsided so that no one will feel he or she is being taken advantage of.

"I Do" Or "I Don't"?

Ask yourself the following questions to help you decide whether forming an alliance is the right move for your business at this point:

○ *Do you need an alliance?* If you can accomplish your strategic goals without an alliance, it's probably best to go it alone.

○ *Will both parties benefit more or less equally?* Alliances that only aid one side are unlikely to last.

○ *Are desired results clearly explained?* You should know what you and your ally want out of the alliance, and clearly communicate it.

○ *Do you have time to manage it?* Alliances are almost as time-consuming for top-level managers as running a separate business.

○ *Is there an exit strategy?* An alliance that doesn't include a clear plan for ending the partnership is headed for trouble.

○ *Set precise goals for what you want to accomplish.* Without goals, an alliance can flounder.

○ *Carefully and frankly communicate expectations, along with the ways performance will be measured, to allies and your own employees.* Describe what and when each party will invest, as well as expected returns and how any disputes will be resolved. Put it in a legal document.

○ *Don't forget to devise an exit strategy.* It's a serious mistake not to have a comprehensive plan for ending the alliance.

Once you've started an alliance, keep it going. Refer frequently to your original objectives. See how you measure up and communicate the results and any changes to everyone involved.

Many alliances are based on hoped-for savings, but alliances involve inevitable costs. Management time is the biggest one. Underestimating the amount of time it will take to manage an alliance is a common cause of failure.

Fast Lane

Alliances can be short cuts to growth. One study found that the average number of alliances fast-growing companies were involved in has increased in the past few years from three to four.

Which Way To Success?

The fact that these roads to growth aren't the ones most companies travel doesn't make them any less effective. Even if you are determined to grow by following conventional routes, you should be aware of the alternatives. After all, you may decide to change your course along the way.

chapter 21

Online
Growth
Opportunities

hould you go online in search of growth?

Experts believe small businesses have the most to gain by offering

their products and services through the Internet. "The Internet is

leveling the playing field for small businesses that compete against

big companies," says Stephen Fickas, a professor of computer and

information science at the University of Oregon in Eugene.

"The wide-open opportunities available online today are like those found in the Wild West."

But don't build a Web site just because it's the trendy thing to do. "The key question is 'Are your customers and potential customers

Dive In! The Water's Fine!

Following are selected statistics detailing the growth of the Internet as compiled by the Rat Report, a service of Cyber-NY, a New York City online marketing company. Can you afford not to be a part of this?

Total Number Of People On The Internet, 1995-2005

- ○ 1995: 25 million
- ○ 1996: 55 million
- ○ 1997: 98 million
- ○ 1998: 147 million
- ○ 1999: 171 million
- ○ 2000: 247 million (projected)
- ○ 2005: 350 million (projected)

Source: Nua Internet Services

Money Spent On Internet Advertising, 1997-2002

- ○ 1997: $650 million
- ○ 1998: $1.5 billion
- ○ 1999: $2.6 billion
- ○ 2000: $4.2 billion (projected)
- ○ 2001: $6.7 billion (projected)
- ○ 2002: $8.9 billion (projected)

Source: Active Media

Total e-Commerce Earnings, 1998-2003

- ○ 1998: $51 billion
- ○ 1999: $95 billion
- ○ 2000: $284 billion (projected)
- ○ 2001: $551 billion (projected)
- ○ 2002: $919 billion (projected)
- ○ 2003: $1.439 trillion (projected)

Source: Forrester Research

> **Fast Lane**
>
> One of the great things about the Web is that it allows you to grow every minute of the day. "Your business can be open 24 hours a day, seven days a week," says Gail Houck, a consultant and Web strategist. When a customer can get answers to questions at any hour of the day or night, it can supercharge your company's growth.

online?'" says Jill Ellsworth, co-author of *New Internet Business Book*. "If your target audience is online, you should be, too." If your customers are not online, spending time and money establishing a Web site could be futile.

Just as with any other marketing strategy, successfully going online requires a plan of attack. You can't just slap up a Web site and expect orders to come pouring in. You have to understand what the Internet offers, what you have to offer online customers, how to add the Internet to your existing business, and the actual mechanics of going online.

What The Internet Can Offer

Start your evaluation of what the Internet can offer by asking yourself what you want your online presence to achieve. Setting up a Web site is not a guarantee of instant riches. Although a few, such as Dell Computer, are racking up millions of dollars in daily online transactions, relatively few companies have seen such substantial sales online. Then why put up a Web page? Because even if your page is little more than an electronic billboard for your company, it's still a powerful tool for building a business. Web sites can economically and effectively serve a number of other goals. Here are legitimate goals for a company Web site:

○ Advertising your products and services
○ Selling your products and services directly to customers
○ Referring customers to brick-and-mortar retailers of your products and services
○ Obtaining information about customers and prospects
○ Receiving instant feedback from customers and prospects
○ Providing information to suppliers
○ Recruiting employees
○ Recruiting investors
○ Trading referrals with other companies' Web sites

- Developing relationships with customers and prospects
- Providing more content than traditional print advertisements allow
- Establishing your company as technologically savvy

Those are some pretty hefty jobs for anything to provide, yet a company Web site is up to the challenge of handling any of these tasks. The Internet is changing society in many ways, and business is no exception. If you don't have a company Web site, at least know that you considered the reasons for having one and decided they aren't sufficient to warrant the time and trouble creating and maintaining a corporate Web site entails.

How many of the Web site goals are you interested in pursuing? Although a pressing need to fulfill just one of these objectives may be enough to convince you to start a Web site, as a rule, the more things you hope to get from your site, the more reason there is to start one up.

> **Viewpoint**
>
> The 10 most common ways consumers use the Internet, according to the PCData User Survey, are as follows, ranked from most common to least: e-mail, researching personal topics, using phone directories, playing games/entertainment, getting news, doing business shopping, checking the weather, sending e-cards, personal shopping, and chatting.

Are You Net-Ready?

Before you are ready to go online, you have to know how having an Internet presence complements your company's goals and objectives. Here are key questions to ask yourself before you go online:

> **Fast Lane**
>
> To get an idea what you want your site to accomplish, identify and visit the three best sites on the Web that relate to your company and your plans. Check out how they look, what they contain and how they attempt to attract and retain visitors. This should give you an idea what you want your site to do and how to do it.

- Are your competitors online? What do they appear to be trying to accomplish? How well do they appear to be accomplishing it?
- If you choose to go online, what will be the primary mission of your online effort?

○ What is the desired outcome, specifically?

○ How much time and money do you have available to accomplish the project?

○ Which are most important to you: quality graphics, constantly updated content, ease of maintenance, speed of preparation, or site performance (speed in loading images, for instance)?

○ What types of visitors do you want to attract?

○ What do you want visitors to do while on your site?

○ Where will you get the content that goes on your site? How will it be updated?

○ What do you want visitors to be able to do? Download software? See animation? Access databases? Buy products? Others?

○ What are the security requirements for your site?

○ What computer systems are you using now? How will these interface with the Web site?

○ What is your long-term plan for the site?

Viewpoint

You don't have to be an Internet-only company to go online. Many companies are so-called "click-and-mortar" operations. That means in addition to an online operation—the click part—they have a physical presence like traditional brick-and-mortar companies.

Assessing Your Prospects As An Online Business

Not every business is right for the online world. The Web is well-suited to selling many types of products and services—but not all. So to begin with, your product or service must be something that is salable over the Internet.

Commodity items, such as books, sell well on the Web. All copies of a given book are alike—if you've seen one, you've seen them all. So a customer can feel confident buying books on the Web. Gifts and impulse items are also popular Web retail items, because much Web shopping is done at home, and it's easy to buy with a click. The Web is also friendly to computer products of all kinds, including software and peripherals. If you are a locomotive mechanic, however, you will have a hard time plying your trade via the Web. That's true of many service businesses, from carpet cleaning to catering. You may decide to have a Web presence to help people become aware of your company, but the chances of you developing significant e-commerce business are low.

> **A**dding an Internet component to your company requires significant investments of time, money and other resources.

Having a product you can sell is only the beginning. Adding an Internet component to your company requires significant investments of time, money and other resources. You have to have the money to hire, either internally or via outsourcing, the Web site designers, programmers and technicians needed to get your site up and keep it up. If you plan to do the technical work yourself, be sure you're really up to the job. Keeping an Internet server up and maintaining a Web site is not a trivial task, not to mention the general business details of pricing, shipping and accounting that may be added to your responsibilities if you go online.

Adding The Internet To Your Mix

Adding an Internet component to your business is not like adding another salesperson or even opening a new location. Doing business on the Internet poses significant challenges from a technical standpoint. Web site designers, programmers and Web server technicians command high salaries and may be hard to find. You may have to alter your product mix to make it more suitable for the Internet. You will find yourself competing with a whole new group of rivals once you set up shop on the Internet.

Perhaps most important, the Internet is a whole new distribution channel. If you are getting most of your sales now from a physical storefront, you need to ask yourself whether having an Internet presence is going to take sales away from that store, with its high fixed costs. If you have franchisees, licensed distributors or retailers who carry your products, you need to know how they are going to feel about having a new channel to compete with.

Taking your business online can add to your business's growth. But it can also give rise to new areas of complexity and challenge. The best time to find ways to deal with these new challenges is now, by asking yourself what adding the Internet to your existing business mix will mean in the long run.

Getting Online

There are a number of ways to do business online—from starting a store on the World Wide Web to using e-mail to entice customers to shop. "Some of these online tactics are very low-cost but still get you a lot of mileage," says Marcia Yudkin, author of *Marketing Online*.

"The cheapest way to get a foothold in the Net is to make your online presence known by using forums," advises Yudkin. The major online services offer hundreds of forums—essentially electronic bulletin boards—where users are welcome to ask questions, give advice and spout opinions. Many thousands of users visit these boards daily, meaning creative marketers can find a large audience.

Because the Internet is not the place for a hard-sell approach, Yudkin avoids overt selling in forum posts and other e-mail communications. However, she often urges users to contact her directly to get her list of FAQs—frequently asked questions—about her areas of expertise. Users who send a message to her e-mail address automatically receive her FAQ list, which provides plenty of useful information as well as plugs for her products.

"E-mail is a great tool for [disseminating] information about what you do at little cost," Yudkin says. How little? Yudkin spends $25 per month to operate several automatic e-mail accounts.

You can also profitably use e-mail to contact customers and prospects, and most businesses would gain by doing so, says Steve Jones, a consultant and communications

Fast Lane

Here's a quick and inexpensive way to raise your company's Web profile: Regularly visit relevant forums, and when you spot a user question that relates to your expertise, post a helpful reply. Along the way, mention your business's services or products. Often, you'll find that these users will come to your Web site ready to buy.

professor. "Ask your customers for their e-mail addresses. Build a list, and use it to send out discount coupons, spec sheets and anything you would otherwise mail or fax," Jones says. "The cost is small, and delivery is instantaneous. The results of creatively using e-mail can be substantial."

Selecting A Web Site Host

Before you set up a Web site, you need to find a place to put it. You can put your Web site up inexpensively by using the often-free Web site-hosting options of an online service or Internet service provider (ISP) such as AOL. There are also a number of companies that specialize in Web hosting.

Louis Silberman began paying $40 per month for a service to host the site for Health4Her.com, the women's nutritional retailer he opened in November 1998. A year later, the 35-year-old Scottsdale, Arizona, entrepreneur had fired four Web-hosting services, finally buying his own $6,000 server and paying a fifth service $400 a month to house and maintain the computer and provide the Internet connection.

Silberman says his former hosts promised reliability and performance they couldn't deliver. As a result, he estimates Health4Her lost $25,000 in sales due to downtime and overloaded host systems that slowed performance to a crawl.

Due to hosting's technical complexity and staffing requirements—and the cost of high-speed Internet lines—most small e-businesses farm the job out. Third-party hosts provide space on a server, usually shared with other companies, as well as a speedy Internet connection and technical support.

Picking a host is tricky. Thousands of services charge all sorts of fees, make all sorts of promises and raise seemingly endless questions. To help you make the decision, here are key questions to ask, answers to insist on and how to get them:

Viewpoint

A Web host computer stores the files that contain the information on an e-business site and keeps it all connected to the Internet.

○ *How reliable is your service?* Surveys show reliability is e-businesses' main concern.

Fast Lane

You can accelerate your search for a Web host by letting a Web site host directory start the work for you. Check out TopHosts at www.tophosts.com, The Ultimate Web Host List at www.webhostlist.com, HostIndex at www.hostindex.com, or Web Host Directory at www.webhostdir.com.

Look for at least a 95 percent uptime guarantee, and find out what that guarantee means. "Get something in writing that says should they not meet the uptime, they will lower your month's cost," advises Jon Landry, sales manager with TopHosts International Inc., a Web site host rating service and directory in Regina, Saskatchewan.

❍ *What kind of performance do you offer?* An ideal host has one or more T3 lines connected directly to the Internet, not through someone else's network operations center, says Landry. Servers should be fast Pentium Pros or Sun SparcStations running Windows NT, Linux or another mainstream, high-performance operating system. Let your host know if you use bandwidth-gobbling features such as streaming audio and video. And know who you share space with, Silberman adds. If other businesses on your server experience large spikes in traffic, you could suffer.

❍ *How good is your support?* Look for 24/7 support available by phone from a live person. And check it. Call the tech support line at 9 p.m. on a Sunday and expect it to be answered by something other than a machine. Send an e-mail with a general support question and see whether it gets answered in a few hours—or a few days.

❍ *What will it cost?* Entry-level service with a single domain name, 20MB of disk space, e-mail service and up to a gigabyte of monthly data transfer (which may also be expressed as hits) should cost about $50. About $200 adds several domain names, 75MB of disk space, several gigabytes of data transfer and facilities for conducting online transactions. For $250 and up, expect a gigabyte of disk space and 50GB of data transfer.

❍ *How do you handle security?* Passwords should be required to manage or modify your site and otherwise control the computer that holds the files and runs the software that make up your online store. All files should be backed up daily. And always look for a host that offers secure online purchase transactions. Even if you don't need it now, ask for it in case you do someday.

○ *How much control do I have?* You want to be able to use a wide variety of background applications, including custom CGI scripts and online forms tailored to your business, says Dave Murphy, president of Damar Group Ltd., a Web site host in Columbia, Maryland. "Otherwise," he warns, "you won't be able to design a site that really meets your needs."

○ *Can you handle the technology I'm using?* If your site software runs on Microsoft Internet Information Server under Windows NT, look for a host that supports that configuration. Asking this question early will narrow your choices quickly.

No matter where you are in the process, don't let anybody snow you, advises Silberman. Some third-party hosts take on more clients than their systems can handle. "Without good service and fast connections," he says, "you are dead in the water."

Creating An Online Presence

Creating an online presence is easier than creating an offline presence. Although the details and expense of selecting a Web host, designing and creating a site and keeping it up and current are significant, they pale compared to the complexities of establishing a physical storefront. The type of site with the most growth potential is an online store.

Setting Up A Store Site

When setting up a Web site to sell, the two most important factors to consider are organization and security. If your site will contain many pages, it's a good idea to draw an orgnizational chart of your entire site before you design it to ensure that all pages are linked to your home page (the first page of your site).

Study Web sites that sell products or services similar to yours. What do you like—and dislike—about them? How easy is

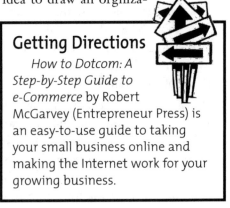

Getting Directions
How to Dotcom: A Step-by-Step Guide to e-Commerce by Robert McGarvey (Entrepreneur Press) is an easy-to-use guide to taking your small business online and making the Internet work for your growing business.

it to place an order? How fast does information download? Can you quickly find what you need?

The old adage that you only have one chance to make a good first impression is absolutely true on the Web. Companies selling their products or services must make sure that visitors can easily move around their Web site, that pages load as quickly as possible, and that there is an e-mail address or phone number for those with questions or comments. Once those pieces are in place, the second most impor- tant factor is security, especially if companies are going to conduct electronic credit card transac- tions over the Web.

Buying online is still a rela- tively new concept, and many potential buyers are concerned about security. They will not fur- nish credit card information unless they know that a site is safe from intruders. When they send electronic order forms, buyers don't want hackers grabbing their account numbers to do a little shopping of their own.

> Look for a program that comes with an assortment of templates. All you have to do is tweak them a little, and you're done.

To show your customers you're thinking about their welfare, you need to offer them choices. They should be able to call a toll-free number, send a check to your street address or fax you an order-form page that they printed from your site. You can also use special pro- grams to conduct online transactions safely.

Getting Outside Help

Designing a Web page used to require hours of laborious wrest- ling with html. But new Web-authoring tools are relatively easy to use. With many programs, building a Web site involves little more than pointing and clicking a mouse.

Visit your local software store or search online, and you'll find a multitude of Web-authoring programs. If you're a beginner, look for a program that comes with an assortment of templates. All you have to do is tweak them a little, and you're done.

Even though setting up a Web site is fairly easy, many busy busi- ness owners have other things to do with their time or simply prefer getting professional help. If that's the case, you have literally hun- dreds of companies to choose from. But these days, with everybody

Danger Ahead! There are more than a billion pages on the Web, so attracting visitors is a constant concern for both established and new Web sites. If you simply slap up a site and expect people to come, odds are you will be seriously disappointed.

and their uncles hanging out a shingle and calling themselves Web page designers, you have to be careful.

"There are people doing this as a business and people just having a good time," cautions Susan Estrada, author of *Connecting to the Internet*. "Select the ones doing it as a business, and make sure the group you are working with is stable."

Before selecting a company to do your site, take a look at other sites they have created. Make sure both graphics and text live up to your expectations. It's a good idea to sketch a rough outline of what you want, says Estrada, so you can find out if the developer can handle it.

Attracting Visitors To Your Site

Setting up a Web site is just the first step. The greatest Web site in the world does you no good if no one visits it. And attracting visitors is getting tougher by the day. With literally thousands of new Web sites created every day, the competition is tough. Here are some ideas for getting visitors to your site:

○ *Promote your Web site in all your marketing materials.* Put your Web site address on your business cards, brochures, letterhead, product packaging, promotional items, in your ads and anywhere else you can think of.

○ *Get listed with the major search engines.* InfoSeek, Excite, AltaVista, Yahoo!, HotBot and Lycos are the most popular search engines. Visit their Web sites for instructions on getting your site's address, or URL, listed with them. That way, when online users do a search for "tennis rackets," your sporting goods shop's Web site address will come up.

○ *In addition to the big-name search engines,* there are hundreds of smaller search engines on the Web. Search online for companies that will do the legwork involved in getting your business listed with these engines.

○ *Enroll in free link exchange programs.* These programs will display your company's banner on other sites if you make space for third-party banners on yours. Just as with search engines, there are many link exchange programs. Search online to find them.

○ *Set up links to related sites.* A "link" allows visitors to your site to click on a Web site address and instantly link to another company's site. Send e-mails to sites related to yours and ask if they would be interested in establishing mutual links. For example, a florist could put up a link to a local bridal shop's site and vice versa.

Holding Their Attention

It's one thing to get visitors to your site and another thing entirely to get them to come back. "A lot of companies just stick their information on the Web and then wonder why people aren't buying," says Rosalind Resnick, co-author of *The Internet Business Guide: Riding the Information Superhighway to Profit.* Here's her advice on setting up a site that tempts users to stay and return:

○ *Hit 'em hard.* Put all your company's key information, including your e-mail address and toll-free number, on the first screen. That way, potential customers won't have to wait until all your information loads to get an idea what your company is all about.

○ *Make connections.* If possible, hyperlink your e-mail address; this means visitors can simply click to open a blank e-mail message and send you a note.

○ *Have fun.* People who surf the Internet are looking for fun. You don't have to be wild and wacky (unless you want to). Just make sure you offer original content presented in an entertaining way.

○ *Don't overdose on graphics.* Since not everyone has high-speed modems, go easy on the art. If it takes too long to download, users will get antsy and go elsewhere.

Danger Ahead!

It's tempting to throw everything but the kitchen sink into a Web site. But you generally should not build a site more than three or four levels deep. Internet users get bored when they have to sift through loads of information to find what they're looking for.

○ *Add value.* Offering something useful customers can do adds tremendous value to your site. For example, customers can track their own packages at FedEx's site or concoct a recipe for a new drink at the Stolichnaya vodka site. You don't have to get quite that elaborate, but offering users the ability to download forms, play games or create something useful or fun will keep them coming back.

○ *Provide a map.* Use icons and button bars to create clear navigational paths. A well-designed site should have a button at the bottom of each subpage that transports the visitor back to the site's home page.

○ *Stage a contest.* Nothing is more compelling than giving something away for free. Have all contestants fill out a registration form so you can find out who's coming to your site.

Keeping It Fresh

Content is king on the Internet. It's essential to have your site packed with a supply of product information, industry news, how-to tips or whatever other information your customers are interested in. More important, that information must also be kept constantly updated. Make sure the Web designer you use is either willing to update your site for you or can show you how to do it yourself. After a Web surfer has visited your site more than a few times and found the same information as the previous visit, odds are good he or she won't come back again.

You can use visitor information collected by your Web site software or Web-hosting service to help you decide how often to update your information. If individual visitors are returning an average of once a week, for instance, you should add to or update your site *at least* once a week. The idea is to give them a reason to come back in hopes of seeing something new.

A Final Word

Before 1995, few people thought of the World Wide Web as a place to do business. However, in the years that followed, advising companies about e-commerce has developed into a distinct specialty. You will find a large number of site designers, programmers, Web site hosts, online marketing consultants, Internet business strategists and others who have spent years steeped in the ins and outs of Internet commerce. It's a good idea to tap into the hard-won expertise of these people before taking your site live or embarking on a major revision of an existing site. Here's how to get an outside opinion you can rely on:

Danger Ahead!
Resist the urge to blast out vast quantities of commercial e-mails to people who haven't asked to receive them. Spamming, which is the indiscriminate sending of messages to Usenet newsgroups, and junk e-mailing, which is sending unsolicited messages to multiple e-mail boxes, may get you some business, but it will just as surely earn you some enemies.

○ *Start by researching your market and deciding how the Internet fits into your business strategy.* Use that information to put down in writing what you want from the site.

○ *Identify several Web designers, programmers, consultants or other experts who fit your needs.* You can find them in the Yellow Pages under "Internet Consultants," "Internet Marketing and Advertising," "Web Site Designers" and the like. Call some of them, get to know more about them and check their references—this should be as simple as typing in URLs for sites they've worked on in the past.

○ *Now, ask a few of them for a bid to do the work or consulting you have in mind.* Companies can spend from a few hundred to a few million dollars developing a Web site. Specify carefully and concisely what you want and when it needs to be delivered.

○ *Take the best overall bid and specify schedule, results, payment terms and exit clauses in detail in writing.* Your Web site should benefit greatly from having an outside consultant advise you, especially if you've chosen wisely.

part three

After You
Arrive

Once you've put your plan into action,
now it's time to manage your business. And just as managing a
start-up is different from managing an established concern,
running a fast-expanding company is a lot different from overseeing a stable one. One of your biggest challenges is covered in
Chapter 22, on managing people, where you'll learn to delegate,
motivate, build teams and otherwise manage a work force geared

for growth. As you take on new challenges while growing your business, you unavoidably encounter new risks. Chapter 23 shows you how to control those risks with the help of insurance and other risk management tools.

Controlling your finances is key to sustaining growth. Chapter 24 will help you understand that; it will also help you manage your cash and other financial resources. Chapter 25 reveals the unfortunate fact that you'll encounter ever-increasing regulation as you grow. But it also demystifies many of the new licenses, permits and certificates you'll need to grow in accordance with applicable regulations.

You're not likely to grow much without having to travel at least occasionally. Chapter 26 shows you how to do business travel right, without spending a bundle or rendering yourself frazzled and jet-lagged. You probably didn't start your business because you love paperwork and bureaucracy. All the more reason to read Chapter 27, "Administering Growing Businesses," for advice on ways to limit paperwork and minimize administrative nuisances while enabling your business to grow to its maximum potential.

Time and tide wait for no business, but, as Chapter 28 on business cycles shows, you may be able to boost your growth rate by waiting for the right wave in the economic surf to launch your ship of growth. Chapter 29, "Time And Stress Management," discusses the potential psychological toll of trying to balance all the issues involved in growing a business.

One of the essential talents of entrepreneurs who enjoy strong growth is the ability to communicate. Chapter 30, on effective communications, tells what effective communication is, how to tell if you are doing it, and how to improve. Chapter 31 deals with the ever-present threat of competition by showing you how it can sometimes help instead of hurt you and how you can effectively deal with the rivalries you are likely to encounter as you grow. And once you've effectively mastered all the challenges and threats of business, there's still one more thing: What are you going to do with the rest of your life? That is the subject of Part 4.

chapter 22

Managing People

To many entrepreneurs running growing businesses, the proof of growth is an increasing personal workload. But the key to growing your company as big and as fast as you want may actually be this: getting good at not doing any work. Here's why: "It's impossible to grow a business without delegating. You can only increase your workload so much," says Ralph Rubio, co-founder and CEO of Rubio's Baja Grill, a $30 million restaurant chain based in San Diego that dominates the fish taco business on the West Coast.

"There's only so much time in a day," adds Don Dailey, partner in charge of PricewaterhouseCoopers' Middle Market Advisory Services for the Midwest region. "When you're encumbered with daily business issues, you're prevented from attending to the larger issues—business vision, customer relations, growth. That's a fatal error we see in many small businesses. Daily stuff has to be done—somebody has to sign the checks—but if you're doing that when you should be developing your next product or service, you're limiting your future growth."

How To Manage
In A Growing Company

It's easy to talk about delegation, but it's not easy to do. "Delegation is very hard to do right," says human resources consultant Susan Leeds. "Smart delegation takes thought and planning." That means delegation isn't simply sweeping your desk clean and blindly handing off all the tasks on your to-do list. "You need to approach delegation with a plan in mind," says Leeds, who teaches a multistep delegation process to clients. The first step is careful thought about what to delegate.

That's a crucial question, mainly because some tasks should be handled only by you. What can't you delegate? There's no rule of thumb; let your instincts guide you. You probably wouldn't delegate deciding what products your company will offer next year, but you might delegate conducting a customer survey regarding improvements they'd like to see in your products. Either way, a building block for effective delegation is knowing what tasks are yours and yours alone.

The next step in Leeds' plan is to determine the results you want to achieve. That doesn't mean telling employees to make some phone calls about past-due invoices. That's too vague. Be specific. A more defined goal might be to get customers with past-due bills to agree to a set payment schedule. Knowing the results you want is your job, not the job of employees to whom you delegate.

Step three is to decide which person is right for the task, says

Leeds. A salesperson might not be the right person to make collection calls, but perhaps your bookkeeper is. Either way, match skills and personality to the task—that will maximize productivity.

The fourth step is to decide what controls and checkpoints you'll put on the person to whom you're delegating. How often will the person report back to you? Under what circumstances should he or she shout for help? Be very specific about these details because that will make delegation work smoothly, both for you and employees.

Fifth, motivate the person to whom you're delegating. If you're handing off important work, you want your subordinate to be fired up to get results. "Link the new job to what motivates that employee," says Leeds. If the employee is there to learn, present the task as a development opportunity. If visibility is important to the employee, present it that way. "Make sure what you delegate is appropriate [for the employee]," Leeds says. And sell what you delegate—don't just hand out tasks.

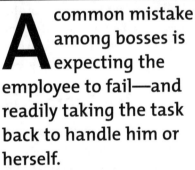

The last step is accountability. "Effective delegation means holding people accountable for the jobs that are assigned to them," Leeds says. A common mistake among bosses is expecting the employee to fail—and readily taking the task back to handle him or herself. Don't. That's a quick way to undermine employee effectiveness and guarantee employees will never develop in the ways you need them to if your business is to reach its potential.

A common mistake among bosses is expecting the employee to fail—and readily taking the task back to handle him or herself.

Provide Clear Goals

Perhaps the most important role of any manager is to provide employees with a clear understanding of what is expected of them at work. That's what Marcus Buckingham and Curt Coffman found when they analyzed surveys of more than 80,000 managers for the Gallup Organization and described the results in their bestselling book *First, Break All the Rules*.

Providing goals is not about telling employees how to do something, emphasize Buckingham and Coffman. Managers should define outcomes, such as sales goals and profit levels. But they should stop short of setting out procedures employees should follow to the letter. When a manager offers employees clear goals and gives them the responsibility and freedom to find their own ways, people respond much better than when being micromanaged every step of the way.

Provide The Tools They Need

Another critical management tip uncovered by the groundbreaking analysis of *First, Break All the Rules* is to provide employees with the materials and equipment required to accomplish goals. This means giving them training and providing them with the people, money and time to do the work you expect of them.

Giving people the tools they need to do the job may seem obvious. But it's not uncommon at all to find managers who assign employees more work than they can do, who strip away resources, including other employees, without changing goals, or who otherwise hamstring the efforts of the most diligent, well-motivated employee to do a good job. If you make sure you only ask people to do the tasks for which they are equipped, you'll be well on your way to becoming a good—or even great—manager.

Tell Them How They're Doing

Too often, managers treat employees like missiles that can be launched at a target and need to be checked only if the resulting explosion misses the target. In fact, employees need frequent positive reinforcement to let them know they are doing a good job, and to encourage them to keep it up.

Buckingham and Coffman zero in on a specific question employees ask themselves when deciding whether they are working for a great manager. That is "In the last seven days, have I received recognition or praise for my work?" In practical terms, this means you should let every employee know about something he or she has done well at least once a week. Recognition costs you nothing to dole out but can be an important tool in your management kit.

Motivating Employees

It's hard to overemphasize the importance of having enthusiastic, committed employees. A well-motivated work force will almost always allow a company to grow faster than one that is lackadaisical or even prone to sabotaging your growth initiatives.

Take This Job And Love It

"**A** CEO's number-one job is to create a mission statement that embraces the corporate culture," says Joseph Minces, president of The CEO Clubs, a New York City-based association of company heads. "Few of us think that's our main job; we are more attuned to sales, marketing or finance. But that is one job you never delegate to someone else."

Charles Hampden-Turner, author of *Creating Corporate Culture*, offers details. Culture, says Hampden-Turner, is a blend of the values, beliefs, taboos, symbols, rituals and myths all companies develop over time. The mission statement mentioned by Minces, for instance, is a vital part of corporate culture. A mission statement is a written document that defines a company's goals and, possibly, the means it will use to achieve those goals and its attitude toward customers and employees. Whether written as a mission statement, spoken or merely understood, culture describes and governs the ways a company's owners and employees think, feel and act.

Your culture may be based on beliefs spelled out in a mission statement. It could consist in part of a corporate symbol, like the rainbow-colored apple that symbolizes Apple Computer. Whatever shape it takes, your corporate culture plays a big role in determining how well your business will do.

You can start changing your culture now. Look for a symbol, story, ritual or other tool you could use to bring out the values and practices you want for your company. Your cultural tool might be a new corporate logo symbolizing your company's personality. Or you could choose a story to embody your approach and make it part of your culture. If you can't find a tool, make one. You can turn an admired former employee into a symbol by giving an award named after that individual, complete with ritual ceremony. Whatever you do, don't be too obvious. "It's best not to do it too overtly or self-consciously," advises Hampden-Turner. "[Culture isn't] necessarily talked about or run up the flagpole and saluted."

Giving Employee Evaluations

Everybody who works for you needs to know where they stand and how they are doing compared to your expectations of them. Many companies have formal review systems to let employees know how their performances stack up. Reviews may be conducted as often as every three months, but annual reviews are most popular.

Each review should go over the goals that were set when the employee started the job or during the last performance evaluation. Then the review should examine how well the employee has done toward reaching these goals. The employee should be asked to rate his or her performance, in addition to relying on objective measurements such as sales figures. You and the employee should then discuss the desirability of trying to reach goals that haven't yet been achieved, and you should both set goals for the future.

But reviews and evaluations are—often justifiably—viewed as little more than formalities that accomplish little or nothing in the way of true feedback. To make formal evaluations go more smoothly, and to eliminate any surprises on the employee's part, give feedback at the time something occurs to warrant it.

Giving Productive Feedback

Do not underestimate the power of feedback. It should be simple, honest and unfailingly constructive. Try to make sure that every piece of feedback you provide contains the following elements. It should:

○ Highlight something good the employee has accomplished.

○ Point out something that needs improvement.

○ Contain specific suggestions about how the employee can improve.

Don't neglect to say something positive. Even making note of the amount of effort the employee has expended can make the employee more receptive to feedback. If you can't think of a positive comment and specific suggestions for improvement, it's better to say nothing.

Inexpensive Perks And Benefits

Value is in the eye of the beholder, and many perks and benefits your employees will see as valuable need not cost you a ton of money—or any money at all. Using inexpensive perks effectively requires knowing your employees well. What one group of workers would perceive as a great work-related benefit might be seen by another bunch as a silly treat nobody uses.

Ask your employees what extras they would like to get as part of

Going To Pieces

When Jim Fall faced the task of building team spirit, explaining his company's mission statement, and helping break the ice before an important trade show, he went to pieces. To focus on the company's goals for the upcoming show, Fall asked the 50 employees of Manufacturing Data Systems Inc. (MDSI), an Ann Arbor, Michigan, factory automation software and services supplier, to assemble a 10-foot jigsaw puzzle. The puzzle's message, "Putting the Pieces of Manufacturing Together," not only unified employees from various parts of the country but revealed MDSI's marketing slogan for the trade show.

The 45-minute exercise challenged everyone and encouraged communication, Fall says. "It went very well," he reports. "Everybody got down on the floor and worked together. It really drove home what we were trying to do. Plus, we had fun."

Businesses smaller than MDSI and even larger than Microsoft are finding that puzzles and brain teasers are fun, effective tools for evaluating job applicants, creating camaraderie, and improving problem-solving and communication skills.

Mark Chester, owner of Rex Games Inc. in San Francisco, says his company has found a growing market for its Tangoes puzzles among trainers. Tangoes, a modern version of the ancient Chinese tangram puzzle, can be played by one or two people, or in teams. Combining artistic and mathematical elements, the puzzle enhances visual perception and helps develop problem-solving, creative thinking and teamwork skills.

Business interest in puzzles can be attributed to the increasing emphasis on teamwork, the switch to an information economy, and the growing need to come up with novel ways to engage employees' attention. Some claim doing puzzles simply makes employees smarter and happier. "Puzzles help develop visual, logical and strategic thinking," Chester says, "and they're entertaining."

being your employee, but don't stop there. One of the most powerful features a perk can have is being unexpected. If you can come up with a fringe benefit that employees love but had never thought of asking for, it will be much more powerful than if they get something to which they already feel entitled. So ask your employees what they would like, but be creative. Here are some inexpensive, offbeat perks that you can use to help employees feel they're special (and that working for your company is special, too).

○ *Free massages:* Hiring a masseuse to come in once a month and roam the cubicles dishing out free neck and back rubs is not something most employees would expect you to do for them. But companies that have done this report that it is widely appreciated and really makes employees feel they are cared about.

○ *Titles:* Few things convey recognition and appreciation as much as a promotion. And while making someone a vice president might cost you a raise, it's easy and cost-free to promote everyone to a nicer-sounding position, such as "associate" or "team member."

○ *On-site conveniences:* More and more businesses are keeping employees happy by providing services such as automotive oil changes, haircuts, manicures and dry cleaning pickup, and help purchasing movie tickets, making dinner reservations and the like.

○ *Humor:* Humor's ability to relieve tension, render points memorable and make work fun are unmatched. You can crack your own jokes, hire a local comic to come in for company meetings or simply encourage the company clown. Take care, however. Inappropriate humor can land you in hot water.

○ *Company apparel:* A T-shirt or cap emblazoned with the company logo advertises your business, encourages employees to identify with your company and provides them with the benefit of free clothing or accessories.

Danger Ahead!

Passing out promotions can be risky. If you promote some people, they may feel they are too good to get their hands dirty anymore. And if the promotion doesn't work out, it may be harder and more costly for you to fire a vice president. So promote carefully.

Wellness Programs

Having a healthier work force can reduce insurance costs while improving productivity. Also, with the emphasis today on fitness and healthy habits, people are glad to get some help in sticking to their resolutions to diet and exercise. There are a number of ways you can help employees with a corporate wellness program, including:

Getting Directions

How to Become an Employer of Choice (Oakhill Press) by Roger E. Herman and Joyce L. Gioia provides proven techniques for becoming an employee-centered company that attracts and retains the best workers at all levels.

○ *Health club memberships:* You can probably negotiate discounts or even barter an even swap for memberships for employees in local health clubs.

○ *Free screenings:* If you have more than a few dozen employees, local hospitals and health organizations will be happy to come out and screen your employees for high blood pressure, elevated cholesterol and other ailments.

○ *On-site health education:* Health-conscious employees will appreciate having a nurse or health counselor come in to give occasional lunchtime presentations on smoking cessation, good nutrition, managing stress, coping with alcohol abuse and other health-related topics.

Compensation Counts

Ask any human resources consultant where financial compensation ranks in the hierarchy of employee requirements, and you are likely to get a range of answers. Some say it's the most important thing. Others declare wages are the only important thing. Still others say that, while financial compensation isn't the most important thing, it's important enough that if your pay isn't fair, all the other employee benefits in the world may not be enough to keep employees on board.

Obviously, it's important to know whether you are paying enough and how to get the most for what you're paying. In addition, you have to know how to bolster the actual dollars you lay out in salary and wages with nonfinancial compensation.

Evaluating Your Compensation Package

You don't pay employees in a vacuum. That's another way of saying that the level of compensation that will attract and keep employees is set primarily by other employers. While there is no formula that will tell you the ideal salary for each position within your company, there are appropriate ranges. Some of the key sources for determining suitable salary ranges for your employees are:

○ Classified ad listings for specific positions, both in your daily newspaper and on the Internet

○ Professional and trade organizations for the specific fields in which you are hiring (most organizations regularly publish salary data)

○ Human resources consultants

○ Specialized recruiters in the appropriate fields

Awarding Raises And Bonuses

After the first flush of excitement from landing a new job or promotion fades, an employee is liable to look around and start noticing that other employees appear to be making more for doing the same job. Employees also experience increases in personal expenses as they start families or incur unpredictable costs due to illness or other misfortune. Finally, everybody wants to raise their standard of living periodically. This means you'll have to offer regular, significant raises and bonuses if you want to keep the best people.

Raises and bonuses are usually determined as a percentage of annual salary. Traditionally, the standard calculation for raises has been based on company performance combined with Consumer Price Index increases, which have averaged about 3 percent nationally in the past five years. However, in the current record-low unemployment environment, you may well have to offer more generous raises to remain competitive.

When deciding on the appropriate mix of salary increases and bonuses, much depends on your corporate philosophy and goals. A growing number of employers are in-

Getting Directions

For a bird's eye view of earnings of people in many different fields, look to the *Occupational Outlook Handbook*. This comprehensive, authoritative study is prepared every two years by the U.S. Bureau of Labor Statistics. It covers hundreds of different job titles, describing everything from duties and working conditions to training and earnings. You can view it online free of charge at http://stats.bls.gov/ocohome.htm.

Getting Directions

Recruiting firm Robert Half International offers several salary guides that contain data on average starting salaries in accounting, finance, law, administration and information systems. You can request a complimentary copy at www.rhii.com.

creasing the portion of compensation that's performance-based, such as bonuses. Through this approach, companies can more directly and immediately reward outstanding achievement. Many firms are basing bonuses on the performance of both the company and the employee to reward personal and team accomplishments. And while we are on the topic of incentives, companies of all sizes (including privately held ones) are increasingly offering stock options to their employees.

Nonfinancial Compensation

While no one can discount the importance of financial rewards, keep in mind that today's job candidates are more concerned with corporate environment and quality-of-life issues than ever before. In an executive survey conducted by Robert Half International, corporate culture rivaled employee benefits in importance for candidates during job interviews. Many small businesses use this trend as a competitive advantage, offering such perks as flexible work schedules, casual dress days, additional vacation time and telecommuting opportunities. The costs of this approach are minimal, particularly when compared to the value-added benefits of improved recruitment, productivity and retention.

Regardless of the monetary and nonmonetary ways you compensate your employees, creating an employee-friendly environment and determining competitive compensation ranges take time. Both require being flexible and adaptable to changing workplace trends and local conditions. The investment is worth it—the difference between a good company and a great company is its

Getting Directions

1001 Ways to Reward Employees (Workman) by Bob Nelson is a management specialist's encyclopedic survey of employee rewards. With more than 1,000 innovative ideas for rewarding employees, this book should give you plenty of inspiration on ways to offer rewards in any situation.

For What It's Worth

Few interactions pack more potential for disagreement than negotiating salaries. Too often, you'll find yourself trying to get the employee to accept less than he or she is worth. Meanwhile, the employee is dead set on getting a more generous salary package than can be objectively justified. This sort of win-lose mentality is exactly what's wrong with negotiating salaries.

Instead of taking the attitude that every penny the employee gets is coming out of your pocket, approach the discussion as if the objective were to decide exactly what that employee's market value is—and then pay them that. Information is the key to doing this. You have to know what similar employees are being paid for comparable work at companies like yours. That entails three things.

1. *Know your employee.* Understand and evaluate all your employee's skills, strengths, weaknesses and potentials.

2. *Know the job.* Assess exactly what is required in the position you are filling, as well as what positions may ultimately be filled by this employee. Evaluate what it's worth to you to have someone performing these duties at whatever level of effectiveness can be expected of this employee.

3. *Know what comparable employees are being paid.* This is the toughest one of all. This will require researching salary directories, talking to recruiters and personnel agencies, and perhaps even quizzing other business owners.

Once you know all this, you have to communicate it. This is where negotiations break down. Instead of a carefully reasoned, well-documented and honest presentation of your logic in arriving at the salary you propose, you may fall into negativity. You may bluff, threaten, shout or even pound the table and walk out. But these tactics can cause more harm by damaging your relationship with your employee than any benefit you might gain in salary savings.

If you feel your argument is weak or if you just can't seem to present it effectively, it may be time to give in to the employee's demands. Don't push a losing argument to the end. Nor is it a good idea to offer an employee half what you know he or she is worth, planning to compromise on a split-the-difference deal that will wind up about where you want to be. Play your cards straight in salary negotiation and, if things don't work out this time, there will always be another chance to negotiate.

people. (For more nonfinancial compensation tips, see the section in this chapter on "Inexpensive Perks And Benefits.")

Extinguishing Employee Burnout

When employees feel they are overworked and unappreciated over a long period of time, the result can be burnout. Burnout usually manifests itself as some combination of high absenteeism, high turnover and poor work quality, such as missed deadlines and increased rework. You may also suspect burnout if you detect a general feel of tension in the workplace.

The causes of burnout may be manifold. If overtime hours are excessive—say, 10 or more hours per week per employee on average—overwork could easily be the cause of burnout. If it's been a long time between raises, celebrations, extra days off or vacations, feeling unappreciated may be at the root of it. Sometimes the cause is poor morale, which itself may be caused by lack of direction (or frequent changes of direction) or a multitude of other factors, including poor training, inadequate equipment or unpleasant working conditions.

You can deal with overwork by adding full-time or part-time employees, hiring temporary workers, farming out jobs to independent contractors, postponing delivery dates, or simply turning down additional business. Paying employees more, increasing their compensation packages with fringe benefits, or giving them extra days off or vacations can boost motivation and relieve overwork. If your strategy is unclear to employees, clarify it. Improving your training, equipment and workplace environment can also help morale.

It's important to carefully think through your evaluation of a burnout problem as well as your response. Work, after all, is work, and few growing companies report that all employees

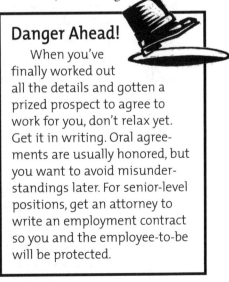

Danger Ahead!
When you've finally worked out all the details and gotten a prized prospect to agree to work for you, don't relax yet. Get it in writing. Oral agreements are usually honored, but you want to avoid misunderstandings later. For senior-level positions, get an attorney to write an employment contract so you and the employee-to-be will be protected.

arrive singing each morning. That's another way of saying that, in an efficient organization, a few cases of burnout are probably inevitable. Don't overreact to a handful of disgruntled employees by declaring companywide pay raises and time off. Carefully match your solution to the actual problem and you can keep everyone performing at near-peak levels while minimizing breakdowns.

Controlling Absenteeism

Everybody misses a day of work now and then. But it's a problem when an employee misses too many days of work. Not showing up for work can cause serious problems when other employees have to cover for the missing worker or, worse, the work simply doesn't get done. Here are keys to controlling absenteeism in your growing company:

O *Find out whether the absent employee missed work voluntarily or involuntarily.* Involuntarily means illness or another unavoidable reason—this is the kind of absenteeism you shouldn't concern yourself with as a manager, unless some kind of counseling or assistance could help the employee regain his or her health. Voluntary absenteeism is the kind you need to worry about. This occurs when an employee is absent without good reason. Get documentation—for example, a doctor's note—to ascertain whether an absence was involuntary or voluntary.

O *Decide whether the absenteeism is excessive.* Compare the employee's attendance record with other employees' records. If one employee's is way out of line, unless there are extenuating circumstances, that's probably excessive absenteeism.

O *Meet with the employee to explore the absences.* Keep your discussion friendly and oriented toward understanding and solving the problem, not placing blame and dispensing discipline.

○ *If things don't get better, explain the problem to the employee and request improved performance.* Employees may not know their absences are affecting others unless you tell them and ask them to improve.

○ *Put the problem in writing.* Make sure the employee and his or her personnel file get a copy of the written notice.

Most employees will straighten up and start coming to work regularly during this process. If they don't, however, you will be prepared to terminate them, if necessary, if you follow these guidelines.

Terminating Employees

The first rule about terminating employees is to do it thoughtfully. That rules out firing someone because you're experiencing a sudden burst of dissatisfaction, except if you caught them stealing or the two of you had a serious disagreement. Barring those situations, here are rules for terminating employees:

○ *If you have a termination policy in place at the time of the firing, follow it to the letter.* Rewriting termination policies to suit an individual case is not a good idea.

○ *Keep a paper trail documenting the employee's performance or other problems that motivate your concern.* Do this while you are pondering whether an employee should be dismissed, not after dismissing them.

○ *Don't give the impression, during hiring interviews or company picnics, that your firm offers lifetime employment.* That means, for instance, that you should avoid referring to your firm as a family. It is always better to say "We're a team." You can't get fired from your family, and you want to keep that option open.

○ *Keep it private.* A termination

Danger Ahead!

Given the popularity of ex-employees bringing wrongful termination lawsuits against former employers these days, it's tempting to inadvertently adopt a policy of never firing anyone. But failing to terminate an employee whose negligence, incompetence or malfeasance may harm other employees could be a bigger risk than being sued by a vengeful former employee.

Getting Directions

The Legal Information Institute of Cornell University maintains a large, free Web-based collection of information about all aspects of law, including a comprehensive selection of employment law resources. Learn more at www.law.cornell.edu/topics/employment.html.

notice should be delivered away from co-workers, perhaps even after hours or off-site. Many employers select Friday as firing day because terminated workers have the weekend to get over the shock.

○ *Be matter-of-fact.* Yelling, screaming, accusing, and recounting past mistakes have no place in a termination notice. Tell the employee things aren't working out and they're being let go.

○ *Accept that the employee may not understand.* Be ready to answer questions, listen to pleas and even accept some criticism for your decision. But don't argue and don't change your mind. If you have good enough reasons to get this far, you should follow through.

Legal Dos And Don'ts

Anytime you let an employee go, you risk running afoul of legal protections afforded to employees to prevent workplace discrimination. Some of these protections may surprise you. You can't, for instance, fire someone solely because of substance abuse. That is a disability under federal law, and it's not grounds for firing without additional justification. And, of course, you can't terminate anyone because of their gender, race, color, religious beliefs, national origin, age or disabilities.

In addition to federal protections, states and many local jurisdictions have laws protecting employees from being fired under a wide range of conditions. Some state laws simply echo federal protections while others cover companies that, because of their small size or other special status, are specifically exempt from federal protections. State laws may cover some new areas as well. For instance, discrimination based on sexual orientation and personal appearance is not prohibited under federal law but may be in the states where you have employees. To learn about employment laws in your state, contact your state Department of Labor.

Noncompete Clauses

Noncompete agreements are contracts between you and your employees in which your employees promise not to take what they learn while working for you and use it against you while working for a competitor. A typical noncompete agreement says the employee agrees not to work for rivals, solicit business from current clients, or otherwise compete with you for some period of time, such as a year, after leaving your company.

Some companies have all employees sign the same noncompete agreement when they join. But this is probably not the best way to do it. General agreements signed by all employees tend not to hold up in court. So it's better to write noncompete agreements only for key employees. And make them specific.

You should also take care to know the laws regarding noncompete agreements in any state in which you do business. California and Texas state laws tend not to support employers in disputes involving noncompete agreements.

Don't keep your noncompete agreements secret. Let employees know the company's policy. Let competitors know it, too, so they won't be tempted to raid your employees. A company that hires a rival's employee in violation of a noncompete agreement may be faced with a lawsuit. Finally, when employees are leaving the company, remind them of the noncompete agreement they signed and go over it with them to make sure they realize what restrictions they may have to observe.

Handling Unemployment Claims

Unemployment insurance helps workers who have been terminated by tiding them over financially for a limited time while they search for another job. For employers, unemployment insurance is primarily a paperwork headache. Tax rates for employers with good records of avoiding layoffs vary by state but are as low as a fraction of a percent of total payroll. For employers who have large numbers of former workers filing claims for unemployment insurance, however, unemployment taxes can be a significant financial burden. Here are three ways to minimize unemployment claim impact:

1. *Understand the laws in your state.* The agency that collects the tax

can provide you with details of the regulations. Know what kinds of layoffs or terminations can trigger unemployment claims, and avoid them whenever possible.

2. *Protest questionable unemployment insurance claims.* Don't allow employees to file unjustifiable claims against you. It can take time and effort to contest questionable claims, but it's worth it in the long run. Your state unemployment benefits administration agency will let you know when someone has filed for benefits and ask for your input. Provide it.

3. *Keep careful records of your tax payments and any charges against your unemployment insurance account by former employees.* Errors have been known to be made. If one is made, protest it and document it. File your tax payments on time to bolster your position as a dutiful corporate citizen.

Severance Pay

Severance pay can be a good investment. That may sound untrue, given that it involves paying money to someone who does not work for you anymore. But when you offer severance benefits, it lets all your employees know that, even if the worst happens, you have some level of regard for them and will not leave them high and dry. It is also a good advertisement for anyone who may be thinking of joining your company.

Severance pay does not have to come in dollar denominations. Sometimes, other benefits may be worth more to a former employee. You may be able to provide paid outplacement counseling or training for a new skill. In some cases, simply allowing the employee to keep a desk at your company for a month or two while he or she searches for a new job may be worth more than a sizable sum of money. Be creative in offering and negotiating severance pay. It can be a good investment.

Danger Ahead!

You are not the only employer who may use noncompete agreements. Be careful any time you are hiring someone away from a competitor. Check to see if the recruit has signed a noncompete agreement, and, if he or she has, obtain legal advice before hiring.

Exit Interviews

Exit interviews are prime opportunities to figure out why someone is leaving your organization. (If you are firing someone, of course, you don't need to know why they are leaving, so exit interviews aren't necessary in this case.) Effective exit interviews can help improve your bottom line by reducing turnover and the associated costs of hiring and training new employees. Bear in mind, too, that nobody will be likely to speak more candidly and knowledgeably about you and your company's failings than an employee who knows what is going on and has nothing to lose by talking. You may get some important tips about the problems and issues that are causing your employees to leave.

> **Viewpoint**
>
> When you ask why someone is leaving, expect to hear one of the following two explanations: Someone offered them a better job, or they have a complaint about your company that hasn't been addressed. The second reason should be of more interest to you because you can do something about it.

To help you prepare for the exit interview, give people who are resigning a questionnaire to be completed before their final day on the job. You can also give a form to ex-employees on their way out and ask them to complete and mail it back. Finally, have a face-to-face or telephone meeting the final day. Ask:

○ What was your favorite part about being an employee here?

○ What was your least favorite part about being an employee here?

○ Have you had complaints? Were they handled fairly?

○ Do you feel you had a clear career path here?

○ What could we do better?

○ What, if anything, would convince you to continue here?

When you have had a few people quit, analyze the results of your exit interviews. Try to figure out trends, such as the main reasons they give for leaving, the typical length of time a person works for you before quitting, the type of jobs that have the most turnover, and patterns of resignation in departments or groups associated with particular managers. The idea is to identify changes you can make to keep people from leaving. So the most important advice of all about exit interviews is to make sure you are really listening and that you will actually do something, including making changes in your company, with the insight you gain.

Employee Training Programs

Employee training is a necessity. You need to get new hires up to speed as quickly as possible so they can become productive members of your team. And you want to update the skills of existing employees so they'll be ready for you to implement new technology, develop new processes and acquire new markets.

> **You need to get new hires up to speed as quickly as possible so they can become productive members of your team.**

You may be able to do much of the training yourself—at significant cost in time, of course. Your more experienced employees are also good sources of training, either on the job or in more formal, off-site sessions held in lunchrooms or classrooms. You can save time—but not money—if you hire third-party trainers to conduct classroom sessions. Inexpensive, easily repeated training can be found in video-based courses, computer-assisted instruction, and Web-based training.

Whatever training mode you go with, here are keys to developing a good training strategy:

○ *Start by asking yourself what you want your people to learn.* Be as specific as possible. ("I want my evening shift workers to be able to use Microsoft Excel to update the day's sales figures.")

○ *Assess your employees' current skill levels.* Evaluate the gap between where you want to be and where you are.

○ *Select one of the training modes described above, based on your time and financial budget.* Don't forget to budget for downtime and lost production while class is in session.

○ *Decide who knows the topic best*—you, your veteran employees or a third-party trainer.

○ *Design a training program that calls for imparting information to trainees,* gives them time to absorb and try out their lessons, provides expert feedback, and gives them a chance to be creative.

Don't forget to make the training enjoyable—even fun. And if you get stuck on what to do about any of these training issues, ask the trainees. Your employees may know more than you give them credit for.

How To Increase Productivity

Since the beginning of time, managers have tried to get more work out of employees and increased productivity from machines and other resources. Everything from time-and-motion studies to complicated piece-rate compensation schemes has been tried, with mixed results. However, some ideas almost always work to improve employee productivity, no matter what industry you are in or what size company you run. Here are some tried-and-true productivity boosters:

○ *Involve employees in making company decisions.* Your workers will appreciate being consulted and listened to when decisions are being made. But more than that, their advice should be sought out because it's likely to be the best available. After all, who know more about how to do the work better? Much of the time, it's the people doing the work.

○ *Provide employees with information.* Informing employees means more than telling them what to do. You need to explain the company's overall strategy and goals, and how each worker's role fits into that overall plan. That may include providing financial information you feel is sensitive, but many studies have shown that the more workers know about what's going on, where things are headed, and what effect his or her efforts have on the organization, the more effective and productive they are.

○ *Provide training in decision-making.* Everybody can make decisions, but not everybody

> **Viewpoint**
>
> Sharing power is not most entre-preneurs' strong suit. After all, many people start their own companies because they want to run the show. It can be difficult for them to accept the fact that if they want to run a real growth race, they're going to have to share the reins. Be aware that you're likely to feel conflicted about empowering employees, and be ready to deal with it.

can make good decisions. Training employees in basic decision-making skills, such as gathering information and evaluating alternatives, can pay off in long-term productivity increases as employees make fewer mistakes.

A work force that assists in making decisions and is well-informed and skilled in decision-making is an ideal work force. If you provide your business with such a labor pool, you can be sure that your growth won't be constrained by low employee productivity.

Updating Your Employee Policy Manual

As companies grow, they encounter issues that smaller firms don't. For instance, many employment laws, such as the federal Family Medical Leave Act, apply only to firms of a certain size or larger. As you grow, your employee policy manual has to grow with you. Simply knowing what's right isn't enough. When the majority of—or even all—employee supervision was handled by you or one or two trusted colleagues, maybe you could survive on faith in them and them in you. But as your company grows, you will hire new employees and new supervisors, and that means you'll need to commit to writing exactly how employees ought to be treated and the behaviors your company will not tolerate.

Laws concerning sexual harassment are steadily evolving, and your policies on harassment in the workplace need to keep pace. For example, one recent ruling says that a company without a strong anti-harassment policy is likely to be held liable if one of its supervisors commits sexual harassment against an employee.

In general, anti-discrimination employment legislation is expanding to cover a larger group of employees. Along with gender, race, color, religious beliefs, national origin, age and disability, some jurisdictions protect employees who are discriminated against on the basis of

Danger Ahead!
Don't trust your instincts when writing an employee policy manual. What you think is right may not be proper under the law. Check with a qualified legal advisor before drawing up or revising your employee policy manual.

appearance or sexual orientation. Your employees may be protected from any retaliation by you because they reported you for violating a law or regulation. Take note of federal, state and local laws regarding discrimination, and make sure their intent is clearly reflected in your employee policy manual.

Smoking Policy

Many workplaces these days are smoke-free. If you wish to ban smoking at your company, you can probably successfully do so. If you do, make sure the policy is written down and contains the following elements:

○ *Explain the reason for the policy.* Health risks to smokers and those exposed to secondhand smoke, effects on absenteeism and productivity, and risks of fire are commonly cited.

○ *Explain the parameters of the ban.* This may be a simple blanket ban on all smoking on and in all company property, including company vehicles. Less restrictive policies might ban smoking in enclosed areas. You should also explain any exemptions, such as special smoking areas in company lunchrooms.

○ *Explain how the policy will be implemented and who is responsible for overseeing it.* This should also state how information about the policy will be disseminated to the work force. For instance, you might place posters announcing the policy on bulletin boards, in a company newsletter and in the employee manual.

○ *Offer and describe assistance you will provide to smokers who want to quit or are having trouble adjusting to the policy.* Smoking is not an easy habit to control, and recognizing this fact will give your policy a friendly face and increase your chances for a successful implementation.

Drug-Free Workplace Policy

Few companies tolerate substance abuse or the presence of illegal drugs in the workplace for good reason. Drug abuse destroys employees' lives and livelihood, harms families, and erodes workplace productivity. You can demonstrate your attitude toward drugs in the workplace with the help of a drug-free workplace policy. Here are keys:

○ *Explain the motivation for the policy.* Serious legal, health and safety risks are associated with the presence of drugs in the workplace.

○ *Explain what you mean by drug-free workplace.* You may simply state that it is a violation of company policy for employees to possess illegal drugs on the job, to report to work under the influence of illegal drugs, or to use prescription drugs in an illegal manner.

○ *Let people know what consequences of misbehavior are.* Typically, this includes disciplinary action up to and including termination for violating the policy.

○ *Encourage employees who may be involved with illegal drug use to seek help.* Offer to assist them whenever possible.

> ## Getting Directions
>
> The Institute for a Drug-Free Workplace is a nonprofit association that provides information, education and advocacy for companies concerned about controlling illicit drug use at work. Learn about drug-testing laws, read model employer guides and more at www.drugfreework place.org, or call (202) 842-7400.

Workplace Violence Policy

Each year, 912 Americans die as a result of violence on the job, and the toll is rising. "Workplace homicide is the fastest-growing form of murder," reports Bruce Blythe, president of Crisis Management International in Atlanta.

"No business is immune," warns Joseph Kinney, executive director of the National Safe Workplace Institute, a nonprofit organization in Chicago that promotes safe and healthy workplaces. "It happens in big businesses and in small ones. The more it happens, the more we ask 'Could it happen to us?'"

Many instances of workplace violence are traced to mental illness and are difficult to predict. However, evidence indicates that your management style can help reduce the chances that it could happen at your company. The key appears to be to treat employees like people and not to rule over them as if they were robots.

"What I have consistently found in workplaces that have suffered homicides is an authoritarian style of management—management by intimidation," says Thomas Harpley, clinical director of National Trauma Services, a San Diego consulting business that specializes in preventing and coping with workplace violence.

Many cases of violence are related to high stress levels at work. "The three chief workplace stressors are lack of control (not being able to pace yourself or make any decisions), uncertainty with respect to job stability and the future, and conflict between the worker and what's expected of him or between him and other people," adds management consultant Frank J. Landy.

So one proven way to ease workplace tensions is to treat your employees as humanely as possible. Says Harpley, "A more sensitive approach to employees as people may well defuse some workplace violence."

Disciplining Employees

There are two main schools of thought on disciplining employees. One says you should follow a series of steps where employees are exposed to increasingly severe penalties for failure to perform as expected. This may start with a verbal warning and end in dismissal. The other school of thought says you should not follow progressive discipline because it limits your ability to move quickly to solve a problem. Probably the best way to discipline employees is to do it on a case-by-case basis, but as you grow larger and have to implement standard policies for taking disciplinary action, you may lose some flexibility. To help provide consistency and effectiveness, follow this three-step process for disciplining employees:

1. *Act immediately.* Justice delayed is justice denied, according to this approach. This means you should see that disciplinary action follows as closely as possible the infraction that calls for it.

2. *Issue a warning first.* Tell employees what the consequences are the first time they break the rules. The next time it happens, follow through with actual disciplinary action.

3. *Be consistent and do not play favorites.* Justice should be blind.

A middle-ground approach is to be consistent by always addressing the behavior that's causing the problem and not attacking the employee. Try to make the punishment fit the

Fast Lane

Want a quick way to save on workers' compensation insurance premiums? Some companies offer a 5 percent discount for simply having a written policy prohibiting drugs in the workplace. It's a cheap trick to save big. Ask your workers' compensation provider for details.

crime, too. In other words, don't fire someone for parking in the wrong spot while ignoring much more serious infractions.

Dealing With Problem Employees

Employees may show up late and leave early, do incomplete or shoddy work, or work long hours and do a top-notch job but something about their attitude just rubs you the wrong way. There is no doubt that problem employees exist, but sometimes it's hard to tell exactly why they are problems. Is it because they have a different style than yours? Perhaps your values are different? Do your goals go in different directions? Maybe they are jealous of your success—or vice versa? Sometimes people just don't like each other, and the reason isn't very clear. However, that doesn't mean you can't still work together.

Since it's easier to control yourself than to control others, the first thing to do when facing a problem employee is to examine your own reactions to the person and the feelings behind them. Try to distance yourself from the problem-causing situation and ask yourself why it bothers you. Try to see things from the employee's perspective—there may be something about the way you are dealing with the person that practically guarantees an aggressive response. Whatever you do, don't respond emotionally to a problem employee. Angry tirades aren't successful with anyone.

It can help to understand the different types of problem employees, including:

○ *Some people can't or won't communicate with you.* Give these people plenty of time to answer questions, and be patient.

○ *Others won't listen.* Give these people summaries, and, if necessary, put it in writing.

○ *Some personalities try to dominate every situation.* Understand that this behavior is frequently rooted in low self-esteem. Stay cool and you'll stay in control.

○ *Others can't relate to anyone else's feelings or interests.* Tell these people clearly what you expect and how it will be monitored. If they still can't do what you ask, let them know that a reassignment may be forthcoming.

○ *Know-it-alls are yet another type of problem employee you are likely to encounter.* Direct such employees into areas such as technical support, where their specialized knowledge will be an attribute.

Investigating Complaints

Sooner or later, as your business grows, you're going to get complaints from employees about how they have been treated. This can be unsettling since you're trying to build a well-oiled machine and now you find out there's rust in the gears. But look at it this way: Complaints from employees can help you identify a problem before it becomes a catastrophe. Here are dos and don'ts for investigating complaints to find out what is going on before you decide how to deal with it:

○ *Do* follow set procedures that are outlined in your policy manual, employment contract or collective bargaining agreement.

○ *Don't* be adversarial.

○ *Do* see that the complaining employee has a chance to tell the whole story. Listen without interrupting until you've heard everything.

○ *Do* make sure you get the whole story. Ask employees to detail the exact nature of the complaint. Ask them to state the precise remedy they are seeking.

○ *Do* conduct additional research to find out about the background of the grievance. Study any previous cases that resemble this one and what happened.

○ *Don't* treat any grievance as if it were inconsequential. Take it seriously and your employee will take you seriously.

Viewpoint

Whenever you are dealing with an employee grievance or disciplinary action, keep an accurate, detailed record of any investigation and action taken. This should include any relevant payroll or attendance records, evidence presented, and names of witnesses or other people involved.

Dealing With Unions

Labor unions exist to help employees, not employers, so it's hard to believe much good can come from having to deal with one. However, if your industry or your company is already unionized, there may be little you can do to avoid it. If you are in a unionized environment, virtually all interaction you have with your employees

Big Brother Meets e-Mail

As an employer, you have the legal right to monitor and regulate the way employees use your company equipment and resources, including e-mail and Internet access. There is also plenty of technology available that will let you do this. Typically, copies of all e-mail emanating from your company will be saved somewhere such as in an electronic mail server or on the employee's own computer, often in multiple copies. This allows you to see not only who your employees are communicating with but what they are saying.

For tracking Internet usage, Sequel Technology in Bellevue, Washington, sells a product called Internet Resource Manager that follows and records all Internet sites visited by people using company computers. Sequel says its software helps companies boost employee productivity, make the most of technology investments and avoid lawsuits. The company notes that its products are intended to monitor only destinations, not content of e-mail, chat and other messages.

This issue is controversial, however. Some employees feel that it's nobody's business whether and how they use a company computer to send e-mail or surf the Web. In a similar vein, some employees feel they should be able to make personal copies on the company photocopier and make personal long-distance calls on the company's account. Some firms overlook these activities with the idea that employees will appreciate the gesture. Others feel the costs should be controlled, if not eliminated. Another consideration is that employees may be engaging in inappropriate or even illegal activities, such as distributing child pornography or illegitimate copies of copyrighted software.

If you plan to monitor and control the way your employees use the Internet, document your policy in your employee manual. The policy should explain what you are doing, why you are doing it and what you intend to do with the information. It should define what is and is not acceptable e-mail and Internet usage. Finally, it should explain the penalties for failing to comply. You can see a sample copy of a company Internet and e-mail usage policy at Sequel Technology's Web site at www.sequel tech.com.

is governed by a collective bargaining agreement. Take care to abide by the requirements of this agreement, as employers have often fared poorly when pitted against labor unions in legal disputes.

If you are not already unionized, chances are you will not have to deal with a union at all. Unionization has been declining for decades. Today, with many of the safety and compensation issues unions were built to remedy being taken care of by government regulation, unions have less appeal to many workers. If you take good care of your workers, pay them fairly and listen to their complaints, you should have little to fear from union organizers. If you are facing a union organization effort, consult an experienced labor attorney or other specialist. The unionization of a nonunion work force, along with the likelihood of restrictive job descriptions and other productivity-damaging rules, can have a serious impact on your company's competitiveness and prospects for growth.

chapter

Risk
Management

There are such things as good luck and bad luck, and it's probably a mistake to think we can have complete control over what happens to us or our businesses. But there are ways to manage the risks faced by growing firms. Risk management is the practice of making as large as possible the areas over which we have some control, while minimizing the areas where we have no control. For instance, you manage risk by wearing a seat belt while riding in an automobile—you enlarge the area where you can influence the outcome of a potentially dangerous crash by using safety equipment. Growing companies manage risk similarly, but instead of wearing seat belts they purchase insurance, implement safety training programs, work to stop theft, and take other recognizable risk management actions. Managing risk is an important part of growing your company.

Measuring Your Risk Exposure

As your firm grows, so does your exposure to risk. There's no escape from this. The more equipment and facilities your business owns, the better the chance that one of them will be damaged by fire, storm or other phenomenon. The more products and services you provide, the greater your exposure to lawsuits from customers or others who claim to have been injured by them. And the greater the value of your inventory, fixtures and cash on hand, the more attractive you are to thieves. You could avoid increasing your exposure to risk by simply not growing. But it makes more sense to manage risk so you can grow without being sunk by a disaster. Managing risk starts with measuring your risk exposure, finding ways to reduce and control risk and obtaining insurance or other protection against unforeseeable loss.

Your three major risks are loss, damage and liability. You could lose assets to a disaster, have goods damaged in shipment, and be found liable for damages resulting from an employee's accident while driving a company car, for example. Of course, there are many other risks lurking under these three umbrellas. Loss of cash due to theft from the till, damage resulting from a supplier's machine, and liability from a classic slip-and-fall accident are also risks you may face.

Liability is a constant risk. Your business could be held accountable if someone is injured or suffers damages to their property because of something your business did—or failed to do. You and your employees also risk medical bills and lost wages due to injuries on the job and job-related illnesses. Vehicles may incur damage and liability claims from other drivers. Crime is another consideration. Theft, burglary, robbery and embezzlement by employees are additional risks.

Reducing And Controlling Risk

You can't eliminate risk, although you can—with the help of insurance policies—limit its impact on your business. But insurance isn't the only answer. You can and should control your exposure to risk by instituting programs to minimize it. Among the things you can do to control risk are to battle theft and other crime.

Controlling Employee Theft

You probably feel you can trust your employees. But that doesn't mean you shouldn't routinely take steps to make sure you can trust them. Putting systems in place to control loss due to employee theft isn't a matter of mistrust—it's just good business.

Screening applicants, including doing background checks, is a starting point for controlling employee theft. You should also closely track valuables, including cash and inventory. For example, know what your average sales are by shift and watch for variances that could indicate theft. You can also use surveillance cameras and even undercover investigators if you suspect theft is occurring.

Controlling Customer Theft

Shoplifting and other theft from stores and other businesses costs many billions of dollars annually. How much? Some retail stores lose 5 percent of their inventory to shrinkage, including shoplifting, an amount that often makes the difference between staying in business and failing. Businesses control customer theft in a variety of ways. Stores may have plain-clothes detectives roaming the floor to catch shoplifters in the act. The use of mirrors and video security cameras is widespread, as are electronic tags that set off alarms if they are removed from the store (on the products they are attached to) without being

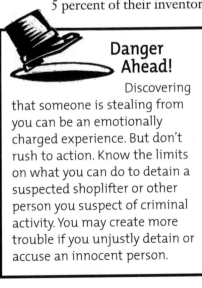

Danger Ahead!

Discovering that someone is stealing from you can be an emotionally charged experience. But don't rush to action. Know the limits on what you can do to detain a suspected shoplifter or other person you suspect of criminal activity. You may create more trouble if you unjustly detain or accuse an innocent person.

deactivated by a cashier. Locking up expensive items, tools, cash and other valuables is nearly universal.

One of the most appealing forms of customer theft prevention essentially allows you to kill two birds with one stone. You can improve your relations with customers and reduce customer theft by improving your customer service. Customers who are being actively attended to don't find the opportunity to steal. And in the vast majority of cases when they have no interest in stealing anyway, they will appreciate the extra attention.

Controlling Computerized Theft

Computer crime can be difficult to prosecute because computer criminals usually work by themselves and don't leave much physical evidence. Prevention, therefore, is the key to control. Surprisingly, technology is less important than low-tech business practices when it comes to controlling computer crime. You need to physically lock up computers, password lists, diskettes and other items that may facilitate computer crime. You need to be careful who you hire because most computer crimes are inside jobs. You need to monitor employees' use of computer systems and let them know you're monitoring them. If they think no one is looking, they're more likely to steal.

Protecting Proprietary Information

As is the case with computer crime, protecting your trade secrets and other proprietary information is largely a matter of common sense. The first thing to do is identify your trade secrets. These are any information you use to operate your business that you consider valuable enough—and secret enough—to give you an edge over your competition. Trade secrets can be product designs, customer lists, sales forecasts and many other types of data.

Once you have conducted an audit of your trade secrets, you need to set up policies to protect them. These can consist of the following:

Viewpoint

A computer crime is a deliberate act that requires knowledge of how a specific computer works and deprives the rightful owner of a benefit. Computer crimes range from vandalizing computer systems to writing programs that deposit small parts of a large number of employee paychecks into the criminal's bank account.

○ *Make sure everyone who sees your secret information is aware that it's secret.* Notify partners, customers, suppliers and employees exposed to proprietary secrets that the material is confidential. Get them to agree not to use it against you or to disclose it to anyone without your written permission. Get this in writing; have them sign these nondisclosure agreements. Stamp documents "Confidential."

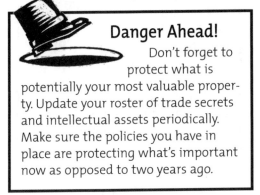

Danger Ahead!

Don't forget to protect what is potentially your most valuable property. Update your roster of trade secrets and intellectual assets periodically. Make sure the policies you have in place are protecting what's important now as opposed to two years ago.

○ *Enforce physical security.* Put up some "No Trespassing" signs, erect fences, lock entrances and exits, and hire security guards. Lock your secrets up.

○ *Use employee and visitor identification badges to control access to your business.* Establish rules requiring people to sign sensitive documents in and out.

○ *Set up passwords.* Use them to access computers, copiers, fax machines and other machines that could be used to copy or transmit secrets.

○ *When employees leave, take measures to ensure that secrets don't leave with them.* Collect sensitive materials from the offices of terminated employees before allowing them to return to their desks. And before they go, remind them of the nondisclosure documents they signed.

General Crime Prevention

According to experts on crime prevention, for a crime to occur, three elements have to be present: ability, motivation and opportunity. Eliminate any one of these, and the crime will not occur. Here's how:

○ Be wary of people who don't appear to belong in or around your business. Ask them questions. If their answers are vague, unconvincing or suspicious, call the police.

○ Encourage employees to keep their personal possessions in sight at all times. Don't leave purses or briefcases unattended in public areas or unlocked offices anywhere. It only takes a matter of seconds for things to disappear.

○ Instruct everyone to lock office doors when they step out, even for just a minute.

○ Install deadbolt locks on external doors. Burglars typically spend no more than a few minutes or even seconds attempting to break into a building. Sturdy, properly installed deadbolt locks on all external doors are a must.

Getting Directions

One of the most effective things you can do to fight crime around your business is to band together with neighboring business owners. Contact your local police department to find out how to form a crime watch organization.

○ Have a trustworthy locksmith rekey locks on all new facilities as soon as you move into them.

○ Install outdoor floodlights to eliminate dark areas where criminals might hide. Make sure parking areas are well-lit.

○ Never leave the keys in company cars or other vehicles. Have a sign-in board where they can be picked up by authorized employees. Also, never leave car doors unlocked.

○ Join business community groups that have the mission of fighting crime. When companies join together to fight crime, they can make a significant difference.

Giving Your Business An Insurance Checkup

It's safe to say that among the 20 million or so businesses in the United States, none of them share the same list of property and possessions. However, the following is a list of the common business assets you should consider protecting against damage and loss:

○ Automobiles, trucks, construction equipment and other mobile property

○ Buildings you own or lease

○ Cash and securities

○ Computer equipment and media, such as diskettes and tapes

○ Furniture, equipment and supplies

○ Improvements to the premises

○ Intangibles such as trademarks and good will

○ Inventory

○ Leased equipment

○ Machinery

○ Outdoor property not attached to a building, such as signs and fences

○ Records and papers, including accounts receivable, books and other documents

After deciding what to insure, the next question is how much to insure it for. There are a few common ways of setting the insurable value of your business assets.

○ *Actual cash value* means the cost of replacing the property. This value is figured including depreciation. That means if your computer cost $2,000 two years ago, it could have already depreciated 50 percent. So if it's lost in a fire, you would get $1,000.

○ *Agreed amount* is typically used to insure unique items such as antiques and art. You agree on the amount the objects will be insured for when you're writing the policy. You'll usually need an appraisal to set the value.

○ *Replacement coverage* is the same as actual cash value, not including depreciation. If you lose your $2,000 computer after two years, replacement coverage would pay you enough to buy a similar machine, whatever that might cost today.

You can get some additional types of insurance policies, such as inflation protection coverage, which will automatically increase the amount of insurance that you are carrying to guard against rising costs.

Updating Your Coverage

Just because you had adequate coverage last month doesn't mean you have adequate coverage today. For instance, your coverage needs may change depending on the season. If you are a retailer whose inventory expands dramatically during the pre-holiday period, you will probably need a policy to reflect that. Similarly, you need to update your coverage before or after you expand significantly. Your coverage may also need to change to reflect a shift in your customers. For instance, if you have been conducting largely business-to-business sales and are moving into consumer marketing, you may need a higher liability limit.

Business policies usually have the flexibility to meet changes in your needs. When you're talking over coverage with your agent, be sure to discuss any change your business is expecting. Your business isn't a static, unchanging entity, and neither should your coverage be.

Basic Types Of Insurance

Business insurance comes in two main varieties: property and liability. Property insurance protects against damage or loss of property. Liability insurance covers the cost of defending and, if necessary, settling lawsuits for damages caused by you, your employees or your company property.

Many small-business owners are covered by a package policy called a business owner's policy (BOP). You can probably save money and get more complete coverage from a BOP than if you bought separate policies for each type of coverage you need. BOPs cover a range of losses, such as loss of business income, and liability, including business and personal liability.

Since all businesses require different coverage, BOPs have built-in flexibility to allow them to be suitable for almost everyone. Restaurants, for example, have special insurance needs that other businesses don't have. (In a restaurant, as opposed to any other kind of business, the risk of fire is greater.) You can get additional coverage under a BOP depending on the type of business you have. You may also need additional coverage for special property, heightened liability risk, dangerous conditions, or other conditions that are normally excluded from BOPs. For instance, you may require flood protection and have to purchase it as an amendment to a standard policy or as a separate policy.

Viewpoint

As you grow into a larger business, you can choose to purchase a commercial package policy (CPP). These policies are available in special configurations for different types of firms, such as manufacturers, retailers, hotels and so forth. CCPs are more flexible and offer larger amounts of coverage than business owner's policies.

Advanced Coverage

As your business grows, you may find you need coverage beyond the BOP, plus any other policies, you started out with. One example is key-man coverage to protect you against the loss of an employee who is important to your business' success. Here are some others:

○ *Builder's risk* insurance covers against loss due to damage to a building during the course of its construction.

○ *Business-interruption* insurance reimburses you for earnings lost due to damage to—or loss of—property. You can include costs such as salaries, taxes and rents in the coverage.

○ *Commercial crime* coverage covers cash, stock, securities and fixtures against theft, burglary and robbery. Coverage includes losses on or off your premises and through the agency of employees or nonemployees.

○ *Debris removal* coverage pays to remove debris after damage such as a fire. This usually must be added as an amendment to a fire insurance policy.

> ## Viewpoint
> Various types of life insurance can be designed to protect your company. Key-man insurance pays the company upon the death of a key person, usually an owner or senior executive, to help the company deal financially with the loss and replace those services.

○ *Equipment breakdown* or mechanical breakdown coverage protects against accidental failure of machines and equipment such as computers, phone systems, boilers and the like. It may include coverage for losses due to business interruption as well as actual property damage.

○ *Fidelity bonds*, also known as honesty insurance, protect you from losses resulting from embezzlement, theft or other dishonest acts by your employees.

○ *Glass breakage* coverage protects against losses from broken store windows and plate glass.

Insurance That Covers You And Your Employees

Don't stop after you have insured the nonhuman assets of your business. Both you and your employees have needs that should be addressed by insurance. Health insurance is often the core of insurance designed to protect you and your employees. There are three basic types of health plans:

1. *Indemnity plans* offer traditional benefits and open access to service

Raise Your Hand If You're Insured

Insurance companies conduct audits to make sure the premiums you're paying are in line with the amount of coverage they're providing. The types of policies most likely to be audited are those for workers' compensation and general liability. Some companies also audit automobile, garage liability, and business-interruption policies.

Insurance companies base initial premiums on estimates a wide range of variables can affect. After a policy period ends, auditors verify the actual payroll numbers and check other issues that might affect the premium, and then the company determines whether they have billed accurately. If they under- or over-billed, you'll receive either an invoice for the additional premium due or a refund.

For other insurance types, auditors examine records that support the basis for the premium, such as sales, purchasing and inventory documentation. If your automobile policy is being audited, for instance, the auditor needs to confirm that the vehicles you are using are the same vehicles described in the policy.

The initial contact from the auditor is either by phone or mail, and you're generally given a week or two to prepare. The auditor will let you know in advance what records will be examined so you can have those documents available.

Rhonda Hamel of Hamel and Associates, an insurance auditing and education firm in Alpharetta, Georgia, offers these tips to make the auditing process go more smoothly:

○ *Have all requested records available.* If, for example, certain records are maintained by your accountant, either have them sent to your office or arrange for the audit to be conducted at your accountant's office.

○ *Get certificates of insurance on any contractors not covered by your workers' comp policy.* Be able to prove that any contract labor source doing work on your premises or on your behalf has coverage, or you may have to pay additional premiums based on those labor costs.

○ *Discuss record-keeping procedures with your insurance agent and accountant.* Proper bookkeeping may reduce your workers' comp premiums. When you pay overtime, for example, you may be entitled to a partial credit against your total payroll for those hours.

providers. These plans tend to be more expensive than the other options.

2. *Preferred Provider Organizations (PPOs)* develop a network of doctors, hospitals and other health-care providers, and negotiate discounts to maintain costs.

3. *Health Maintenance Organizations (HMOs)* contract with doctors, hospitals and other service providers to deliver care. Patients are typically required to see a plan provider for care.

Some issues to consider when choosing a health plan and provider include:

○ *Financial stability:* Check out the insurer's financial health by contacting your state insurance department and reviewing the insurer's ranking from rating agencies such as A.M. Best Co. Inc., Duff & Phelps Credit Rating Co., and Standard & Poor's. Your agent can help you with this.

○ *Plan features, limitations and exclusions:* Find out what the plan does and doesn't cover; then compare that with your employees' needs.

○ *Service record:* How well (and how quickly) does the insurer pay claims and respond to customer service and administrative requests? Check with your state's department of insurance and the Better Business Bureau to see if any complaints are on file. Ask to see the plan's latest member satisfaction survey results. And always ask for and check references.

If your employees are paying all or a portion of their health insurance premiums, allow them to pay with pretax dollars. Michael Hart, president and principal of Hart Associates Inc., an advertising agency in Maumee, Ohio, does just that for his 60 employees. "We were able to help our employees by creating a Section 125 program, which our agent administers for us, that allows our employees to pay their part of their health insurance premiums with pretax dollars," Hart says.

Viewpoint

Cafeteria plans and flexible spending plans allow
employees to use pre-tax dollars to choose among different types of benefits. Cafeteria plans typically have
core benefits such as medical and life insurance, sick leave, and
sometimes disability benefits. Option benefits may include anything from dental insurance to elder care to vision coverage. They
can't, however, include transportation assistance, tuition assistance or, unless part of a 401(k) plan, retirement benefits.

Similarly, a medical savings account (MSA) is a popular tax-deferred savings account set up by the Health Insurance Portability Act of 1996, which allows employees to accumulate long-term tax-free savings to pay for future medical expenses. MSAs can replace all or part of health insurance coverage, saving on premiums while allowing patients to make their own health-care decisions, such as choosing physicians, without consulting insurance companies.

In addition to health insurance, consider other types of coverage as part of your benefits package. Many health insurers also offer dental and vision plans. Group life and disability coverage can help employees plan for their futures and protect their families, usually at rates lower than they can obtain on their own.

One of the most common objections to obtaining disability insurance is the cost—it's one of the more expensive types of coverage. That's because rates are based on the amount of risk the insurer is taking, and there is a much higher chance people will use their disability insurance than their life insurance. But group disability coverage is more affordable than individual policies.

Setting Up A Workplace Safety Program

Requirements for workplace safety vary widely from business to business. But some components of an adequate workplace safety program are universal.

○ Make employees aware that safety is a priority at your workplace. Draft a statement saying you are committed to providing a safe and healthy environment.

○ Make it a policy for all employees to report any unsafe conditions and to stop work until the situation has been corrected. Require all employees to know and follow rules set forth in your safety program.

○ Assign a safety coordinator to whom employees are to report all accidents, injuries, breaches of safety rules, or problem situations.

○ Hold regular meetings of a Safety Committee, made up of both management and employees, to review and update safety rules, provide safety training, and evaluate employee accident and illness prevention programs.

○ Train all employees from day one to make sure they understand all safety rules and policies, and job-specific procedures.

○ Have supervisors train employees to perform assigned tasks safely and observe them to make sure they follow the procedures they were taught.

Viewpoint

It's important to properly investigate workplace accidents. Assign and train one or more supervisors to secure accident scenes, identify and interview witnesses, fill out investigative reports, review equipment or procedures involved, and follow up on recommendations. Be sure to perform these duties as soon as possible after accidents.

○ Instruct all employees on how to safely operate any new equipment before using the equipment.

○ Retrain employees periodically on safety rules, polices and procedures any time changes are made to your workplace safety manual and following any work-related injury.

Government Assistance Programs

If your business suffers physical damage as a result of a hurricane, flood or other natural disaster and is located in a declared disaster area, you may be eligible for assistance from the Small Business Administration. You can apply for a loan to help repair or replace damaged property to the way it was before trouble struck. Disaster loans of up to $1.5 million can be used to repair or replace buildings, machinery, equipment, fixtures and inventory, and make improvements. SBA loans can help cover physical damage that is not protected by conventional insurance.

In addition to SBA disaster loans to cover physical damage, the government offers Economic Injury/Disaster Loans that provide working capital to small businesses to help them survive disaster. These loans are available only to applicants who can't get credit through conventional means.

When A Lawsuit Strikes...

At one time or another, many businesses find themselves getting hauled into court. What should you do if you get sued? First, don't wait until it happens. Make sure you have adequate liability insurance coverage. Then, if you are sued by someone, your liability insurance coverage will pay for an attorney to defend you, saving you a bundle in legal fees. Plus, your insurance company is likely to find a better, more experienced attorney than you could find on your own. This makes paying liability insurance premiums practically a bargain.

Your next step is obvious: Contact your attorney immediately. When you receive a summons notifying you that someone has filed a complaint against you, you have a limited time to respond. If you ignore the summons or wait until the period has expired, the plaintiff may proceed without your input. So don't delay.

A competent attorney can make sure you respond appropriately, perhaps including filing a counterclaim against the party suing you. If you don't already have access to an attorney, look in the Yellow Pages for your local lawyer referral service or legal aid office.

Dealing With Negative Publicity

Negative publicity can come in a variety of forms. It might be a televised consumer report about a local resident who feels cheated by your company, or a newspaper article about someone who had a bad

Crisis Cleanup

If an event is serious enough to warrant an insurance claim, it will have a psychological impact on you and your employees. Dealing with your staff's problems is every bit as important as dealing with your insurance company.

"Grieving the loss caused by a disaster is a natural process, and to ignore that can have a negative impact on your recovery," says Jennell Evans, vice president of Strategic Interactions Inc., an organizational development firm in Vienna, Virginia. "While you have to attend to the business side of rebuilding, you also have to attend to the emotional functions of the group."

To do that, Evans advises, talk about the future and communicate the status of the recovery. If your employees' jobs are secure, they need to know that; if the future looks shaky, they have a right to know that, too.

Ron Ellman's experience supports Evans' position. Ellman is president of Ellman Batteries and Power Systems Inc., an industrial battery distributor in Orlando, Florida. In 1983, an electrical fire destroyed his former business. While insurance covered the building and its contents, replaced lost income and paid for other recovery efforts, Ellman was so devastated that he neglected his business, and two years later, it failed. "When [there's] a catastrophe, your employees will be as affected as you are," Ellman says. "I lost track of what was going on, and that crippled us."

If you're so distressed you don't feel capable of handling a crisis, consider bringing someone in to help with trauma counseling. Some insurance policies will pay for what Evans calls "critical incident debriefing."

experience with the products or services you sell. Wherever it comes from, negative publicity can interrupt the operation of your business and requires an immediate response. Here are keys to dealing with negative publicity:

○ Make it clear that no employees may speak to the media on behalf of the company. This should be the case in normal business operations as well as during a crisis. The CEO, public relations or media liaison, or other selected individual should be the sole official spokespersons for the company.

- Be cooperative with the media. Always know who is calling and why. Then make sure calls from news media are sent to the right person and satisfactory information is offered. Never ignore media inquiries during a crisis.
- Answer questions candidly with facts. Don't evade questions. Never say "No comment." Many people see this as an admission of guilt. If you don't know, say so. If you need to and can, look it up.
- Don't say it unless you are ready to see it in print. Do not give off-the-record comments or answer hypothetical "what if" questions.
- Avoid arguments with journalists, even if the person pressures you.
- Don't fall into an interviewer's trap of repeating a question containing language you don't like.

Handling Stress

Stress is unavoidable when you're growing a business. In moderate amounts, it's even helpful because it focuses your attention. But too much stress can lead to poor decisions and even damage your physical, emotional and mental health. Here are tips for controlling and handling stress:

- *Avoid it.* If you know that you are headed for a stressful situation, avoid it if possible. If you find yourself dreading about going to an upcoming industry convention, why not send somebody else?
- *Limit the number of major changes you make simultaneously.* When you are rolling out a new product is probably not the best time to refinance your debt, fire and hire a new vice president, and open up a new territory. Sometimes you must do everything at once, but if you're stressing, trying to do too much may be the cause.

Fast Lane

If a camera crew is at the door and you only have time to think about one thing, think attitude. Your attitude toward news media is critical. You want to come across as honest, sensible, willing to cooperate, and ready to provide information.

- *Exercise.* Regular exercise gives you a chance to work through tension and will also help boost your body's resistance to stress-induced medical problems.
- *Hang onto your sense of humor.* Laughter can be the best medicine for stress. When you can laugh at

Danger Ahead!

Stress can be more than an irritation. You should contact your doctor if you experience any of the following: 1) trouble concentrating enough to complete your work, 2) significant changes in appetite, sleep or sex drive, 3) uncontrollable crying spells, 4) thoughts of harming yourself or others, or 5) severe mood swings.

yourself and the world, you will get relief from stress.

○ *Take some time off.* Relaxing and unwinding is a powerful stress-buster. It's not always possible to take a lot of time off, but a little is better than none. Even spending a few minutes alone each day can break the stress-building routine.

○ *Watch your diet.* Alcohol, sugar and caffeine can contribute to stressful feelings.

○ *Find a sounding board.* You are not alone. Getting feedback from others may be more helpful than you think. Talking through your problems and concerns puts them into perspective.

○ *Set realistic goals.* Be ambitious, but if the source of your stress is self-induced performance pressure, it might be time to give yourself a break. If you can't rein in your aspirations, break them into small daily goals and build from there.

○ *Set priorities.* List tasks in order of urgency and importance. Focus on what's important and let the time- and energy-wasters slide.

Using Risk Management: The Only Way To Grow

It's possible to grow your business without using risk management strategies, but not indefinitely. If your business is inadequately insured, you're lackadaisical about theft prevention, and you don't institute workplace safety programs, your business will surely suffer. Be smart. Use the risk management strategies discussed in this chapter, and your business will have the best chance of not only surviving, but living up to its greatest potential.

chapter 24

Financial
Management

Just as your heart rate, blood pressure and
other vital signs indicate bodily health, financial measures such
as profit margin and cash flow are indicators of your business's
health. You can't grow unless your body is healthy, and your
business can't grow unless it's healthy. The way you tell
whether and how fast your business can grow is by checking its
vital signs—the financial measures of a business's health.

Financial Management For Growing Companies

Managing the finances of a growing company is different from managing the finances of a company that isn't growing. Here's the problem: Your business could grow so fast that generating enough cash (through profits or borrowing) to pay for expanding bills for materials, supplies, payroll, etc., is impossible. When that happens, you can run out of cash and be out of business even though you are growing profitability.

You can avoid growing yourself out of business by sticking to your affordable growth rate. Your affordable growth rate is tied to your firm's assets. The basic idea is that your sales shouldn't grow more quickly than your assets. As a rule, this means if your sales double, your assets—including inventory, receivables and fixed assets—should also double. Assets are important because your lender may be unwilling to loan you any more money if your debt-to-equity ratio exceeds a certain figure. If sales and assets grow at the same rate, your debt-to-equity ratio should remain within the lender's limit, allowing you to borrow to finance growth forever.

Cash Flow Management

Cash is king when it comes to the financial management of a growing company. The lag between the time you have to pay your suppliers and employees and the time you collect from your customers is the problem, and the solution is cash flow management. At its simplest, cash flow management means delaying outlays of cash as long as possible while encouraging anyone who owes you money to pay it as rapidly as possible.

Measuring Cash Flow

Prepare cash flow projections for next year, next quarter and, if you're on shaky ground, next week. An accurate cash flow projection can alert you to trouble well before it strikes.

Understand that cash flow plans are not glimpses into the future. They're educated guesses that balance a number of factors, including

> **Danger Ahead!**
> Cash and profits are not the same thing. You could have hefty profits and rising sales, but if all your cash is tied up in accounts receivable at the time payroll is due and vendors are complaining, you could be headed for bankruptcy.

your customers' payment histories, your own thoroughness at identifying upcoming expenditures, and your vendors' patience. Watch out for assuming without justification that receivables will continue coming in at the same rate they have recently, that payables can be extended as far as they have in the past, that you have included expenses such as capital improvements, loan interest and principal payments, and that you have accounted for seasonal sales fluctuations.

Improving Receivables

If you got paid for sales the instant you made them, you would never have a cash flow problem. Unfortunately, that doesn't happen, but you can still improve your cash flow by managing your receivables. The basic idea is to improve the speed with which you turn materials and supplies into products, inventory into receivables, and receivables into cash. Here are specific techniques for doing this:

○ Offer discounts to customers who pay their on time.
○ Ask customers to make deposit payments at the time orders are taken.
○ Require credit checks on all new noncash customers.
○ Get rid of old, outdated inventory for whatever you can get.
○ Issue invoices promptly and follow up immediately if payments are slow in coming.
○ Track accounts receivable to identify and avoid slow-paying customers. Instituting a policy of cash on delivery (c.o.d.) is an alternative to refusing to do business with slow-paying customers.

Managing Payables

Top-line sales growth can conceal a lot of problems—sometimes too well. When you are managing a growing company, you have to watch expenses carefully. Don't be lulled into complacency by simply expanding sales. Any time and any place you see expenses growing faster than sales, examine costs carefully to find places to cut or control them. Here are some more tips for using cash wisely:

Go With The (Cash) Flow

Cash flow projections are important for every small business. You may already do income and balance sheet projections, but no matter how carefully you prepare other financial documents, the cash flow projection is still essential.

Start your cash flow projection by adding cash on hand at the beginning of the period with other cash to be received from various sources. In the process, you will wind up gathering information from salespeople, service representatives, collections, credit workers and your finance department. In all cases, you'll be asking the same question: How much cash in the form of customer payments, interest earnings, service fees, partial collections of bad debts, and other sources are we going to get in, and when?

The second part of making accurate cash flow projections is detailed knowledge of amounts and dates of upcoming cash outlays. That means not only knowing when each penny will be spent, but on what. Have a line item on your projection for every significant outlay, including rent, inventory (when purchased for cash), salaries and wages, sales and other taxes withheld or payable, benefits paid, equipment purchased for cash, professional fees, utilities, office supplies, debt payments, advertising, vehicle and equipment maintenance and fuel, and cash dividends.

"As difficult as it is for a business owner to prepare projections, it's one of the most important things one can do," says accountant Steve Mayer. "Projections rank next to business plans and mission statements among things a business must do to plan for the future."

○ *Take full advantage of creditor payment terms.* If a payment is due in 30 days, don't pay it in 15 days.

○ *Use electronic funds transfer to make payments on the last day they are due.* You will remain current with suppliers while retaining use of your funds as long as possible.

○ *Communicate with your suppliers so they know your financial situation.* If you ever need to delay a payment, you'll need their trust and understanding.

○ *Carefully consider vendors' offers of discounts for earlier payments.*

These can amount to expensive loans to your suppliers, or they may provide you with a chance to reduce overall costs. The devil is in the details.

◯ *Don't always focus on the lowest price when choosing suppliers.* Sometimes more flexible payment terms can improve your cash flow more than a bargain-basement price.

Surviving Shortfalls

Sooner or later, you will foresee or find yourself in a situation where you lack the cash to pay your bills. This doesn't mean you're a failure as a businessperson—you're a normal entrepreneur who can't perfectly predict the future. And there are normal, everyday business practices that can help you manage the shortfall.

The key to managing cash shortfalls is to become aware of the problem as early and as accurately as possible. Banks are wary of borrowers who have to have money today. They'd much prefer lending to you before you need it, preferably months before. When the reason you are caught short is that you failed to plan, a banker is not going to be very interested in helping you out.

If you assume from the beginning that you will someday be short on cash, you can arrange for a line of credit at your bank. This allows you to borrow money up to a preset limit any time you need it. Since it's far easier to borrow when you don't need it, arranging a credit line before you are short is vital.

If bankers won't help, turn next to your suppliers. These people are more interested in keeping you going than a banker, and they probably know more about your business. You can often get extended terms from suppliers that amount to a hefty, low-cost loan just by asking. That's especially true if you've been a good customer in the past and kept them informed about your financial situation.

Consider using factors. These are financial service businesses that can pay you today for receivables you may not otherwise be able to collect on for weeks or months. You'll receive as much as 15 percent less than you would otherwise, since factors demand a discount, but you'll eliminate the hassle of collecting and be able to fund current operations without borrowing.

Ask your best customers to accelerate payments. Explain the situation and, if necessary, offer a discount of a percentage point or two off the bill. You should also go after your worst customers—those whose invoices are more than 90 days past due. Offer them a steeper discount if they pay today.

You may be able to raise cash by selling and leasing back assets such as machinery, equipment, computers, phone systems and even office furniture. Leasing companies may be willing to perform the transactions. It's not cheap, however, and you could lose your assets if you miss lease payments.

Choose the bills you'll pay carefully. Don't just pay the smallest ones and let the rest slide. Make payroll first—unpaid employees will

These Don't Get Better With Age

By studying customers who are reluctant to fork over the dough, you can learn to avoid slow payers in the future and possibly make a dramatic improvement in your cash flow. "It's not nuclear science," says Ron Torrence, author of *10 Keys to Sales and Financial Success for Small Business.* "It's just having a good system of aged receivables reports, reviewing those reports, and making collection calls."

You can't learn from late payers until you know you have them and who they are. That begins with basic accounts receivables aging. Any legitimate business bookkeeping software will produce reports giving at least a few different views of a company's outstanding receivables.

Like a youth soccer coach, a typical receivables aging report breaks accounts into age groups. Rows in an aging report might be labeled "current" for accounts that are up to date, "31 to 60 days" for accounts with outstanding invoices at least a month old but not two, "61 to 90 days" for those getting into more serious trouble, "91 to 120 days" for the critically late, and "more than 120 days" for ones you'll likely never collect.

Another column will show the total dollar amount of receivables outstanding for each age group. For instance, one figure will total "current" receivables, the next will sum up "31 to 60 days," and so on.

The most important column gives the percentage of your receivables represented by each age group. A glance will tell you in an instant whether most of your accounts are current, starting to get behind or calling for instant action.

soon be ex-employees. Pay crucial suppliers next. Ask the rest if you can skip a payment or make a partial payment.

Setting Your Salary

There is no place where self-discipline plays a more important role than in setting your own salary. As the owner and founder, you can allocate as much or as little of the company's profits as you want to your own paycheck. You can even decide to go further. You can tell your accountant to cut you a check equal to the entire month's sales. That will be a high-water mark for your earnings, however, since draining that much cash will ensure that it is your last month in business.

There are two groups of interested parties in the decision about how much to pay yourself. First, you have to do right by your partners (if any), employees, suppliers, creditors and customers. If you take money out of your company for yourself, to the extent that any of these parties are damaged, it could be a mistake.

But you also have to consider yourself (and perhaps your spouse and your children), as well as any charitable causes you support out of your earnings. These interested parties deserve a fair cut of the bounty, too. You should get a decent return on the labor and risk you have invested. Your family should, of course, share in those benefits.

Complicating the issue is the fact that there is no set amount an entrepreneur should earn. Strictly speaking, it's all yours, or as much of it as you retain ownership of. Of course, a board of direc-tors, partners, other owners and lenders may also have a say in this. Absent all limits, in a world where only you and your company are involved in the decision, you have to choose between taking money out to spend on yourself and your interests outside work, or reinvesting it in the company, where it can power further growth. The decision to take or reinvest profits is a highly personal one that turns on the ful-

Getting Directions

You can find factors by looking in the Yellow Pages under the "Commercial Finance Companies" heading. The *Edwards Directory of American Factors* (Edwards Research), a comprehensive directory, is available at many libraries. Learn more at www.edwardsresearch.com.

crum where your interests and those of your business coincide.

Other than taking a salary, there are several ways you can get value out of your business.

○ *Dividends:* You can elect to pay yourself any amount you want by declaring it as a dividend.

○ *Paying family members:* You can hire your family members and pay them just like

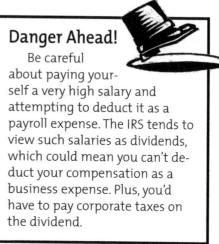

Danger Ahead!

Be careful about paying yourself a very high salary and attempting to deduct it as a payroll expense. The IRS tends to view such salaries as dividends, which could mean you can't deduct your compensation as a business expense. Plus, you'd have to pay corporate taxes on the dividend.

your regular employees (as long as they are working just like your regular employees). This way it will at least keep the money in the family.

○ *Fringe benefits:* You may be able to pay for country club memberships, company cars, luxury business trips to popular destinations, and give yourself other attractive perks—and have them treated as tax-deductible business expenses. Just make sure you offer them to other employees as well.

○ *Delayed compensation:* If you chose to forgo compensation during your start-up phase, when cash was critical, you can take larger compensation now without fear of being accused by the IRS of taking excessive compensation—as long as you have carefully documented your delayed-compensation plan when you were carrying it out.

○ *Don't forget loans:* You may be able to take a loan from your business as long as you make sure to document it in writing, pay a market rate of interest, and have a definite schedule for repaying it. Without those features, a loan between a business and its owner may run afoul of the IRS.

Tax Concerns

As your sales and profits grow, your obligations for federal, state and local taxes grow as well. That's why it is important to stay abreast of your business's tax situation and work with a qualified accountant to understand all that's required by federal and state governments. The task is by no means simple. Owners of growing businesses face a host of tax requirements and ever-changing rules.

For instance, the IRS requires any business paying more than $200,000 annually in payroll taxes or other federal taxes to pay through the Electronic Federal Tax Payment System (EFTPS). Don't risk being charged a penalty. It's your responsibility to do your homework and check with the IRS before you pay your taxes to determine if you're required to pay electronically.

Planning For Taxes

The key to tax planning is making accurate estimated tax payments to cover your income, payroll and other tax liability. A variety of rules affect when your payments are due and how much they should be. The simplest approach for your personal federal return is to base your payments on the previous year's income. If your adjusted gross income last year was less than $150,000, your estimated tax payments must be at least 90 percent of your current year's tax liability or 100 percent of the prior year's liability, whichever is less.

According to the Taxpayer Relief Act of 1997, estimated tax payments must be made for income not subject to withholding if you owe at least $1,000 in federal taxes for the year. The federal government allows sole proprietors to pay estimated taxes in four equal amounts throughout the year on the 15th of April, June, September and January. Here are additional form filing requirements for other business structures:

○ *Partnerships and limited liability companies (LLCs):* Companies set up with these structures must file Form 1065, U.S. Partnership Return of Income. The partnership must furnish copies of Schedule K-1 (Partner's Share of Income, Credits, Deductions),

Getting Directions

To help you wade through all the tax laws and regulations, the IRS offers free publications including *Tax Guide for Small Business* (Publication No. 334), *Business Expenses* (Publication No. 535), *Travel, Entertainment, Gift and Car Expenses* (Publication No. 463), *Circular E, Employer's Tax Guide* (Publication No. 15), and *Employer's Supplemental Tax Guide* (Publication No. 15-A). To order copies of these publications, call (800) TAX-FORM or download them from the IRS Web site at www.irs.gov.

which is part of Form 1065, to the partners or LLC members by the filing date for Form 1065. The due dates are the same as those for sole proprietors.

○ *Corporations:* If your business is structured as a standard corporation, you must file Form 1120, U.S. Corporation Income Tax Return. For calendar-year taxpayers, the due date for the return is March 15. For fiscal-year corporations, the return must be filed by the 15th day of the third month after the end of the corporation's tax year.

○ *S corporations:* Owners of these companies must file Form 1120S, U.S. Income Tax Return for an S Corporation. Like partnerships and LLCs, shareholders must receive a copy of Schedule K-1, which is part of Form 1120S. The due dates are the same as those for standard corporations.

Sales Tax

Sales taxes vary by state and are imposed at the retail level. It's important to know the rules in the states and localities where you do business because if you are a retailer, you must collect state sales tax on each sale you make.

While many states and localities exempt service businesses from sales taxes, some have recently begun to change their laws in this area and are applying the sales tax to some services. If you are a service business, contact your state and/or local revenue offices for information on the laws in your area.

If you are a mail order seller who ships and sells goods in other states, be careful. In the past, many retailers have not collected sales taxes on the sale of these goods. Ralph Anderson, a CPA and partner in charge of tax and financial services with accounting firm M.R. Weiser, says to make sure you or your accountant knows the state sales tax requirements where you do business. The definition of your business's physical presence—or "nexus" as it's sometimes referred to in tax jargon—varies from state to state. In some cases, merely having a telecommuter located in a state

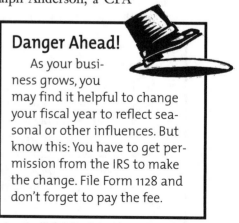

Danger Ahead!

As your business grows, you may find it helpful to change your fiscal year to reflect seasonal or other influences. But know this: You have to get permission from the IRS to make the change. File Form 1128 and don't forget to pay the fee.

may constitute a nexus, requiring you to collect and pay taxes there. Warns Anderson, "Just because you don't have a physical location in a state doesn't mean you don't have to collect the sales tax."

Many states require business owners to make an advance deposit against future taxes. Some states will accept a surety bond from your insurance company in lieu of the deposit. It's possible for retailers to defer paying sales taxes on merchandise they purchase from suppliers. Once the merchandise is sold, however, the taxes are due. The retailer adds the sales taxes (where applicable) to the purchase. To defer sales taxes, you need a reseller permit or certificate. For details on obtaining a permit, contact your state tax department.

Alternative Minimum Tax

The alternative minimum tax (AMT) is a separate tax system designed to keep high-earning corporations and individuals from reducing their taxes to a level that the federal government considers too low. It amounts to a second tax system under which you may be required to figure your tax if your income exceeds a certain level. To calculate the income at which you'll fall under AMT, you have to add various tax preferences and adjustments to your taxable income, and a $33,750 exemption ($45,000 for married filing jointly and $22,500 for married filing separately) is deducted. The exemption starts to phase out once AMT income exceeds certain levels. Determining exactly what that level is in your case is tricky, however. So it's recommended that you consult a tax advisor to find out whether you may be subject to the AMT.

Two things don't require much analysis, however. Since the AMT amounts are not indexed to inflation, with each year that passes, you are more likely to fall under AMT. And if your company and your wealth are growing, you are more likely to become subject to the AMT as well.

Depreciation

As your business grows, you'll likely accumulate assets. Anytime you acquire an asset, depreciation comes into play. Depreciation is an accounting trick that allows you to claim as an expense the loss in value of the property that occurs after you have bought it. In some cases, you can take all the value of the property as a depreciation in the first year you bought it. In other instances, such as those involving real estate, you will have to deduct a portion of the value over several years. The IRS has different rules for automobiles, software, furniture, buildings and other classes of property. You have to know—or have an accountant who knows—about these rules and their latest updates to make sure you are accurately depreciating your business's property.

Tax Deductions

What makes the tax code complex is not the taxes themselves.

Fast Lane

If you lost money in your business's operations, you may be able to get some tax relief from something called net operating loss deduction. It allows you to offset one year's losses against another year's income. The IRS lets you carry this operating loss back two years and use it to offset the income of those previous two years.

It's the deductions. There is a wide variety of deductions you can use to reduce the taxes you'll pay as your business grows. You'd be foolish not to take advantage of as many of them as you legally can. Here are some of the more important tax deductions your growing business may quality for:

○ *Equipment purchases:* If you buy equipment for your business, you can deduct a portion of the cost of that equipment in the year you placed the equipment in service. Under current law, the deduction cannot exceed the taxable income derived from your business. There's also an absolute limit to the deduction for equipment purchase. It will be set at $25,000 after 2003.

○ *Business expenses:* Common expenses for running a growing business for which you can take a deduction include advertising, employee benefits, insurance, legal and professional services, telephone and utilities, rent, office supplies, wages, dues to professional associations, and subscriptions to business publications.

○ *Auto expenses:* For a car you own and use in your business, the IRS allows you to either deduct your actual business-related expenses or claim the standard mileage rate, which is a specified amount of money you can deduct for each business mile you drive. The IRS generally adjusts the rate each year. To calculate your deduction, multiply your business miles by the standard mileage rate for the year. For tax purposes, be sure to keep a log of your business miles, as well as the costs of business-related parking fees and tolls because you can deduct these expenses, too.

With the actual cost method, the IRS allows you to deduct various expenses, including depreciation, gas, insurance, cleaning, leasing fees, routine maintenance, tires, and personal property taxes. If you use this method, keep records of your car's costs during the year and multiply those expenses by the percentage of total car mileage driven for business purposes. While using the standard mileage rate is easier for record-keeping, you may receive a larger deduction using the actual cost method. If you qualify to use both methods, the IRS recommends figuring your deduction both ways to see which gives you a larger deduction. Just make sure you've kept detailed records to substantiate the actual cost method.

○ *Meal and entertainment expenses:* To deduct business meals and entertainment, you must discuss business during, immediately before or immediately after the event. Your deduction is limited to 50 percent of the cost of qualified expenses, and you must have receipts for any cost of $75 or more. If you have an individual entertainment expense of less than $75, you can record the necessary information in an expense account book and not worry about keeping receipts. Record the reason for the expense, amount spent, dates, locations, and people entertained.

○ *Travel expenses:* You can deduct ordinary and necessary travel expenses you incur while traveling on business. Your records should show the amount of each expense for items such as transportation, meals and lodging. Be sure to record the date of departure and return for each trip, the number of days you spent on business, the name of the city, and the business reason for the travel or the business benefits you expect to achieve. Keep track of your cleaning and laundry expenses while traveling because these are also deductible.

Audit Red Flags

Nobody wants to get audited. The existence of specific traits that attract the eyes of IRS auditors is part of tax lore. And it seems likely that, faced with tens of millions of returns

Danger Ahead!
As a rule, expenses the IRS judges ordinary and necessary will stand up in court. But finding your way through all the exemptions, exceptions and limitations can be tricky, and the stakes are high. So always consult with a tax professional before making any tax-related move.

to either audit or pass, the IRS uses some red flags to identify those it will delve into further. Exactly what these flags are, however, has never been conclusively proven. Here are some of the most commonly mentioned audit red flags:

○ *Independent contractors:* If you use workers who claim independent contractor status, the IRS may suspect you are doing so to avoid paying employment taxes, which may attract an audit.

○ *Loans from your business:* If you borrow from your business, make sure you do it properly, paying a market rate of interest and repaying it on a set schedule. The IRS reportedly looks extra closely at returns showing loans from a business to the owner.

Getting Directions

What if you get audited? You can get IRS-published guides to the audit process that will tell you what to expect if you get audited. The main one is Publication No. 556, *Examination of Returns, Appeal Rights and Claims for Refund.* Check it out on the IRS Web site at www.irs.gov.

○ *High travel and entertainment amounts:* Any auditor can find a T&E expense to disallow. Allowable deductions have to include a record of the time, place, and business purpose of the expense. Large amounts may attract audits regardless.

Do Or Die

Now that you've finished reading this chapter, you know how important financial management is for a business. Well, it's even more important for a growing business. If you have hopes of growing to a certain size or revenue level, keep your eyes on the prize—and by all means, stay on top of financial management. You'll be glad you did.

Regulatory
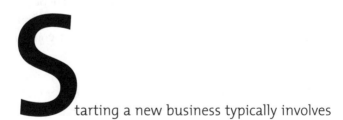
Roadblocks

Starting a new business typically involves obtaining a raft of licenses and certificates certifying that you comply with regulations ranging from the rules for doing business under a fictitious name to conforming to city zoning laws. As your business grows, don't neglect this important side of managing a firm.

You may need updated or new licenses and permits as your business enters new markets, commences new operations or simply gets larger.

State And Local Licenses And Permits

Most of the licenses and permits you are likely to need as your business grows will be issued by your city or state agencies. Events that may trigger a need for a new certificate or license range from changing your business's name to entering a new market.

○ *If you change the name of your company or the names it operates under, you may have to obtain a new dba or fictitious name certificate.* Procedures for doing this vary by state. The cost of filing a fictitious name notice ranges from $10 to $100. In most states, corporations don't have to file fictitious business names unless the corporations do business under names other than their own.

○ *Most cities license businesses, essentially granting them the right to operate in that city.* If you open a location in a new city, you may have to pay a fee and file for a new license.

○ *If you start selling food, either directly to customers as in a restaurant or as a wholesaler to other retailers, you'll need a county health department permit.* This costs about $25, but that varies depending on the size of the business and the amount and type of equipment you have. The health department will want to inspect your facilities before issuing the permit.

○ *If you add liquor, wine or beer to the products you sell, you will need liquor licenses.* In most states, you'll need to get one type of license to serve wine and beer and another to serve hard liquor.

○ *You may need to get a permit from your fire department if your business starts using any flammable materials or if your premises will be open to the public.* Other areas don't require permits but simply schedule periodic inspections of your business to see if you meet fire safety regulations. If you don't, the fire department will issue a citation.

○ *Many cities now have departments that work to control air and water pollution.* If you begin burning materials, discharging anything into the sewers or waterways, or using products that produce gas (such as paint sprayers), you may have to get a special permit from this department in your city or county.

○ *To attract more customers, you may want a different or larger sign.* Some cities and suburbs have sign ordinances that restrict the size, location and sometimes the lighting and type of sign you can use outside your business. Landlords may also impose restrictions. Malls, for instance, enforce stringent rules. Check regulations and secure the written approval of your landlord before you go to the expense of having a sign designed and installed.

Zoning Concerns

Don't forget to check zoning regulations when you relocate or expand. When you file your license application, the city planning or zoning department will check to make sure your area is zoned for the purpose you want to use it for and that there are enough parking spaces to meet the codes.

Asking For An Exception

You may be able to operate in an area that is not zoned for your type of business if you get a variance or conditional-use permit. To get a variance, you will need to present your case before the planning commission in your city. In many cases, variances are quite easy to get, as long as you can show that your business won't disrupt the character of the neighborhood where you plan to locate.

Fast Lane
Zoning laws can be hard to interpret. Luckily, if you relocate or expand your business in a location that previously housed a similar business, you're not likely to run into any problems.

Safety Regulations

Encouraging and enforcing safety in your workplace makes good sense. Unintentional injuries are the fifth leading cause of death in this country and the leading cause of death for Americans under 45 years old. Besides the human loss, workplace accidents cost money and time in lost productivity.

That's not all. You could be liable for substantial penalties that could wipe out your business's cash flow if you're found to have willfully violated safety rules. The federal Occupational Safety and Health Administration (OSHA), for example, can impose a minimum penalty of $70,000 for willful violations of safety rules that could result in death or serious physical harm. So paying attention to safety is definitely worth your while.

OSHA

OSHA was created by law in 1970 to oversee workplace safety and health. Today, it covers more than 100 million employees and six and a half million employers. Miners, transportation workers, many public employees, and those who are self-employed are about the only ones not covered by OSHA. OSHA itself employs more than 2,000 inspectors, plus hordes of investigators, engineers, physicians, educators and others in more than 200 offices nationwide.

OSHA has a labyrinth of rules regarding everything from asbestos to workplace violence. There are regulations on how to report injuries, document your safety program and on countless other topics, all of which vary by industry and even by the size of your firm. Many businesspeople complain about the burdens of complying with OSHA rules, but there is no doubt that the end result—a safer workplace—is a worthwhile goal. There is also no doubt that compliance with OSHA is not optional.

Getting Directions

You can learn more about workplace safety from the National Safety Council (NSC), a private-sector source of information and recommendations about safety, at www.nsc.org or by calling the NSC in Itasca, Illinois, at (630) 285-1121.

Getting Directions

If your state does not have its own workplace safety plan that is at least as strict at OSHA, then you have to follow OSHA. You can learn more about the rules in your state from your state's labor department. About half the states have their own safety agencies and regulations.

Even OSHA realizes its rules can be daunting for small businesses. So the agency maintains an extensive online database of articles, handbooks, frequently asked questions, guidelines and more, especially for small businesses, at its Web site. Go to www.osha-slc.gov/smallbusiness/index.html to view the small-business-specific materials, or check out www.osha.gov for general information about OSHA.

Other Regulations Affecting Growing Companies

Regulations can be a burden to small companies. A 1995 study by Hopkins and Diversified reported that regulatory costs per employee were highest for firms with one to four employees at $31,748. For firms with more than 500 employees, the regulatory burden was $16,241 per employee. It's no wonder that regulation and associated paperwork are commonly listed as significant burdens by small-business owners.

Since the regulatory cost per employee is higher for small firms, one way to reduce the overall impact of regulations on your company is to grow your business. Becoming larger will reduce the percentage of resources you have to devote to keeping up with regulations and will allow you to grow still larger.

Don't expect the regulatory burden to decline sharply any time soon. While there have been some sporadic moves to reduce regulation of growing companies, as a general rule, any lightening of regulations in one area is soon followed by an increase of regulations in another. Following are a few of the regulations that your growing company will find itself subject to.

The Family Medical Leave Act

The Family Medical Leave Act (FMLA), enacted in 1993, entitles eligible employees to take up to 12 weeks of unpaid, job-protected leave in a 12-month period for specified family and medical reasons. It covers all public agencies, including state, local and federal employers, and schools. However, the FMLA only covers private companies that employ 50 or more employees in 20 or more workweeks in the current or preceding calendar year. As a result, the FMLA is one of the regulations you'll be affected by as you grow. You can learn more about the FMLA at the Department of Labor's Web site at www.dol.gov.

Americans With Disabilities Act

The Americans With Disabilities Act (ADA), which went into effect in 1992, is a federal civil rights law prohibiting businesses from excluding people with disabilities from activities such as patronizing stores and restaurants. The ADA's rules require such things as removing narrow doors, steps and other physical barriers to wheelchair access, providing handicapped-accessible parking, and installing signage informing patrons of your compliance. The requirements for facilities built before 1993 are less strict than for ones built or modified later. However, nearly all private businesses that serve the public are covered, regardless of size. Also, if you own, operate, lease, or lease to a business that serves the public, you are covered by the ADA.

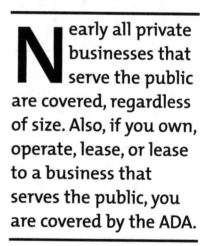

Nearly all private businesses that serve the public are covered, regardless of size. Also, if you own, operate, lease, or lease to a business that serves the public, you are covered by the ADA.

You can find a great deal of useful information at the Department of Justice's ADA home page at www.usdoj.gov/crt/ada/adahom1.htm, or call (800) 514-0301. TDD users can call (800) 514-0383.

Minimum Wage Rules

The federal Fair Labor Standards Act (FLSA) sets a minimum wage that most employees must be paid. At this writing, the federal minimum wage is $5.15 per hour, where it was set in 1997, but pending legislation would increase the wage to keep pace with inflation. In addition, some states have already set their minimum wages higher than the federal minimum wage. If your state's minimum wage is higher, you are subject to that law, which will be enforced by your state's Department of Labor. The U.S. Department of Labor's Wage and Hour Division enforces the federal minimum wage law.

The federal minimum wage law applies to employees of companies with $500,000 or more in annual sales, about 100 million employees in all. About one in 10 U.S. workers receives the federal minimum wage. The law may also cover smaller firms that are engaged in interstate commerce or produce goods for commerce. There are a number of specific exemptions, including a youth sub-minimum wage law that allows teenage employees to earn lower wages during their first 90 days on the job. Learn more about it at the Department of Labor's Web site at www.dol.gov.

Overtime Regulations

Federal overtime regulations require that most employees be paid overtime rates of at least one and one-half times their regular rates of pay for any hours over 40 in a workweek. The rules do not, however, limit the number of hours in a day or days in a week an employee may be asked to work, including overtime. You are required to keep payroll and schedule records to show compliance with the law, which is enforced by the Department of Labor. The federal overtime rules generally apply to the same types of businesses that are covered by minimum wage rules, so overtime regulations are something you will become more exposed to as you grow. There are several partial or full exemptions for specific employees, such as retail salesclerks, taxi drivers and farm workers, that apply only to overtime. Learn more about federal overtime regulations at the Department of Labor's Web site at www.dol.gov.

chapter 26

Business
Travel Tips

or the most part, only the light characters

travel," said Ralph Waldo Emerson. "Who are you that have no

task to keep you at home?" Not every entrepreneur loves busi-

ness travel, but most know different from Emerson: Far from

being a way to avoid tasks at home, business travel can be an im-

portant job and a spur to growth. That's true for several reasons:

○ *Traveling gives you an opportunity to improve and deepen critical business relationships.* Many people like to "put a face with a name" and prefer to deal with those they have met in person. By traveling to meet important suppliers and customers, you can make it easier for them to do more business with you, leading to growth.

○ *Travel can help you recognize promising new opportunities.* "Be there," was the two-word advice handed down by revered sports journalist Red Smith. It's as true for entrepreneurs as for sportswriters. When you experience a new market in person, you'll pick up nuances no research report or secondhand account could provide.

○ *Travel is all but essential for many formalities.* This includes signing legal documents and appearing in court for business purposes.

○ *When you travel to other branches of your expanding business, you can personally observe the ways these far-flung outposts are doing things better—or worse, as the case may be—than they are being done back in the home office.* Other people in your company may see the same things, but their reports wouldn't have the same impact as seeing it for yourself.

Business Travel Issues

For every way business travel can help, it may hurt. Business travel is expensive, time-consuming, exhausting and distracting. You are out of touch much of the time on airplanes, meaning you may be hard to reach in the event of a business emergency. It is difficult to work effectively in hotel rooms and airport lounges, where you don't have support staff and may lack important files. Jet lag is just the best-known manifestation of the physical effects of business travel. Riding in cramped seats, dining on fatty restaurant meals, imbibing too much alcohol at business functions and being away from your usual exercise equipment and venues can all lead to worse health than you would have if you never left home.

Fast Lane

You can track airline flights using the World Wide Web with Trip.com's online flight tracker at www. trip.com. Just type in the airline and flight number and get a route map with a tiny aircraft winging across it. You get departure and arrival times—even the airplane's actual airspeed, altitude and heading.

If none of these get you, toting an overloaded shoulder bag through three or four concourses of an international airport will probably do the job. But business travel is a powerful tool and one you will almost certainly have to use. It's something to be used judiciously—only when you need it and can justify it. If you have to be on the road 200 days a year, then you have to. But embracing the road warrior credo to excess can hurt you more than it can help.

Controlling Business Travel Costs

Entrepreneurs can be as avid about travel as anyone. But since their travel expenses are usually paid out of their own wallets and not out of some deep corporate kitty, entrepreneurs travel differently than average business travelers. Unlike expense-account-backed corporate travelers who concern themselves with frequent flier miles, upgrades and the contents of the hotel minibar, small-business owners zero in on costs. Unfortunately, those costs keep creeping up. But even in times of rising travel prices, there are still ways to keep things affordable—especially if you use suppliers that consistently offer affordable options to overpriced travel. The two biggest costs of travel are transportation and lodging. Here are some ideas to help you keep those costs from taking you for a ride.

Flying High Without High Prices

Cutting transportation costs is one of the first things budget-minded business travelers look to do. One of the best things that they can do is to try to travel routes served by Southwest Airlines (SWA), the "granddaddy" of the low-fare airlines. True to its name, Southwest has long dominated the budget-travel scene between many Sunbelt cities. But due to overwhelming success, it has become strong enough to take on the major airlines in their high-priced turf in the Northeast, and, most important, the giant New York City market by serving Long Island's Islip-MacArthur airport.

When Southwest announced plans to invade these areas, fares plummeted on not only Southwest, but also the major carriers serving those markets. For business travelers, Southwest offers more than

Viewpoint

Sending a salesperson to a moderate-sized U.S. city costs around $1,000 to $2,000 per day.

just low fares. It has one of the youngest fleets in the industry (an average of 8.4 years old) and leads the pack in on-time performance. Its simple frequent flier program is one of the easiest for securing award seats. Its no-nonsense Web site lets you make a reservation with as few as 10 clicks of the mouse. It serves less crowded, smaller and often gentler airports, eschewing most giant airline hubs. And, best of all, its average one-way fare is a very wallet-pleasing $79.

Don't expect a first-class section, an airport lounge or any on-board fare. Southwest proudly serves just light snacks and drinks, encouraging customers to bring their own food on board. So even if you don't fly SWA, you can thank the airline for keeping fares affordable—and for providing a role model for other low-fare carriers doing the same in your hometown. For more information, call (800) 435-9792 or visit www.IFlySWA.com.

Southwest is fine for low-priced domestic travel, but what about when you're bound for the Continent? Most Europe-bound business travelers aren't able to take advantage of the deep discounts usually offered to vacation travelers. That's because low trans-Atlantic fares must be booked far in advance and carry penalties for changes or refunds—restrictions business travelers find hard to live with. Even worse, a business traveler who has paid $1,500 for a last-minute coach-class ticket is usually seated next to a family of six (including two screaming babies), who paid $399 for a round-trip special they booked more than a year ago.

Leave it to kicky Virgin Atlantic Airways to provide a solution to this seeming inequity: the Virgin Atlantic Premium Economy Cabin. Premium Economy tickets are fully flexible and won't penalize you for changing flight dates or times. You avoid lengthy airport lines, thanks to its dedicated check-in desk and use of Fast Track immigration (a shorter passport line). On board, there's a separate Premium Economy cabin featuring extra-wide seats with headrests, footrests and generous amounts of legroom. You can make your selection from a menu that offers three different meals, including a vegetarian option. Best of all, you can leave vacationers in the back of the plane and even get some work done. Virgin Atlantic currently flies to London from Athens, Newark, JFK, Chicago, Miami, Orlando, Washington-Dulles, San Francisco, Los Angeles and Las Vegas. For details, call (800) 862-8621 or visit www.virgin.com.

Solid Choices For Cost-Efficient Business Lodging

Lodging is the next-biggest expense for cost-cutting business travelers to home in on. Here, the growth of good-quality budget hotel chains is a boon. Holiday Inn Express, for instance, won't give you bells, whistles or chocolates on the pillows—just a fresh, clean room, uncomplicated amenities, a good location and a decent price. Each Holiday Inn Express offers comfortable rooms, a free breakfast bar featuring fresh fruit, cereal and pastries, free local phone calls in the United States, voice mail, and points in the popular Priority Club Worldwide frequent-stay program that can be redeemed for merchandise, airline miles or free stays in the more than 2,800 hotels owned by its parent company, Bass Hotels and Resorts. Holiday Inn Express locations are ubiquitous—initially, many were built along or near freeways, but now many are springing up in downtown areas, suburban office parks and even small towns. Rates generally run from $60 to $90 per night but can vary. For details, visit www.hiexpress.com or call (800) Holiday.

All Wingate Inns offer free high-speed Internet access in every guest and meeting room. Each hotel also provides thoughtful amenities, like automated check-in and check-out, in-room cordless phones, two-line desk phones with all the necessary features, free breakfast, and free local and toll-free calls. There's also free 24-hour access to fax, printing and copying equipment, and wireless phones can be checked out from the front desk for use anywhere within the hotel. Each location also has a whirlpool and fitness

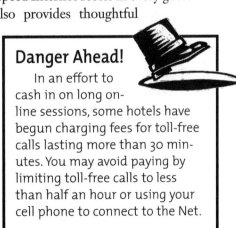

Danger Ahead!

In an effort to cash in on long on-line sessions, some hotels have begun charging fees for toll-free calls lasting more than 30 minutes. You may avoid paying by limiting toll-free calls to less than half an hour or using your cell phone to connect to the Net.

room. You'll find the price competitive, too (from $69 to $99 per night). For details, call (800) 228-1000 or visit www.wingateinns. com.

Starwood Hotels' latest brand, W Hotels, is a prototype of the new generation of modern boutique-style hotels offering both style and funk. You'll notice details like quick and easy Internet connections, voice mail, good coffee, comfortable beds, a healthy room service menu, and a lobby that's hip to hang out in. W Hotels are now open in Atlanta, Honolulu, Los Angeles, Miami, New York City, San Francisco and Seattle. Twenty more are scheduled to open by the end of 2001 in Boston, Chicago, Denver, Los Angeles, New Orleans and Washington, DC. For more information, call (877) W-Hotels or visit www.whotels.com.

Online Travel Booking

Once you've selected your low-cost travel and accommodations, you need to make your reservations. Online travel booking is convenient, fast and cost-effective. Here are reviews of a few of the most popular sites for booking your travel needs online:

○ *Priceline.com (www.priceline.com):* For last-minute travel, Priceline. com remains a hot destination. Know what the lowest published fare is on a route, and chances are you can get that price if you bid at the last minute. The same rule applies for bidding on rental cars: Know what the going rate is before sending in a bid.

○ *Trip.com (www.trip.com):* This site works with unmanaged business travelers, offering a whole suite of applications that help you track your travel expenses and make the most of your frequent flier miles. Of interest to frequent travelers is the IntelliTrip function, a program that scours the Internet and finds the best travel deals for you.

○ *Biztravel.com (www.biztravel.com):* Here's another site that lets you book trips and track your travel. This site lets you accomplish many of the same things Trip.com does, with a few variations. For example, a new feature called FareGuard ensures you the lowest fare until you depart. Another program sends flight information to your pager.

Insider tip: Don't forget travel agents. Brick-and-mortar outfits may be passé, but with airline commissions cut again, real-life retailers want to show their value. Agents are newly resolved to act as travel consultants.

Regaining Productivity

Travel is supposed to be about increasing productivity. But you don't have to return from many trips to an overflowing inbox to realize that being out of the office can really put you off your stride. Luckily, there are ways you can regain productivity so that you almost won't lose anything by being on the road.

First, always let someone know where you are and how you can be reached. Many things can be taken care of by a quick "yes" or "no" delivered over a pay phone or a borrowed desk phone at a customer's site. If you wait until you get back or call that evening, the problem may have gotten worse and require serious effort to solve.

Second, computerize your files. You can carry more information in the hard drive of a midrange laptop computer than a pickup truck could carry if it were in paper form. Each gigabyte of electronic data is equal to well over 1,000 printed books. If you computerize your files and take them with you, either by scanning in paper documents or simply transferring those in electronic form to your laptop, you will never have to be without critical information again.

Third, get wired. Use e-mail throughout your organization. Keep important company information on a secure Web site that you can access from anywhere over the Internet—using a password to keep out snoops and vandals, of course. Use cell phone modems and laptops and wireless-equipped palmtops so you can surf the Web, receive pages and check and send e-mail from anywhere.

Avoiding Employee Burnout

Business travel gets old quickly, and it's difficult to inject freshness to it. For employees who are carrying punishing schedules of business travel, it can be a major source of burnout. Most employees will eventually wear down under the strain of always being out of town, missing family events, living out of a suitcase, eating hotel food, driving rented cars, working in airplane seats and sleeping in hotel beds. Excessive travel is a frequent reason cited in exit interviews by employees who are leaving firms.

So although business travel can spur growth, it can also hinder growth if excessive use of it leads to the loss of critical employees and

Viewpoint

Common sense says business travelers can't check laptop computers as airline baggage. Common sense, however, is wrong. A number of cases are made strong and shock-resistant enough to let a laptop travel safely through a baggage carousel. The $280 Model 1009 AC computer attaché from Tenba Cases of Brooklyn, New York, foils brutish baggage handlers but still looks good enough to carry into a business meeting.

resulting poor productivity. The best thing to do with an employee showing signs of travel burnout is simply to take him or her off the road, at least for a while. But what will happen to the business while your ex-road warrior has been demobilized and is away from the front lines? Fortunately, there are many alternatives to travel you can use to grow while staying close to home.

Teleconferencing

You don't necessarily have to travel to get the benefits of a face-to-face meeting. Video teleconferencing is an increasingly popular way to hold business meetings among small groups of people who never leave their offices. It's relatively cheap, fast and flexible, and you're able to join people on short notice, at low cost and at any time or place. However, teleconferencing can also be dehumanizing. It's disliked by many people and considered a waste of time by others.

For the most part, professional teleconferencing facilities are still limited to the city centers of large metropolitan areas. And although it can be cheap compared to flying a group of people halfway across the country and lodging them overnight, video teleconferencing can still cost thousands of dollars per hour.

A much less costly option is to use some form of Internet-based videoconferencing. CUseeMe is an inexpensive Internet videoconferencing program that, along with some low-cost digital video cameras, can allow you to set up your

Danger Ahead!

When you're involved in a teleconference, remember that the people you are talking with can't see you anymore than you can see them. If you use a lot of body language when you speak, you will have to make up for it with more verbal communication when teleconferencing. Otherwise, you risk having your message get seriously lost in the translation to teleconferencing.

Do Leave Home Without Your Laptop

Can in-room personal computers liberate travelers from the heavy laptops they tote around with them? At least one hotel chain thinks so. Choice Hotels International is installing PCs with high-speed Internet connections in its hotel rooms. Choice Hotels' project could represent the single largest investment in hotel computer technology ever, if not the beginning of a new trend in the hospitality industry. Guests will have free access to the Internet, but they will be charged a fee to utilize the word-processing and spreadsheet programs on the computer. Think of it as an in-room premium similar to pay TV or a minibar.

But will the offering attract business travelers trying to lighten their loads? Choice Hotels' Anne Curtis says it's looking that way. "So far, the four test hotels have been extremely well-received," Curtis says. "More than 50 percent of our guests are going online. Guests are delighted with the amenity." The next six months will dictate this trend's future.

Insider tip: Even if in-room PCs become commonplace, they won't eliminate the need for portable computers. Some business travelers get a lot of their work done on planes, where we're still a decade away, at best, from having reliable computing devices installed in seatbacks. In-room PCs may be best for travelers just looking for an easy way to check e-mail.

own videoconference using a couple of PCs connected to the Internet. You can learn more about CUseeMe's desktop video collaboration software at its Web site at www.cuseeme.com, or by calling CUseeMe Networks at (800) 241-7463.

Branch Offices

When you find yourself and your people traveling often to a specific locale, it may be time to consider opening a branch office there. That will reduce the need to travel and greatly improve your coverage of the remote office. For many locations, such as international markets many time zones away, a branch office may be the only feasible way to serve a particular market.

Be careful about opening a large number of branch offices simply to reduce travel time and costs, though. It can cost far more to staff, lease, equip and maintain an office than to conduct numerous business trips. Cost out the alternatives carefully, and only commit when you can find the right location, the right personnel and the right price.

Getting Directions

A series of printed tables from a practice called "Guerrilla Linguistics" can clue you in on a country's money, language and culture before you ever go there. Minneapolis-based publisher John Freivalds says his charts give users "the ability to speak a client's culture, not just their language." For more information, call (612) 525-0731.

chapter 27

Administering Growing Businesses

lot of entrepreneurs are refugees

from the corporate world who left specifically because of the

paperwork, bureaucracy and administrative hassles of working for

a large company. The good news is they'll get a lot less of that in a

smaller company. The bad news is as a company grows, it's inevitable

that forms, policies and turf-protecting staffers will increase.

There's no way around an increase in the complexity of a growing organization. It's fine to be lean and flat. But there comes a time when not all decisions can be handled by you. You'll need other employees to handle some of them. That leads to more staff. And those staff will have to know what to do. That leads to more policies. And you'll need to know what those staffers did during the week or month. That leads to more reports. Luckily, as you grow your company, you have an excellent opportunity to make sure that the administrative overhead you add is only what is strictly necessary. It's a lot easier to keep complexity from invading an organization than it is to root it out once it's taken hold.

Minimizing Paperwork

Every time you hire an employee, acquire a new customer, take out a new loan or close the books on another year, you have to create a new file—or several. It's impossible to avoid it. The paperwork is going to mushroom.

And as your organization grows, you will need more and more forms filled out, memos written and reports issued for each one of these events. Paperwork serves a purpose by keeping people informed, and the more people you have, the more paperwork it will take to see that sales managers know what the sales are, production supervisors know what the error rates are, and everybody has the information they need to do their jobs.

Paperwork seems to mushroom as a business grows, but you don't have to give in to it. By steadily working to reduce the spread of papers, you can keep it to a minimum. Here are ways to reduce paperwork as much as possible:

○ *Create form letters for responding to frequent requests* such as those for product information, em-

Danger Ahead!
Hang onto tax records for at least seven years. The IRS can audit you up to three years after you file under normal circumstances, but the period extends to six years if you are suspected of under-reporting income by more than 25 percent. Audits of filings that are outright fraudulent have no statute of limitations. It's not a bad idea to hang onto accounting ledgers, check registers and employment contracts for a decade.

Taming The Paper Tiger

Suppliers are significant generators of paperwork and administrative clutter. Not only do you have your purchase orders and specifications to deal with, but you have their invoices, bills of lading and other requirements. The administrative hassles of dealing with large numbers of suppliers are significant. As your product line grows and you begin seeking out additional sources for key materials and supplies, the number of suppliers you deal with will grow. Combine these forces and the administrative clutter can expand exponentially.

This is the key reason many large purchasers have trimmed the number of suppliers they do business with. The automotive industry has led the charge in using fewer suppliers. You may not have as many suppliers as an automaker, but the point is still valid. You'll add unnecessary complexity and administrative overhead if you let your suppliers get too numerous. Try working more closely with fewer suppliers—as your big customers are probably already doing, especially if you sell to large corporations—and you will find you can grow without losing ground to clutter.

ployment and sales opportunities and the like. Being able to whip one out and slap a signature on it—or even use one with a preprinted signature—can save you considerable time and hassle in many situations.

○ *Be ruthless when deciding whether to keep or scrap questionable documents.* Have a set procedure when scanning incoming mail and messages—look at it once. Decide then whether to read it, file it or toss it. If you are going to file it, do so. If you are going to read it, do so. If you are going to toss it, do so. This will reduce the

Viewpoint

As your company gets larger, it will come to the attention of more regulators and fall within the guidelines of more regulations. The good news is that as you get larger, the financial impact of dealing with regulations will be less than when you were a smaller company. (See Chapter 25, "Regulatory Roadblocks," for more information.)

towers of backlogged items you are going to get around to when you have the time—which, let's face it, you'll never have.

○ *Use forms with checklists to avoid having to write memos and notes for routine matters.* Being able to place an "X" in the box for "I will be able to attend the meeting" or "I can't make it" can improve clarity of communication while reducing paper backup and saving time.

○ *Delegate paperwork to others.* Hiring employees is a prime cause of paperwork, so there is no reason employees can't help alleviate some of its pressure on you. Having other people handle routine paperwork can let your business grow without you growing frazzled.

Creating Filing Systems

Your files are to your business what your memory is to your brain. If you can't lay your hands on a customer's folder when you need it, you might as well be an amnesiac. Creating an effective filing system is an important component of making it easy for your company to grow.

Like most things, the time to do it right is when you're just getting started. If you wait until you've grown significantly to set up your files properly, the job is going to be very difficult. And think about all the sales you'll miss in the meantime because you couldn't help those customers with information when they needed it. Here are tips to creating a filing system that can grow with your company:

○ *When creating a filing system, think "hierarchy."* Organize your files first under major topics such as "clients," "vendors," "equipment," "accounts receivable/payable," and "operations." Subcategories such as customers' names or types of equipment come next.

○ *Centralize files wherever possible.* It may seem wasteful to devote an entire room to files when you could stash them all over the company in various nooks and crannies. But when files are centralized, it's much easier to keep them updated and purge old or duplicate files, not to mention to find what you're looking for.

○ *Use technology to make your filing system more compact and useful.* Use a scanner to save documents in electronic format. You can put several filing cabinets full of files on a modest-sized hard drive, and using rewritable CD-ROMs gives you nearly unlimited storage in a closet-sized file room. Electronic files are also easier to index and search through than paper files.

Off-Site Record Storage

One of the best moves you can make to reduce clutter is to store archived records off-site. Every business generates files, such as old tax returns and customer records, that should not be destroyed but are unlikely to be referred to again. Keeping them in the office takes up space that could be used more effectively and may cost you more than the records are worth, given the expenses of renting the office space where they are stored. You will have to fork over even more money to move unused records if you relocate.

Getting those boxes and cartons out of the office will give you more room to get work done and reduce overall clutter. You get a one-price-for-everything quote from an archiving center specializing in off-site record storage. These companies are equipped with the security, tracking systems and climate control to keep your records cheaply and safely. And because these companies specialize in record retrieval, you may be able to obtain an infrequently used file more quickly from an off-site archive than if you kept it in your own file room.

Office Design For Growth

Offices and other company facilities tend to grow as the companies themselves do—with a spurt here and a new addition there. Often, years of haphazard office space expansion means you wind up with a hodgepodge of chopped-up rooms, winding hallways and disconnected departments.

Good office design involves selecting the proper furniture, allocating adequate space, addressing file and storage needs, lighting work areas properly, pro-

Danger Ahead!

It's been said before, but it's worth saying again. Back up computer files daily. You'll reduce paper clutter because you won't need hard-copy backups. And when the inevitable day comes that your electronic files are lost or damaged, you'll be eternally grateful for those backup copies.

viding work surfaces for computers and peripherals, and taking into account your personal work style and those of your employees. In a

Making The Most Of The Mail

The mail room is a vital part of any business. Important items come in the mail, yet business owners don't pay much attention to how mail gets to them. Mail rooms are frequently staffed by high-turnover part-timers. Ergonomics often stop at the mail room, which are often furnished with old desks and unwanted rather than productivity-enhancing workstations. Here's how to get your growing mail room running efficiently:

○ Hire a mail clerk with previous experience running a company mail room—someone who is knowledgeable about mail and postal service regulations.

○ Be sure your mail room is well-equipped. A postage meter adds to your business's professional image and dissuades employees from mailing personal letters at company expense. You can also control postage by using one of the online postage services, such as Stamps.com.

○ Reduce incoming junk mail by removing your name from catalog mailing lists unless you order from them regularly.

○ Reduce outgoing mail by asking yourself, before you mail something, "Is this letter really necessary? Could it be more easily faxed, e-mailed or handled with a phone call?"

○ Control costs by using appropriate delivery services. Business owners often overpay for postage because they don't know the differences between certified and registered mail. (Certified is when you just want to ensure a letter arrives by requiring a signature; registered is for mailing valuables.) Establish and enforce policies governing the use of overnight delivery and second-day air. If something doesn't have to be there overnight, there's no point in paying for it.

○ Keep mailing lists up to date. Computerizing your list and checking it regularly for outdated addresses cuts down on duplicate and unnecessary mailings.

○ Keep postage scales in good working order. Scales occasionally get out of whack, so you could be paying more postage than necessary.

growing company, you have to do this with an eye toward providing for future requirements.

Start by addressing work area needs. Determine how much space you will require for filing systems, office and computer supplies, company literature such as brochures and letterhead, and equipment such as fax machines, printers and copiers. Don't forget room for phones and answering machines and the full array of compute peripherals: monitors, hard drives, scanners, backup drives, speakers and the like. When designing your layout, consider how work flows—do you take printouts directly from the printer to the fax frequently?—and do what you can to help tasks get done easily and quickly.

Lighting is a key element of effective office design. You should know whether you and your employees prefer natural or electrical lighting, ambient overheads or indirect task fixtures, and incandescent or fluorescent lamps.

Work-related injuries are often traced directly to office layout, so ergonomics should play a significant role in your office design. Adjustability is the watchword when it comes to furniture and fixtures. Chairs, monitor stands, keyboards trays, mouse rests and footrests should be adjustable to a variety of heights and angles to allow for variety in the posture required to work at them. Here are ergonomic considerations when setting up workstations:

○ Computer monitors should be 24 to 36 inches from the worker's eyes, with the center of the screen just below eye level, requiring the neck to be bent at no more than a 15-degree angle up or down.

○ The worker should be able to work sitting firmly against the back of the chair, with back and shoulders in a relaxed, natural position.

○ Armrests should support elbows at a 90-degree angle close to the body. Wrists should extend at the same angle. Keyboards should be usable with fingers slightly arched.

○ Chairs should be at a height so that knees are at a 90-degree angle to the floor. Feet should be securely on the floor or on a footrest.

chapter 28

Beating
Business
Cycles

Savvy entrepreneurs are skeptical of sales

charts without dips and profit projections without valleys.

Forecasts that repeat last month's numbers reflect wishful

thinking—not reality. The truth is, no business is insulated from

industry cycles, economic trends and seasonal fluctuations.

Even in the most consistently growing real-world companies,

sales don't go straight up, and expenses don't remain level as sales increase. A sensible growth plan takes into account the cycles of business and finds ways to minimize and exploit them.

Types Of Business Cycles

Business cycles are periods during which a business, an industry or the entire economy expands and contracts. Many business cycles are anything but regular. They vary in intensity and length. Others are based on seasons of the year, holidays and other recurring events.

Seasonal Fluctuations

Bathing suits and sunscreen sell well in spring and summer, poorly in fall and winter. The opposite is true of coats and gloves. Those are just a few of the more obvious examples of the seasonality that affects many, if not most, businesses. Less well-known examples include fast-food outlets and other restaurants regularly suffering sales declines in the winter and boosts in the summer, especially in northern climes. Don't underestimate the potential effect of seasonality. Cooler maker Igloo's sales during its busiest month, June, are 10 times those in its slowest months.

There are many things you can do to smooth out seasonality—and you should do some or all of them if you want to grow steadily. Seasonality is a management challenge; it makes it harder for your company to grow when you experience wide swings in demand. If seasonality is causing you problems, think of ways to generate steady sales. For example, one mail order flower company gets as much as 40 percent of its revenue from a flower-of-the-month-club program, which helps smooth out the seasonality of this business.

Viewpoint

Not all seasonal fluctuations are natural. Well-known man-made seasonal effects include the rush accountants experience before each tax filing deadline and the back-to-school busy season for apparel makers and merchants.

Timing Of Holidays

One of the best-known examples of the power of seasons on business is the year-end holiday sales boom that

Danger Ahead!
Companies that supply capital goods to industries that are going through severe fluctuations usually experience those fluctuations far more acutely. When the notoriously cyclical semiconductor business is in a down phase, for example, semiconductor equipment suppliers frequently struggle to survive. The same goes for toolmakers in the auto industry. If you supply a cyclical industry, increase your reserves so you can better weather the bad times.

packs half the year's sales into a few months for many retailers. But the timing of holidays is even more sensitive than it may appear. Holidays that do not occur on the same calendar date each year may have different effects on business, depending on when they actually take place. Easter is a good example. It may occur during a broad spread of weeks in March and April. If it's early, retailers in the North may be hurt because they have displayed swimming suits that don't appeal to shoppers who are still wearing their winter coats. If it's late, on the other hand, retailers have to be ready to supply summer tastes in goods along with their Easter displays.

Your business may not be influenced by the same holidays everyone else's are influenced by. That's true for companies that do the majority of their business overseas, where different laws and customs mean different holidays. But don't forget the effect of holidays in foreign countries. Trying to reach decision-makers in France during August, when the entire nation seemingly takes a mass vacation, is usually fruitless, for example. Know the customs and holidays of whatever countries you do business in, and you will avoid being blindsided by holiday-related fluctuations.

Economic Cycles

Expansions and contractions of the economy, also sometimes referred to as booms and busts, are broad economic events that affect many industries and companies. The United States economy has experienced approximately 10 of these boom-and-bust business cycles since 1945. They have varied in length from the abbreviated six-month contraction that followed the five-year expansion from 1975 to 1980, to the 106-month expansion that spanned the 1960s.

At this writing, the longest expansion, which began in 1991, was still ongoing. The characteristics of economic cycles include:

○ Fluctuations tend to affect durable manufactured goods more than services.

○ Wholesale and industrial prices tend to be affected more than retail prices.

○ Short-term interest rates track and amplify the cycles, moving in an exaggerated manner along with the economy.

Random Events

Don't ignore the influences of fortune on your business. Wars, hurricanes, floods and fires can all have powerful effects on your business. These tend to be bad influences, as when you have your inventory destroyed by high water or a warehouse that collapses in an earthquake. They may affect just you, in the case of a fire, or they may affect the entire industry or nation, as in the case of the oil embargoes of the 1970s. Wars in particular have a tendency to affect the entire economy, producing booms in their early years as government spending mushrooms and followed by the dampening effects of inflation and, later, recession as the economy cools down.

Some random events can be beneficial to some businesses. A roofing company, for example, could see a boom in business immediately after a destructive hailstorm strikes its service area. Likewise, many companies have built their businesses on lucrative defense contracts obtained during wartime. It doesn't pay to structure your business around hoping for disaster, but you should be ready to swing into action when random events create extra demand for your products and services.

Tracking And Taming Business Cycles

Much effort has been expended trying to develop ways to predict the turning points of business cycles. Few things are widely agreed upon, however. For example, falls in stock prices, profit margins and finally profits are generally seen as precursors of downturns. However, even experts disagree on the timing of these so-called leading indica-

Viewpoint

Want to know about an industry that isn't usually affected by broad economic cycles? Two types of businesses that are less affected than most by expansions and recessions are agricultural and natural resources companies.

tors. It may be weeks or months after a stock market crash before the economy begins to show signs of receding. Then again, it may never happen. And there are many other indicators, such as housing starts, interest rates and price indices, that economists look to for help tracking and forecasting changes in business cycles.

Economic Forecasts

The Conference Board Inc., a private, nonprofit New York City research organization, produces a monthly report that looks at recent figures on employment, income, prices, costs, inventories and many other factors. One of the most interesting features of these reports is the index of leading indicators, which is an attempt to peek at the near future of the economy. The leading indicators include average weekly hours worked by manufacturing employees, unemployment claims, new orders for consumer goods, building permits, interest rates, and an index of consumer expectations. Unfortunately, because of difficulties in the timely collection of all this data, it is subject to revision for some months after a report has been released. Therefore, the "forecasts" of an upcoming recession are often made after the recession has arrived.

It may be weeks or months after a stock market crash before the economy begins to show signs of receding.

In general, economic forecasts are not perfectly reliable. Neither, of course, are the hunches and intuitions of entrepreneurs. However, taken together and applied carefully in view of what you know about your particular industry and company, economic forecasts can help you to prepare for changes in the direction of the economy—before or soon after these changes occur.

Planning For Cycles

Highly seasonal businesses must avoid the tempting budgeting short cut of taking the projection for first-year sales and dividing it by 12. If you have wide-ranging changes in cash flow needs, that kind of budgeting error could sink you. So enter sales and cash needs on a monthly basis, taking into account the expected effect of the seasons on each month. Otherwise, planning for cycles is largely a matter of recognizing that they exist. This may mean not assuming that the current good times will go on forever. Plan for tougher times by limiting the costs you add to your business. In particular, be wary of paying higher recurring expenses such as rent.

Fast Lane

When business booms, you may want to outsource or hire temporary workers until you are sure the expansion will be a long-lasting one. Using flexible workers and outsourcing nonessential functions allows you to not only grow faster, but to shrink faster if the need arises.

Entrepreneurs tend to take on unnecessary expenses when times are good, but this can sink you if a recession strikes. Look out for overly lavish expense accounts, over-reliance on high-priced professional advisors, products that don't carry their weight, and even marginal customers you'd be better off without. Trimming these costs when times are good will help your profits now and may make the difference between success and failure when the cycle turns the other way.

Also think twice before adding expenses that may be hard to cut, or even cost more to cut than they do to keep. Chief among these costs is people. It can be emotionally as well as financially painful to lay off workers in the event of an economic downturn. And the costs for severance pay, unemployment insurance, outplacement and retraining may also be steep. Remember: Even if your income statement and balance sheet are strong now, you have to practice cost containment to be ready for the next recession.

Getting Directions

Agile Manager's Guide to Cutting Costs (Velocity Business Publishing) by Jeff Olson is a manual full of practical cost-control tips and techniques in a concise format. Learn more at www.agilemanager.com or call (888) 805-8600.

chapter 29

Time ~~And Stress~~ Management

 business owner can ignore employee stress if he or she doesn't care about employee productivity and creativity," says Allan Rabinowitz, owner of Stress Strategies Resources in Los Angeles. "We know that when stress goes up, work quality goes down—and absenteeism and conflicts between employees increase. If you want your employees doing

their best work, you simply have to care about their stress levels."

Stress overload hurts a growing business in several areas, including:

○ *Decision-making:* The best decisions are often made when we are in a relaxed, relatively unfocused state, as opposed to a tightly focused state of teeth-clenching. You can not make your best decisions when you are dealing with unmanaged stress.

Fast Lane

It's counterintuitive to think that adding a task to your already-overstuffed day could make it easier to accomplish the rest of your work. But it's a fact when you're allocating extra time to save time. Plan to spend at least five minutes each day on time management. It will regularly be the best-spent five minutes of your day.

○ *Health:* Excessive stress levels have been tied to many health conditions, from hives to heart disease. Considering the costs of health insurance and medical care—not to mention downtime and lost productivity due to replacing stressed-out, burned-out employees—you can't afford to ignore stress.

○ *Employee retention:* Replacing burned-out employees is something you will have to do unless you deal with the stress levels in your company. It's never easy to find good people, and good people will stay away in droves once word gets out that your workplace has a stressful environment.

The bottom line: Working to cut employee stress is not feel-good management; it's dollars-and-cents management. If you don't attend to the waves of tension washing over your workers, you just might find that your plans for growing your business have been wiped out.

Reasons To Control Stress

Maybe you're thinking that stress is simply an inescapable part of the entrepreneurial environment. And for you that might be true. It's even arguable that good entrepreneurs thrive on stress—the more stress they're under, the tougher they fight. "But you need to recognize that employees aren't entrepreneurs—they aren't as driven as you are," says Richard Hagberg, an organizational psychologist and CEO of Hagberg Consulting Group in Foster City, California.

"The name of the entrepreneurial game is getting long-term results," adds Hagberg, whose consulting practice centers around high-flying Silicon Valley computing companies. "To survive, you may have to push your people occasionally. But when stress becomes a way of life in your company, employees will leave, because in today's full-employment economy, people have lots of choices."

Look at your balance sheet, and the math is compelling. When stress is out of control, productivity tumbles, creativity sags, and good employees take flight. So how can you lower stress levels in your company? One way to start is to break stress into two clusters: stressors that you as the business owner can control and those you can't. Despite your best intentions, you can't change how your competitors behave, and you can do little to impact the conduct of customers.

But there are stressors you can change. "For instance, is there ambiguity about job descriptions and the responsibilities of individual workers?" asks David Munz, a St. Louis University professor of

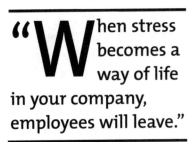

"When stress becomes a way of life in your company, employees will leave."

psychology who consults with businesses on stress-reduction programs. "Employees tell us that's a big stressor, and it's common. Do employees have the information and resources they need to complete their tasks in a timely and satisfactory fashion? When they don't, they'll feel a lot of stress."

Managing Stress Levels

One way to combat stress in your workplace is to look around for glaring trouble spots. Then ask workers what bugs them, and listen carefully. You won't be able to resolve every annoyance they pinpoint, but odds are you'll be able to reduce at least some of their tension.

Another stress buster—and morale booster—is giving employees more control over their workload and pace. "When employees don't have that control, they feel substantial stress, especially in small businesses, where many workers feel the boss is always looking over their shoulder," says Paul Spector, an industrial and organizational psychology professor at the University of South Florida in Tampa.

Getting Directions

Looking for more stress-busting tips? Try www.jobstresshelp.com, an online consulting resource developed by psychotherapist Bill DeLeno that provides loads of free information.

It's easy to put too much on an employee's plate—especially when you have a high performer who is always willing to do more. But eventually, stress will set in and performance will suffer. The antidote is to give your employees more control—but how? Make it clear that when employees feel overloaded, you want them to speak up so you can find ways to lighten their burden. And if they do speak up, be grateful for their honesty—don't make them feel they can't pull their weight.

While you're at it, empower your employees to set limits on how many hours they'll work. "We're seeing more of this, even in Silicon Valley," reports Hagberg. "Employees are putting caps on how many hours they'll work, and they're flatly refusing to work weekends."

Your first reaction may be "How dare they!" But lighten up. It's genuinely for the good of your company to have employees set limits on work hours. Why? Research clearly shows that when employees have abundant and satisfying lives outside the office, they cope better with workplace stress. Granted, there will be times—during crises and emergencies—that you'll need to ask workers to put in extra hours. But on the whole, respect their desire to set boundaries.

Another step in the right direction is to "create a compelling vision for the company and its future, and link current activities to achieving that vision," says Hagberg. "When people clearly see what they are striving for and how what they're doing today relates to that, they can live with a much higher level of stress for a longer period of time. When they feel they're on a mission, their ability to cope with stress increases." It's up to you to articulate a vision your employees will buy into.

You and your employees can also develop stress-management skills that will help all of you cope when busy times hit. "While you have to be commit-

Fast Lane

Exercise is a quick, proven stress buster. It need not be much—just going for a walk or engaging in some brisk exercise such as a few push-ups or climbing up several flights of stairs. A few minutes spent elevating your heart rate can lower your stress level.

Here's The Rub

Here's one answer to your and your employees' stress—on-site massage. It can reduce stress, help manage work-related pain from carpal tunnel syndrome or neck cramps, and even enhance productivity.

A growing number of big corporations, small businesses and even government agencies have found massage to be a low-cost investment that produces big returns. The Touch Research Institute at the University of Miami in Florida has documented the positive effects of massage therapy with research that indicates a basic 15-minute chair massage, provided twice weekly, results in decreased stress and increased productivity.

Clients remain fully dressed and sit in a specially designed chair while the massage therapist works on their neck, back and shoulders, explains Marilyn Kier, a nationally certified massage therapist and owner of Wellness at Work in Wheeling, Illinois. Though pricing varies, the average hourly rate for workplace massage is $60, and Kier says she completes an average of three employees massages per hour. Companies handle the fees differently: Some pay the entire fee, others split the cost with employees, and still others provide the space and opportunity but ask employees to pay the full amount.

To locate a certified massage therapist in your area, contact the American Massage Therapy Association at (847) 864-0123 or visit its Web site at www.amtamassage.com.

ted to reducing stressors in the environment, employees need to develop skills so they don't experience so much wear and tear from the stressors you can't change," says Munz.

Stress-reduction techniques can be relatively simple. "I teach people to relax and count their own breaths as they breathe deeply, for instance," says Rabinowitz. "It takes only a few seconds, but it works." Master that technique and then teach it to employees. Ask them to use it when their stress levels jump off the meter.

You can also deflate stress by meditating on your favorite vacation spot or counting down slowly from 100 to zero. "People can learn to relax," says Spector. "And every employee should know a few relaxation techniques they can depend on in tough moments."

Post four or five stress-busting techniques where employees can see them, such as in the break room or kitchen. Ask them to add ideas they find useful—and encourage all the employees to put stress-reduction techniques into practice whenever the need arises.

As in most workplace situations, communication is crucial to keeping stress in check. "If employees feel there are avenues [of communication], their stress goes down," says Dr. Venetta Campbell, a psychology professor at Mt. St. Mary's College in Los Angeles. "You can get good results just by encouraging employees to get together over a brown-bag lunch once a week to share concerns and to relate stress-management tools that work for them."

Whether it's encouraging workers to blow off steam with vigorous lunch-time walks or just holding a one-hour meeting to talk about stress and its solutions in your business, know that whatever you do to help your workers cope with stress, good things will result. "The fact that you acknowledge stress is an issue and showing a willingness to work on it reduces stress in the workplace," says Munz. "Take steps, and employees will appreciate it."

How Do You Handle Time?

Everybody has a relationship with time. Some see it as an enemy, some as a friend. Some people never seem to have enough time, while others manage to get more done in a day than seems humanly possible. Energy level has something to do with that, as do organizational ability and various hard-to-control factors such as the number of interruptions other people make in your day, and even the time relationship sported by people at your company. But one thing is the same everywhere: As your company grows, the demands on your time will grow, too. Learning to handle time and developing a good working relationship with it is an important part of heading up a growing company.

Managing Time Wisely

Often, it seems time is managing us more than we're managing time. But managing time is actually a simple proposition. If you're going to manage time well, there are just four things you have to do consistently:

1. *Track your time usage.* Photocopy a page from your daily planner and instead of planning the day on it, record the time you actually spend doing things. After a week or two of this, patterns will start

Danger Ahead!

"If you want something done, ask a busy person"—ever heard that? It's probably good advice as long as you're not the busy person being asked to do more. When you're overloaded, let people know it. Don't accept more work if you can avoid it. Don't even let people pitch you more work if there's no way you can do it. If they want something done, refer them to someone less busy.

to emerge that reveal how you are actually spending your time.

2. *Allocate your time wisely.* Armed with facts from tracking your time usage, you can start allocating time wisely. You'll know, for instance, that it takes you 15 minutes to run out and get coffee and a bagel, not the five minutes you have been unwisely allocating. Another aspect of wise time allocation is prioritizing. It may be that a quarter-hour for a midmorning snack makes it just too expensive timewise. If you'd be better off spending that time returning phone calls, allocate it that way.

3. *Stick to the schedule.* "No battle plan ever survived contact with the enemy," said military master Karl von Clausewitz. It's much the same with a daily schedule. Too often, by lunch time, your plans are shattered, and your day may be spiraling out of control. Try, for just a few days, to stick to the schedule. If the schedule says it's time to switch tasks, switch. You may want to make some adjustments, but whenever possible, make them to the next day's schedule, not today's.

4. *Delegate what you can.* Doing other people's work is an excellent way to get behind on yours. You're much better off delegating work to others in your organization who might have more time on their hands or more skill in a particular area, allowing them to complete a task more quickly than you can. As your company grows, you'll spend more time strategizing and less time on the daily components of running a business. So hand off the time-eating details and concentrate on the big picture.

Victory Over Voice Mail

Depending which side of the beep you're on, voice mail can be a stress easer and a timesaver or a stress creator and time destroyer. You can take the stress out of voice mail by doing the following:

○ *When recording your message, if your system has the capability, let the caller know within the first few seconds how he or she can bypass your greeting to leave a message.* In your contact management software, card file or the address book within your planner, note how you can bypass others' messages.

○ *Keep your greeting short, simple and professional.* Include the basics and exclude extraneous information. Don't forget to include your Web address for callers who need more information. Review your message after you've recorded it to ensure your voice sounds clear and that there are no unwanted background noises.

○ *During your greeting, ask the caller to indicate the best time to return his or her call, and do this when you leave messages for others.* This simple request spares you the agony of phone tag (and let's be honest—you'll also know the best time to call and leave a message for a long-winded client or friend). Also, ask the caller to leave his or her phone number in case you don't have it with you while you're out of your office.

○ *If you're out of your office most of the time, consider combining your voice-mail system with a paging system.* When someone calls, you can give them the option of paging you immediately.

○ *Don't save all your voice messages.* Instead, take action. After writing down the message and number, delete it.

chapter 30

Communicating
Effectively

S uccessful entrepreneurs are rarely considered poor communicators. True, entrepreneurs have many
styles of communication, from go-go cheerleading to dignified
vision setting. But good communicators have one thing in common: They are more likely to lead their companies to success
and growth than those who can't say what they mean and
understand what others are saying back.

Are You A Good Communicator?

Good communication isn't complicated. At its most basic, it involves saying what you mean clearly, concisely and politely and then listening courteously and attentively to what is said in return. Some secondary skills include summarizing and repeating information for clarity, and encouraging others to inject their comments to expand the flow of communication. But essentially, it's nothing more than speaking (or writing) and listening with care and courtesy.

Getting Directions

Thousands of people have learned to give speeches, chair meetings and provide constructive feedback through Toastmasters International. Learn how to find a local branch of this nonprofit, low-cost organization by writing to Toastmasters at P.O. Box 9052, Mission Viejo, CA 92690, calling (949) 858-8255, or visiting www.toastmasters.org.

Perhaps a better way to tell whether you are a good communicator is to find out if you practice bad communications. Examples of bad communications include being unclear and asking the wrong kinds of questions.

Many people who are worried about their communications skills try to avoid the issue by being ambiguous whenever possible. This is a big mistake. Ambiguous instructions lead to ambiguous outcomes. If you want an employee to do exactly what you say, say exactly what you want and don't leave anything to chance.

It's also important to use the right kinds of questions. Use open-ended questions when you want to give people a way out, as when you are trying to probe someone's feelings on a sensitive topic. An open-ended question is one that can't be answered with a simple yes or no, such as "What do you think of that new report?" If you're after information, you can use closed-ended questions, such as "Are you going to have that report ready Monday?" It's hard to give an ambiguous answer to that one.

Listening Skills

Being able to listen well is a valuable skill. It encourages others to come to us with their problems and opportunities, and it greatly enhances our ability to lead and make decisions. What is even more surprising is its rarity. Everyone wants to be listened to, it seems, but few are willing to take the time to listen to others. But being a good listener is not an obscure skill. You can become perceived as a good listener by following a few simple rules.

> **Getting Directions**
>
> More than 1 million copies have been sold of the Gentle Art book series on practical communication by linguist Suzette Haden Elgin, Ph.D. *The Gentle Art of Verbal Self-Defense at Work* (Prentice Hall Press) is Haden's translation of her techniques for listening and self-expression for the working world.

- ○ *Never interrupt.* Let the other person finish speaking before you start, no matter how much you may disagree with what he or she is saying.

- ○ *Give the speaker your full attention.* Don't check your watch, sip your coffee, flip through a file folder or otherwise divert your attention from what's being said.

- ○ *Encourage the speaker by making reassuring sounds such as "uh-huh" and saying "yes" or "I see."* Lean forward slightly and face the speaker to make sure your body language says the same thing. And smile.

In addition to being perceived as a good listener, it's a good idea to actually be a good listener. That means not drifting off in a daydream, formulating a response to what's being said or in any other unseen way failing to pay attention to the person speaking to you.

Offering Constructive Criticism

It would be nice if the best way to offer criticism were to be honest and upfront. Telling someone exactly what you think of him or her sometimes seems like the right way to clear the air, especially when you're angry or disappointed about something they have done. However, that is not a prescription for getting people on your side. Rarely should you offer unvarnished opinions of others' performances. Instead, follow these techniques to get your point across without making an opponent in the process:

- ○ *Make sure you're addressing constructive criticism to the behavior and not the person.* Explain to a chronically tardy employee that coming in late to meetings interferes with productivity. Don't call the person a lazy loafer who can't get out of bed in the morning.

Meetings That Matter

The secret to holding an effective meeting is to know why you are holding it. Then you have to communicate that reason to the people participating. Finally, you have to evaluate how well the meeting has met its goals. At the meeting, you need to be sure you are dealing with problems effectively, gathering input from all sides, keeping on track and, above all, keeping the meeting from becoming a time waster. Here are five steps to holding effective meetings:

1. *Before you call it, ask yourself: What's the purpose of this meeting?* What will I consider a successful outcome? Who will have to attend for the meeting to accomplish its goals?

2. *Prepare a clearly written agenda and make sure everyone invited gets a copy.* Include a brief description of each item, the time allotted for each item, and how each item will be dealt with, such as generating a report, further discussion, making a decision, etc.

3. *Assign roles to key meeting participants.* For example, assign someone to take notes, another to facilitate, another to keep time, etc.

4. *Follow established problem-solving procedures during the meeting.* Identify the issue, create a goal, gather input, and create a plan including a schedule and individual responsibilities for carrying it out.

5. *Follow up your meeting with a written summary of what was accomplished, including any decisions, schedules and responsibilities that were established.* Note any items that were carried forward to the next meeting. Summarize progress made on them and other items that weren't resolved. Finally, set a time, place and agenda for the next meeting.

Try to make meetings feel inviting, and encourage everyone to participate. Concentrate on seeking solutions. Try to provide closure when moving from one item to another. And always acknowledge other people's contributions to making your meetings successful.

Viewpoint

It's tough to say "no" nicely and even tougher to give criticism and impart bad news. You can help, however, by making sure people's feelings are separated from what you're saying. For example, if you have to refuse a request, clarify that you are nixing the request, not the person making it. Criticize behavior, not people. And cushion bad news by sandwiching it between two pieces of good news.

○ *Avoid saying "you" and focus on saying "I" and including your feelings.* For instance, instead of saying "You failed to make quota last month," say "I'm worried about the failure to make quota last month."

○ *Mix negative feedback with positive feedback.* The sugarcoating technique is one of the oldest around because it works. Before you point out someone has messed up, take note of where they have done well.

Taking Criticism

People who love to be criticized are hard to find. But you have to do the best job you can of listening to it, or risk alienating and perhaps angering the person giving it. Plus, honest criticism can be a powerful tool to help you learn to be a better entrepreneur. Here is a three-step process for taking criticism well:

1. *Acknowledge the critic.* Simply acknowledge that you hear what is being said. Do not agree or disagree at this stage. Just demonstrate, with eye contact, a nod and a simple summary of what was said, that you heard it.

2. *Ask gentle questions.* Request more information. Don't be challenging. Just ask for more details. Focus on issues, not feelings.

3. *Respond honestly.* If the criticism seems justified, accept it and say so. If you disagree, you might ask permission to state your opinions. In either case, say what you will do differently to respond to the criticism. Finally, thank the person who offered the criticism and ask if they have further response to your comments.

Handling criticism gracefully isn't always easy. You may have to bite your tongue when you feel you're being unfairly attacked. But remember the other person has a point of view, too. Being respectful of that viewpoint will pay dividends in more open communication.

chapter 31

Coping With Competition

Competition is good for you. Competition drives innovation, inspires perseverance and builds team spirit. And that's not all. Many times, the presence of competition increases the market for everyone. For instance, when a Wal-Mart goes up on the edge of a small town, not all local businesses get hurt. Nearby restaurants, gas stations, jewelers

Getting Directions

The Internet Age of Competitive Intelligence (Quorum Books) by John J. McGonagle and Carolyn M. Vella discusses the impact of the Internet on the acquisition and use of information about business opponents.

and personal service providers such as hair salons benefit from added traffic and, often, have higher sales than before.

Competition isn't all good, of course. While using the presence of threatening rivals to focus and motivate employees, you also have to make sure your competitors aren't going to steal your customers. Meanwhile, you will be doing everything you can to grab sales from your rivals. Step one in both of these processes is to identify and know your competitors.

Know Thy Enemy

Not all businesses are your competitors. If you own a bookstore, for instance, you don't have to worry about the coffee bar next door siphoning off your sales. Quite the reverse, in fact, as book buyers may be lured by the scent of java, and coffee lovers may wander over for some reading material to peruse as they sip. Many other businesses are essentially irrelevant to your business. If your motorcycle dealership sits adjacent to a day-care center, the odds aren't good that many of the day-care clientele—parents or children—will turn out to be hot prospects for a bike.

Determining exactly who is your competition is pretty easy. Companies that offer the same or similar products as you do may be competitors. If their geographical market areas overlaps with yours and their price points also resemble yours, it's almost a certainty that they're competitors. But you may also be in competition with companies that offer products that are sub-

Getting Directions

The Society of Competitive Intelligence Professionals (SCIP) is an international group that sets standards, provides education, hosts events and publishes information about competitive intelligence. Contact the SCIP at 1700 Diagonal Rd., #600, Alexandria, VA 22314. You can call (703) 739-0696, fax (703) 739-2524, send e-mail to info@scip.org, or visit www.scip.org.

stitutes for yours. Look at companies that sell accessories to your products—they may want to begin offering a complete solution. In general, it's safe to say that anyone who sells anything that is related to your offerings, either as an accessory or a replacement, is an actual or potential competitor.

Monitoring The Competition

You can develop your own competitive monitoring system by tracking the flow of information about your business and your market. The key question is "How do you make your money, and what other profit opportunities exist in your field?" This is the information that will inspire and guide competitors, and you can follow its flow to learn who those competitors are likely to be, explains Paul Geroski, an economics professor at London Business School.

Tracking information is largely a matter of networking, according to business professor Philip C. Anderson. Talk to vendors, customers, consultants and others who do business with companies in and around your field to find out whether and when new competitors are likely to pop up, he says. Felicia Lindau, CEO and founder of online greeting card retailer Sparks.com in San Francisco, says venture capitalists represent a fruitful source of competitive information for her because due diligence requires investors to research related businesses before backing a company.

Fast Lane

Use Internet indices and search engines to stay abreast of new rivals cheaply and quickly. Once a week or so, type search words describing your market offerings into a Web-based search engine and see what turns up. Use terms your customers might use to describe your product or service, as opposed to technical or insider terms.

Also look in related product markets, adds Geroski. These are the markets whose participants are most likely to understand your customers' needs. For example, he points to the way magazine publishers complement book publishers. Books provide content for periodicals, while magazines provide book publishers with publicity and reviews. Companies whose products complement each other in this way are more likely to become competitors than firms in unrelated industries, he says.

In addition, scan the value chain for your product or service. Geroski points to Microsoft's efforts to use its strength in personal computer operating systems to move up the value chain to sell in markets ranging from word-processing software to online travel services. Companies that occupy spots on your value chain often understand your business and customers well enough to become rivals.

Danger Ahead!

You can damage your business by appearing overly concerned about competitors. Asking customers and vendors whether and why they do business with other firms may be perceived as a sign of weakness. In the process of pumping customers, vendors and others for information, you inevitably reveal your concerns. Be careful not to give away too much proprietary information in the pursuit of knowledge about others.

Also suspect firms with related competencies. Carefully scrutinize companies that have mastered technology similar to yours, even if they appear to operate in distant sectors, Geroski warns. He points to the way companies such as Motorola have used technologies originally developed for the defense industry to become powerful competitors in consumer markets such as those for cellular phones. Competencies can also concern nontechnological skills such as management of retail outlets, new product development or even customer service, he adds.

Responding To Threats

Once you track information, complementary products and related competencies to identify potential competitors, prepare a plan to beat them. The best way may be to preempt them, introducing a new offering so appealing to consumers that competitors decide to look elsewhere for profit opportunities. You may also successfully plan to move second, quickly adopting and improving on ideas that others pioneer, adds George E. Cressman Jr., a consultant on competitive strategy with Strategic Pricing Group Inc. in Marlborough, Massachusetts.

How will you know whether you are successfully detecting and countering competitors? By noting how and to whom you are losing sales, says Cressman. No one wins every sale, but if you start to lose

David Vs. Goliath

It takes a special approach to compete against a firm that is many times your size. Low prices, vast selection, plenty of parking and the simple allure of newness have led many shoppers to abandon small retailers and others for Wal-Mart, Target and other giant firms. Many small stores that tried to compete on service found that attentive service had limited appeal. Yet there are ways to compete effectively against the giants, including:

○ *Hit 'em where they ain't.* Wal-Mart and Target don't sell haircuts, travel services, liquor, and many other products and services. It will take effort to change your business, but it might be your only choice.

○ *Go upscale.* By offering hard-to-find, high-priced goods that aren't suitable for mass discounters, you may be able to do an end run around giant competitors.

○ *Dominate a niche.* Wal-Mart may stock 70,000 items, but it covers a broad range of products. If you focus on a narrow niche, you can cover it better than even the largest mass merchandiser.

○ *Market creatively.* Home Depot may have millions to spend on advertising in your market, but the ads will be the same ones they run everywhere else, perhaps slightly modified to address regional differences. If your hardware store hires a hula dancer to entertain at midnight cabinet-making classes, Home Depot will be hard pressed to follow.

○ *Know your customers.* All the database marketing in the world can't take the place of recognizing your best customers by name—and knowing their favorites items and special needs. Make an effort to get to know your customers as personally and as well as possible. With the high employee turnover at large retailers, that's one thing customers will never find at a giant.

sales to companies you've never heard of, you may be witnessing the birth of a new and unexpected competitor, and your early warning system may be faulty.

part four

The Next
Journey

Y ou can easily spend the majority of your lifetime establishing and growing a business. But that still leaves many years when you may not be actively involved in your business. Chapter 32, on succession planning, lays out rules for finding good hands in which to leave your business. Why would you want to leave your own business? Retirement is the most common reason. But as Chapter 33 shows, without planning, your retirement may not be as secure as you'd like it to be. Fortunately, business owners are in a good position to do something about providing for retirement, and this chapter provides you with a road map to a comfortable one.

What if you're not ready to quit learning? One of the entrepreneurship programs described in Chapter 34 may be for you. And if you want to try a high-powered growth strategy, consider franchising your business, the topic of Chapter 35. Franchising isn't for everyone, but if you can make it work, it can produce growth like practically nothing else.

Finally, you may have never thought about selling your business, but after reading Chapter 36, you should start mulling over the possibilities. Having a good exit strategy is as important as having a good plan for entering and expanding a business. Selling well, it turns out, is all part of ending well when it comes to growing your business.

chapter 32

Succession
Planning

For years, all you thought about was how to get

your business going. Now that you're actually making money

from your idea, it is time to think about your future. Even

though retirement may seem far off now, it's worth it to think

about what issues you may face once you stop actively partici-

pating in your business. Lyle Benson, a CPA in Baltimore, notes,

"In most cases, your business is going to be your largest asset. Even if you don't want to retire, even if you just want to get out of this venture and into another one, you still have to sell your share of the business to someone—and that could mean hefty capital gains." And that, of course, means hefty taxes.

Here is where succession planning comes in. Death and taxes, while inevitable, shouldn't have to be dealt with at the same time. Savvy business owners need an exit plan. A succession plan aims to ensure that when you retire or die, not only will your business continue according to your vision, but your heirs won't be saddled with a huge tax bill for carrying out your plans.

There are several reasons to have a succession plan in place. First and foremost, family businesses in particular need to make sure they

Who'll Fill Your Shoes?

It's up to you to ensure that your business has a capable CEO to lead it into the future after you've left the business. Making that happen requires a multipronged attack consisting of finding, training and, if necessary, hiring a successor to your throne.

Among your offspring is the most obvious place to look for future leaders. But don't make the mistake of assuming a son or daughter will take over your company without checking to see if they can and will. A child who expresses interest and ability in working for your company is a good candidate for succession. One who doesn't seem to care—or who doesn't seem to be up to the challenge—is a poor choice, whether or not they are your offspring.

You can preempt some of the shortfalls of second-generation business owners by training them for the job they will face. This may include giving them experience in a number of jobs in the company to cross-train them as well as uncover their innate talents. It will probably also include outside training, such as working toward a college business degree or working at another company.

If all else fails, you can look to hire an outsider to run your company, either for the foreseeable future or until a family member acquires the maturity and skills to take on the job. In this case, it's essential that any outsider understand the caretaking nature of their role and be ready to hand over the reins when the time comes.

Danger Ahead!

According to the Center for Applied Research at the University of Pennsylvania in Philadelphia, only one-third of all family businesses pass successfully to the second generation, and of those, only 15 percent reach the third generation.

have some kind of succession plan, says Barton Francis, a partner in the accounting and consulting firm Shellenhamer & Co. in Palmyra, Pennsylvania. A succession plan for a family business should address the following questions: Do you want your children to take over the business? Some children but not others? Are your children able to take over the business? Or should they just own it and someone else manage it? If you die, will your spouse get control of the business? If you sell your business outright to your children, will you pay capital gains?

Another important reason to create a succession plan is tax savings. "If you die without some kind of plan in place, estate taxes start at 37 percent and ratchet up to a whopping 55 percent fairly quickly," warns Scott H. Mustin, a partner with the law firm of Krekstein, Wolfson, Mustin & White LLC in Philadelphia. The government gives heirs only nine months to pay this tax, notes Mustin. Given this fact, says Mustin, "it's easy to see why some businesses don't make it to the next generation."

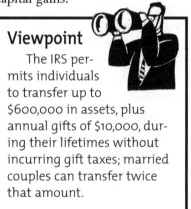

Viewpoint

The IRS permits individuals to transfer up to $600,000 in assets, plus annual gifts of $10,000, during their lifetimes without incurring gift taxes; married couples can transfer twice that amount.

Preparing For Succession

The first thing to do in preparation for succession, according to Francis, is to decide who gets the business next. Keeping in mind that there is a big difference between who runs the company and who owns the company, be realistic in your choice, he says. If your kids don't want anything to do with the business, don't force them. An uncooperative heir can scuttle the whole estate plan after you are gone.

Once you have made the ownership decision, it's a good idea to get a business valuation, says Francis. He suggests using a valuation specialist who has a successful history with the IRS. Most entrepreneurs are shocked to find out how the IRS would value their businesses. "Highest and best use" is the phrase most often bandied about. That means that while you think you could realistically get $100,000 for your business assets, in the eyes of the IRS, they might go for $200,000.

In addition to giving you an idea of what your business is worth, a valuation provides a good starting point for projecting what your tax liability would be if you (or your heirs) were to sell the business. Minimizing this tax liability is at the core of any succession plan, says Mustin.

And, of course, all succession plans must comply with the tax code. The good news here is that in the event of your unexpected demise, there are a few sections in the tax code that might give your heirs a break. For example, IRS Code Section 303 permits, under certain circumstances, the corporation to cash out the owner's stock (upon his or her death) if the proceeds are used to pay estate taxes and administrative expenses. There's also Section 6166, which allows a portion of the federal estate tax to be deferred for up to 15 years (with interest) if the estate qualifies.

It's crucial that your succession plan be structured to take advantage of these sections by meeting their rather exacting circumstances, says Francis. Once you're gone, it's too late to go back and restructure your affairs to meet IRS criteria.

Hiring A Successor

Before you can hand the reins over, you must have someone in place who you are confident can run your business. The natural and easy thing to do is to look for someone who is exactly like you, notes Paul Karofsky, executive director of the Center for Family-Owned Business at Northeastern University in Dedham, Massachusetts. Entrepreneurs often want to pass the reins to someone exactly like themselves to feed family pride, assuage the entrepreneur's own anxiety, or even foster a sense of immortality, Karofsky says.

There's also an inclination to hand control over to someone who will make decisions the same way as the founder did. Potential acquirers of a successful company that is being harvested by the founder naturally want to feel the enterprise will continue to be run in much the same way as when it was run by its successful founder. Just as powerful are the emotional attachments entrepreneurs feel to their own way of doing things. "It's the notion that if you do things differently from the way I do them, you're not doing them well," says Karofsky.

If you decide to try to locate someone who'll run your business as you've run it, don't focus solely on skills. Instead, look at the candidates' styles. You want people who think like you and feel like you, even if they don't necessarily have the same set of abilities.

Finally, don't restrict your search for a successor to outside your company. In fact, the best successors come from inside the organization. "You grow [a suc-

As the company's founder, you may have an almost mythical standing among your employees.

cessor]," says Katharine Paine, founder of the Delahaye Group, a 50-person marketing consulting firm in Portsmouth, New Hampshire. "Find somebody in your company who understands the goals and principles of the [business] and who the other people of the company trust."

Training And Communication

Grooming a successor isn't an overnight operation. Be prepared for it to take time—and lots of it. "It's going to take two or three years," says Paine. While training in management skills and operational issues may take that long, the more important issue is letting trust develop between your candidate and the rest of the company, she says. "You can buy training," Paine notes. "You can't buy trust."

Communication also plays an important role. As the company's founder, you may have an almost mythical standing among your employees. You can't expect anyone to fill your shoes in the eyes of others in the company unless you have personally, convincingly designated them as the heir apparent. You communicate your choice by consistently, plainly saying with words and actions that this is your choice—the person who will run the company after you leave. This job also takes time, but it will pay off in improved effectiveness of the person you leave in charge and, with luck, will lead to equal or even better growth prospects for your company after you leave.

'Til Death Do Us Part

H e that dies pays all debts." Shakespeare no doubt believed in the truth of that line when he wrote it. But then the Bard never had the gut-wrenching experience of American Fastsigns Inc. CEO Gary Salomon. In 1988, Salomon's partner in the fast-growing Austin, Texas, sign company was diagnosed with terminal cancer. Six months later, 37-year-old Bob Schanbaum died.

Grief-stricken at his friend's personal tragedy, it took a while for Salomon to realize the dimensions of the business calamity. The emotionally precarious task of negotiating with Schanbaum's heirs to buy out his interest in the company was bad enough. But that wasn't all. The partner had put off taking a medical exam that—aside from possibly saving his life with an early diagnosis—would have qualified him for a life insurance policy. The proceeds of that policy would have set up his heirs with a half-million dollars. And that policy would also have provided the funds for Salomon to buy out his partner's interest. After his diagnosis, it was too late.

So in reality, the deficits created by Schanbaum's untimely death were sizable. Not only was Schanbaum's family financially short-changed, but Salomon had to reach into his own pocket to buy out his deceased partner's interest. "It was a lose-lose deal," Salomon says, "all the way around."

To minimize death's sting in a business partnership, set up a method of valuing the company and a way of funding a buyout. The popular "King Solomon" agreement says either partner can make an offer to buy out the other's interests. The other partner has the option to accept the buyout offer or to buy the offering partner's stock at the same price.

Most partners cross-purchase life insurance policies on each other to solve the problem of coming up with the money to buy out a partner's interest. The benefit amount of each policy is calculated to be enough to buy out the insured partner's interest in the company, and the beneficiary is the other partner.

Cross-purchasing insurance can get costly, and valuing businesses is always tricky. But making plans for the worst can go a long way toward paying any debts that would arise from the death of a partner.

Transferring Assets

There are infinite ways to divest yourself of your company. Even more so than other areas of estate planning, this is a potential minefield for the novice, filled with such options as trusts, private annuities and self-canceling annuities. Enlisting the right professional is of paramount importance. Among the more popular methods of transferring family businesses, Mustin says, are:

○ *Gifting to family members:* This is one of the simpler means of transferring your business. Individuals may give ownership interest worth up to $10,000 per year (or $20,000, split between husband and wife) to each heir without tax consequences. This is in addition to the $600,000 or $1.2 million in allowable transfers.

○ *Recapitalizing the business:* The departing business owner exchanges his or her common stock in the business for preferred and common stock. He or she then keeps the preferred portion and sells or gifts the common stock to the junior members. All future appreciation of the business is attached to the common shares.

○ *Family limited partnerships:* The owner transfers stock or real estate to a limited partnership. Typically, he or she retains a 1 percent general partnership interest and a 99 percent limited partnership interest, which can be transferred to junior family members by gift or sale.

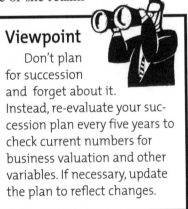

Viewpoint

Don't plan for succession and forget about it. Instead, re-evaluate your succession plan every five years to check current numbers for business valuation and other variables. If necessary, update the plan to reflect changes.

The myriad options available to business owners in transferring their businesses to the next generation should not obscure the real reason for undertaking succession planning. Any plan can maximize tax savings, but if you don't take into account family dynamics, says Francis, you could destroy the business. The basic idea is to shift some of the ownership to the next generation so the growth of the business is not considered part of your estate.

Transferring Control

While transferring assets is a legal and financial operation, transferring control is more psychology-oriented. Here are some major concerns when you are handing over the reins to your successor:

○ Make sure that the successor is clearly seen by other employees as your successor, not an interloper or pretender to the throne who can safely be ignored or discounted.

○ Make sure that you are really ready to hand over control. An entrepreneur who lurks around his or her business after ostensibly handing over the reins is only undermining the effectiveness of the person he or she has chosen to lead the business. So when you leave, leave.

chapter 33

Retirement
Planning

ant to set yourself apart from

other small businesses and appear to be someone with vision,

foresight and a concerned and caring attitude toward employ-

ees? Then set up a plan to provide for a financially secure

retirement for you and your employees. It'll sharply distinguish

you from most other small firms.

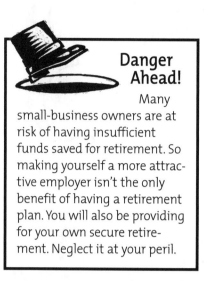

Danger Ahead!

Many small-business owners are at risk of having insufficient funds saved for retirement. So making yourself a more attractive employer isn't the only benefit of having a retirement plan. You will also be providing for your own secure retirement. Neglect it at your peril.

While 80 percent of big businesses offer retirement plans, only 20 percent of small companies offer these plans. So having a retirement plan will make you a more attractive employer than four out of five comparably sized companies right off the bat.

Retirement plans have a current financial benefit as well. Besides the long-term benefit of providing for your future, setting up a retirement plan also provides the immediate gratification of cutting taxes. That's because there are many options for plugging pre-tax funds into retirement savings, reducing the amount of income and other taxes you'll have to pay today.

Tools For Retirement Planning

Here's a closer look at a range of retirement plans for yourself and your employees.

Individual Retirement Accounts

One of the greatest advantages of the Individual Retirement Account (IRA) is its relative simplicity, although the Taxpayer Relief Act of 1997 has made this retirement vehicle a bit more complex. For the most part, however, the paperwork and tax reporting requirements are minimal, and you are not obligated to cover any of your employees, as you are required to do with other types of retirement plans. You can set up or make annual contributions to an IRA any time up to the date your federal income tax return is due.

The biggest drawback to an IRA is that your maximum annual contribution is limited to the lesser of your earned income or $2,000. If you're not covered by an employer-provided retirement plan, then you can make a tax-deductible IRA contribution, regardless of your income.

For joint tax filers, even if one spouse is covered by an employer-provided retirement plan, the spouse who is not covered by a plan may make a tax-deductible IRA contribution if the couple's adjusted gross income is $150,000 or less. The amount you can deduct is decreased in stages above that income level and is eliminated entirely for couples with income over $160,000. Previously, the IRA deduction for a working or nonworking individual whose spouse was covered by a retirement plan was decreased between $40,000 and $50,000. Nonworking spouses and their partners can contribute up to $4,000 to IRAs ($2,000 apiece), provided the working spouse earns at least $4,000.

You may also want to consider the Roth IRA, a variety of IRA created by the Taxpayer Relief Act of 1997. Unlike the rules for traditional IRAs, contributions to a Roth IRA are nondeductible, but withdrawals are tax-free if certain conditions are met. Joint filers can make the full contribution ($2,000) to a Roth IRA as long as their joint income is less than $150,000. For those with income between $150,000 and $160,000, the contribution amount is decreased until it is eliminated completely at $160,000.

Savings Incentive Plans for Employees

The main drawback of the Savings Incentive Match Plan for Employees (SIMPLE) is that it is limited to companies with 100 or fewer employees. Otherwise, a SIMPLE is one of the most attractive options available to small-business owners. With a SIMPLE, you can decide whether to use a 401(k) or an IRA as your retirement plan. A SIMPLE is just that—simple to administer. It does not come with a lot of paperwork or reporting requirements.

SIMPLE is one of the most attractive options available to small-business owners.

The employer must make contributions to the plan by either matching each participating employee's contribution dollar for dollar, which can be up to 3 percent of each participating employee's pay, or by making an across-the-board 2 percent contribution for all the employees, even if the employees don't participate in the plan, which can be very expensive. The maximum amount each employee can contribute to the plan is only $6,000 a year. This is one of the lowest maximum contributions of all the available plans. Therefore, the tax deduction for the contribution will not be as great as it could be with some of the other plans.

Simplified Employee Pension Plans

As its name implies, the Simplified Employee Pension Plan (SEP) is the simplest type of retirement plan available. Essentially, this is a glorified IRA that allows you to contribute a set percentage up to a maximum amount each year. Paperwork is minimal, and you don't have to contribute every year. The catch is, employees do not make any contributions to SEPs. Employers must pay the full cost of the plan, and whatever percentage you contribute for yourself must be contributed to all eligible employees. The maximum contribution is 15 percent of an employee's salary or $24,000, whichever is less.

401(k) Plans

401(k) plans take their name from the section of the federal tax code that provides for them. These plans let you and your employees set aside a percentage of salary tax-free every year. As a kicker, the funds grow tax-free until they're withdrawn. 401(k) plans are very popular benefits with employees because they allow you—the employer—to essentially pay workers more without that income being taxed. Compared to SEPs, 401(k) plans are more popular with employers because most of the contribution comes from the employees.

The Employee Retirement Income Security Act of 1974 (ERISA) governs the way 401(k) plans are set up and managed. There are many responsibilities that go with setting up a 401(k) plan. For instance, you or someone you select has to determine the investment options employees will get to choose from. You have to monitor the investments' performance as well as the service provided by whomever is administering your plan. ERISA exists to make sure any fees that are charged are "reasonable." Setting up a 401(k) is a complicated procedure governed by many arcane rules. You should never do it without consulting with a qualified tax advisor. You can learn more about 401(k) plans at the Department of Labor's Pension and Welfare Benefits Administration Web site at www.dol.gov/dol/pwba.

Getting Directions

With so many retirement plans available, it's a good idea to talk to your accountant about what type of plan is the best for you. Banks, investment companies, full-service or discount brokers, and independent financial advisors can also help you set up a plan that meets your needs.

Profit-Sharing Plans

Profit-sharing plans are defined contribution-type plans that many companies find attractive because of their combination of tax advantages and performance incentives. The key features of profit-sharing plans are that the money put into them comes from a portion of the company's profits that are shared with employees, and that the money grows tax-free. You can't put an amount exceeding 15 percent of your payroll into a profit-sharing plan. Also, allocations to each participant's account are limited to $30,000 per year.

Employee Stock Ownership Plans

Employee Stock Ownership Plans (ESOPs) allow you to make contributions to retirement programs in the form of company stock rather than cash. Aside from that, they are similar to profit-sharing plans. ESOPs are good ways to motivate employees and increase the distribution of company shares and create markets for them. In many cases, ESOPs are used to find ways for company owners to sell the company to employees when the owner wishes to retire.

Viewpoint

Retirement plans can be divided into two types, dubbed defined-benefit and defined-contribution plans. Defined-benefit plans promise to pay a predetermined amount to each employee who retires after working a certain number of years. Defined-contribution plans set the amount that employer and employee will put into the plan each year but don't guarantee that any amount will be paid out.

Planning For Retirement

The key question about retirement planning is "How much money will I need to maintain my lifestyle?" The answer varies, but most financial experts say that you should plan to have about 70 percent of whatever your income will be at the time you retire. That means if you expect to have an income of $100,000 at retirement, a post-retirement income of $70,000 should allow you to maintain the same lifestyle. The smaller amount required for retirement income reflects the fact that you will not have work-related expenses and may also have paid off your mortgage and otherwise reduced living expenses.

Another important question is "At what age should I retire?" As you approach retirement age, postponing your retirement from age 62 to age 65 can make a significant difference in the amount of cash you retire with—and therefore on your retirement income.

Getting Directions

Want to know how you're doing on your retirement investment plan? Check out Financial Engines' online financial forecaster at www.financialengines.com. It's an easy, accurate way to answer the question "Will I be able to retire when I want to, with the income I want?" Plus, it's free.

You'll also have to decide how you plan to generate income from your assets after retirement. Many investors choose popular income-oriented investment vehicles such as CDs, U.S. Treasury bills, corporate bonds, and money market funds. These instruments yield rates of interest that typically vary between 3 percent and 8 percent. They also carry varying degrees of risk, with Treasury obligations generally considered to have no risk and corporate bonds considered to be the riskiest of this group. Municipal bonds and municipal bond funds generate income that is sheltered from U.S. income tax and, in some cases, from state income taxes.

Your Retirement Plan

Before you can decide how to spend your retirement, you have to fund your retirement. The best way to accumulate funds for retirement, both for you and your employees, is through a steady process of saving that starts early. You should select an amount, either a percentage or a flat amount of your income, that you will devote each year to retirement savings. Then you should put that amount of money into whatever investment vehicle you find suitable.

Don't try to time the market by contributing larger amounts when the investment market is booming and smaller amounts during downtimes. Instead, use a trick called dollar-cost averaging to boost your overall returns. Dollar-cost averaging means that if you put the same amount in each year, you will buy more investments, such as

Holding Your Interest

Don't ignore the value of investing early. The power of compound interest, coupled with regular contributions and tax-sheltered treatment, means that an early start to investing will put a powerful ally—time—squarely on your side.

If, starting at age 35, you invested $3,000 each year with a 14 percent annual return, you would have an annual retirement income of nearly $60,000 at age 65. But $5,000 invested at the same rate of return beginning at age 45 only results in $30,700 in annual retirement income.

The benefit of retirement plans is that savings grow tax-free until you withdraw the funds—typically after age 59. If you withdraw funds before that age, the withdrawn amount is fully taxable and also subject to a 10 percent penalty. The value of tax-free investing over time means it's best to start right away, even if you start with small amounts.

shares of a stock mutual fund, when prices are down and fewer when prices are up. The end result will be that you will pay a lower average price than the actual average price of the investment during that period.

The most popular and reliable single investment during the last few decades has been U.S. growth stocks. However, investment experts say you should invest in a variety of investment vehicles, including large- and small-growth stocks and funds, stocks and funds that offer a balance of potential for equity appreciation and reliable dividend income, bonds and bond funds, cash, and, in smaller amounts, perhaps real estate and collectibles such as art. In addition, it's a good idea to diversify your portfolio by investing in international markets. Over decades, a portfolio with a properly balanced allocation of assets should do reasonably well in up markets and down markets, and reliably outperform most other types of investment approaches.

chapter 34

Entrepreneur Study Programs

If you're a business owner with most of your growth ahead of you, one place you may want to go to finance your expansion—as well as to learn how to manage it—is back to school. At least that is the advice of Mark Rice, director of the Severino Center for Technological Entrepreneurship at Rensselaer Polytechnic Institute (RPI) in Troy, New York.

Rice, whose staid title belies his contribution to making Rensselaer one of the powerhouse entrepreneurship schools in the country, has seen the same scenario happen over and over again. Young growth companies tap into the activity surrounding a university and find themselves awash in the kinds of resources—capital included—that help turn great ideas into great companies.

"Creating an environment where companies can thrive requires an important underlying fabric," Rice says. This fabric consists of an active angel network, a source of technology or new business ideas, a large number of entrepreneurs, a base of professionals—such as lawyers, bankers, accountants and marketing consultants—who understand entrepreneurial companies and are prepared to assist them, and a state or local government that maintains a pro-business stance

> Young growth companies tap into the activity surrounding a university and find themselves awash in the kinds of resources—capital included—that help turn great ideas into great companies.

Rice says universities are uniquely qualified to promote and integrate these diverse elements, and as a result, they're havens for entrepreneurs seeking capital as well as the technical resources that are often part of a great success story.

To see just how fertile a university environment can be for raising capital and promoting success, consider the story of Michael Marvin, once an RPI employee who ran the school's manufacturing center and now an entrepreneur with several successful ventures under his belt.

His tale dates back to December 1985, when four RPI students who were completing an entrepreneurship class wrote the course's required business plan. The quartet, who envisioned a company that would create and distribute in-car navigation systems, approached Marvin. Would he help them put the plan into action? Marvin, who gravitated to the university because of its stable of new business opportunities, anted up $12,000. The funds were critical—they put the first breath into the company that was to become MapInfo Corp., a mapping software company in Troy.

Marvin, who joined MapInfo's board, says that RPI "friends and family"—trustees, board members and affiliated angels—immediately invested another $70,000. In June of 1987, investors within the university community kicked in another $500,000, and one year later, yet another $500,000. All told, as part of RPI's affiliate program that allows off-campus companies to participate in various university-sponsored programs, MapInfo raised nearly $1.1 million in its own backyard.

But Marvin, who joined the company full time in 1986, says the university's help didn't stop there. When MapInfo went outside RPI to raise institutional venture capital, the university movers and shakers who sat on the company's board added a lot of weight. "They met with the investors and gave the company a lot more credibility," says Marvin.

As a result, the company raised another $1 million in institutional venture capital. Four years later, the company went public, raising $26 million from a syndicate of underwriters led by technology investment banking firms BancBoston, Robertson Stephens and BT Alex. Brown Inc. with First Albany Corp. also provided regional support. Today, MapInfo boasts annual sales of more than $74 million.

While MapInfo was reaching critical mass, Marvin and RPI were also nurturing LearnLinc Corp., which was founded by RPI professor Jack Wilson and graduate students interested in advancing distance learning (learning via the Internet, videotapes, TV and other technologies). Research and development for LearnLinc, which is also in Troy, began in 1992. Marvin, who now had a seed fund called Exponential Business Development Co. LP, with many in the RPI community as limited partners, kicked in seed financing in 1995 and joined the LearnLinc's board.

Executives from a technology company touring RPI in 1996 learned about LearnLinc and eventually became clients. This was followed by several rounds of institutional venture capital funding and an investment from Intel. In February 1998, Marvin took the helm of LearnLinc to help manage the company's rapid expansion. Now vice chairman, Marvin says it's been a wild ride, but one made possible by the entrepreneurial momentum established by the RPI community. More important, he says, "It's a path other entrepreneurs can take to help realize their vision."

How To Pick A Study Program

If you need help and feel that a university environment might be right for you, your first task is to find the institution that best fits

Fast Lane

If you happen to be located deep in the heart of Texas, the University Of Texas at Austin has one of the country's better entrepreneurship deals. The UT B-school hosts the International Moot Corp. business plan contest, one of the oldest and most popular such contests. UT is also a bargain—with tuition of less than $20,000 a year, it costs around half what schools such as MIT and Columbia charge.

your needs. Experts like Rice and Marvin suggest that not every educational institution is capable of delivering the assistance you need. In particular, they say you should focus your energy on working with a university that has an entrepreneurship program. The different mindsets at different schools are subtle but important. At most universities, for instance, professors prepare students to join a company as an employee after graduation. At schools with entrepreneurship programs, you'll find professors and students preparing to build businesses.

Even schools with fledgling entrepreneurship programs are worth checking out. Bob Tosterud, head of the Council of Entrepreneurship Chairs, a group of business schools with endowed entrepreneurship professorships, says entrepreneurship is a hot topic in universities these days.

"People who are hired by schools to cultivate entrepreneurship chairs are often highly qualified and have lots of contacts in business and academia," says Tosterud. "I recommend calling any university nearby, and if they have even a rudimentary entrepreneurship program, schedule an appointment to talk to the person running it."

Marvin also advises that if you want to approach a university for funding, keep in mind that they offer many ports of entry. "Go in as many doors as possible," he says, "but don't stay anywhere too long if it doesn't look productive." For instance, a school like RPI, which has an active entrepreneurship program, might have affiliate programs in which off-campus companies can get involved. Other options include:

○ *SBA-sponsored Small Business Development Centers (SBDCs):* SBDCs frequently offer a variety of seminars on topics from marketing to finance. Although usually not offered for college credit, these courses can help small-business owners develop their skills.

○ *Alumni outreach programs:* Successful graduates of universities often offer to help current students, recent graduates and even unaffiliated businesses in the university's community by sharing their information, expertise and, sometimes, financial help.

○ *Campus networking events:* You might learn a lot just by hanging out and talking to people at business mixers, management lectures and the like.

○ *Business incubators:* Many universities are setting up business incubators, frequently to help commercialize university research.

○ *Manufacturing assistance centers:* Numerous colleges and universities have government-assisted centers with the mandate of helping local factories improve their competitiveness.

○ *Entrepreneurial resource centers:* Miscellaneous resources could help entrepreneurs range from using university libraries to taking part in research projects to recruiting business students to work as interns.

○ *Continuing education programs:* Continuing education classes in business are often full of working students who add their wealth of real-world experience to what the lecturer may have to offer.

○ *Night schools:* They may not have the cachet of regular daytime courses, but night classes are often taught by the same professors and cover the same material, for the same credit.

○ *Community colleges:* The nation's thousands of community colleges provide low-cost, convenient educational opportunities for entrepreneurs who need basic instruction in topics such as information technology, accounting, marketing and management.

○ *Executive MBA programs:* If you want to get your driver's license for the business fast lane, two to six years in an executive MBA program, usually meeting only at night and on weekends, can get you there.

In addition to trying out these formal and semiformal resources, try approaching professors, deans, executive directors and even students informally. With LearnLinc and MapInfo, for instance, Marvin says the companies got their strongest support and best contacts through alumni.

Getting Directions

You can find a list of top entrepreneurship programs and gain some framework for evaluating them by reading "Measuring Progress in Entrepreneurship Education" in the *Journal of Business Venturing*, published by Elsevier Science. Call (800) 282-2720 for a reprint of this article, which appeared in volume 12, issue 5 of the publication, pages 403 to 421. The cost is approximately $45.

chapter 35

Franchising Your Business

I am looking to expand my employment service into other cities in the United States. Which method is better—franchising or satellite offices?" The questioner is Bill Poindexter, owner of Career Services Inc., a Springfield, Missouri, employment agency. Like a lot of entrepreneurs, he is wondering whether his business is well-suited for the franchising mechanism that made global corporations out of companies such as Century 21 and McDonald's.

The answer to Poindexter's question depends on two things: what kind of business you want to have and what kind of business you have now. The kind of business you have now determines whether your business *can* be franchised. The kind of business you want to have decides whether franchising *is the best way* to build it.

Why Would You Want To Franchise?

Let's start with what you want out of franchising and your business. If you plan to rapidly expand your concept nationwide, franchising is probably your best bet, says Robert Barbato, director of the Small Business Institute at the Rochester Institute of Technology in Rochester, New York.

Because the franchisee—rather than the franchisor—provides the capital for expansion, a business can grow much larger and faster than if it were funded by bank loans or internally generated funds. "You could probably sell a few hundred franchises in several years, but you probably couldn't open a few hundred company-owned offices that fast," says Barbato.

Danger Ahead!

Franchisees can be difficult. A renegade franchisee could seriously harm a business's image in the marketplace. Yet the franchisor may have granted a 10-year license and have few options to stop the franchisee's activities. Choose franchisees and franchise terms carefully.

If, on the other hand, you plan to add only a handful of offices in a few new markets, company-owned satellites are probably a better choice. The heavy legal and regulatory costs involved in creating a franchise will make it impractical for limited expansions, Barbato says.

Also, seriously ask yourself whether you want to become a franchisor, which is very different from being in business for yourself. Are you prepared to handle the more extensive staffing demands necessary to support an entire franchise system? And what about the competition? In an industry with many large, well-established franchises, are you prepared to be the new kid on the block?

Even your management style will likely need to be revised. For example, "A person good at selling employment services may not be good at selling franchises," says Barbato. "For one thing, it's a different customer you're going to be selling to now."

A company-owned office, as opposed to a franchise, is run by a manager who is hired by—and can be fired by—you. However, what a company-owned office gains in control it may lose in terms of the extra dedication a franchisee is likely to show as compared to a hired gun.

What Is A Franchisable Business?

The other key consideration in deciding whether or not to go the franchising route is what kind of business you have now. Even if you think franchising is for you, that doesn't mean your business is franchisable, says Geoffrey Stebbins, president of World Franchise Consultants in Southfield, Michigan. No matter how successful your business is, it won't work as a franchise unless it appears to be a good business opportunity.

"People get too caught up in the actual product," says Stebbins. For example, "we're not talking about selling employment services. We're talking about [whether] the employment service appeals to people as a business opportunity."

What makes an appealing business opportunity? The franchise should be based on a concept with pizzazz, says Stebbins, such as a new kind of fast food or a patented technology for repairing automobile finishes. That's because to really be successful, a franchise has to capture the imaginations of would-be business owners. It's much easier to market a franchise with built-in appeal than one that sounds like some humdrum business.

Needless to say, your franchise must produce a superior product or service. Nobody wants to purchase and run a franchise whose success is based on being the lowest-cost producer. That doesn't necessarily mean that all successful franchises cater to the silk-stocking trade, but it does mean that you need some clearly distinguishing, positive characteristics in the marketplace.

If you produce a superior product or service, it also has to be possible for you to control the quality of that product or service. Much of the appeal of a franchise system to consumers lies in the fact that, no matter where they go, if they patronize one of that system's franchises, they will get the same quality of service and product they would get anywhere else. Unless your product or service is one that lends itself to that kind of standardization, you're going to have trouble franchising your concept.

> Your franchisable business should be thoroughly systemized and its operations documented so it can be copied by others.

If you have a good product, a good market and plenty of pizzazz, you need to look for some security. Specifically, you should have—or try to develop—a strong trademark. Most of the best franchises, such as Subway and ServiceMaster, have spent lots of time and money creating strong trademarks that convey a consistent and appropriate message about the product and the franchise. Of course, to be effective, any trademark you have has to be yours and yours alone—meaning it can't be too similar to ones other businesses are using. It also has to be one that is—or could be—registered for federal trademark protection.

The Importance of A System

A good franchise concept has to be teachable. That means it has to be something you can explain to other people and that they can be expected to grasp readily. To accomplish that, your franchisable business should be thoroughly systemized and its operations documented so it can be copied by others. In addition, it must be a business that can be run in a noncentralized way.

If your business is run on the basis of knowledge that exists only in your head and requires your personal involvement every step of the way, you'll have trouble franchising it. Successful franchisors create detailed operating manuals that set standards and describe procedures for every facet of the business. They also create training programs for franchise owners, managers and employees.

Repeatibility is an essential component of a franchisable business. That means your business must be one that can be replicated over and over in many places by many people. If it can only work in one location—a business offering tours of the Grand Canyon, for instance—it's not repeatable and not franchisable. The same is true if the business can only be run successfully by one person.

Obviously, incorporating all these features into your business is going to take time and energy. In fact, franchising is a very different business from whatever business you're in now. Instead of the customers you are used to dealing with, once you franchise, your customers will be your franchisees. Franchisees invest time and money in your concept, and they can be demanding when it comes to training and support. Make sure you have the time and inclination to support multiple franchisees before you commit to franchising.

Navigating Regulatory Roadblocks

There are many regulatory and legal hoops you have to jump through before you can sell franchises. The federal government has rules, and many states also have specific requirements that must be met for you to sell franchises. These rules often require you to register with the state or federal authorities before selling franchises, as well as meet certain standards as to the way the franchise is set up. Once you're underway, some states stay involved with the relationship between you and your franchisees, controlling or limiting the way franchises can be transferred or renewed, territorial rights can be distributed, and franchisees can be terminated.

The Uniform Franchise Offering Circular (UFOC) is a regulatory document describing your franchise opportunity that prospective franchisees have to receive before they pay any money, sign any papers or, in some cases, even meet with you. If you give a franchisee any details about his or her prospects for making money from a franchise you're offering, those claims have to be made in writing according to certain guidelines.

Danger Ahead! Franchise regulations are taken seriously. If you violate them, you could be subject to civil or criminal penalties, so make sure you know the law and follow it. Consult an attorney who specializes in franchises.

There are a lot of regulatory hurdles to be cleared in franchising. They're primarily designed to protect franchisees. But if your franchisees become dissatisfied and attempt to do things you don't want them to, the franchise agreement and accompanying regulations can work to your advantage as well.

The Finances of Franchising

The final requirement of a franchisable concept is that it must produce an adequate profit. This is a more significant concern than with many other businesses because of the extra costs franchisees must bear. These extra costs come in the form of the upfront franchise fees that are paid to you, the franchisor, as well as the royalties franchises must pay to you in the form of an ongoing percentage of sales.

So the profit-making power of the business has to be sufficient to allow franchisees to pay you a royalty while still leaving enough income for the franchisee. Don't forget that the franchisee has likely had to invest significant amounts to get started. So the business must, in addition to providing the franchisee with income, yield an adequate return for the franchisee's investment.

You're also going to have to pony up significant cash to get the franchise up and running. You have to pay attorneys to create your UFOC document. More attorney's fees will be required to get the franchise registered. You will need accountants to prepare audited financials. Additional costs come from creating marketing materials and running advertising to promote the franchise to prospective franchisees. Don't forget the training staff, manuals and other systems you'll need to run the franchise.

All told, you could easily be looking at a quarter of a million dollars or more to create a workable franchise system, in addition to the everyday costs of running your business in the meantime. While the upfront fees franchisees pay are designed to help you, the franchisor, recover your development costs rapidly, you

Danger Ahead!
When designing a franchise, it is tempting to set high royalties to generate maximum income from franchisees. However, setting royalties is a balancing act. You want a fair financial return, but if you set royalties too high, the financial burden may mean franchisees can't compete with other businesses. If that happens, you will wind up with less in the end.

need to budget for these investments and be sure you see your way clear to recovering them before you embark on a franchise plan.

Does all that describe you and your business? The fact is, few businesses are likely candidates for franchising. Regardless, there are thousands of franchises out there. Ask yourself what it is that makes you different. If your business passes these tests, go for it. Nothing grows quite like a successful franchise.

chapter 36

Selling Your Business

There is a season for all things, and even the most enjoyable entrepreneurial career must come to an end. Unfortunately, for many entrepreneurs, this means the demise of an enterprise that ultimately could not financially justify its existence. Once a business passes a certain anniversary—say, five years—chances of its long-term survival go up.

But long-term viability brings problems of its own. Your business may last forever, or at least many years. But will you last that long? Longing for retirement, a change in interests, a desire to pass the torch or simple boredom may play a role in your decision to exit a business that has brought you satisfaction and accomplishment.

What's Your Exit Strategy?

Just as you needed a plan to get into business, you will need a plan to get out of it. Selling or otherwise disposing of a business requires some forethought, strategizing and careful implementation. In some ways, it is a little more complicated than starting a business. For instance, while there's really only one way to start a company, there are at least three primary methods for entrepreneurs to leave the businesses they founded: selling, merging and closing.

Selling

Deciding to sell the business you've worked so hard to grow is rarely an easy decision. However, it may be the right one under some common circumstances. Selling may be preferable to owning if:

Fast Lane

You may be able to consummate a quick, profitable sale of your business to your employees. These are knowledgeable buyers who are likely to make a go of the business under new ownership. Employees may lack financial resources to make the purchase, but if they can raise the money and manage the business, you may never have to look outside for a buyer.

○ You or another owner get divorced and need cash for a settlement.

○ Partners who own the business decide to dissolve their partnership.

○ One of the owners dies or becomes disabled.

○ You are ready to retire and have no heir to continue the company.

○ You may want to do something more challenging, more fun or less stressful.

○ You do not have enough working capital to keep going.

○ The company needs new skills, a new approach or resources you can't provide.

If you are aware of the factors that indicate selling is a good idea, you can time the sale to take advantage of high prices. Usually, you will get the most for your company when sales are climbing and profits are strong. If you have an unblemished history of solid performance, by all means sell the company before trouble strikes. Other factors that may affect the timing of a sale are availability of bank financing, interest rate trends, changes in tax law, and the general economic climate.

You can sell your business yourself, but many owners contract with a professional business broker to handle the job. In addition to the training and awareness of relevant legal, tax and accounting considerations, a good reason to use a broker is to protect your anonymity and confidentiality. If you're advertising your business for sale and showing it to prospects, it compromises your ability to continue leading the firm. A broker can front for you, screening prospects and keeping the identity of the business owner secret from all but qualified buyers.

Viewpoint

Before selling your business through a broker, ask: Is this a full-time business broker or someone who does it as a sideline? Does the broker belong to professional groups such as the International Business Brokers Association? Who has your broker worked with in the past? Get references from former clients and customers, and check his or her reputation with other professionals.

Merging

Most business buyers are individuals like you who want to become small-business owners. But sometimes you can transfer ownership of a business to another business in a merger or acquisition. As a rule, businesses have deeper pockets and borrowing power than individuals, and they may be willing to pay more than individuals. Businesses also tend to be more savvy buyers than individuals, increasing the chances your business will survive, albeit perhaps as a division or subsidiary of another company. However, businesses can't move as fast as individuals. It may take you a year or more to get your company ready to be merged or acquired. You'll need to:

○ Clean up the balance sheet.

○ Drop poorly performing products.

○ Terminate insider deals, such as property the company is renting from you or family members.

○ Trim excessive fringe benefits.

○ Make sure you're paid up on all taxes.

○ Make sure to have at least two years' worth of audited financial statements.

The best candidate for a merger is a company that sees yours as a strategic fit with their own firm. If you have something they want and can't find elsewhere, such as a unique product or distribution channel, they may be willing to pay a premium price. A competitor who only wants to put you out of business is usually a poor merger prospect, however. This buyer is motivated only by price and probably isn't interested in preserving the business.

Danger Ahead!

An acquirer may ask you to stay on to run the merged company. It's flattering, but get the details in writing. Ask: Will I have to relocate? Who will I report to? What if I want to leave? You will be in a strong position to negotiate terms because you are the new owner's best insurance policy for keeping the business going.

Closing

Sometimes, the best thing to do is simply sell your inventory and fixtures, pay your creditors and employees, close your doors, and walk away. Closing may be the best option if your business is failing, isn't valuable enough for anyone to want to acquire it, or is the type of business that is unlikely to be valuable without you personally operating it. (A law office is a good example of this.) If you can't raise enough money by disposing of your assets to pay everyone off, you can give them what you have and promise to pay the rest later on. You can avoid legal wrangles if the debts are small enough.

Danger Ahead!

You may be forced into involuntary liquidation if you fail to keep happy a large creditor who can foreclose on you and seize all your assets. After paying your employees and key suppliers, keep banks and tax authorities happy. These are the creditors most likely to put a padlock on your door and auction off your equipment, leaving you with nothing.

Variations on this theme include making formal or informal arrangements to pay off your creditors, filing for voluntary liquidation, and declaring bankruptcy. Only bankruptcy is intended to give you a second chance. The others are almost certain to result in the end of your business.

The Ins And Outs
Of Business Valuation

Value, like beauty, is in the eye of the beholder. There are probably as many ways to define value as there are businesses. The basic definition is how much money the business could be expected to sell for on the open market. But that's dependent on what a hypothetical buyer is looking for, how the business has positioned itself, and exactly who is doing the valuing.

"In finance, any asset has value based on its expected future cash flows," says Glen Larsen, professor of finance and chairperson of undergraduate programs in the Kelley School of Business at Indiana University in Indianapolis. "So in the purest sense of the word, you build value by building up expectations of future cash flow to the holder of that asset."

In this sense, value doesn't necessarily equal net profits or even break-even performance. Cash flow is usually more important than profits are when valuing small businesses. Unlike publicly held firms that want to maximize reported profits to attract investors, entrepreneurs often minimize profits for tax or other reasons, notes Karl Vesper, a University of Washington professor and author of *New Venture Experience*.

> **C**ash flow is usually more important than profits are when valuing small businesses.

An entrepreneur may chalk up a trip to Hawaii for a meeting as a business cost or keep a spouse or child on the company payroll when a publicly held company would not. To accurately assess the value of a business, the ability to employ family members and mix business with pleasure must be accounted for. And, Vesper notes, these may have values beyond financial considerations. "Quite aside from the dollar value of these things, there's the psychological value," he says. "Would you take less pay to sleep in in the morning?"

Value may also come in other forms. Ownership of a patent, proprietary process or trade secret may, by promising exceptional future cash flow, increase the value of a business. Companies that dominate a market, no matter how small, are often sought out for purchase at premium prices by other firms that, for one reason or another, want

For What It's Worth

It can be a little unnerving to think about placing a hard cash value on something that, for many entrepreneurs, represents their lives. But there are sound reasons for coming up with a firm figure for what your business is worth. Sometimes valuation is a response to adversity; sometimes it's an attempt to exploit an opportunity. Specific reasons for valuing a business include:

○ To calculate the financial amount of damages if you are suing for damages suffered by your business

○ To calculate your personal net worth for purposes of estate planning

○ To figure your personal net worth to plan for your retirement

○ To prepare an equitable division of family assets in a divorce

○ To guide negotiations connected to a purchase or sale of the business

○ To allow you to place an accurate value on what you're bringing to a merger with another company

○ To assist you in purchasing adequate life insurance, both for yourself and for key executives

○ To fund buy/sell agreements that would activate in the event of the death of a partner

○ To place an accurate value on charitable donations of company stock

○ To make sure you have adequate business disruption insurance to compensate you in the event of a disruption

○ To evaluate a plan for an Employee Stock Ownership Plan

○ To prepare for an initial public offering of stock

Being able to make a convincing case for what your business is worth is invaluable when you're seeking financing. You almost can't do succession planning without knowing the value of the business. And, if part of your growth plan is to grow the value of your business—as it should be—then knowing your business's worth is an essential part of your management plan for growth.

to add that niche to their existing businesses. There are different kinds of value for different kinds of people.

Many businesses count their physical location as a primary component of value. That's especially true in the case of restaurants and other retail businesses and, again, is not necessarily connected to cash flow or profit. Some retailers make a practice of buying businesses only for their locations rather than how much or what they sell, or who they sell it to, figuring that a high-traffic spot will eventually prove a winner for some business combination. The business itself may not be doing well, but if the business got good terms and conditions on its lease, and it's in an excellent location, sometimes they can switch what they sell there.

Location may also play a starring role in value if a company is located in a resort community that has a lifestyle that's attractive to would-be business owners. Other businesses, such as bed-and-breakfasts and bookstores, may have higher values because they appear glamorous or simply interesting to potential buyers.

On the other hand, a business may be worth more if the buyer never has to venture near it. "Certain types of businesses have higher value because the owner is not required to be there," explains Larsen.

The intangible known as goodwill is another key consideration in a business's value. Goodwill may range from a long-established distribution network to a sterling market reputation. And sometimes a buyer will pay top dollar to obtain a business with great goodwill.

For Haim Ariav, chief creative officer of DVCI Technologies, a New York City multimedia production company, goodwill is the kind of value that counts most. Ariav started his company using credit cards for financing. Now he can get regular bank financing, and he says it's because of the reputation he has established by handling six-figure accounts such as Cadbury Schweppes PLC, Nickelodeon, and JVC.

"We show them who our clients are, what we were working on, and what we are going to be working on," says

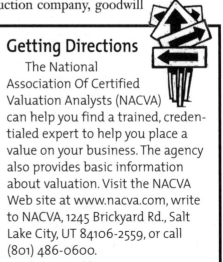

Getting Directions

The National Association Of Certified Valuation Analysts (NACVA) can help you find a trained, credentialed expert to help you place a value on your business. The agency also provides basic information about valuation. Visit the NACVA Web site at www.nacva.com, write to NACVA, 1245 Brickyard Rd., Salt Lake City, UT 84106-2559, or call (801) 486-0600.

Ariav. Because of the size and stability of Ariav's clients, banks are willing to treat projected revenues that will come from DVCI's future jobs almost as if they were physical collateral.

All told, Ariav counts his firm's reputation as the most critical component of its value. "Can you put a dollar on it?" he asks. "I don't know if you can. How much is a reputation worth?"

While Ariav has a point, other important factors that influence value are easier to pin down. Experts agree that if you want to boost your business's value, pay close attention to the bottom line of your cash flow statement. That is because most of the time, the value of your business is simply a multiple of the cash flow it generates.

Life After Business

Whether you sell your business, pass it on to a descendent or simply close it, one thing is certain: Life will go on. But what will be your part in it? The answer depends entirely on you. Here are some of the most popular activities—besides golf and bridge—ex-entrepreneurs use to keep their post-business lives as active and enjoyable as always:

○ The Service Corps of Retired Executives (SCORE) is a national organization of businesspeople who have left their businesses, but not the world of business, behind. In this Small Business Administration program, SCORE members share their hard-won expertise with less-experienced business owners. You can learn more about SCORE at its Web site at www.score.org. You can also call (800) 634-0245 to find the nearest of SCORE's nearly 400 chapters in the United States and Puerto Rico.

○ Philanthropy lures many entrepreneurs to begin giving away the assets they have accumulated over their business careers. The idea of helping others is attractive, and the not-too-pleasant prospect of losing large amounts of wealth to the inheritance tax is another motivation for giving to charities. The difficult part of philanthropy is finding a cause you believe in and that has good opportunities for giving. You can search for causes that meet your requirements at PhilanthropySearch at www.philanthropysearch.com.

Many well-off former and current entrepreneurs, including the likes of Bill Gates, prefer to delegate all or part of the task of distributing their wealth to experts. You can locate an individual giving advisor to help you make philanthropic decisions through such organizations as the National Society of Fund Raising Executives in Alexandria, Virginia, at (703) 684-0410 or on the Web at www.nsfre.org.

○ Teaching is an increasingly appealing prospect for many ex-entrepreneurs. There is a growing interest in entrepreneurship among young businesspeople, and the number of college-level programs teaching entrepreneurship is mushrooming. You do not necessarily have to have a Ph.D. to teach in these programs. Even a high school dropout may be a welcome guest lecturer for a professor who wants his or her students to get a lesson about the real world of starting and growing a business. Teaching, as always, doesn't pay as well as many pursuits. But if you like to share your knowledge and are interested in encouraging others to follow the same track of growing a business that you did, teaching can be an enjoyable and rewarding way to do that.

Fast Lane Want to become a philanthropist before you are rich? You can—through organizations like the entrepreneurs' foundations in Silicon Valley, Austin, Texas, and other places. These organizations accept donations of stock and options in companies that, in some cases, are still quite small. When the firms grow, the theory is, the shares could be worth millions. Meanwhile, although they may be relatively cash-poor, the entrepreneurs have given sizable gifts.

In Closing

For many entrepreneurs, the prospect of not being connected with their company, or even in business at all, is unsettling. But think back to *A Sense of Where You Are*, the account of former U.S. Senator Bill Bradley's college basketball career. The title hints at one of Bradley's most useful talents as an athlete, and later, as a politician—the ability to know where he is on any court and on any issue. The same thing holds true for entrepreneurs. If you didn't have a sense of where you were, you wouldn't have been able to get to where you are now. And when you know where you are, you can be at home there. That's true whether you are in business or involved in some other pursuit. And it's true whether the company you started is still growing or, like an adult child, has already grown up and gone on.

appendix

Government
Listings

Government Agencies

Copyright Clearance Center, 222 Rosewood Dr., Danvers, MA 01923, (978) 750-8400, fax: (978) 750-4470, www.copyright.com

Export-Import Bank of the United States, 811 Vermont Ave. NW, Washington, DC 20571, (202) 565-3946, fax: (202) 565-3380, www.exim.gov

Internal Revenue Service, 1111 Constitution Ave. NW, Washington, DC 20224, (202) 622-5000, www.irs.ustreas.gov

U.S. Copyright Office, Library of Congress, 101 Independence Ave. SE, Washington, DC 20559-6000, (202) 707-3000, fax: (202) 707-6859, www.loc.gov/copyright

U.S. Department of Agriculture, 1400 and Independence Aves. SW, Washington, DC 20250, (202) 720-7420, www.fas.usda.gov

U.S. Department of Commerce, 14th St. and Constitution Ave. NW, Washington, DC 20230, (202) 482-2000, fax: (202) 482-5270, www.doc.gov

U.S. Department of Energy, 1000 Independence Ave. SW, Washington, DC 20585, (202) 586-5000, www.doe.gov

U.S. Department of Interior, 1849 C St. NW, Washington, DC 20240, (202) 208-3100, www.doi.gov

U.S. Department of Labor, 200 Constitution Ave. NW, Rm. S-1032, Washington, DC 20210, (202) 693-4650, www.dol.gov

U.S. Department of Treasury, Main Treasury Bldg., 1500 Pennsylvania Ave. NW, Washington, DC 20220, (202) 622-2000, fax: (202) 622-6415, www.ustreas.gov

U.S. Patent and Trademark Office, Washington, DC 20231, (800) 786-9199, www.uspto.gov

U.S. Printing Office, Superintendent of Documents, Washington, DC 20402, (202) 512-1800, fax: (202) 512-2250, www.access.gpo.gov/sudocs

U.S. Securities and Exchange Commission, 450 Fifth St. NW, Washington, DC 20549, (202) 942-7040, e-mail: help@sec.gov, www.sec.gov

U.S. Small Business Administration, 409 Third St. SW, Washington, DC 20416, (800) 827-5722, www.sba.gov

SBA District Offices

Alabama: 2121 Eighth Ave. N., Birmingham, AL 35203-2398, (205) 731-1344, fax: (205) 731-1404, www.sba.gov/regions/states/al

Alaska: 222 W. Eighth Ave., #67, Anchorage, AK 99513-7559, (907) 271-4022, fax: (907) 271-4545, www.sba.gov/regions/states/ak

Arizona: 2828 N. Central Ave., #800, Phoenix, AZ 85004-1093, (602) 745-7200, fax: (602) 745-7210, www.sba.gov/regions/states/az

Arkansas: 2120 Riverfront Dr., #100, Little Rock, AR 72202, (501) 324-5871, fax: (501) 324-5491, www.sba.gov/regions/states/ar

California: 2719 N. Air Fresno Dr., #200, Fresno, CA 93727-1547, (209) 487-5791, fax: (209) 487-5636, www.sba.gov/regions/states/ca/fresno

330 N. Brand Blvd., #1200, Glendale, CA 91203-2304, (818) 552-3210, fax: (818) 552-3286, www.sba.gov/regions/states/ca/la

550 W. C St., #550, San Diego, CA 92101, (619) 557-7250, fax: (619) 557-5894

455 Market St., 6th Fl., San Francisco, CA 94105-1988, (415) 744-6820, www.sba.gov/ca/sf

660 J St., Rm. 215, Sacramento, CA 95814-2413, (916) 498-6410, fax: (916) 498-6422, www.sba.gov/regions/states/ca/sacr

200 W. Santa Ana Blvd., #700, Santa Ana, CA 92701-4134, (714) 550-7420, fax: (714) 550-0191, www.sba.gov/regions/states/ca/sant. html

Colorado: 721 19th St., #426, Denver, CO 80202-2599, (303) 844-2607, fax: (303) 844-6468, www.sba.gov/regions/states/co

Connecticut: 330 Main St., 2nd Fl., Hartford, CT 06106, (860) 240-4700, fax: (860) 240-4659, www.sba.gov/regions/states/ct

Delaware: 824 N. Market St., Wilmington, DE 19801-3011, (302) 573-6294, fax: (302) 573-6060, www.sba.gov/regions/states/de

District of Columbia: 1110 Vermont Ave. NW, 9th Fl., Washington, DC 20005, (202) 606-4000, fax: (202) 606-4225, www.sba.gov/regions/states/dc

Florida: 100 S. Biscayne Bl., 7th Fl., Miami, FL 33131, (305) 536-5521, fax: (305) 536-5058, www.sba.gov/regions/states/fl

7825 Baymeadows Wy., #100-B, Jacksonville, FL 32256-7504, (904) 443-1900, fax: (904) 443-1980, www.sba.gov/regions/states/fl/north

Georgia: 233 Peachtree St. NE, Harris Tower - 1900, Atlanta, GA 30309, (404) 331-0100, fax: (404) 331-0101, www.sba.gov/regions/states/ga

Hawaii: 300 Ala Moana Blvd., Rm. 2-235, Box 50207, Honolulu, HI 96850-4981, (808) 541-2990, fax: (808) 541-2976, www.sba.gov/regions/states/hi

Idaho: 1020 Main St., #290, Boise, ID 83702-5745, (208) 334-1696, fax: (208) 334-9353, www.sba.gov/regions/states/id

Illinois: 500 W. Madison St., #1250, Chicago, IL 60661-2511, (312) 353-4528, fax: (312) 866-5688, www.sba.gov/regions/states/il

511 W. Capitol Ave., #302, Springfield, IL 62704, (217) 492-4416, fax: (217) 492-4867, www.sba.gov/regions/states/il

Indiana: 429 N. Pennsylvania, #100, Indianapolis, IN 46204-1873, (317) 226-7272, fax: (317) 226-7259, www.sba.gov/regions/states/in

Iowa: Mail Code 0736, 215 Fourth Ave. SE, #200, The Lattner Bldg., Cedar Rapids, IA 52401-1806, (319) 362-6405, fax: (319) 362-7861, www.sba.gov/regions/states/ia/cedar

210 Walnut St., Rm. 749, Des Moines, IA 50309-2186, (515) 284-4422, fax: (515) 284-4572, www.sba.gov/regions/states/ia/desmo

Kansas: 271 W. 3rd St. N, #2500, Wichita, KS 67202, (316) 269-6616, fax: (316) 269-6499, www.sba.gov/regions/states/ks

Kentucky: 600 Dr. Martin Luther King Jr. Pl., Louisville, KY 40202, (502) 582-5761, fax: (502) 582-5009, www.sba.gov/regions/states/ky

Louisiana: 365 Canal St., #2250, New Orleans, LA 70130, (504) 589-6685, fax: (504) 589-2339, www.sba.gov/regions/states/la

Maine: 40 Western Ave., Rm. 512, Augusta, ME 04330, (207) 622-8274, fax: (207) 622-8277, www.sba.gov/regions/states/me

Maryland: 10 S. Howard St., 6th Fl., Baltimore, MD 21201-2525, (410) 962-4392, fax: (410) 962-1805, www.sba.gov/regions/states/md

Massachusetts: 10 Causeway St., Rm. 265, Boston, MA 02222-1093, (617) 565-5590, fax: (617) 565-5598, www.sba.gov/regions/states/ma

Michigan: 477 Michigan Ave., Rm. 515, Detroit, MI 48226, (313) 226-6075, fax: (313) 226-4769, e-mail: michigan@sba.gov, www.sba.gov/regions/states/mi

Minnesota: 610-C Butler Square, 100 N. 6th St., Minneapolis, MN 55403-1563, (612) 370-2324, fax: (612) 370-2303, www.sba.gov/regions/states/mn

Mississippi: 210 E. Capitol St., #900, Jackson, MS 39201, (601) 965-4378, fax: (601) 965-4294, www.sba.gov/regions/states/ms

Missouri: 323 W. Eighth St., #501, Kansas City, MO 64105, (816) 374-6708, fax: (816) 374-6759, www.sba.gov/regions/states/mo/kansas

815 Olive St., Rm. 242, St. Louis, MO 63101, (314) 539-6600, fax: (314) 539-3785, www.sba.gov/regions/states/mo/stlouis

Montana: 301 S. Park Ave., Rm. 334, Helena, MT 59626-0054, (406) 441-1081, fax: (406) 441-1090, www.sba.gov/regions/states/mt

Nebraska: 11145 Mill Valley Rd., Omaha, NE 68154, (402) 221-4691, fax: (402) 221-3680, www.sba.gov/regions/states/ne

Nevada: 300 S. Las Vegas Blvd., #1100, Las Vegas, NV 89101, (702) 388-6611, fax: (702) 933-6469, www.sba.gov/regions/states/nv

New Hampshire: 143 N. Main St., Concord, NH 03302-1248, (603) 225-1400, fax: (603) 225-1409, www.sba.gov/regions/states/nh

New Jersey: 2 Gateway Center, 15th Fl., Newark, NJ 07102, (973) 645-2434, fax: (973) 645-6265, www.sba.gov/regions/states/nj

New Mexico: 625 Silver SW, Albuquerque, NM 87102, (505) 346-7909, fax: (505) 346-6711, www.sba.gov/regions/states/nm

New York: 111 W. Huron St., Rm. 1311, Buffalo, NY 14202, (716) 551-4301, fax: (716) 551-4418, www.sba.gov/regions/states/ny/buffalo

26 Federal Plaza, #3100, New York, NY 10278, (212) 264-4354, fax: (212) 264-7751, www.sba.gov/regions/states/ny/ny

401 S. Salina St., 5th Fl., Syracuse, NY 13202-2415, (315) 471-9272, fax: (315) 471-9288, www.sba.gov/regions/states/ny/syracuse

North Carolina: 200 N. College St., Ste. A-2015, Charlotte, NC 28202-2137, (704) 344-6563, fax: (704) 344-6769, www.sba.gov/regions/states/nc

North Dakota: 657 Second Ave. N., Rm. 219, Fargo, ND 58102, (701) 239-5131, fax: (701) 239-5645, www.sba.gov/regions/states/nd

Ohio: 1111 Superior Ave., #630, Cleveland, OH 44114-2507, (216) 522-4180, fax: (216) 522-2038, www.sba.gov/regions/states/oh/cleveland

2 Nationwide Plaza, #1400, Columbus, OH 43215-2542, (614) 469-6860, fax: (614) 469-2391, www.sba.gov/regions/states/oh/columbus

Oklahoma: 210 Park Ave., #1300, Oklahoma City, OK 73102, (405) 231-5521, fax: (405) 231-4876, www.sba.gov/regions/states/ok

Oregon: 1515 SW Fifth Ave., #1050, Portland, OR 97201-6695, (503) 326-2682, www.sba.gov/regions/states/or

Pennslyvania: 900 Market St., 5th Fl., Philadelphia, PA 19107, (215) 580-2722, fax: (215) 580-2762, www.sba.gov/regions/states/pa/phil

1000 Liberty Ave., Rm. 1128, Pittsburgh, PA 15222-4004, (412) 395-6560, fax: (412) 395-6562, www.sba.gov/regions/states/pa/pitt

Puerto Rico: 252 Ponce de Leon Blvd., Rm. 201, Hato Rey, PR 00918, (809) 766-5572, fax: (809) 766-5309, www.sba.gov/regions/states/pr

Rhode Island: 380 Westminster Street, Providence, RI 02903, (401) 528-4562, fax: (401) 528-4539, www.sba.gov/regions/states/ri

South Carolina: 1835 Assembly St., Rm. 358, Columbia, SC 29201, (803) 765-5377, fax: (803) 765-5962, www.sba.gov/regions/states/sc

South Dakota: 110 S. Phillips Ave., #200, Sioux Falls, SD 57102-1109, (605) 330-4231, fax: (605) 330-4215, www.sba.gov/regions/states/sd

Tennessee: 50 Vantage Wy., #201, Nashville, TN 37228-1500, (615) 736-5881, fax: (615) 736-7232, www.sba.gov/regions/states/tn

Texas: 4300 Amon Carter Blvd., #114, Ft. Worth, TX 76155, (817) 684-5500, fax: (817) 684-5516, www.sba.gov/regions/states/tx/dallas

9301 Southwest Fwy., Houston, TX 77074-1591, (713) 773-6500, fax: (713) 773-6550, www.sba.gov/regions/states/tx/hous

222 E. Van Buren St., Rm. 500, Harlingen, TX 78550-6855, (956) 427-8533, fax: (956) 427-8537, www.sba.gov/regions/states/tx/harlingen

1205 Texas Ave., #408, Lubbock, TX 79401-2693, (806) 472-7462, fax: (806) 472-7487, www.sba.gov/regions/states/tx/lubbock

727 E. Durango Blvd., Rm. A-527, San Antonio, TX 78206-1204, (210) 472-5900, fax: (210) 472-5935, www.sba.gov/regions/states/tx/sanantonio

Utah: 125 S. State St., Rm. 2231, Salt Lake City, UT 84138-1195, (801) 524-3209, fax: (801) 524 4160, www.sba.gov/regions/states/ut

Vermont: 87 State St., Rm. 205, P.O. Box 605, Montpelier, VT 05602, (802) 828-4422, fax: (802) 828-4485, www.sba.gov/regions/states/vt

Virginia: 400 North 8th St., #1150, Richmond, VA 23240, (804) 771-2400, fax: (804) 771-8018, www.sba.gov/regions/states/va

Washington: 1200 Sixth Ave., # 1700, Seattle, WA 98101-1128, (206) 553-7310, fax: (206) 553-7099, www.sba.gov/regions/states/wa

801 W. Riverside Ave., #200, Spokane, WA 99201-0901, (509) 353-2800, fax: (509) 353-2829, www.sba.gov/regions/states/wa

West Virginia: 320 West Pike St., #330, Clarksburg, WV 26301, (304) 623-5631, fax: (304) 623-0023, www.sba.gov/regions/states/wv

Wisconsin: 740 Regent St., #100, Madison, WI 53715, (608) 264-5261, fax: (608) 264-5514, www.sba.gov/regions/states/wi

Wyoming: 100 E. B St., Rm. 4001, P.O. Box 2839, Casper, WY 82602-2839, (307) 261-6500, fax: (307) 261-6535, www.sba.gov/regions/states/wy

Small Business Development Centers

Alabama: Small Business Development Center, University of Alabama, Box 870397, Tuscaloosa, AL 35487, (205) 348-7011, fax: (205) 348-9644, http://sbdc.cba.ua.edu

Alaska: UAA Small Business Development Center, 430 W. Seventh Ave., #110, Anchorage, AK 99501, (907) 274-7232, fax: (907) 274-9524

Arizona: Small Business Development Center Network, 2411 W. 14th St., Tempe, AZ 85281, (602) 731-8720, fax: (602) 731-8729, www.dist.maricopa.edu/sbdc

Arkansas: Small Business Development Center, 100 S. Main, #401, Little Rock, AR 72201, (501) 324-9043, fax: (501) 324-9049, www.ualr.edu/~sbdcdep

California: Small Business Development Center, Office of Small Business Certification & Resources, 1531 I St., 2nd Fl., Sacramento, CA 95814-2016, (916) 323-5478, fax: (916) 442-7855, www.omsb.dgs.ca.gov

Colorado: Business Assistance Center, 1625 Broadway, #805, Denver, CO 80202, (800) 333-7798, (303) 592-5720, fax: (303) 592-8107, www.state.co.us/govdir/oed/bac.html

Connecticut: Small Business Development Center, University of Connecticut, 2 Bourn Pl., U-94, Storrs, CT 06269-5094, (860) 486-4135, fax: (860) 486-1576, www.sbdc.uconn.edu

Delaware: Small Business Development Center, Delaware Technology Park, 1 Innovation Way, #301, Newark, DE 19711, (302) 831-1555, fax: (302) 831-1423, www.delawaresbdc.org

District of Columbia: Small Business Development Center, Howard University, School of Business, Rm. 128, 2600 Sixth St. NW, Washington, DC 20059, (202) 806-1550, fax: (202) 806-1777

Florida: Small Business Development Center, 19 W. Garden St., #300, Pensacola, FL 32501, (904) 444-2060, fax: (904) 444-2070, www.floridasbdc.com

Georgia: Business Outreach Services, Small Business Development Center, Chicopee Complex, University of Georgia, 1180 E. Broad St., Athens, GA 30602-5412, (706) 542-7436, fax: (706) 542-6803, www.sbdc.uga.edu

Guam: Pacific Islands Small Business Development Center Network, UOG Station, Mangilao, Guam 96923, (671) 734-2590, fax: (671) 734-2002, http://uog2.uog.edu/sbdc

Hawaii: University of Hawaii at Hilo, Small Business Development Center Network, 100 Pauahi St., #109, Hilo, HI 96720, (808) 969-1814, fax: (808) 969-7669, www.hawaii-sbdc.org

Idaho: Small Business Development Center, Boise State University, 1910 University Dr., Boise, ID 83725-1655, (208) 426-3875, fax: (208) 426 3877, www.idbsu.edu/isbdc

Illinois: Greater North Pulaski Small Business Development Center, 4054 W. North Ave., Chicago, IL 60639, (773) 384-2262, fax: (773) 384-3850

Indiana: Small Business Development Center, 1 N. Capitol, #1275,

Indianapolis, IN 46204, (888) ISBD-244, (317) 264-2820, fax: (317) 264-2806, www.isbdcorp.org

Iowa: Small Business Development Center, 137 Lynn Ave., Ames, IA 50014, (800) 373-7232, (515) 292-6351, fax: (515) 292-0020, www.iabusnet.org/sbdc/index.html

Kansas: Small Business Development Center, 1501 S. Joplin, Pittsburg, KS 66762, (316) 235-4920, fax: (316) 235-4919, www.pittstate.edu/bti/sbdc.htm

Kentucky: Small Business Development Center, 225 Gatton College of Business and Economics Bldg., Lexington, KY 40506-0034, (606) 257-7668, fax: (606) 323-1907, www.ksbdc.org

Louisiana: Small Business Development Center, Northeast Louisiana University, College of Business Administration, Room 2-57, Monroe, LA 71209-6435, (318) 342-5506, fax: (318) 342-5510

Maine: University of Southern Maine, Maine Small Business Development Centers, 96 Falmouth St., P.O. Box 9300, Portland, ME 04104-9300, (207) 780-4420, fax: (207) 780-4810, www.mainesbdc.org

Maryland: Small Business Development Center, 7100 E. Baltimore Ave., #401, College Park, MD 20740-3627, (301) 403-8300, fax: (301) 403-8303, www.mbs.umd.edu/sbdc

Massachusetts: Small Business Development Center, University of Massachusetts, P.O. Box 34935, Amherst, MA 01003, (413) 545-6301, fax: (413) 545-1273

Michigan: Small Business Development Center, 2727 Second Ave., #107, Detroit, MI 48201, (313) 577-4850, fax: (313) 577-8933, http://bizserve.com/sbdc

Minnesota: Small Business Development Center, Dept. of Trade and Economic Development, 500 Metro Square, 121 Seventh Pl. E., St. Paul, MN 55101-2146, (651) 297-5770, fax: (651) 296-1290

Mississippi: Small Business Development Center, P.O. Box 1848, B19 Track Dr., University, MS 38677, (662) 915-5001, (800) 725-7232 (in MS), fax: (662) 915-5650, e-mail: msbdc@olemiss.edu, www.olemiss.edu/depts/mssbdc

Missouri: Small Business Development Center, 1205 University Ave., #300, Columbia, MO 65211, (573) 882-0344, fax: (573) 884-4297, www.mo-sbdc.org/index.html

Montana: Small Business Development Center, Department of Commerce, 1424 Ninth Ave., Helena, MT 59620, (406) 444-4780, fax: (406) 444-1872

Nebraska: Business Development Center, 1313 Farnam St., #132, Omaha, NE 68102, (402) 595-2381, fax: (402) 595-2385, www.nbdc. unomaha.edu

Nevada: Small Business Development Center, University of Nevada at Reno, College of Business Administration, Business Bldg., Room 411, Reno, NV 89557-0100, (702) 784-1717, fax: (702) 784-4337, www.nsbdc.org

New Hampshire: Small Business Development Center, 1000 Elm St., 12th Fl., Manchester, NH 03101, (603) 624-2000, fax: (603) 647-4410, e-mail: sbdcinfo@nhsbdc.org, www.nhsbdc.org

New Jersey: Small Business Development Center, 49 Bleeker St., Newark, NJ 07102-1913, (973) 353-1927, fax: (973) 353-1110, www.nj.com/smallbusiness

New Mexico: Small Business Development Center, Santa Fe Community College, 6401 S. Richards Ave., Santa Fe, NM 87505, (505) 428-1343, fax: (505) 428-1469, www.nmsbdc.org

New York: Small Business Development Center, SUNY at Albany, 1 Pinnacle Place, #218, Albany, NY 12203-3439, (518) 453-9567, fax: (518) 453-9572, www.nys-sbdc.suny.edu

North Carolina: Small Business and Technology Development Center, 333 Fayetteville Street Mall, #1150, Raleigh, NC 27601, (919) 715-7272, (800) 258-0862 (in NC), fax: (919) 715-7777, www.sbtdc.org

North Dakota: Small Business Development Center, 202 N. 3rd St., #200, Grand Forks, ND 58202, (701) 772-8502, fax: (701) 772-9238, http://bpa.und.nodak.edu/sbdc

Ohio: Small Business Development Center, P.O. Box 1001, Columbus, OH 43261-1001, (614) 466-2711, fax: (614) 466-0829

Oklahoma: Small Business Development Center, 517 University, Durant, OK 74701, (580) 924-0277, fax: (580) 920-7471, www.osbdc.org

Oregon: Small Business Development Center Network, 44 W. Broadway, #501, Eugene, OR 97401-3021, (541) 726-2250, fax: (541) 345-6006, www.efn.org/~osbdcn

Pennsylvania: Small Business Development Center, State Director's Office, 3733 Spruce St., 4th Fl., Philadelphia, PA 19104, (215) 898-1219, fax: (215) 573-2135, e-mail: pasbdc@wharton.upenn.edu, www.pasbdc.org

Rhode Island: Small Business Development Center, Bryant College, 1150 Douglas Pike, Smithfield, RI 02917, (401) 232-6111, fax: (401) 232-6933, e-mail: admin@risbdc.org, www.risbdc.org

South Carolina: Small Business Development Center, The Darla Moore School of Business, University of South Carolina, Columbia, SC 29208, (803) 777-4907, fax: (803) 777-4403, e-mail: abdc@darla. badm.sc.edu, http://sbdcweb.badm.sc.edu

South Dakota: Small Business Development Center, 414 E. Clark St., Vermillion, SD 57069-2390, (605) 677-5287, fax: (605) 677-5427, www.usd.edu/brbinfo/sbdc

Tennesee: Small Business Development Center, 320 South Dudley St., Memphis, TN 38104-3206, (901) 527-1041, www.tsbdc.memphis. edu

Texas: Small Business Development Center, 1100 Louisiana, #500, Houston, TX 77002, (713) 752-8404, fax: (713) 756-1515, http:// smbizsolutions.uh.edu

Utah: Small Business Development Center, 1623 S. State St., Salt Lake City, UT 84111, (801) 957-3840, fax: (801) 524-4160

Vermont: Small Business Development Center, P.O. Box 188, Randolf Center, VT 05061-0188, (802) 728-9101, fax: (802) 728-3026, www.vtsbdc.org

Virginia: Small Business Development Center, P.O. Box 446, Richmond, VA 23218-0446, (804) 371-8200, fax: (804) 371-8111, www.dba. state.va.us

Washington: Small Business Development Center, Washington State University, P.O. Box 644851, Pullman, WA 99164-4851, (509) 358-7765, www.sbdc.wsu.edu

West Virginia: Small Business Development Center, 950 Kanawha Blvd. E., #200, Charleston, WV 25301, (304) 558-2960, fax: (304) 558-0127, www.wvsbdc.org

Wisconsin: University of Wisconsin at Whitewater, Small Business Development Center, Carlson 2000, Whitewater, WI 53190, (414) 472-3217, fax: (414) 472-5692

Wyoming: Small Business Development Center, 111 W. Second St., #502, Casper, WY 82601, (307) 234-6683, fax: (307) 577-7014

State Commerce And Economic Development Departments

Alabama: Development Office, 401 Adams Ave., #670, Montgomery, AL 36130, (800) 248-0033, e-mail: idinfo@ado.state.al.us, www.ado.state.al.us

Alaska: State Dept. of Community and Economic Development, P.O. Box 110800, Juneau, AK 99811-0800, (907) 465-2500, fax: (907) 465-5442, www.dced.state.ak.us

Arizona: State Dept. of Commerce Business Assistance Center, 3800 N. Central Ave., Phoenix, AZ 85012, (602) 280-1300, fax: (602) 280-1339, www.commerce.state.az.us

Arkansas: Economic Development Commission, Advocacy and Business Services, 1 State Capitol Mall, Little Rock, AR 72201, (501) 682-1121, fax: (501) 324-9856, www.aedc.state.ar.us

California: Trade and Commerce Agency, Office of Small Business, 801 K St., #1700, Sacramento, CA 95814, (800) 303-6600, (916) 324-5790, fax: (916) 322-5084, www.commerce.ca.gov

Colorado: Office of Business Development, 1625 Broadway, #1710, Denver, CO 80202, (303) 892-3840, fax: (303) 892-3848, www.state.co.us/govdir/oed.htm

Connecticut: Economic Resource Center, 805 Brook St., Bldg. 4, Rocky Hill, CT 06067, (800) 392-2122, fax: (860) 571-7150, www.cerc.com

Delaware: Economic Development Office, 99 Kings Hwy., Dover, DE 19901, (302) 739-4271, fax: (302) 739-5749, www.state.de.us

District of Columbia: Office of Economic Development, 441 Fourth St. NW, Ste. North-1140, Washington, DC 20001, (202) 727-6365, fax: (202) 727-6703

Florida: Enterprise Florida, 390 N. Orange, #1300, Orlando, FL 32801, (407) 316-4600, fax: (407) 316-4599, www.floridabusiness.com

Georgia: Dept. of Community Affairs, 60 Executive Park S., NE, Atlanta, GA 30329-2231, (404) 679-4940, fax: (404) 679-4940, www.dca.state.ga.us

Hawaii: Business Action Center, 1130 N. Nimitz Hwy., Second Level, Ste. A-254, Honolulu, HI 96817, (808) 586-2545, fax: (808) 586-2544, www.hawaii.gov/dbedt

Idaho: State Dept. of Commerce, P.O. Box 83720, Boise, ID 83720-0093, (208) 334-2470, (800) 842-5858, fax: (208) 334-2631, www.idoc.state.id.us

Illinois: Dept. of Commerce and Community Affairs, 620 E. Adams St., Springfield, IL 62701, (217) 782-7500, fax: (217) 524-3701, www.commerce.state.il.us

Indiana: State Dept. of Commerce, 1 N. Capitol, #700, Indianapolis, IN 46204-2288, (317) 232-8782, fax: (317) 233-5123, www. indbiz.com

Iowa: Dept. of Economic Development, 200 E. Grand Ave, Des Moines, IA 50309, (800) 532-1216, fax: (515) 242-4776, e-mail: smallbiz@ided.state.ia.us, www.state.ia.us/sbro

Kansas: Dept. of Commerce and Housing, Business Development Division, 700 SW Harrison St., #1300, Topeka, KS 66603, (785) 296-5298, fax: (785) 296-3490, www.kansascommerce.com

Kentucky: Cabinet for Economic Development, 2400 Capital Plaza Tower, 500 Mero St., Frankfort, KY 40601, (800) 626-2930, fax: (502) 564-3256, e-mail: econdev@mail.state.ky.us, www.edc.state.ky.us/ kyedc/entrance.html

Louisiana: Dept. of Economic Development, P.O. Box 94185, Baton Rouge, LA 70804-9185, (225) 342-3000, fax: (225) 342-5349, www.lded.state.la.us

Maine: Business Answers, Dept. of Economic and Community Development, 33 Stone St., 59 Statehouse Station, Augusta, ME 04333-0059, (207) 287-2656, fax: (207) 287-2861, www.econdev.maine.com

Maryland: Dept. of Business and Economic Development, Division of Regional Development, 217 E. Redwood St., 10th Fl., Baltimore, MD 21202, (410) 767-0095, fax: (410) 338-1836, www. mdbusiness.state.md.us

Massachusetts: Office of Business Development, 10 Park Plaza, #3720, Boston, MA 02116, (617) 973-8600, (800) 5-CAPITAL, fax: (617) 973-8797, e-mail: mobd@state.ma.us, www.state.ma.us/mobd

Michigan: Economic Development Corp., 201 N. Washington Square, 4th Fl., Lansing, MI 48913, (517) 373-9808, fax: (517) 335-0198, http://medc.michigan.org

Minnesota: Small Business Assistance Office, 500 Metro Square, 121 Seventh Pl. E., St. Paul, MN 55101, (800) 657-3858, (651) 282-2103, www.dted.state.mn.us

Mississippi: Dept. of Economic and Community Development, Division of Existing Industry and Business, New Business, P.O. Box 849, Jackson, MS 39205-0849, (601) 359-3449, fax: (601) 359-2832, www.decd.state.ms.us

Missouri: Dept. of Economic Development, P.O. Box 118, Jefferson City, MO 65102, (573) 751-4982, fax: (573) 751-7384, www.ecodev. state.mo.us/mbac

Montana: Dept. of Commerce, Economic Development Division,

1424 Ninth Ave., Helena, MT 59620, (406) 444-3814, fax: (406) 444-1872, http://commerce/mt.gov

Nebraska: Dept. of Economic Development, 301 Centenial Mall S., P.O. Box 94666, Lincoln, NE 68509-4666, (402) 471-3111, (800) 426-6505, fax: (402) 471-3778, www.ded.state.ne.us

Nevada: State Dept. of Business and Industry, 555 E. Washington Ave., #4900, Las Vegas, NV 89104, (702) 486-2750, fax: (702) 486-2758, www.state.nv.us/b&i

New Hampshire: Office of Business and Industrial Development, P.O. Box 1856, Concord, NH 03302-1856, (603) 271-2591, fax: (603) 271-6784, http://ded.state.nh.us/obid

New Jersey: Dept. of Commerce and Economic Development, 20 State St., CN 820, Trenton, NJ 08625, (609) 292-2444, fax: (609) 292-9145, www.nj.com/business

New Mexico: Economic Development Dept., P.O. Box 20003-5003, Santa Fe, NM 87504, (505) 827-0300, fax: (505) 827-0300, www.edd.state.nm.us

New York: Division for Small Business, Empire State Development, 1 Commerce Plaza, Albany, NY 12245, (518) 473-0499, (800) STATE-NY, fax: (518) 474-1512, www.empire.state.ny.us

North Carolina: Small Business and Technology Development Center, 333 Fayetteville Street Mall, #1150, Raleigh, NC 27601-1742, (919) 715-7272, fax: (919) 715-7777, www.sbtdc.org

North Dakota: Center for Innovation, 4300 Dartmouth Dr., Grand Forks, ND 58202, (701) 777-3132, fax: (701) 777-2339, www.innovators.net

Ohio: One-Stop Business Center, 77 S. High St., 28th Fl., P.O. Box 1001, Columbus, OH 43216-1001, (614) 644-8748, fax: (614) 466-0829

Oklahoma: Department of Commerce, P.O. Box 26980, Oklahoma City, OK 73126-0980, (405) 815-6552, (800) 879-6552, fax: (405) 815-5142, www.odoc.state.ok.us

Oregon: Economic Development Dept., 775 Summer St. NE, Salem, OR 97310, (503) 986-0123, fax: (503) 581-5115, www.econ.state.or.us

Pennsylvania: Small Business Resource Center, Rm. 374, Forum Bldg., Harrisburg, PA 17120, (717) 783-5700, fax: (717) 234-4560, www.dced.state.pa.us

Rhode Island: Economic Development Corporation, 1 W.

Exchange St., Providence, RI 02903, (401) 222-2601, fax: (401) 222-2102, e-mail: riedc@riedc.com, www.riedc.com/startframe.html

South Carolina: Enterprise Inc., SC Department of Commerce, P.O. Box 927, Columbia, SC 29202, (803) 737-0238, www.callsouth carolina.com

South Dakota: Governor's Office of Economic Development, 711 E. Wells Ave., Pierre, SD 57501-3369, (800) 872-6190, (605) 773-5032, fax: (605) 773-3256, e-mail: goedinfo@state.sd.us, www.state.sd.us/goed

Tennessee: Small Business Service, Dept. of Economic and Community Development, 320 Sixth Ave. N., 7th Fl., Rachel Jackson Bldg., Nashville, TN 37243-0405, (615) 741-2626, fax: (615) 532-8715, www.state.tn.us/ecd

Texas: Dept. of Economic Development, Office of Small Business Assistance, P.O. Box 12728, Austin, TX 78711-2728, (512) 936-0223, fax: (512) 936-0435, www.tded.state.tx.us/SmallBusiness

Utah: Dept. of Community and Economic Development, 324 S. State St., #500, Salt Lake City, UT 84111, (877) 4UT-DCED, (801) 538-8700, fax: (801) 538-8888, www.dced.state.ut.us

Vermont: Agency of Commerce and Community Development, Department of Economic Development, National Life Bldg., Drawer 20, Montpelier, VT 05620-0501, (802) 828-3080, (800) Vermont, fax: (802) 828-3258, www.thinkvermont.com

Virginia: Dept. of Business Assistance, Small Business Development Center Network, 707 E. Main St., #300, Richmond, VA 23219, (804) 371-8200, fax: (804) 371-8111, www.dba.state.va.us

Washington: Business Assistance Division, Community Trade and Economic Development, 906 Columbia St. SW, P.O. Box 48300, Olympia, WA 98504-8300, (360) 753-7426, fax: (360) 586-3582, www.cted.wa.gov

West Virginia: Small Business Development Center, 950 Kanawha Blvd. E., #200, Charleston, WV 25301, (304) 558-2960, fax: (304) 558-0127, www.wvsbdc.org

Wisconsin: Department of Commerce, 201 W. Washington Ave., Madison, WI 53703, (608) 266-1018, fax: (608) 267-2829, www.commerce.state.wi.us

Wyoming: Business Council, 214 W. 15th, Cheyenne, WY 82002, (307) 777-2800, (800) 262-3425, fax: (307) 777-2838, www.wyoming tourism.org/wbc

Index

About The Author

Mark Henricks is the author of *Business Plans Made Easy*. His column "Cutting Edge" appears monthly in *Entrepreneur* magazine. One of the country's most experienced business writers, he has written more than 1,300 articles on business, technology and investing. He lives in Austin, Texas.

Current titles from Entrepreneur Press:

Benjamin Franklin's 12 Rules Of Management:
The Founding Father of American Business Solves Your Toughest Problems

Business Plans Made Easy:
It's Not as Hard as You Think

Creative Selling:
Boost Your B2B Sales

Extreme Investor:
Intelligent Information From The Edge

Financial Fitness in 45 Days:
The Complete Guide to Shaping Up Your Finances

Gen E:
Generation Entrepreneur is Rewriting the Rules of Business—And You Can, Too!

Get Smart:
365 Tips to Boost Your Entrepreneurial IQ

How to be a Teenage Millionaire:
Start Your Own Business, Make Your Own Money and Run Your Own Life

How to Dotcom:
A Step-by-step Guide to e-Commerce

Knock-Out Marketing:
Powerful Strategies to Punch Up Your Sales

Radicals & Visionaries:
Entrepreneurs Who Revolutionized the 20th Century

Start Your Own Business:
The Only Start-up Book You'll Ever Need

Success for Less:
100 Low-Cost Businesses You Can Start Today

303 Marketing Tips
Guaranteed to Boost Your Business

Where's The Money?
Sure-Fire Financial Solutions for Your Small Business

Young Millionaires:
Inspiring Stories to Ignite Your Entrepreneurial Dreams

2 5/02

"Business Plans Made Easy is a practical, common-sense guide not only to planning but to the markets for the multiple uses of a good plan."

RON TORRENCE
Business Advisor and Author of
Ten Keys to Sales & Financial Success for Small Business

Creating Winning Business Plans Is Not As Hard As You Think!

An easy-to-use, no-nonsense guide for creating and using successful business plans

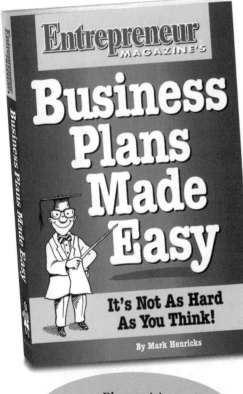

Whether you're just starting out or already running a business, a business plan can be the most important factor in your success. Unfortunately, many entrepreneurs neglect this important step because the thought of writing a business plan can be intimidating. But creating an effective business plan doesn't have to be difficult.

In this enjoyable, easy-to-read guide, Mark Henricks shares with you proven techniques, hints and tips for easily creating results—getting business plans that match your exact needs.

Unlike many books, which only cover the basics, this comprehensive guide is packed with easy-to-follow advice, hints and tips, including:

- Why you need a business plan
- When to write your business plan
- What to include in your business plan
- What a business plan can and cannot do
- Where to get more information, including reviews of business plan software
- PLUS, actual business plans from successful companies such as Dell Computer and Southwest Airlines offer you real-life inspiration and guidance

Please visit
www.smallbizbooks.com
for more information or to order

$19.95 paperback

Help ensure your success with this easy-to-understand guide.

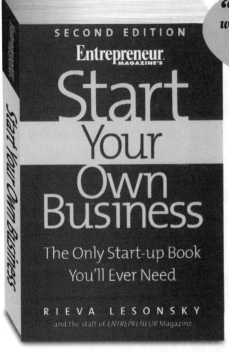

" ...all true entrepreneurs won't want to put this book down."
LILLIAN VERNON
Chairman and CEO
Lillian Vernon Corporation

Whether you're just thinking of starting a business, have taken the first few steps, or already have your own business, this comprehensive, easy-to-understand guide can help ensure your success.

Written in a friendly, down-to-earth style, *Start Your Own Business* makes it easy to understand even the most complex business issues so you can reach your goals and enjoy the rewards of owning your own business. This new edition has been substantially updated to include sections on e-commerce, homebased businesses, and how to add a web site to an existing business.

Inside you'll find:

- Our easy-to-navigate format loaded with work sheets, tip boxes, charts, graphs and illustrations.
- Practical, proven, hands-on techniques so you can get started right away.
- Expert guidance from the nation's leading small-business authority, backed by over 20 years of business experience.
- And much more!

Please visit
www.smallbizbooks.com
for more information or to order

Entrepreneur Press

$24.95 paperback

"Mandatory reading for any small-business owner who is serious about success."

— Jay Conrad Levinson,
author, *Guerrilla Marketing*
series of books

Powerhouse Marketing Tactics for Making Big Profits

Written for both new and established small-business owners, this nuts-and-bolts guide gives you the marketing firepower you need to satisfy customers, attract prospects, boost your profits and blast the competition.

Packed with proven techniques, tips and advice, this easy-to-read guide covers every aspect of marketing, including:

- How to think like a marketer
- How to select the best market for your products and services
- 4 common marketing mistakes and how to avoid them
- Tips for writing your marketing plan
- Sure-fire selling tactics that get results
- Building your presence on the Internet

Available at **www.smallbizbooks.** and at local and online bookstor

ISBN 1-891984-04-7
$19.95
paperback
296 pages